Language Awareness

FOURTH EDITION

Language
Awareness

EDITORS
Paul Eschholz
Alfred Rosa
Virginia Clark

ST. MARTIN'S PRESS   New York

For information, write St. Martin's Press, Inc.,
175 Fifth Avenue, New York, N.Y. 10010

cover design: Darby Downey

ISBN: 0-312-46695-1

Acknowledgments

I LANGUAGE AWARENESS

"Coming to an Awareness of Language" from *The Autobiography of Malcolm X*,
by Malcolm X, with the assistance of Alex Haley. Copyright © 1965 by Alex Haley
and Betty Shabazz. Copyright © 1964 by Alex Haley and Malcolm X. Reprinted
by permission of Random House, Inc.

"Man the Talker" by Peter Farb. From *Word Play: What Happens When People
Talk*, by Peter Farb. Copyright © 1973 by Peter Farb. Reprinted by permission of
Alfred A. Knopf, Inc.

"A Brief History of English" from *Understanding English* by Paul Roberts. Copyright © 1958, by Paul Roberts. Reprinted by permission of Harper & Row, Publishers, Inc.

"Are You Making Yourself Clear?" by Norman Cousins. © 1969 *Saturday Review*
magazine. Reprinted by permission.

"The Sounds of Silence" by Edward T. Hall and Mildred Reed Hall originally appeared in *Playboy* Magazine: copyright © 1971 by Playboy. Reprinted by permission of Edward T. Hall and Mildred Reed Hall.

II AMERICAN ENGLISH TODAY

"Language on the Skids" by Edwin Newman reprinted with permission from the
November 1979 *Reader's Digest*, the *Naval War College Review*, and Edwin Newman. © 1979 by The Reader's Digest Assn., Inc.

"Is There Really a Language Crisis?" from *Famous Last Words: The American
Language Crisis Reconsidered*, by Harvey A. Daniels. Copyright © 1983 by Southern Illinois University Board Trustees. Reprinted by permission of the Southern Illinois University Press.

Acknowledgments and copyrights continue at the back of the book on pages
457–460, which constitute an extension of the copyright page.

PREFACE

Since the first edition of *Language Awareness* appeared in 1974, its purpose has been twofold: to foster an appreciation of the richness, flexibility, and vitality of the English language and to encourage and help students to use their language more responsibly and effectively in speech and particularly in writing. Because of these twin purposes, *Language Awareness* has been used in a variety of different courses over the years. Its primary use, however, has been and continues to be in college composition courses. Clearly, many instructors believe as we do that the study of language and the study of writing go hand in hand. Thus, many of the changes in this fourth edition have been made with an eye toward the college writing classroom.

First, we have added an alternate table of contents that classifies the reading selections in *Language Awareness* according to the rhetorical strategies they exemplify. Next, our new general introduction provides a discussion of reading and writing that includes guidelines and questions students can use to increase their abilities as thoughtful, analytical readers, as well as explanations of how the various writing strategies can be put to work. Concluding this introduction is a sample student paper demonstrating how language issues (in this case, the use of language in advertising) can suggest fascinating topics for research and writing. Finally, at the end of the text we have appended a detailed glossary that defines rhetorical terms and concepts important to the study of writing.

As in previous editions, the readings have been chosen not only for their subject matter but also to provide students of composition with practical illustrations of rhetorical principles and techniques. After each selection, in addition to questions on the content of the essay, we have provided questions that address these rhetorical concerns, adding cross-references to the new glossary where useful. The vocabulary list after each selection calls attention to a few words that students will find worth adding to their own active vocabularies. Finally, each reading is followed by two or more writing topics. In our own teaching we have found such topics helpful in promoting both writing and classroom discussion of language issues.

At the end of each section in *Language Awareness,* we provide topics and instructions for writing several short essays. Usually these topics direct students to make use of what they have learned from two or more of the readings in the section. Each section also concludes with a list of quotations that can provide further effective stimuli for writing or for class discussion. At the end of the book is a list of possible topics for longer papers that may involve some library work.

None of this attention to and emphasis on the study of writing should suggest that we have neglected our other primary goal: encouraging students to recognize and appreciate the complex nature of language itself. Thus, our selection of essays continues to be careful and wide-ranging. Guided by comments and advice from many colleagues across the country who have used the third edition, we have retained those essays that teachers and students have valued most. But over half of the selections in *Language Awareness* are new to this edition. As always, we have emphasized pieces written in nontechnical language on topics and issues of current interest. We have added Peter Farb's fascinating discussion of the miracle of language; Harvey Daniels's timely piece on the language "crisis" in America; Richard Rodriguez's personal view of the question of bilingual education; and Casey Miller and Kate Swift's examination of sexist language in the workplace. Many users asked us to include more on advertising, so we have expanded that section, adding David Ogilvy's classic advice on writing successful ad copy and the Consumers Union report on the current buzz words in advertising food products—"natural" and "organic." In addition, to meet the requests for more material on the language of the professions, we have included such pieces as Kenneth Hudson's essay on jargon and technical language and Stephen Hilgartner's examination of the specialized vocabulary of nuclear war strategists.

Of the ten thematic sections into which the essays are grouped, three are new to this edition. "American English Today" considers the state of the language in this country by examining three key issues: grammar, spelling, and the "back to basics" movement; Black English; and bilingual education. "Words, Meanings, and Dictionaries" explores our fascination with words and how these words acquire meaning. And "Language and Sexism," which includes essays by some of the best known writers on this problem—Alleen Pace Nilsen, Robin Lakoff, Casey Miller, and Kate Swift—addresses the question of sexist language in America. (Because sexism in language is not a topic without controversy, we have chosen Cyra McFadden's essay to present an opposing point of view.) The final section, "Writing Well: Using Language Responsibly," has been significantly revised for this edition, to focus more specifically on providing advice to students as writers.

All of our aims in *Language Awareness* are serious ones, but a serious book need not be humorless. Jim Quinn's irreverent essay about political language and its critics not only teaches us a number of things about language and human nature but is funny besides. So, we think, are William Safire's "Vogue Words Are Trific, Right?" Noel Perrin's "Tell Me, Pretty Billboard," Mary Ruth Yoe's "How to Interpret an Annual Report," and *English Highlights* magazine's "Does Language Libel the Left-Handed?"—among others. Indeed, we like to think that readers of *Language Awareness* will have as much fun using this edition as we have had in preparing it.

ACKNOWLEDGMENTS

We are grateful to the following colleagues across the country who have sent us helpful reactions and suggestions for this fourth edition: Mark Allen, University of Texas at San Antonio; Philip Bishop, Edison Community College; David Bradt, New Hampshire College; Anne Burley, Towson State University; Greg Candela, University of New Mexico; Margaret Clark, Edison Community College; Paul R. Cockshutt, North Carolina State University; Dorothy A. Cook, Central Connecticut State University; Wayne Cook, Central Connecticut State Univesity; David H. Covington, North Carolina State University; David Critchett, Community College of Rhode Island; Bernard Crook, University of Texas at San Antonio; Eva Crook, Nassau Community College; Jeremiah J. Cullinane, University of Charleston; Trudy Drucker, Bergen Community College; Barbara DuBois, University of New Mexico; Thomas J. Duffy, Bergen Community College; Walter Everett, Indiana State University; John Ferstel, University of Louisiana; Michael Finney, Youngstown State University; Gretchen Flesher, University of California at Los Angeles; Olivia Frey, St. Olaf College; Susan R. Gannon, Pace University; Sharlene Glock, New Mexico State University; Clare R. Goldfarb, Western Michigan University; Kathleen Greenfield, Drexel University; Dominick Grundy, Nassau Community College; Heather Hardy, North Texas State University; Susan Harland, University of Pittsburgh; Patricia Hartman, Ohio University; Lynn Haywood, North Carolina State University; Lynn Hildenbrand, Chesapeake College; Jeffrey Jeske, University of California at Los Angeles; Sonia Kaleb, Indiana State University at Evansville; Frank Kelly, SUNY Agricultural and Technical College at Farmingdale; Larry B. Kent, William Rainey Harper College; Mary King, University of Akron; Deborah Kiser, Boise State University; Sandra Lason, Oklahoma City Community College; Eileen Lothamer, California State University at San Bernardino; Audrey Lattie, Charles

Stuart Mott College; Anne LeCroy, East Tennessee State University; Francis Lyvers, Kentucky State University; John Mascaro, University of California at Los Angeles; Alfred McDowell, Bergen Community College; Susan Meisenhelder, California State University at San Bernardino; John Morris, University of Wisconsin at Eau Claire; Michael T. Motley, University of California at Davis; Fred Paulenich, Youngstown State University; Dennis Perzanowski, Utica College; Jennifer Petersen, University of Wisconsin at Milwaukee; Carol Pollard, North Carolina State University; Mary Purcell, California State University at Long Beach; Jennifer Randisi, California State University at San Bernardino; Mary Redding, San Diego State University; John R. Rodman, Chesapeake College; Jack Rollow, Bergen Community College; August Rubrech, University of Wisconsin at Eau Claire; Leone Scanlon, Clark University; Wayne Schow, Idaho State University; Ida Shaker, Charles Stuart Mott Community College; Frank Shivers, Towson State University; Robert N. Shorter, Wake Forest University; Jeffrey Skoblow, University of California at Los Angeles; Clay Smith, Kentucky State University; Frank Smith, William Rainey Harper College; Uwe Stuecher, University of Minnesota; Samuel J. Umland, University of Nebraska; Thomas C. Ware, University of Tennessee at Chattanooga; Lawrence Watson, University of Wisconsin at Stevens Point; Edith J. Wynne, East Texas State University; Jacquelin Webber, American River College; Keith Welsh, Indiana University; M. Wigam, Bunker Hill Community College; Thomas A. Wilhelmus, Indiana State University at Evansville; John B. Williams, California State University at San Bernardino; James Willis, Charles Stuart Mott Community College; Keith Wilson, New Mexico State University; Paul Witherington, South Dakota State University; Susan Yates, Nebraska Wesleyan University; and Nancee I. Young, Millikin University.

We would also like to express our appreciation of our helpers at St. Martin's Press, especially Nancy Perry and Mark Gallaher. Finally, we are grateful to all our students at the University of Vermont for their enthusiasm for language study and writing and their invaluable responses to materials included in this book. They teach us something new every day.

PAUL ESCHHOLZ
ALFRED ROSA
VIRGINIA CLARK

CONTENTS

RHETORICAL TABLE OF CONTENTS

The essays in *LANGUAGE AWARENESS* are arranged in ten sections according to their subjects. The following alternate table of contents, which is certainly not exhaustive, classifies the essays according to the rhetorical strategies they exemplify.

On the Relation of Language to Public Policy
Resolved, That the National Council of Teachers of English find means to study the relation of language to public policy, to keep track of, publicize, and combat semantic distortion by public officials, candidates for office, political commentators, and all those who transmit through the mass media.

On Dishonest and Inhumane Uses of Language
Resolved, That the National Council of Teachers of English find means to study dishonest and inhumane uses of language and literature by advertisers, to bring offenses to public attention, and to propose classroom techniques for preparing children to cope with commercial propaganda.

Resolutions Passed by the National Council of Teachers of English

Introduction

Language Awareness is a collection of readings aimed at college writing students and designed to emphasize the crucial role language plays in virtually every aspect of our lives. Most of us think of language as we think of the air we breathe: we cannot survive without it, but we take it for granted nearly all of the time. Seldom are we conscious of language's real power to lead us (or mislead us) or of the effect our own use of language has on others. Even rarer is the recognition that our perceptions of the world are influenced, our very thoughts at least partially shaped, by language. But, if it is true that we are all in some sense prisoners of our language, it is also true that liberation begins with our awareness of that fact. To foster such an awareness is one of the goals of this book. We hope, therefore, that as you use this text you will gain a heightened appreciation of the richness, flexibility, and vitality of your language and be moved to explore its possibilities further.

THE STUDY OF LANGUAGE

Language is one of humankind's greatest achievements and most important resources, and it is a subject endlessly fascinating in itself. *Language Awareness* represents the most immediate and interesting fields of language study with a diverse range of thought-provoking essays, grouped into ten broad units. The first unit, "Language Awareness," provides an overview of the central issues: the power of words to shape our perceptions, the way language evolves, our responsibilities as users of language, even how communication transcends language. Next, in "American English Today," we present some of the arguments that characterize the contemporary debate over what has been called a decline in our general standard of language ability. Unit III, "Language, Politics, and Propaganda," points out the ways language can be used to manipulate our thinking (or to keep us from thinking at all), as well as the abuses language suffers at the hands of politicians. In "Words, Meanings, and Dictionaries" you will find discussions of how our vocabularies are shaped; how expressions differ among regions, among generations, and among social classes; and how we come to determine what a word in fact means. The following unit, "Advertising and Language," considers some of the ways advertisers use language to create a positive image of a product, to imply what they cannot say directly, to exploit consumer vulnerability, and to insinuate their way into our lives.

Next, in "Prejudice and Stereotypes," we look at the way words can lock us into particular categories, create powerfully discriminatory impressions, and deeply affect our judgments about others. Then, Unit VII, "Language and Sexism," concentrates specifically on stereotypical images of women implied in our language and suggests some of the difficulties involved in overcoming such linguistic prejudice. In the next unit, "Euphemisms and Professional Jargon," the readings raise an important question about the language used in specialized fields of work—when is complex, technical language necessary, and when is it merely a pretentious smokescreen for a writer's hidden intentions or simple lack of ideas? And in Unit IX, "Taboos," we confront some of our culture's "dirty words" to determine how and why they may seem offensive.

Finally—because our further purpose in this fourth edition of *Language Awareness,* as in earlier editions, is to encourage you to write more responsibly and effectively—we have included in our final section, "Writing Well," five essays in which professional writers reflect on their craft, on the way they write. Each writer offers practical advice on the qualities of good writing and the writing process—getting started, drafting, identifying an audience, being truthful to yourself and your audience, revising, and editing. Although this section is at the end of the book, you may find the readings useful as you start your writing course, because together they provide a detailed overview of the composing process. Or, as you work on particular assignments during the school term, you may want to look at one or more of these essays for direction and encouragement about specific aspects of your writing.

The common denominator of all good writing is the writer's conscious concern for language, and this concern is emphasized, in various ways, by every essay in *Language Awareness.* We have chosen them not only because they explore important issues of language and communication, but also because they provide excellent models of how writers give effective expression to their thoughts. Thus, reading and studying the selections throughout the text, by making you more sensitive to how you use language yourself and to how the language of others affects you, can help you become a better reader and, perhaps most important, a better writer. The more aware you are of the many subtleties and complexities of language use, the greater your mastery and control of language will be. This sense of control will, in turn, allow you to read more thoughtfully and critically and to achieve greater competence and confidence in your own writing.

THE IMPORTANCE OF READING WELL

Reading, whatever your reason for doing so, is most rewarding when you do it actively, in a thoughtful spirit, and with an alert and inquiring mind. For writers—and in one way or another we are all writers—there are special reasons to cultivate the habits and skills of careful, attentive reading. By analyzing the ideas and techniques of the writers you read, you can increase your mastery and refine your own personal style as a writer. Furthermore, for everything you write you will be your own first reader and critic. How well you are able to read your own drafts will powerfully affect how well you can revise them; and revising well is crucial to writing well. So, close, critical reading of what others have written is useful and important practice for anyone who wishes to improve his or her writing skills.

Your first important task as a reader sensitive to language is to read every essay assigned from this text at least twice. In your first reading you will be concerned primarily with understanding the points about language a writer is trying to make. In your second reading—and perhaps even a third—you can refine and develop your understanding of the content, working especially at the difficult passages and analyzing more carefully the author's purpose and his or her means of achieving that purpose. You should determine which features of the essay's organization and style seem particularly successful, so you can learn from them and, perhaps, adapt them to your own work. You may also begin to look for the general strategy or strategies a writer uses to develop the essay's ideas. For example, Malcolm X uses *narration* to tell the story of his "Coming to an Awareness of Language." In "Bugs Bunny Says They're Yummy" Dawn Ann Kurth analyzes *cause and effect* to explain the results of vitamin advertisements on children. And in her essay "Black Children, Black Speech," Dorothy Z. Seymour uses *comparison and contrast* to detail the similarities and differences between Black English and Standard English. These and the other rhetorical forms—*description, definition, analogy, division and classification, process analysis, example* (or *illustration*), and *argument/persuasion*—are important ways of structuring our thoughts and getting our point across to others. (The Glossary at the end of *Language Awareness* explains these and other rhetorical terms in detail. In developing your understanding of these rhetorical forms, you may find it helpful to consult the Glossary as well as the alternate table of contents at the beginning, which classifies the essays in the text according to the rhetorical patterns that they demonstrate.)

Expanding your awareness of how writers use language, then, will require you to pay careful attention not only to what an essay says but also to the way it has been put together. To do so most effectively, as you read, keep a pencil in your hand and use it. Make note, first, of your own responses. If you disagree with a fact or a conclusion, object in the margin: *"NO!"* If you feel skeptical, indicate that response: *"Why?"* If you are impressed by an argument or a turn of phrase, compliment the writer: *"Good!"* Mark words or passages you don't understand at first reading. A question mark in the margin may do the job, or you may want to circle words or phrases in the text. During the second reading you can look up the words and puzzle out the difficult passages. Be sure, as well, to highlight key points. Mark off the essay into its main sections, such as the introduction, body, and conclusion.

Write in whatever marginal notes come naturally to you. These quick, brief responses will help you later when you begin asking and answering for yourself more specific analytical questions. When annotating a text, don't be timid. Mark up your book as much as you like. But don't let annotating become burdensome or meaningless. It should be an aid, not a chore, and a word or phrase is usually as good as a sentence. To avoid annotating or underlining more than necessary, always ask yourself why you believe the sentence or paragraph is important. You may, in fact, want to delay much of your annotating until a second reading, so that your first reading can be fast and free.

Once you've finished reading and annotating an essay, you'll want to make sure that you've gotten everything from it you can. One good way to complete your analysis is to answer some basic questions about the essay's content and form. Here are several such questions that you may find useful:

1. What does the author want to say about language? What is the essay's main idea or thesis?
2. What are the chief supporting ideas, and how do they relate to the main idea?
3. What is the author's general purpose? Is it to *persuade* you to a particular point of view? to *explain* a subject to you? to *entertain* you? to *tell* a story? or to *describe* a language phenomenon? Does the author state his or her purpose directly? If not, how do you know what the author's purpose is?

4. What strategy or rhetorical form—narration, comparison and contrast, definition, argument, etc.—does the author use as the principal form for the essay?

5. Why and how does the author's writing strategy suit both the subject and the purpose?

6. What other strategies or rhetorical forms does the author use? Where and for what reason(s)?

7. How is the essay structured? How does its organization relate to its main idea and to the author's purpose?

8. What is the author's attitude toward the essay's subject—enthusiastically positive, objective, ironic, hostile, etc.?

9. To whom is the essay addressed? What should the audience expect from this particular type of essay—to find out how something works, to discover what something means, to understand why something happened?

10. Does the author supply enough information to support the essay's ideas and enough details to make its descriptions precise? Is all of the information relevant and, as far as you can tell, accurate?

11. Has the author left out any information that you think might be relevant to the thesis? Does he or she fail to consider any important views—including perhaps your own view?

12. Does the author assume anything without supporting the assumption or even stating it? Are these assumptions acceptable, or would you challenge them?

13. Overall, how effective is the essay? Has the writer accomplished his or her purpose?

Each of the essays in *Language Awareness* is followed by questions for analysis similar to the ones suggested above, but usually more specific. In addition to content questions on the language issues explored in each essay, we have provided questions that direct your attention to specific rhetorical principles and techniques illustrated by the selection. Each essay is also followed by a list of words that you will find worth adding to your active vocabulary, including paragraph references to help you see each word in its original context in the essay. The questions on content and rhetoric as well as the vocabulary items work best when you try to answer them as fully as you can, remembering and considering many details from the selection to support your answers.

LEARNING TO WRITE WELL

As we suggested before, one of our main purposes in encouraging you to give such thoughtful attention to the essays in *Language Awareness* is to help increase your own competence and confidence as a writer. By considering how a variety of writers have solved the problem of providing an opening and closing paragraph for their essays, you can achieve a fuller understanding of the possibilities available to you as you work on introductions and conclusions in essays of your own. Similarly, the essays you read in *Language Awareness* will show you how writers develop coherent paragraphs, how they use transitional words and phrases to create clear connections among the parts of their essays, how they choose words carefully to bring about an appropriate response in their readers. Increasing your sensitivity to matters like these can have a big impact on your own writing.

Furthermore, recognizing how and why the writers in *Language Awareness* have used certain rhetorical strategies will help you put these powerful patterns of thought and organization into practice for yourself. You'll see, for example, that a writer who wants to explain the differences between the language of men and the language of women will naturally choose the strategy of *comparison and contrast* to provide her essay's structure. On the other hand, if a writer wants to explain *why* such differences exist, you'll see that no amount of comparing will do the job: it will be necessary to use the strategy of analyzing *cause and effect*. If a writer wants to communicate the meaning of a term like "jargon" or "euphemism," the strategy of *definition* suggests itself naturally. Every topic and purpose for writing will suggest one or another writing strategy. As you write, you may often wish to plan your strategy before you start, consciously deciding which one or which combination of strategies best fits what you have to say and what you want to accomplish. When you've completed a rough draft, you need to read what you've written, making sure that your choice of strategy was a good one and that it expresses your content accurately and effectively. The sort of reading *Language Awareness* encourages will help you become more skilled at making the decisions that lead to such improvement in your own writing.

Language Awareness will also provide you with many possibilities for practicing your writing skills. Each essay in the text is followed by two or more writing assignments based upon the essay's content and/or its rhetorical features. These assignments will give you a chance to use the essay as a model or as a starting point for an essay of your own. At the end of each section of the text, we have provided further topics and instructions for writing that bring together ideas from several different selections, allowing you to synthesize your thoughts about the overall subject of a section. Finally, at the end of the book there is a list of suggested topics for longer papers involving some library research. Each of the many suggestions is designed to help you think more closely about some particular aspect of language as you refine your ability to express your thoughts forcefully and coherently in writing.

A SAMPLE STUDENT ESSAY

Rekha Mirchandani, a student at the University of Vermont, wrote the following paper after her composition class had studied the "Language and Advertising" section in *Language Awareness*. She first chose a broad subject—a comparison of today's advertising techniques with those practiced fifty years ago—from the list of suggested topics at the end of the text. Then she narrowed the focus of her research to concentrate on five specific language techniques that she had learned from her reading were commonly found in contemporary ads. Once she had decided on this basis of comparison, she began to gather examples of specific ads—first from current magazines, then from popular periodicals of the 1920s and 1930s, which she was able to locate in the library. She classified each ad according to the language technique it exemplified, so that she could compare how frequently each technique had occurred in the past with the frequency of its occurrence in the present. As she continued to work with her materials and to read further about her subject, a tentative thesis began to emerge: Advertisers today, she discovered, use basically the same techniques that their counterparts in the past used; one technique, however, weasel words, has increased in the last fifty years, probably because a direct statement of unsubstantiated claims—possible before 1938—is no longer permissible by law. At this point, after briefly outlining the order in which she would discuss each technique and choosing which ads she would refer to in her comparison, Rekha was ready to write her first draft. Her essay, however, went through two further drafts before she felt satisfied that she had made her point as effectively as she wished. Although we only present her final version here, you should be aware that this is the result of a number of revisions made over the course of several weeks.

HAVE WE COME A LONG WAY, BABY?

The communications field is bursting with new technology that increases our television reception, spreads news through computer systems, and programs radio stations to run without DJs. We might expect that advertising, the life support of the media, would reflect this increase in sophistication. But, according to David Ogilvy, one of advertising's major tycoons, the advertising business has undergone only one significant change since he entered it in 1949: Television has become an important transmitter of the advertising word (7). The actual techniques that work today have been in use since the beginning of the twentieth century.

One way to see if advertising has changed at all is to contrast methods used today with those used years ago. In his book *I Can Sell You Anything,* Paul Stevens points out some fifteen language techniques copywriters use to make products attractive (23–76); five stand out as being especially pervasive. To determine the existence or non-existence of change, I examined a large number of ads—both old and new—for the use of these five techniques.

One common method of manipulating words is to imply an association between the accomplishments of a hero and the product. In a 1952 ad for Ballantine Ale, Ernest Hemingway is shown on one page looking up from a book, while on an adjacent page a letter signed by him praises the ale. The intended message is clear: if you want to be like this prestigious person, do as he does, drink Ballantine Ale. The same technique is at work in a 1981 advertisement for Campari. Actress Geraldine Chaplin is pictured, along with a written interview describing her experiences with the aperitif; hinted at is a relationship between movie stars and those who drink Campari.

Another technique used by advertisers is what Stevens calls the "noncomparative comparative claim" (73). This is an assertion that compares the product to some deliberately vague item or items. In 1928, for example, an ad for sanitary napkins read, "Modess: so infinitely finer." The question that should come to mind is, finer than what? Than they were before? Finer than other companies' sanitary napkins? finer than no sanitary napkin at all? In 1984 an ad for Atune uses the same technique: "Introducing Atune. Shampoo. Conditioner. Hair Spray. The first system that keeps permed or colored hair looking good longer." Longer than what is not made clear. In each case the advertiser attempts to make a particular brand of sanitary napkins or shampoo sound better, but we may infer that there is no evidence that the products really are "finer" or "last longer." As Stevens points out, if there were proof, the advertiser would not hide it under unclear generalizations (74).

A third method of manipulating words is inventing names that make the product or its key ingredient sound more important, more advanced, or more effective than it actually is. In 1936 Woodbury's Germ-free Beauty Cream, which supposedly protected skin from blemishes, attributed its effectiveness to Element 576, which "aids in combatting skin dryness." Exactly what Element 576 is remains a mystery, but it is surely meant to sound scientific. A classic example of the same technique being used today is an advertisement for Certs that says "Retsyn is the reason that it works." Retsyn is simply a fancy name for vegetable oil, used to imply something special about the product. A case where the product itself has an invented name is the "Nobody Else Like You Service" provided by Equitable Life Insurance in 1971. The name hints that other companies do not cater to the individual. Another invented name is "The Penna Method of Scientific Face Lifting by Bloodless Surgery," advertised in 1927. It sounds magical, but as you read on you discover that the "method" consists only of various creams, oils, and astringents. In each case very ordinary products are made to sound revolutionary through an important-sounding name.

Stevens also discusses how advertisers use adjectives when they have nothing substantial to say about a product. As he puts it, "There is a direct, inverse proportion between the number of adjectives and the number of facts" (38). An ad for Ivory soap in 1918 said, "It's so mild and pure that no matter how often it is used, it leaves the tenderest skin soft, smooth, and white." Cross out the modifying words, and relatively little remains. Similarly, an ad for Neutrogena in 1984 claims, "Skin silkening: The unique body oil that is so light and absorbent that it leaves your skin soft, caressable, and immediately dressable." Again, no worthwhile message.

A final technique, "weasel words," is used by copywriters to avoid a direct statement of fact (Stevens, 23). The most common weasel word is "help," used in phrases like "helps stop . . . ," "helps prevent . . . ," "helps fight. . . ." Other words such as "like" and "as" allow the advertiser to compare his goods to something much larger ("For a diamond as valuable as the love you've found . . ."). "Virtually" and "quite possibly" are words often used at the beginning of a sentence to avoid a direct claim ("Quite possibly, the purest, clearest, mildest cleansing bar. . . ."). These words are little noticed because they fall into the flow of the sentence in which they are found. The consumer may well believe that each statement presents a straight claim.

Although weasel words are prominent in ads today, I found that they are rare in ads written at the beginning of the century. I examined fifty early ads, and few used "help" in their copywriting. Stevens estimated that this word is used in 75 percent of all contemporary advertising (24).

A possible explanation for the lack of weasel words in early ads is that there were no strong laws to forbid false advertising. Before 1938 the Federal Trade Commission was able "to take action only when competition was adversely affected" (Stuart, 3). During the Depression, Fleischmann's yeast ads contained the endorsement of a "doctor": "If you would 'tune up' your system and keep it free of the poisons that lead to coated tongue, bad breath, bad skin, etc., try Fleischmann's yeast. Just eat it regularly like any other food—three cakes each day." The *Journal of American Medicine* did a study disproving most of this "evidence," but the FTC would not act, because they could not prove that the ad hurt competition. In 1938, however, Congress passed the Wheeler-Lea Act, which gave the FTC power to punish false advertisers. Manufacturers had to find other ways of making statements without offending the letter of the law. Words such as "help" and "quite possibly"—not needed before—became an indispensable part of the vocabulary of advertising.

An increase in the use of weasel words is very noticeable in a comparison of ads published before and after 1938. Before the Wheeler-Lea Act was passed, beauty products made many radical claims. In a 1927 ad, Elizabeth Arden said that regular use of her creams "will revive the elastic firmness of the muscles and restore the smooth curve of your contour." In the same year Helena Rubinstein said that her Velaze Beautifying Skin Food "removes tans, freckles, sallowness and discolorations." These are in contrast with later ads. In 1945, for example, Dorothy Grey's Extra Rich Skin Cream claimed that it *"Helps* overcome flaky dryness," and *"Hastens* the return of softness and smoothness to your weather-dried complexion." And Tussy Rich Cream's "fine emollient oils *help* smooth away fine lines due to dryness."

Another example of the need to use weasel words after 1938 is the advertising for Air Step shoes—shoes with a new type of cushiony sole. In 1936 an ad read, "You're actually walking on Air! The effortless ease of wearing them ends fatigue, erases aging fatigue lines from your face. You feel younger, vibrantly alive—ready for anything!" In 1945 an ad for similar shoes said, "Air Borne. It's *like* floating through the air." The need to modify claims without changing the intention of the words is illustrated by the increase in use of weasel words after 1938.

Despite the appearance of sophistication and rapid change in the world of advertising, much remains the same. Advertisers today use basically the same techniques that their counterparts used forty or fifty years ago. I found hero association, non-existent comparison, name-inventing, and adjectival padding in early as well as contemporary advertising. One change, however, was the increased use of weasel words to avoid a direct statement of the sort of unsubstantiated claims that are no longer permissible. Otherwise, comparing ads from today and yesterday shows David Ogilvy to be correct: methods of manipulating words have changed little throughout the century.

Works Cited

Ogilvy, David. *Ogilvy on Advertising.* New York: Crown Publishers Inc., 1983.

Stevens, Paul. *I Can Sell You Anything.* New York: Ballantine Books, 1973. (Paul Stevens is the pen name of Carl P. Wrighter.)

Stuart, Fredric. *Consumer Protection from Deceptive Advertising.* Hempstead, New York: Hofstra University, 1974.

Not every assignment you complete in conjunction with *Language Awareness* will involve the kind of outside research that Rekha's paper did (although it is very possible that your instructor at some point will ask you to complete a longer research paper on some language-related topic). However, the thoughtful attention Rekha has given to the ads she analyzes, the clearly organized structure of her essay, and the awareness she demonstrates in her use of language should give you some idea of the work this text will encourage you to pursue. We hope you will find much here to spark your interest in language, much to increase your understanding of the power of language, and, most important, much to help you develop greater control over your own abilities as an effective user of language, in speech as well as in writing.

I

Language Awareness

The future exists only in language.

S. I. Hayakawa

The limits of my language stand for the limits of my world.
Ludwig Wittgenstein

Every human language has been shaped by, and changes to meet, the needs of its speakers.
Harvey A. Daniels

It is impossible to dissociate language from science or science from language, because every natural science always involves three things: the sequence of phenomena on which the science is based; the abstract concepts which call the phenomena to mind; and the words in which the concepts are expressed. To call forth a concept, a word is needed; to portray a phenomenon, a concept is needed. All three mirror one and the same reality.
Antoine Laurent Lavoisier

To keep informed—even to stay alive—our citizens and voters must demand that linguistic knowledge become public knowledge far more than ever before.
Dwight Bollinger

1
Coming to an
Awareness of Language

MALCOLM X

On February 21, 1965, Malcolm X, the Black Muslim leader, was shot to death as he addressed an afternoon rally in Harlem. He was thirty-nine years old. In the course of his brief life he had risen from the world of thieving, pimping, and drug pushing to become one of the most articulate and powerful blacks in America during the early 1960s.

With the assistance of Alex Haley, later the author of Roots, *Malcolm X told his story in* The Autobiography of Malcolm X, *a moving account of his search for fulfillment. In the following selection taken from the* Autobiography, *Malcolm X narrates the story of how his frustration at not being able to express himself in the letters he wrote led to his discovery of the power of language.*

I've never been one for inaction. Everything I've ever felt strongly about, I've done something about. I guess that's why, unable to do anything else, I soon began writing to people I had known in the hustling world, such as Sammy the Pimp, John Hughes, the gambling house owner, the thief Jumpsteady, and several dope peddlers. I wrote them all about Allah and Islam and Mr. Elijah Muhammad. I had no idea where most of them lived. I addressed their letters in care of the Harlem or Roxbury bars and clubs where I'd known them.

I never got a single reply. The average hustler and criminal was too uneducated to write a letter. I have known many slick sharp-looking hustlers, who would have you think they had an interest in Wall Street; privately, they would get someone else to read a letter if they received one. Besides, neither would I have replied to anyone writing me something as wild as "the white man is the devil."

What certainly went on the Harlem and Roxbury wires was that Detroit Red was going crazy in stir, or else he was trying some hype to shake up the warden's office.

During the years that I stayed in the Norfolk Prison Colony, never did any official directly say anything to me about those letters, although, of course, they all passed through the prison censorship. I'm sure, however, they monitored what I wrote to add to the files which every state and federal prison keeps on the conversion of Negro inmates by the teachings of Mr. Elijah Muhammad.

But at that time, I felt that the real reason was that the white man knew that he was the devil. 5

Later on, I even wrote to the Mayor of Boston, to the Governor of Massachusetts, and to Harry S. Truman. They never answered; they probably never even saw my letters. I handscratched to them how the white man's society was responsible for the black man's condition in this wilderness of North America. 6

It was because of my letters that I happened to stumble upon starting to acquire some kind of a homemade education. 7

I became increasingly frustrated at not being able to express what I wanted to convey in letters that I wrote, especially those to Mr. Elijah Muhammad. In the street, I had been the most articulate hustler out there—I had commanded attention when I said something. But now, trying to write simple English, I not only wasn't articulate, I wasn't even functional. How would I sound writing in slang, the way I would *say* it, something such as, "Look, daddy, let me pull your coat about a cat. Elijah Muhammad—" 8

Many who today hear me somewhere in person, or on television, or those who read something I've said, will think I went to school far beyond the eighth grade. This impression is due entirely to my prison studies. 9

It had really begun back in the Charlestown Prison, when Bimbi first made me feel envy of his stock of knowledge. Bimbi had always taken charge of any conversation he was in, and I had tried to emulate him. But every book I picked up had few sentences which didn't contain anywhere from one to nearly all of the words that might as well have been in Chinese. When I just skipped those words, of course, I really ended up with little idea of what the book said. So I had come to the Norfolk Prison Colony still going through only book-reading motions. Pretty soon, I would have quit even these motions, unless I had received the motivation that I did. 10

I saw that the best thing I could do was get hold of a dictionary—to study, to learn some words. I was lucky enough to reason also that I should try to improve my penmanship. It was sad. I couldn't even write in a straight line. It was both ideas together that moved me to request a dictionary along with some tablets and pencils from the Norfolk Prison Colony school. 11

I spent two days just riffling uncertainly through the dictionary's pages. I'd never realized so many words existed! I didn't know *which* words I needed to learn. Finally, just to start some kind of action, I began copying. 12

In my slow, painstaking, ragged handwriting, I copied into my   13
tablet everything printed on that first page, down to the punctuation
marks.

I believe it took me a day. Then, aloud, I read back, to myself,   14
everything I'd written on the tablet. Over and over, aloud, to myself, I
read my own handwriting.

I woke up the next morning, thinking about those words—im-   15
mensely proud to realize that not only had I written so much at one
time, but I'd written words that I never knew were in the world. Moreover, with a little effort, I also could remember what many of these
words meant. I reviewed the words whose meanings I didn't remember. Funny thing, from the dictionary first page right now, that "aardvark" springs to my mind. The dictionary had a picture of it, a long-
tailed, long-eared, burrowing African mammal, which lives off ter-
mites caught by sticking out its tongue as an anteater does for ants.

I was so fascinated that I went on—I copied the dictionary's next   16
page. And the same experience came when I studied that. With every
succeeding page, I also learned of people and places and events from
history. Actually the dictionary is like a miniature encyclopedia. Finally the dictionary's A section had filled a whole tablet—and I went
on into the B's. That was the way I started copying what eventually
became the entire dictionary. It went a lot faster after so much practice
helped me pick up handwriting speed. Between what I wrote in my
tablet, and writing letters, during the rest of my time in prison I would
guess I wrote a million words.

I suppose it was inevitable that as my word-base broadened, I   17
could for the first time pick up a book and read and now begin to understand what the book was saying. Anyone who has read a great deal
can imagine the new world that opened. Let me tell you something:
from then until I left that prison, in every free moment I had, if I was
not reading in the library, I was reading on my bunk. You couldn't
have gotten me out of books with a wedge. Between Mr. Muhammad's
teachings, my correspondence, my visitors . . . and my reading of
books, months passed without my even thinking about being imprisoned. In fact, up to then, I never had been so truly free in my life.

QUESTIONS ON CONTENT

1. What motivated Malcolm X "to acquire some kind of a homemade
education"(7)?

2. What does Malcolm X mean when he says that he was "going
through only book-reading motions"(10)? How did he decide to solve
this problem?

3. In paragraph 8 Malcolm X points to the difference between being "articulate" and being "functional" in his speaking and writing. What exactly is the distinction that he makes?

4. Why did the word *aardvark* spring to mind when Malcolm X recalled his study of the first page of the dictionary?

5. In what ways is the dictionary like a "miniature encyclopedia"(16)? How are dictionaries and encyclopedias different?

6. What is the nature of the freedom that Malcolm X refers to in the final sentence?

QUESTIONS ON RHETORIC

1. Malcolm X narrates his experiences as a prisoner in the first person. Why is the first person particularly appropriate? (Glossary: *Point of View*)

2. How has Malcolm X organized his essay? (Glossary: *Organization*)

3. The first sentences of paragraphs 1 and 2 are both short declarative sentences. Why are they especially effective as introductory sentences?

4. Could paragraphs 12, 13, and 14 be combined into a single paragraph? What would be gained or lost if they were to be combined?

5. Why is Malcolm X's relatively simple vocabulary in this narrative appropriate? (Glossary: *Diction*)

VOCABULARY

frustrated (8)   functional (8)   inevitable (17)
articulate (8)   emulate (10)

WRITING TOPICS

1. All of us have been in situations in which our ability to use language seemed inadequate—for example, when taking an exam; being interviewed for a job; giving directions; or expressing sympathy, anger, or grief. Write a brief essay in which you recount one such frustrating incident in your life. In preparing to write your narrative, you may find it helpful to ask yourself such questions as: Why is the incident important to me? What details are necessary for me to re-create the incident in an interesting and engaging way? How can my narrative of the incident be most effectively organized? Compare your experiences with those of your classmates.

2. Malcolm X solved the problems of his own illiteracy by carefully studying the dictionary. Would this be a practical solution to the national problem of illiteracy? Are there any alternatives to Malcolm X's approach? What are they?

2
Man the Talker

PETER FARB

Although the ability to use language is perhaps the most distinguishing character-istic of human beings, most people underestimate the miracle of language, the linguistic creativity involved "in exploiting a language's total resources." This linguistic creativity is the birthright of every human being, as Peter Farb reminds us in this selection from his provocative book Word Play: What Happens When People Talk. *Farb uses striking examples to illustrate the complexity and the in-finitely flexible nature of the English language, which he compares and contrasts to other human languages as well as to animal sounds.*

Some twenty-five hundred years ago, Psamtik, an Egyptian pharaoh, 1
desired to discover man's primordial tongue. He entrusted two infants to an isolated shepherd and ordered that they should never hear a word spoken in any language. When the children were returned to the pharaoh several years later, he thought he heard them utter *bekos,* which means "bread" in Phrygian, a language of Asia Minor. And so he honored Phrygian as man's "natural" language. Linguists today know that the story of the pharaoh's experiment must be apocryphal. No child is capable of speech until he has heard other human beings speak, and even two infants reared together cannot develop a language from scratch. Nor does any single "natural" language exist. A child growing up anywhere on earth will speak the tongue he hears in his speech community, regardless of the race, nationality, or language of his parents.

Every native speaker is amazingly creative in the various strategies 2
of speech interaction, in word play and verbal dueling, in exploiting a language's total resources to create poetry and literature. Even a monosyllabic *yes*—spoken in a particular speech situation, with a cer-tain tone of voice, and accompanied by an appropriate gesture—might constitute an original use of English. This sort of linguistic creativity is the birthright of every human being on earth, no matter what language he speaks, the kind of community he lives in, or his degree of intelli-gence. As Edward Sapir pointed out, when it comes to language "Plato

walks with the Macedonian swineherd, Confucius with the head-hunting savage of Assam."

And at a strictly grammatical level also, native speakers are unbelievably creative in language. Not every human being can play the violin, do calculus, jump high hurdles, or sail a canoe, no matter how excellent his teachers or how arduous his training—but every person constantly creates utterances never before spoken on earth. Incredible as it may seem at first thought, the sentence you just read possibly appeared in exactly this form for the first time in the history of the English language—and the same thing might be said about the sentence you are reading now. In fact, if conventional remarks—such as greetings, farewells, stock phrases like *thank you,* proverbs, clichés, and so forth—are disregarded, in theory all of a person's speech consists of sentences never before uttered.   3

A moment's reflection reveals why that may be so. Every language   4 groups its vocabulary into a number of different classes such as nouns, verbs, adjectives, and so on. If English possessed a mere 1,000 nouns (such as *trees, children, horses*) and only 1,000 verbs (*grow, die, change*), the number of possible two-word sentences, therefore, would be 1,000 × 1,000, or one million. Of course, most of these sentences will be meaningless to a speaker today—yet at one time people thought *atoms split* was a meaningless utterance. The nouns, however, might also serve as the objects of these same verbs in three-word sentences. So with the same meager repertory of 1,000 nouns and 1,000 verbs capable of taking an object, the number of possible three-word sentences increases to 1,000 × 1,000 × 1,000 or one billion. These calculations, of course, are just for minimal sentences and an impoverished vocabulary. Most languages offer their speakers many times a thousand nouns and a thousand verbs, and in addition they possess other classes of words that function as adverbs, adjectives, articles, prepositions, and so on. Think, too, in terms of four-word, ten-word, even fifty-word sentences—and the number of possible grammatical combinations becomes astronomical. One linguist calculated that it would take ten trillion years (two thousand times the estimated age of the earth) to utter all the possible English sentences that use exactly twenty words. Therefore, it is improbable that any twenty-word sentence a person speaks was ever spoken previously—and the same thing would hold true, of course, for sentences of greater length, and for most shorter ones as well.

For a demonstration of just why the number of sentences that can   5 be constructed in a language is, at least in theory, infinite, show twenty-five speakers of English a cartoon and ask them to describe in a single sentence what they see. Each of the twenty-five speakers will come up with a different sentence, perhaps examples similar to these:

> I see a little boy entering a magic and practical-joke shop to buy some-
> thing and not noticing that the owner, a practical joker himself, has laid a
> booby trap for him.
> The cartoon shows an innocent little kid, who I guess is entering a magic
> shop because he wants to buy something, about to be captured in a trap by
> the owner of the shop, who has a diabolical expression on his face.

It has been calculated that the vocabulary and the grammatical structures used in only twenty-five such sentences about this cartoon might
provide the raw material for nearly twenty *billion* grammatical sentences—a number so great that about forty human life spans would be
needed to speak them, even at high speed. Obviously, no one could
ever speak, read, or hear in his lifetime more than the tiniest fraction
of the possible sentences in his language. That is why almost every
sentence in this book—as well as in all the books ever written or to be
written—is possibly expressed in its exact form for the first time.

This view of creativity in the grammatical aspects of language is a   6
very recent one. It is part of the revolution in ideas about the structure
of language that has taken place since 1957, when Noam Chomsky, of
the Massachusetts Institute of Technology, published his *Syntactic
Structures.* Since then Chomsky and others have put forth a theory of
language that bears little resemblance to the grammar most people
learned in "grammar" school. Not all linguists accept Chomsky's
theories. But his position, whether it is ultimately shown to be right or
wrong, represents an influential school in theoretical linguistics today,
one that other schools often measure themselves against.

Chomsky believes that all human beings possess at birth an innate   7
capacity to acquire language. Such a capacity is biologically determined—that is, it belongs to what is usually termed "human nature"—and it is passed from parents to children as part of the offspring's biological inheritance. The innate capacity endows speakers
with the general shape of human language, but it is not detailed
enough to dictate the precise tongue each child will speak—which accounts for why different languages are spoken in the world. Chomsky
states that no one learns a language by learning all of its possible sentences, since obviously that would require countless lifetimes. For example, it is unlikely that any of the speakers who saw the cartoon of
the child entering the magic store ever encountered such a bizarre situation before—yet none of the speakers had any difficulty in constructing sentences about it. Nor would a linguist who wrote down these
twenty-five sentences ever have heard them previously—yet he had no
difficulty understanding them. So, instead of learning billions of sentences, a person unconsciously acquires a grammar that can generate
an infinite number of new sentences in his language.

Such a grammar is innately within the competence of any native   8 speaker of a language. However, no speaker—not even Shakespeare, Dante, Plato, or the David of the Psalms—lives up to his theoretical competence. His actual performance in speaking a language is considerably different, and it consists of numerous errors, hesitations, repetitions, and so forth. Despite these very uneven performances that a child hears all around him, in only a few years—and before he even receives instruction in reading and writing in "grammar" school— he puts together for himself the theoretical rules for the language spoken in his community. Since most sentences that a child hears are not only unique but also filled with errors, how can he ever learn the grammar of his language? Chomsky's answer is that children are born with the capacity to learn only grammars that accord with the innate human blueprint. Children disregard performance errors because such errors result in sentences that could not be described by such a grammar. Strong evidence exists that native speakers of a language know intuitively whether a sentence is grammatical or not. They usually cannot specify exactly what is wrong, and very possibly they make the same mistakes in their own speech, but they know—unconsciously, not as a set of rules they learned in school—when a sentence is incorrect.

The human speaker—born with a capacity for language, infinitely [9] creative in its use, capable of constructing novel utterances in unfamiliar speech situations—shares the globe with a variety of animals that whistle, shriek, squeak, bleat, hoot, coo, call, and howl. And so it has been assumed, ever since Aristotle first speculated about the matter, that human speech is only some superior kind of animal language. Alexander Graham Bell saw nothing odd about his attempts to teach a dog to speak by training it to growl at a steady rate while he manipulated its throat and jaws. The dog finally managed to produce a sequence of syllables which sounded somewhat like *ow ah oo gwah mah*—the closest it could come to "How are you, Grandma?" And Samuel Pepys, in his *Diary* entry for August 24, 1661, noted:

> by and by we are called to Sir W. Batten's to see the strange creature that Captain Holmes hath brought with him from Guiny; it is a great baboon [apparently not a baboon at all but rather a chimpanzee], but so much like a man in most things, that though they say there is a species of them, yet I cannot believe but that it is a monster got of a man and a she-baboon. I do believe that it already understands much English, and I am of the mind it might be taught to speak or make signs.

Other experimenters concluded that animals could not be taught [10] human languages, but they saw no reason why they themselves should not learn to speak the way animals do. A few enthusiasts have even published dictionaries for various bird and animal languages—among them E. I. Du Pont de Nemours, the French-born founder of the

American chemical firm, who in 1807 compiled dictionaries for the languages of such birds as crows and nightingales. These efforts are ludicrous because human speech is quite different from most animal communication. Between the bird's call to its mate and the human utterance *I love you* lie a few hundred million years of evolution, at least one whole day of Biblical Creation. St. Francis of Assisi, talking to the birds, may have had much to say to them, but they had nothing to discuss with him.

Human speech seemingly resembles animal calls in that it employs a small number of sounds, often no more than the number emitted by many species of birds and mammals. But, unlike animal calls, human sounds are combined to form a vast vocabulary, which in turn is structured into an infinite number of utterances. The number of different units of sound in each human language, such as the *m* in *man* or the *ou* in *house,* varies between about a dozen and a little more than five dozen. English recognizes about 45 units, Italian 27, Hawaiian 13. This range is not notably different from the separate units of sound emitted by many kinds of animals: prairie dog, 10; various species of monkeys, about 20; domestic chicken, 25; chimpanzee, 25; bottlenosed dolphin, 28; fox, 36.

Chimpanzees, with their 25 units of sound, are incapable of speech, while Hawaiians, with only 13 units, possess a very expressive language. That is because the chimpanzee employs one unit of sound in social play, another when a juvenile is lost, a third when attacked, and so on—but two or more calls cannot be combined to generate additional messages. In contrast, the 13 sounds of Hawaiian can be combined to form 2,197 potential three-sound words, nearly five million six-sound words—and an astronomical number if the full repertory of 13 sounds is used to form longer words. In the same way, a speaker of English can select three units of sound out of his store of 45, such as the sounds represented in writing by *e, n,* and *d*—and then combine them into such meaningful words as *end, den,* and *Ned.* But the chimpanzee cannot combine the three units of sound that mean play, lost juvenile, and threat of attack to form some other message. Nor can the chimpanzee's call that means "Here is food" ever be changed to talk about the delicacies it consumed yesterday or its expectations about finding certain fruits tomorrow. Generation after generation, as far into the future as the chimpanzee survives as a species, it will use that call solely to indicate the immediate presence of food.

Certain animals—most notably parrots, mynahs, and other mimicking birds—can emit a wide repertory of sounds, and they also have an uncanny ability to combine them into longer utterances. Nevertheless, they do not exploit their abilities the way human beings do. A trained mynah bird can so unerringly repeat an English sentence that it is scarcely distinguishable on a tape recording from the same sentence spoken by a human being. Parrots also can duplicate human speech with awesome fidelity, and they have been taught vocabularies of more than a hundred words. A parrot can easily enough be trained to mimic the utterance *a pail of water* and also to mimic a variety of nouns such as *sand* and *milk.* But, for all its skill, the parrot will never substitute nouns for each other and on its own say *a pail of sand* or *a pail of milk.*

Even the most vocal animals are utterly monotonous in what they say in a given situation. The well-known nursery rhyme does not reveal what Jack said to Jill when they went up the hill to fetch a pail of water, and in fact no way exists to predict which of the tremendous strategies two people will select in such a speech situation. But everyone knows what a male songbird will say when another male enters its territory during the breeding season. It will emit a distinctive series of sounds that signify "Go away!" It cannot negotiate with the intruder, nor can it say "I'm sorry that I must ask you to depart now, but I will be happy to make your acquaintance after the breeding season is concluded." The male defender of the territory is simply responding to the stimulus of an intruder at a certain time of the year by uttering a general statement about the existence of such a stimulus.   14

Specialists in animal behavior infer the "meaning" of animal sounds from the behavior of the animals at the time they emit sounds, but it is safe to conclude that the sounds express only indefinable emotions. Individuals belonging to the same animal species emit approximately the same sounds to convey the same emotions. All expressions of pain uttered by any individuals of a monkey species are very much the same, but in the human species the sounds that a speaker uses to communicate his pain are quite arbitrary. A speaker of English says *ouch,* but a Spaniard says *ay* and a Nootka Indian *ishka-takh.* Jill might have emitted an animal-like cry of pain as she came tumbling down the hill—but, as a speaker of English, she also had the choice of saying *I hurt my head* or *Please take me to a doctor.* Even if Jill merely uttered the conventional word *ouch,* which signifies pain in English, this sound is nevertheless considerably different from an animal's cry of pain. An animal's cry cannot be removed from its immediate context, but Jill's *ouch* can. She could, for example, tell someone the next day about her accident by saying *When I fell down the hill, I cried "ouch."* Or she could utter *ouch* in a completely different context, as when someone makes a feeble pun and she wishes to convey that her sensibilities, not her bones, have been wounded.   15

An animal, though, has no such choices. As Bertrand Russell re-   16

marked about a dog's ability to communicate, "No matter how eloquently a dog may bark, he cannot tell you that his parents were poor
but honest." Despite the variety of sounds in the babel of the animal
world, nonhuman calls are emotional responses to a very limited number of immediate stimuli. Every other kind of sound made by living
things on the planet belongs to human speech alone.

QUESTIONS ON CONTENT

1. What does Farb mean when he says that "native speakers are unbelievably creative in language" (3) and that "linguistic creativity is
the birthright of every human being on earth" (2)?

2. Who is Noam Chomsky? Why, according to Farb, is he important?

3. What, according to Farb, is the central tenet of Chomsky's theory
of language?

4. What evidence does Farb present to support Chomsky's claim that
"no one learns a language by learning all of its possible sentences" (7)?

5. What distinctions, according to Farb, does Chomsky draw between
competence and *performance?*

6. In paragraphs 11–16 Farb discusses the differences between human
language and animal sounds. What are the essential differences that
Farb sees?

7. Farb states that "strong evidence exists that native speakers of a
language know intuitively whether a sentence is grammatical or not"
(8). As an experiment, examine the following sentences. Which ones
do you believe are grammatical; which are not? Try to explain what is
wrong with the ones you believe are ungrammatical.

   a. That student continually sleeps in class.
   b. Student in class continually that sleeps.
   c. The basketball player were trying to stall at the end of the game.
   d. The chicken is too hot to eat.
   e. Colorless green ideas sleep furiously.
   f. The band marched smooth in the parade.

QUESTIONS ON RHETORIC

1. Farb opens his essay with the brief story of the Egyptian pharaoh
and his search for man's earliest language. How is this story related to
the subject of Farb's essay? Did you find his opening effective? Why,
or why not? (Glossary: *Beginnings*)

2. What is the relationship between paragraph 4 and paragraph 3? between paragraph 5 and paragraph 4?

3. Writers use transitions to make natural and logical connections between sentences as well as between paragraphs. Such transitions are one way of giving an essay coherence. Discuss the kinds of transitions that Farb uses to link the paragraphs in his essay. (Glossary: *Transitions* and *Coherence*)

4. Farb's essay breaks nicely into three major sections: (1) a discussion of linguistic creativity, (2) a description of Noam Chomsky's theory of language, and (3) an explanation of the differences between human languages and animal "languages." How are these three sections related to Farb's title "Man the Talker"? Why are they presented in the order that they are? What would happen if they were to be rearranged?

5. How does Farb organize his discussion of the differences between human language and animal sounds in paragraphs 11–16? (Glossary: *Comparison* and *Contrast*)

VOCABULARY

primordial (1)	clichés (3)	innate (7)
apocryphal (1)	repertory (4)	ludicrous (10)
arduous (3)	grammar (6)	awesome (13)

WRITING TOPICS

1. As Peter Farb suggests, "show twenty-five speakers of English [e.g., the members of your class] a cartoon and ask them to describe in a single sentence what they see" (5). Compare and contrast the sentences produced. What conclusions can you draw?

2. As a native speaker of English, you have several basic language competencies. For example, you can determine whether or not an utterance is a grammatical sentence. Other competencies include the ability to tell when two or more sentences are synonymous, recognize ambiguity in a sentence, and interpret completely novel utterances. Discuss these competencies in a brief essay that uses examples to illustrate your points.

3. Pet lovers will tell you that their animals can communicate with them. Using your own personal experience or that of someone you know, describe how people and pets communicate with each other. Do you think that this communication fits Farb's definition of language?

3
A Brief History of English

PAUL ROBERTS

In the following selection from his book Understanding English, *the late Professor Paul Roberts recounts the major events in the history of England and discusses their relationship to the development of the English language. He shows us how the people who invaded England influenced the language and how, in recent times, the rapid spread of English has resulted in its becoming a major world language.*

HISTORICAL BACKGROUNDS

No understanding of the English language can be very satisfactory without a notion of the history of the language. But we shall have to make do with just a notion. The history of English is long and complicated, and we can only hit the high spots.

The history of our language begins a little after A.D. 600. Everything before that is pre-history, which means that we can guess at it but can't prove much. For a thousand years or so before the birth of Christ our linguistic ancestors were savages wandering through the forests of northern Europe. Their language was a part of the Germanic branch of the Indo-European Family.

At the time of the Roman Empire—say, from the beginning of the Christian Era to around A.D. 400—the speakers of what was to become English were scattered along the northern coast of Europe. They spoke a dialect of Low German. More exactly, they spoke several different dialects, since they were several different tribes. The names given to the tribes who got to England are *Angles, Saxons,* and *Jutes.* For convenience, we can refer to them as Anglo-Saxons.

Their first contact with civilization was a rather thin acquaintance with the Roman Empire on whose borders they lived. Probably some of the Anglo-Saxons wandered into the Empire occasionally, and cer-

tainly Roman merchants and traders traveled among the tribes. At any
rate, this period saw the first of our many borrowings from Latin. Such
words as *kettle, wine, cheese, butter, cheap, plum, gem, bishop, church*
were borrowed at this time. They show something of the relationship
of the Anglo-Saxons with the Romans. The Anglo-Saxons were learning, getting their first taste of civilization.

They still had a long way to go, however, and their first step was to   5
help smash the civilization they were learning from. In the fourth century the Roman power weakened badly. While the Goths were
pounding away at the Romans in the Mediterranean countries, their
relatives, the Anglo-Saxons, began to attack Britain.

The Romans had been the ruling power in Britain since A.D. 43.   6
They had subjugated the Celts whom they found living there and had
succeeded in setting up a Roman administration. The Roman influence did not extend to the outlying parts of the British Isles. In Scotland, Wales, and Ireland the Celts remained free and wild, and they
made periodic forays against the Romans in England. Among other
defense measures, the Romans built the famous Roman Wall to ward
off the tribes in the north.

Even in England the Roman power was thin. Latin did not become   7
the language of the country as it did in Gaul and Spain. The mass of
people continued to speak Celtic, with Latin and the Roman civilization it contained in use as a top dressing.

In the fourth century, troubles multiplied for the Romans in Brit-   8
ain. Not only did the untamed tribes of Scotland and Wales grow more
and more restive, but the Anglo-Saxons began to make pirate raids on
the eastern coast. Furthermore, there was growing difficulty every-
where in the Empire, and the legions in Britain were siphoned off to
fight elsewhere. Finally, in A.D. 410, the last Roman ruler in England,
bent on becoming emperor, left the islands and took the last of the legions with him. The Celts were left in possession of Britain but almost
defenseless against the impending Anglo-Saxon attack.

Not much is surely known about the arrival of the Anglo-Saxons in   9
England. According to the best early source, the eighth-century historian Bede, the Jutes came in 449 in response to a plea from the Celtic
king, Vortigern, who wanted their help against the Picts attacking
from the north. The Jutes subdued the Picts but then quarreled and
fought with Vortigern, and, with reinforcements from the Continent,
settled permanently in Kent. Somewhat later the Angles established
themselves in eastern England and the Saxons in the south and west.
Bede's account is plausible enough, and these were probably the main
lines of the invasion.

We do know, however, that the Angles, Saxons, and Jutes were a   10 long time securing themselves in England. Fighting went on for as long as a hundred years before the Celts in England were all killed, driven into Wales, or reduced to slavery. This is the period of King Arthur, who was not entirely mythological. He was a Romanized Celt, a general, though probably not a king. He had some success against the Anglo-Saxons, but it was only temporary. By 550 or so the Anglo-Saxons were firmly established. English was in England.

OLD ENGLISH

All this is pre-history, so far as the language is concerned. We have no record of the English language until after 600, when the Anglo-Saxons were converted to Christianity and learned the Latin alphabet. The conversion began, to be precise, in the year 597 and was accomplished within thirty or forty years. The conversion was a great advance for the Anglo-Saxons, not only because of the spiritual benefits but because it reestablished contact with what remained of Roman civilization. This civilization didn't amount to much in the year 600, but it was certainly superior to anything in England up to that time.   11

It is customary to divide the history of the English language into three periods: Old English, Middle English, and Modern English. Old English runs from the earliest records—i.e., seventh century—to about 1100; Middle English from 1100 to 1450 or 1500; Modern English from 1500 to the present day. Sometimes Modern English is further divided into Early Modern, 1500–1700, and Late Modern, 1700 to the present.   12

When England came into history, it was divided into several more or less autonomous kingdoms, some of which at times exercised a certain amount of control over the others. In the century after the conversion the most advanced kingdom was Northumbria, the area between the Humber River and the Scottish border. By A.D. 700 the Northumbrians had developed a respectable civilization, the finest in Europe. It is sometimes called the Northumbrian Renaissance, and it was the first of the several renaissances through which Europe struggled upward out of the ruins of the Roman Empire. It was in this period that the best of the Old English literature was written, including the epic poem *Beowulf.*   13

In the eighth century, Northumbrian power declined, and the center of influence moved southward to Mercia, the kingdom of the Midlands. A century later the center shifted again, and Wessex, the country of the West Saxons, became the leading power. The most famous king of the West Saxons was Alfred the Great, who reigned in the second half of the ninth century, dying in 901. He was famous not only as   14 a military man and administrator but also as a champion of learning. He founded and supported schools and translated or caused to be translated many books from Latin into English. At this time also much of the Northumbrian literature of two centuries earlier was copied in West Saxon. Indeed, the great bulk of Old English writing which has come down to us is in the West Saxon dialect of 900 or later.

In the military sphere, Alfred's great accomplishment was his successful opposition to the Viking invasions. In the ninth and tenth centuries, the Norsemen emerged in their ships from their homelands in Denmark and the Scandinavian peninsula. They traveled far and attacked and plundered at will and almost with impunity. They ravaged Italy and Greece, settled in France, Russia, and Ireland, colonized Iceland and Greenland, and discovered America several centuries before Columbus. Nor did they overlook England. 15

After many years of hit-and-run raids, the Norsemen landed an army on the east coast of England in the year 866. There was nothing much to oppose them except the Wessex power led by Alfred. The long struggle ended in 877 with a treaty by which a line was drawn roughly from the northwest of England to the southeast. On the eastern side of the line Norse rule was to prevail. This was called the Danelaw. The western side was to be governed by Wessex. 16

The linguistic result of all this was a considerable injection of Norse into the English language. Norse was at this time not so different from English as Norwegian or Danish is now. Probably speakers of English could understand, more or less, the language of the newcomers who had moved into eastern England. At any rate, there was considerable interchange and word borrowing. Examples of Norse words in the English language are *sky, give, law, egg, outlaw, leg, ugly, scant, sly, crawl, scowl, take, thrust.* There are hundreds more. We have even borrowed some pronouns from Norse—*they, their,* and *them.* These words were borrowed first by the eastern and northern dialects and then in the course of hundreds of years made their way into English generally. 17

It is supposed also—indeed, it must be true—that the Norsemen influenced the sound structure and the grammar of English. But this is hard to demonstrate in detail. 18

A Specimen of Old English

We may now have an example of Old English. The favorite illustration is the Lord's Prayer, since it needs no translation. This has come to us in several different versions. Here is one: 19

Fæder ure,
þu þe eart on heofonum,
si þin nama gehalgod.
Tobecume þin rice.
Gewurþe ðin willa on eorðan swa swa on heofonum.
Urne gedæghwamlican hlaf syle us to dæg.
And forgyf us ure gyltas, swa swa we forgyfað urum gyltendum.
And ne gelæd þu us on costnunge,
ac alys us of yfele. Soþlice.

Some of the differences between this and Modern English are [20] merely differences in orthography. For instance, the sign *æ* is what Old English writers used for a vowel sound like that in modern *hat* or *and*. The *th* sounds of modern *thin* or *then* are represented in Old English by *þ* or *ð*. But of course there are many differences in sound too. *Ure* is the ancestor of modern *our,* but the first vowel was like that in *too* or *ooze*. *Hlaf* is modern *loaf;* we have dropped the *h* sound and changed the vowel, which in *hlaf* was pronounced something like the vowel in *father*. Old English had some sounds which we do not have. The sound represented by *y* does not occur in Modern English. If you pronounce the vowel in *bit* with your lips rounded, you may approach it.

In grammar, Old English was much more highly inflected than [21] Modern English is. That is, there were more case endings for nouns, more person and number endings for verbs, a more complicated pronoun system, various endings for adjectives, and so on. Old English nouns had four cases—nominative, genitive, dative, accusative. Adjectives had five—all these and an instrumental case besides. Present-day English has only two cases for nouns—common case and possessive case. Adjectives now have no case system at all. On the other hand, we now use a more rigid word order and more structure words (prepositions, auxiliaries, and the like) to express relationships than Old English did.

Some of this grammar we can see in the Lord's Prayer. *Heofonum,* [22] for instance, is a dative plural; the nominative singular was *heofon*. *Urne* is an accusative singular; the nominative is *ure*. In *urum glytendum* both words are dative plural. *Forgyfaþ* is the first person plural form of the verb. Word order is different: "urne gedæghwamlican hlaf syle us" in place of "Give us our daily bread." And so on.

In vocabulary Old English is quite different from Modern English. [23] Most of the Old English words are what we may call native English: that is, words which have not been borrowed from other languages but which have been a part of English ever since English was a part of Indo-European. Old English did certainly contain borrowed words. We have seen that many borrowings were coming in from Norse.

Rather large numbers had been borrowed from Latin, too. Some of these were taken while the Anglo-Saxons were still on the Continent (*cheese, butter, bishop, kettle,* etc.); a large number came into English after the conversion (*angel, candle, priest, martyr, radish, oyster, purple, school, spend,* etc.). But the great majority of Old English words were native English.

Now, on the contrary, the majority of words in English are bor-   24
rowed, taken mostly from Latin and French. Of the words in *The American College Dictionary* only about 14 percent are native. Most of these, to be sure, are common, high-frequency words—*the, of, I, and, because, man, mother, road,* etc.; of the thousand most common words in English, some 62 percent are native English. Even so, the modern vocabulary is very much Latinized and Frenchified. The Old English vocabulary was not.

MIDDLE ENGLISH

Sometime between the years 1000 and 1200 various important changes   25
took place in the structure of English, and Old English became Middle English. The political event which facilitated these changes was the Norman Conquest. The Normans, as the name shows, came originally from Scandinavia. In the early tenth century they established themselves in northern France, adopted the French language, and developed a vigorous kingdom and a very passable civilization. In the year 1066, led by Duke William, they crossed the Channel and made themselves masters of England. For the next several hundred years, England was ruled by kings whose first language was French.

One might wonder why, after the Norman Conquest, French did   26
not become the national language, replacing English entirely. The reason is that the Conquest was not a national migration, as the earlier Anglo-Saxon invasion had been. Great numbers of Normans came to England, but they came as rulers and landlords. French became the language of the court, the language of the nobility, the language of polite society, the language of literature. But it did not replace English as the language of the people. There must always have been hundreds of towns and villages in which French was never heard except when visitors of high station passed through.

But English, though it survived as the national language, was pro-   27
foundly changed after the Norman Conquest. Some of the changes—in sound structure and grammar—would no doubt have taken place whether there had been a Conquest or not. Even before 1066 the case system of English nouns and adjectives was becoming simplified; peo-

ple came to rely more on word order and prepositions than on inflectional endings to communicate their meanings. The process was speeded up by sound changes which caused many of the endings to sound alike. But no doubt the Conquest facilitated the change. German, which didn't experience a Norman Conquest, is today rather highly inflected compared to its cousin English.

But it is in vocabulary that the effects of the Conquest are most obvious. French ceased, after a hundred years or so, to be the native language of very many people in England, but it continued—and continues still—to be a zealously cultivated second language, the mirror of elegance and civilization. When one spoke English, one introduced not only French ideas and French things but also their French names. This was not only easy but socially useful. To pepper one's conversation with French expressions was to show that one was well-bred, elegant, *au courant.* The last sentence shows that the process is not yet dead. By using *au courant* instead of, say, *abreast of things,* the writer indicates that he is no dull clod who knows only English but an elegant person aware of how things are done in *le haut monde.* 28

Thus French words came into English, all sorts of them. There were words to do with government: *parliament, majesty, treaty, alliance, tax, government;* church words: *parson, sermon, baptism, incense, crucifix, religion;* words for foods: *veal, beef, mutton, bacon, jelly, peach, lemon, cream, biscuit;* colors: *blue, scarlet, vermilion;* household words: *curtain, chair, lamp, towel, blanket, parlor;* play words: *dance, chess, music, leisure, conversation;* literary words: *story, romance, poet, literary;* learned words: *study, logic, grammar, noun, surgeon, anatomy, stomach;* just ordinary words of all sorts: *nice, second, very, age, bucket, gentle, final, fault, flower, cry, count, sure, move, surprise, plain.* 29

All these and thousands more poured into the English vocabulary between 1100 and 1500 until, at the end of that time, many people must have had more French words than English at their command. This is not to say that English became French. English remained English in sound structure and in grammar, though these also felt the ripples of French influence. The very heart of the vocabulary, too, remained English. Most of the high-frequency words—the pronouns, the prepositions, the conjunctions, the auxiliaries, as well as a great many ordinary nouns and verbs and adjectives—were not replaced by borrowings. 30

Middle English, then, was still a Germanic language, but it differed from Old English in many ways. The sound system and the grammar changed a good deal. Speakers made less use of case systems and other inflectional devices and relied more on word order and structure words to express their meanings. This is often said to be a simplification, but 31 it isn't really. Languages don't become simpler; they merely exchange one kind of complexity for another. Modern English is not a simple language, as any foreign speaker who tries to learn it will hasten to tell you.

For us Middle English is simpler than Old English just because it is   32 closer to Modern English. It takes three or four months at least to learn to read Old English prose and more than that for poetry. But a week of good study should put one in touch with the Middle English poet Chaucer. Indeed, you may be able to make some sense of Chaucer straight off, though you would need instruction in pronunciation to make it sound like poetry. Here is a famous passage from the *General Prologue to the Canterbury Tales,* fourteenth century:

> *Ther was also a nonne, a Prioresse,*
> *That of hir smyling was ful symple and coy,*
> *Hir gretteste oath was but by Seinte Loy,*
> *And she was cleped° Madame Eglentyne.*   named
> *Ful wel she song the service dyvyne,*
> *Entuned in hir nose ful semely.*
> *And Frenshe she spak ful faire and fetisly,°*   elegantly
> *After the scole of Stratford-atte-Bowe,*
> *For Frenshe of Parys was to hir unknowe.*

EARLY MODERN ENGLISH

Sometime between 1400 and 1600 English underwent a couple of   33 sound changes which made the language of Shakespeare quite different from that of Chaucer. Incidentally, these changes contributed much to the chaos in which English spelling now finds itself.

One change was the elimination of a vowel sound in certain un   34 stressed positions at the end of words. For instance, the words *name, stone, wine, dance* were pronounced as two syllables by Chaucer but as just one by Shakespeare. The *e* in these words became, as we say, "silent." But it wasn't silent for Chaucer; it represented a vowel sound. So also the words *laughed, seemed, stored* would have been pronounced by Chaucer as two-syllable words. The change was an important one because it affected thousands of words and gave a different aspect to the whole language.

The other change is what is called the Great Vowel Shift. This was   35 a systematic shifting of half a dozen vowels and diphthongs in stressed syllables. For instance, the word *name* had in Middle English a vowel something like that in the modern word *father; wine* had the vowel of modern *mean; he* was pronounced something like modern *hey; mouse* sounded like *moose; moon* had the vowel of *moan.* Again the shift was thoroughgoing and affected all the words in which these vowel sounds occurred. Since we still keep the Middle English system of spelling these words, the differences between Modern English and Middle English are often more real than apparent.

The vowel shift has meant also that we have come to use an entirely different set of symbols for representing vowel sounds than is used by writers of such languages as French, Italian, or Spanish, in which no such vowel shift occurred. If you come across a strange word—say, *bine*—in an English book, you will pronounce it according to the English system, with the vowel of *wine* or *dine.* But if you read *bine* in a French, Italian, or Spanish book, you pronounce it with the vowel of *mean* or *seen.*   36

These two changes, then, produced the basic differences between Middle English and Modern English. But there were several other developments that had an effect upon the language. One was the invention of printing, an invention introduced into England by William Caxton in the year 1475. Where before books had been rare and costly, they suddenly became cheap and common. More and more people learned to read and write. This was the first of many advances in communication which have worked to unify languages and to arrest the development of dialect differences, though of course printing effects writing principally rather than speech. Among other things it hastened the standardization of spelling.   37

The period of Early Modern English—that is, the sixteenth and seventeenth centuries—was also the period of the English Renaissance, when people developed, on the one hand, a keen interest in the past and, on the other, a more daring and imaginative view of the future. New ideas multiplied, and new ideas meant new language. Englishmen had grown accustomed to borrowing words from French as a result of the Norman Conquest; now they borrowed from Latin and Greek. As we have seen, English had been raiding Latin from Old English times and before, but now the floodgates really opened, and thousands of words from the classical languages poured in. *Pedestrian, bonus, anatomy, contradict, climax, dictionary, benefit, multiply, exist, paragraph, initiate, scene, inspire* are random examples. Probably the average educated American today has more words from French in his vocabulary than from native English sources, and more from Latin than from French.   38

The greatest writer of the Early Modern English period is of course Shakespeare, and the best-known book is the King James Version of the Bible, published in 1611. The Bible (if not Shakespeare) has made many features of Early Modern English perfectly familiar to many   39 people down to present time, even though we do not use these features in present-day speech and writing. For instance, the old pronouns *thou* and *thee* have dropped out of use now, together with their verb forms, but they are still familiar to us in prayer and in Biblical quotations: "Whither thou goest, I will go." Such forms as *hath* and *doth* have been replaced by *has* and *does;* "Goes he hence tonight?" would now be "Is he going away tonight?"; Shakespeare's "Fie, on't, sirrah" would be "Nuts to that, Mac." Still, all these expressions linger with us because of the power of the works in which they occur.

It is not always realized, however, that considerable sound changes   40 have taken place between Early Modern English and the English of the present day. Shakespearian actors putting on a play speak the words, properly enough, in their modern pronunciation. But it is very doubtful that this pronunciation would be understood at all by Shakespeare. In Shakespeare's time, the word *reason* was pronounced like modern *raisin; face* had the sound of modern *glass;* the *l* in *would, should, palm* was pronounced. In these points and a great many others the English language has moved a long way from what it was in 1600.

RECENT DEVELOPMENTS

The history of English since 1700 is filled with many movements and   41 countermovements, of which we can notice only a couple. One of these is the vigorous attempt made in the eighteenth century, and the rather half-hearted attempts made since, to regulate and control the English language. Many people of the eighteenth century, not understanding very well the forces which govern language, proposed to polish and prune and restrict English, which they felt was proliferating too wildly. There was much talk of an academy which would rule on what people could and could not say and write. The academy never came into being, but the eighteenth century did succeed in establishing certain attitudes which, though they haven't had much effect on the development of the language itself, have certainly changed the native speaker's feeling about the language.

In part, a product of the wish to fix and establish the language was   42 the development of the dictionary. The first English dictionary was published in 1603; it was a list of 2,500 words briefly defined. Many others were published with gradual improvements until Samuel Johnson published his *English Dictionary* in 1755. This, steadily revised, dominated the field in England for nearly a hundred years. Meanwhile in America, Noah Webster published his dictionary in 1828, and before long dictionary publishing was a big business in this country. The last century has seen the publication of one great dictionary: the twelve-volume *Oxford English Dictionary*, compiled in the course of seventy-five years through the labors of many scholars. We have also, of course, numerous commercial dictionaries which are as good as the public wants them to be if not, indeed, rather better.

Another product of the eighteenth century was the invention of "English grammar." As English came to replace Latin as the language of scholarship, it was felt that one should also be able to control and dissect it, parse and analyze it, as one could Latin. What happened in practice was that the grammatical description that applied to Latin was removed and superimposed on English. This was silly, because English is an entirely different kind of language, with its own forms and signals and ways of producing meaning. Nevertheless, English grammars on the Latin model were worked out and taught in the schools. In many schools they are still being taught. This activity is not often popular with school children, but it is sometimes an interesting and instructive exercise in logic. The principal harm in it is that it has tended to keep people from being interested in English and has obscured the real features of English structure. 43

But probably the most important force on the development of English in the modern period has been the tremendous expansion of English-speaking peoples. In 1500 English was a minor language, spoken by a few people on a small island. Now it is perhaps the greatest language of the world, spoken natively by over a quarter of a billion people and as a second language by many millions more. When we speak of English now, we must specify whether we mean American English, British English, Australian English, Indian English, or what, since the differences are considerable. The American cannot go to England or the Englishman to America confident that he will always understand and be understood. The Alabaman in Iowa or the Iowan in Alabama shows himself a foreigner every time he speaks. It is only because communication has become fast and easy that English in this period of its expansion has not broken into a dozen mutually unintelligible languages. 44

QUESTIONS ON CONTENT

1. What are the three major periods in the history of the English language? When did each occur?

2. Roberts is careful to describe the relationship between historical events in England and the development of the English language. In what ways did historical events affect the English language?

3. When the Anglo-Saxons invaded England, their language, with some modifications, became the language of the land. How does Roberts explain the fact that French did not become the language of England after the invasion of William the Conqueror?

4. How would you characterize in social terms the French words that were brought into English by the Norman Conquest? In what areas of life did French have the greatest influence?

5. Explain what changes the English language underwent as a result of the Great Vowel Shift. What is the importance of this linguistic phenomenon for the history of English?

6. Why, according to Roberts, have school children tended not to be interested in the study of the English language?

QUESTIONS ON RHETORIC

1. What is Roberts's thesis in this essay? (Glossary: *Thesis*) Where is it stated?

2. Why is a chronological organization appropriate for this essay? (Glossary: *Organization*)

3. Roberts makes extensive use of examples in his essay. Of what value are these examples for the reader? (Glossary: *Examples*)

4. How does Roberts use comparison and contrast to help him discuss Old English? (Glossary: *Comparison and Contrast*)

5. Roberts uses the pronouns *we, our,* and *us* throughout his essay. What effect does this have on you?

VOCABULARY

forays (6)	impunity (15)	zealously (28)
siphoned (8)	facilitated (25)	linger (39)
conversion (11)		

WRITING TOPICS

1. Using your dictionary, identify the language from which each of the following words was borrowed:

barbecue	hustle
buffalo	marmalade
casino	orangutan
decoy	posse
ditto	raccoon
fruit	veranda

What other examples of borrowed words can you find in your dictionary? Write an essay in which you show with examples that today "the majority of words in English are borrowed" (24).

2. During its relatively brief 1400-year history, the English language has consistently been characterized by change. How is American English still changing today? What effects, if any, have the Vietnam War, the NASA space program, the drug culture, computers and other new technology, the women's movement, and/or recent waves of immigration had on American English?

4

Are You Making Yourself Clear?

NORMAN COUSINS

Norman Cousins has had a long and industrious career as a journalist and writer. He is perhaps best known as the editor of Saturday Review, *a position he held for thirty-five years. His long-standing interest in language and his concern for clear thinking are reflected in the following article, in which he argues for clarity of purpose and organization in conversation and writing. Cousins believes that schools need to give more attention to developing the individual's communication skills.*

In the present scratchy and undiscriminating national mood, educa- 1
tion is an easy target. I deplore the tendency but would like to get into
the act nonetheless. One of the prime weaknesses of education, it
seems to me, is that it doesn't give enough attention to the need for developing the individual's communications skills. It is concerned with
his ability to absorb knowledge but it assigns somewhat lesser importance to his need to make himself clear. This is less a matter of vocabulary range than of vocabulary control. It has to do with the entire process by which an individual organizes his thoughts for purposes of
transmission.

The prime element in this process is sequence. Ideas have to be fit- 2
ted together. The movement of a concept or an image from the mind of
the speaker to the mind of the listener is retarded when words become
random chunks rather than sequential parts of an organized and ordered whole. This doesn't rule out unhurried allusions; these can give
color to an account and help to make a claim on the imagination
and memory. But it does rule out ungoverned circling and droning,
reminiscent of buzzards hovering and swooping over a victim until
he drops.

It contributes nothing to a conversation to have an individual in- 3
terrupt himself in order to insert sudden thoughts. The abuse is compounded when these obtrusive thoughts are invaded by yet others so
that nothing is complete, neither the sentence, nor the paragraph, nor

any of the vagrant incidents or ideas that are strewn around like fragments of an automobile wreck.

The following quotation is a fair approximation drawn from a recent conversation:

> "This book I want to talk to you about," a visitor told me, "is one of the finest novels that I—well, let me put it this way, when I first heard about it I said to myself—actually, I told my wife, who asked me if we were publishing anything exciting; you know, my wife is one of the finest assets I have in my job. She doesn't come to the office or anything like that, you know, but—well, first let me tell you that she did disagree with me about two manuscripts I turned down and they were published by another house and of course they became best sellers. First let me tell you I once had a manuscript reader who was working for me and, well, she was two years out of Radcliffe but she had taken Levin's course in writing at Yale. I don't agree that writing can't be taught. I remember my own lit course with Jenney, who told me—well, you know, he had the highest standards and I was really pleased to see him publish last month in *Saturday Review*. What I meant was, someone always publishes the manuscript that everyone considers unpublishable, and this is what one always hears about and it is what always comes up in conversation. One always hears about *A Tree Grows in Brooklyn*—it was rejected by a dozen publishers—or *The Naked and the Dead*—it must have been turned down by ten publishers. Of course, Norman Mailer has turned out to be quite different from what everyone expected. His report on the Chicago convention was one of the finest—I don't know whether you saw it in *Harper's*—it was better, you know, than his piece on the Pentagon riots in *Commentary* which—well, let me put it this way, the best writing is being done by—I mean the best reporting—no one has come close, you know, to Truman Capote and this is where we go, you know, when we want to find out what is really—you know, nothing in any of the newspapers can tell us what it is like, especially if you want to know what the real facts were . . ."

He was at least two hundred words and three minutes beyond his topic sentence, and I had yet to hear the title of the book. The passage quoted is not a parody. If you want its equivalent, I suggest you take a tape recording of a cross section of an average day's office interviews or serious conversations. Chances are you will be appalled by the sprawling and fragmented character of the transcript. Complete sentences will be largely nonexistent; central ideas will emerge as from a deep mist. The surprise will not be that the meaning should be as obscured as it is by the unrelated turnings and self-interruptions, but that there should be any meaning at all. Oral communications in our society come close to being a complete bust. . . .

If there is no excuse for blurring and meandering in conversation, there is even less excuse for it in written forms of communication. The daily correspondence basket is a greater source of fatigue than anything that has been invented to harass a man whose work requires him to be in almost constant communication. I have a vivid picture in my mind of Dr. Albert Schweitzer at the age of eighty-four spending most of his time struggling with his correspondence. Every day two sacks of mail would arrive at the hospital at Lambaréné—letters from people who wanted to visit the hospital or work there; letters from Schweitzer Fellowship members all over the world; letters from admirers and readers of his books, letters from doctors and theologians, musicologists, and scientists, all of them writing on matters within his professional competence.

Late at night, long after the hospital was put to bed, Schweitzer would be bent over his desk, working on his correspondence. One night, during my visit in 1958, I was unable to sleep. I left my bunk and walked toward the river. I saw a light in Dr. Schweitzer's quarters and peeked in. There was Le Grand Docteur, struggling with his correspondence at 2 A.M.   7

We discussed the matter the next day.   8

"My correspondence is killing me," he said, "I try to answer all my letters, but I keep falling further and further behind. I get great joy out of reading my letters. It keeps me in touch with the outside world. I like to hear from people. But most of the time, I don't really know what my letters are trying to tell me. They wander so!"   9

Is it unreasonable to expect education to attach primary importance to the techniques of clarity, either oral or written? Is it unreasonable to suggest that respect for the next man's time is one of the most essential and useful lessons a person can learn? Time is capital. Time is finite. Clarity is a coefficient of time.   10

I should like to think that the school provided an environment conducive to the development of habits of clarity. But I am troubled by what I know. A recent high school test in English composition that came to my attention called upon the student to write descriptive material of 1,000 words or more in ninety minutes. If the school allowed (or even required) the student to spend half a day thinking about such a writing assignment, and a full day for the actual writing, the time would not be excessive. A writer like Thomas Mann felt he had put in a productive day if he had been able to write 500 words. Good writing, most of all, is clear writing. This is painstaking and often painful work. It requires time. It requires sustained and sequential thought.   11

But the school itself is not yet a model of organization, either in its internal structure or in its relationship to the student. I see very little evidence of total time-management in the demands made by the school on the student. Each course of study has its own claim. Unable to get it all in, the student is often under pressure to cut corners. He finds himself forced into a strategy of intellectual merchandising and   12 packaging; he becomes more concerned with the voluminous trappings and the appurtenances of surface scholarship than with genuine achievement. He learns the tricks of glibness. . . .

All this has to do with the student's ability to organize his time, to give his total attention to a difficult problem or objective, and to make himself clear. The school is not the only conditioning agent in the thought patterns and habits of the student, but it is possibly the dominant one. 13

Meanwhile, there is the ongoing problem of all those who are beyond the reach of the school. It is churlish and absurd to take the position that a poor communicator is locked into his low-level condition. The key to his liberation is the realization that effective communications, oral and written, depend absolutely on a clear understanding of his purpose. That purpose should be clearly defined and identified. It should be developed point by point, with the rigorous attention to sequence of a professional bead-stringer at work. 14

In verbal communication, the prime requisite is to anticipate the circumstances of a meeting or encounter. If it seems likely that the time available for meeting will be limited, then it is obviously suicidal to use up most of the time in clearing one's throat. Nor does it seem especially perspicacious to have overly long agenda, saving the most important items for last, when there is every likelihood that time will run out long before the main event. 15

In written communication, no better advice can be offered than to cite the favorite six-word question of Harold Ross, late editor of the *New Yorker.* "What the hell do you mean?" Ross was a great editor because he was death on ambiguities. Though he edited one of the most sophisticated magazines in the nation, he cherished the simplicities. He insisted on identifications for all names and places. And he hated extraneous words or observations. Under his rule, the *New Yorker* became a model of clear, effective writing. 16

My purpose here is not to drum up business for the *New Yorker,* but to point out that institutions can be built on clarity. Also that clarity is one of the truly distinguishing characteristics of the educated man. 17

QUESTIONS ON CONTENT

1. What does Cousins feel is the prime weakness of education today?

2. What does he feel is wrong with contemporary oral and written communication? What does he offer as a solution to this problem?

3. What, according to Cousins, is good writing?

4. What does Cousins mean when he says that the student is "forced into a strategy of intellectual merchandise and packaging" (12)?

QUESTIONS OF RHETORIC

1. What is Cousins's purpose in this essay? (Glossary: *Purpose*)

2. Is Cousins's essay both clear and unified? Why do you think so? (Glossary: *Unity*)

3. Cousins says there is a lack of sequence of ideas and a purposelessness in communication today. What technique does he use to make these claims clear for the reader? (Glossary: *Examples*)

4. Identify several similes and metaphors that Cousins uses in the essay. What do they contribute to his writing? (Glossary: *Figures of Speech*)

5. Cousins argues that sequence is important, that "ideas have to be fitted together" (2). The following six sentences form a paragraph. However, the sentence order has been changed, destroying the logical sequence. Place the sentences in what seems to you the most logical order. Explain why you placed the sentences in the order that you did.

    a. These circumstances and forces are largely beyond our control.
    b. A vocabulary is a tool which one uses in formulating the important questions of life, the questions which must be asked before they can be answered.
    c. At least it helps us call things by their right names.
    d. To a large extent, vocabulary shapes all the decisions we make.
    e. But our speech is a sort of searchlight that helps us to see these things more clearly and to see ourselves in relation to them.
    f. Most decisions, of course, are shaped by our emotions, by circumstances, and by the forces which may hold us back or urge us on.

VOCABULARY

obtrusive (3)   voluminous (12)   churlish (14)
parody (5)   glibness (12)   perspicacious (15)
coefficient (10)

WRITING TOPICS

1. How well did your high school develop your communication skills? Do you feel confident as a speaker? as a writer? Why, or why not? What can you do to improve your own communication skills?

2. Cousins stresses the importance of "purpose" and "organization" in communication. Write a brief essay in which you discuss how you identify and define your purpose and how you determine an appropriate organization when writing.

3. Cousins boldly states that "oral communications in our society come close to being a complete bust" (5). Using examples from your own experiences, write an essay in which you either agree or disagree with Cousins's assessment.

5

The Sounds of Silence

EDWARD T. HALL and MILDRED REED HALL

Until recently, few Americans were aware of the significance of body language. In this article, Edward and Mildred Hall discuss the crucial effects that "your posture, gestures, facial expressions, costume, the way you walk, even your treatment of time and space and material things" may have. The Halls use numerous examples as they contrast the body language of Americans with that of other cultures both to explain what body language is and to emphasize the importance of respecting the power and diversity of "the sounds of silence."

Bob leaves his apartment at 8:15 A.M. and stops at the corner drug-   1
store for breakfast. Before he can speak, the counterman says, "The
usual?" Bob nods yes. While he savors his Danish, a fat man pushes
onto the adjoining stool and overflows into his space. Bob scowls and
the man pulls himself in as much as he can. Bob has sent two messages
without speaking a syllable.

Henry has an appointment to meet Arthur at 11 o'clock; he arrives   2
at 11:30. Their conversation is friendly, but Arthur retains a lingering
hostility. Henry has unconsciously communicated that he doesn't
think the appointment is very important or that Arthur is a person who
needs to be treated with respect.

George is talking to Charley's wife at a party. Their conversation is   3
entirely trivial, yet Charley glares at them suspiciously. Their physical
proximity and the movements of their eyes reveal that they are powerfully attracted to each other.

José Ybarra and Sir Edmund Jones are at the same party and it is   4
important for them to establish a cordial relationship for business reasons. Each is trying to be warm and friendly, yet they will part with
mutual distrust and their business transaction will probably fall
through. José, in Latin fashion, moved closer and closer to Sir Edmund as they spoke, and this movement was miscommunicated as

pushiness to Sir Edmund, who kept backing away from this intimacy, and this was miscommunicated to José as coldness. The silent languages of Latin and English cultures are more difficult to learn than their spoken languages.

In each of these cases, we see the subtle power of nonverbal communication. The only language used throughout most of the history of humanity (in evolutionary terms, vocal communication is relatively recent), it is the first form of communication you learn. You use this preverbal language, consciously and unconsciously, every day to tell other people how you feel about yourself and them. This language includes your posture, gestures, facial expressions, costume, the way you walk, even your treatment of time and space and material things. All people communicate on several different levels at the same time but are usually aware of only the verbal dialog and don't realize that they respond to nonverbal messages. But when a person says one thing and really believes something else, the discrepancy between the two can usually be sensed. Nonverbal-communication systems are much less subject to the conscious deception that often occurs in verbal systems. When we find ourselves thinking, "I don't know what it is about him, but he doesn't seem sincere," it's usually this lack of congruity between a person's words and his behavior that makes us anxious and uncomfortable.

Few of us realize how much we all depend on body movement in our conversation or are aware of the hidden rules that govern listening behavior. But we know instantly whether or not the person we're talking to is "tuned in" and we're very sensitive to any breach in listening etiquette. In white middle-class American culture, when someone wants to show he is listening to someone else, he looks either at the other person's face or, specifically, at his eyes, shifting his gaze from one eye to the other.

If you observe a person conversing, you'll notice that he indicates he's listening by nodding his head. He also makes little "Hmm" noises. If he agrees with what's being said, he may give a vigorous nod. To show pleasure or affirmation, he smiles; if he has some reservations, he looks skeptical by raising an eyebrow or pulling down the corners of his mouth. If a participant wants to terminate the conversation, he may start shifting his body position, stretching his legs, crossing or uncrossing them, bobbing his foot or diverting his gaze from the speaker. The more he fidgets, the more the speaker becomes aware that he has lost his audience. As a last measure, the listener may look at his watch to indicate the imminent end of the conversation.

Talking and listening are so intricately intertwined that a person cannot do one without the other. Even when one is alone and talking to oneself, there is part of the brain that speaks while another part listens. In all conversations, the listener is positively or negatively reinforcing the speaker all the time. He may even guide the conversation without knowing it, by laughing or frowning or dismissing the argument with a wave of his hand.

The language of the eyes—another age-old way of exchanging feelings—is both subtle and complex. Not only do men and women use their eyes differently but there are class, generation, regional, ethnic and national cultural differences. Americans often complain about the way foreigners stare at people or hold a glance too long. Most Americans look away from someone who is using his eyes in an unfamiliar way because it makes them self-conscious. If a man looks at another man's wife in a certain way, he's asking for trouble, as indicated earlier. But he might not be ill mannered or seeking to challenge the husband. He might be a European in this country who hasn't learned our visual mores. Many American women visiting France or Italy are acutely embarrassed because, for the first time in their lives, men really look at them—their eyes, hair, nose, lips, breasts, hips, legs, thighs, knees, ankles, feet, clothes, hairdo, even their walk. These same women, once they have become used to being looked at, often return to the United States and are overcome with the feeling that "No one ever really looks at me anymore."

Analyzing the mass of data on the eyes, it is possible to sort out at least three ways in which the eyes are used to communicate: dominance *vs.* submission, involvement *vs.* detachment and positive *vs.* negative attitude. In addition, there are three levels of consciousness and control, which can be categorized as follows: (1) conscious use of the eyes to communicate, such as the flirting blink and the intimate nose-wrinkling squint; (2) the very extensive category of unconscious but learned behavior governing where the eyes are directed and when (this unwritten set of rules dictates how and under what circumstances the sexes, as well as people of all status categories, look at each other); and (3) the response of the eye itself, which is completely outside both awareness and control—changes in the cast (the sparkle) of the eye and the pupillary reflex.

The eye is unlike any other organ of the body, for it is an extension of the brain. The unconscious pupillary reflex and the cast of the eye have been known by people of Middle Eastern origin for years—although most are unaware of their knowledge. Depending on the context, Arabs and others look either directly at the eyes or deeply *into* the eyes of their interlocutor. We became aware of this in the Middle East several years ago while looking at jewelry. The merchant suddenly started to push a particular bracelet at a customer and said, "You buy this one." What interested us was that the bracelet was not the one that had been consciously selected by the purchaser. But the merchant, watching the pupils of the eyes, knew what the purchaser really wanted to buy. Whether he specifically knew *how* he knew is debatable.

A psychologist at the University of Chicago, Eckhard Hess, was the first to conduct systematic studies of the pupillary reflex. His wife remarked one evening, while watching him reading in bed, that he must be very interested in the text because his pupils were dilated. Following up on this, Hess slipped some pictures of nudes into a stack of photographs that he gave to his male assistant. Not looking at the photographs but watching his assistant's pupils, Hess was able to tell precisely when the assistant came to the nudes. In further experiments, Hess retouched the eyes in a photograph of a woman. In one print, he made the pupils small, in another, large; nothing else was changed. Subjects who were given the photographs found the woman with the dilated pupils much more attractive. Any man who has had the experience of seeing a woman look at him as her pupils widen with reflex speed knows that she's flashing him a message. 12

The eye-sparkle phenomenon frequently turns up in our interviews of couples in love. It's apparently one of the first reliable clues in the other person that love is genuine. To date, there is no scientific data to explain eye sparkle; no investigation of the pupil, the cornea or even the white sclera of the eye shows how the sparkle originates. Yet we all know it when we see it. 13

One common situation for most people involves the use of the eyes in the street and in public. Although eye behavior follows a definite set of rules, the rules vary according to the place, the needs and feelings of the people, and their ethnic background. For urban whites, once they're within definite recognition distance (16–32 feet for people with average eyesight), there is mutual avoidance of eye contact—unless they want something specific: a pickup, a handout or information of some kind. In the West and in small towns generally, however, people are much more likely to look at and greet one another, even if they're strangers. 14

It's permissible to look at people if they're beyond recognition distance, but once inside this sacred zone, you can only steal a glance at strangers. You *must* greet friends, however; to fail to do so is insulting. Yet, to stare too fixedly even at them is considered rude and hostile. Of course, all of these rules are variable. 15

A great many blacks, for example, greet each other in public even if they don't know each other. To blacks, most eye behavior of whites has the effect of giving the impression that they aren't there, but this is due to white avoidance of eye contact with *anyone* in the street. 16

Another very basic difference between people of different ethnic   17
backgrounds is their sense of territoriality and how they handle space.
This is the silent communication, or miscommunication, that caused
friction between Mr. Ybarra and Sir Edmund Jones in our earlier example. We know from research that everyone has around himself an
invisible bubble of space that contracts and expands depending on several factors: his emotional state, the activity he's performing at the time
and his cultural background. This bubble is a kind of mobile territory
that he will defend against intrusion. If he is accustomed to close personal distance between himself and others, his bubble will be smaller
than that of someone who's accustomed to greater personal distance.
People of North European heritage—English, Scandinavian, Swiss
and German—tend to avoid contact. Those whose heritage is Italian,
French, Spanish, Russian, Latin American or Middle Eastern like
close personal contact.

People are very sensitive to any intrusion into their spatial bubble.   18
If someone stands too close to you, your first instinct is to back up. If
that's not possible, you lean away and pull yourself in, tensing your
muscles. If the intruder doesn't respond to these body signals, you may
then try to protect yourself, using a briefcase, umbrella or raincoat.
Women—especially when traveling alone—often plant their pocket-
book in such a way that no one can get very close to them. As a last
resort, you may move to another spot and position yourself behind a
desk or a chair that provides screening. Everyone tries to adjust the
space around himself in a way that's comfortable for him; most often,
he does this unconsciously.

Emotions also have a direct effect on the size of a person's territory.   19
When you're angry or under stress, your bubble expands and you require more space. New York psychiatrist Augustus Kinzel found a difference in what he calls Body-Buffer Zones between violent and nonviolent prison inmates. Dr. Kinzel conducted experiments in which
each prisoner was placed in the center of a small room and then Dr.
Kinzel slowly walked toward him. Nonviolent prisoners allowed him
to come quite close, while prisoners with a history of violent behavior
couldn't tolerate his proximity and reacted with some vehemence.

Apparently people under stress experience other people as looming   20
larger and closer than they actually are. Studies of schizophrenic patients have indicated that they sometimes have a distorted perception
of space, and several psychiatrists have reported patients who experience their body boundaries as filling up an entire room. For these patients, anyone who comes into the room is actually inside their body,
and such an intrusion may trigger a violent outburst.

Unfortunately, there is little detailed information about normal   21
people who live in highly congested urban areas. We do know, of

course, that the noise, pollution, dirt, crowding and confusion of our cities induce feelings of stress in most of us, and stress leads to a need for greater space. The man who's packed into a subway, jostled in the street, crowded into an elevator and forced to work all day in a bull pen or in a small office without auditory or visual privacy is going to be very stressed at the end of his day. He needs places that provide relief from constant overstimulation of his nervous system. Stress from overcrowding is cumulative and people can tolerate more crowding early in the day than later; note the increased bad temper during the evening rush hour as compared with the morning melee. Certainly one factor in people's desire to commute by car is the need for privacy and relief from crowding (except, often, from other cars); it may be the only time of the day when nobody can intrude.

In crowded public places, we tense our muscles and hold ourselves   22 stiff, and thereby communicate to others our desire not to intrude on their space and, above all, not to touch them. We also avoid eye contact, and the total effect is that of someone who has "tuned out." Walking along the street, our bubble expands slightly as we move in a stream of strangers, taking care not to bump into them. In the office, at meetings, in restaurants, our bubble keeps changing as it adjusts to the activity at hand.

Most white middle-class Americans use four main distances in   23 their business and social relations: intimate, personal, social and public. Each of these distances has a near and a far phase and is accompanied by changes in the volume of the voice. Intimate distance varies from direct physical contact with another person to a distance of six to eighteen inches and is used for our most private activities—caressing another person or making love. At this distance, you are overwhelmed by sensory inputs from the other person—heat from the body, tactile stimulation from the skin, the fragrance of perfume, even the sound of breathing—all of which literally envelop you. Even at the far phase, you're still within easy touching distance. In general, the use of intimate distance in public between adults is frowned on. It's also much too close for strangers, except under conditions of extreme crowding.

In the second zone—personal distance—the close phase is one and   24 a half to two and a half feet; it's at this distance that wives usually stand from their husbands in public. If another woman moves into this zone, the wife will most likely be disturbed. The far phase—two and a half to four feet—is the distance used to "keep someone at arm's length" and is the most common spacing used by people in conversation.

The third zone—social distance—is employed during business   25 transactions or exchanges with a clerk or repairman. People who work together tend to use close social distance—four to seven feet. This is also the distance for conversations at social gatherings. To stand at this distance from someone who is seated has a dominating effect (e.g., teacher to pupil, boss to secretary). The far phase of the third zone— seven to twelve feet—is where people stand when someone says, "Stand back so I can look at you." This distance lends a formal tone to business or social discourse. In an executive office, the desk serves to keep people at this distance.

The fourth zone—public distance—is used by teachers in class-   26
rooms or speakers at public gatherings. At its farthest phase—25 feet and beyond—it is used for important public figures. Violations of this distance can lead to serious complications. During his 1970 U.S. visit, the president of France, Georges Pompidou, was harassed by pickets in Chicago, who were permitted to get within touching distance. Since pickets in France are kept behind barricades a block or more away, the president was outraged by this insult to his person, and President Nixon was obliged to communicate his concern as well as offer his personal apologies.

It is interesting to note how American pitchmen and panhandlers   27
exploit the unwritten, unspoken conventions of eye and distance. Both take advantage of the fact that once explicit eye contact is established, it is rude to look away, because to do so means to brusquely dismiss the other person and his needs. Once having caught the eye of his mark, the panhandler then locks on, not letting go until he moves through the public zone, the social zone, the personal zone and, fi- nally, into the intimate sphere, where people are most vulnerable.

Touch also is an important part of the constant stream of commu-   28
nication that takes place between people. A light touch, a firm touch, a blow, a caress are all communications. In an effort to break down bar- riers among people, there's been a recent upsurge in group-encounter activities, in which strangers are encouraged to touch one another. In special situations such as these, the rules for not touching are broken with group approval and people gradually lose some of their inhibi- tions.

Although most people don't realize it, space is perceived and dis-   29
tances are set not by vision alone but with all the senses. Auditory space is perceived with the ears, thermal space with the skin, kines- thetic space with the muscles of the body and olfactory space with the nose. And, once again, it's one's culture that determines how his senses are programmed—which sensory information ranks highest and lowest. The important thing to remember is that culture is very persis- tent. In this country, we've noted the existence of culture patterns that determine distance between people in the third and fourth generations of some families, despite their prolonged contact with people of very different cultural heritages.

Whenever there is great cultural distance between two people,   30
there are bound to be problems arising from differences in behavior
and expectations. An example is the American couple who consulted a
psychiatrist about their marital problems. The husband was from New
England and had been brought up by reserved parents who taught him
to control his emotions and to respect the need for privacy. His wife
was from an Italian family and had been brought up in close contact
with all the members of her large family, who were extremely warm,
volatile and demonstrative.

When the husband came home after a hard day at the office, drag-   31
ging his feet and longing for peace and quiet, his wife would rush to
him and smother him. Clasping his hands, rubbing his brow, crooning
over his weary head, she never left him alone. But when the wife was
upset or anxious about the day, the husband's response was to with-
draw completely and leave her alone. No comforting, no affectionate
embrace, no attention—just solitude. The woman became convinced
her husband didn't love her and, in desperation, she consulted a psychiatrist. Their problem wasn't basically psychological but cultural.

Why has man developed all these different ways of communicating   32
messages without words? One reason is that people don't like to spell
out certain kinds of messages. We prefer to find other ways of showing
our feelings. This is especially true in relationships as sensitive as
courtship. Men don't like to be rejected and most women don't want to
turn a man down bluntly. Instead, we work out subtle ways of encouraging or discouraging each other that save face and avoid con-
frontations.

How a person handles space in dating others is an obvious and very   33
sensitive indicator of how he or she feels about the other person. On a
first date, if a woman sits or stands so close to a man that he is acutely
conscious of her physical presence—inside the intimate-distance
zone—the man usually construes it to mean that she is encouraging
him. However, before the man starts moving in on the woman, he
should be sure what message she's really sending; otherwise, he risks
bruising his ego. What is close to someone of North European background may be neutral or distant to someone of Italian heritage. Also,
women sometimes use space as a way of misleading a man and there
are few things that put men off more than women who communicate
contradictory messages—such as women who cuddle up and then act
insulted when a man takes the next step.

How does a woman communicate interest in a man? In addition to   34
such familiar gambits as smiling at him, she may glance shyly at him,
blush and then look away. Or she may give him a real come-on look
and move in very close when he approaches. She may touch his arm

and ask for a light. As she leans forward to light her cigarette, she may brush him lightly, enveloping him in her perfume. She'll probably continue to smile at him and she may use what ethologists call preening gestures—touching the back of her hair, thrusting her breasts forward, tilting her hips as she stands or crossing her legs if she's seated, perhaps even exposing one thigh or putting a hand on her thigh and stroking it. She may also strike her wrists as she converses or show the palm of her hand as a way of gaining his attention. Her skin may be unusually flushed or quite pale, her eyes brighter, the pupils larger.

If a man sees a woman whom he wants to attract, he tries to present himself by his posture and stance as someone who is self-assured. He moves briskly and confidently. When he catches the eye of the woman, he may hold her glance a little longer than normal. If he gets an encouraging smile, he'll move in close and engage her in small talk. As they converse, his glance shifts over her face and body. He, too, may make preening gestures—straightening his tie, smoothing his hair or shooting his cuffs. 35

How do people learn body language? The same way they learn spoken language—by observing and imitating people around them as they're growing up. Little girls imitate their mothers or an older female. Little boys imitate their fathers or a respected uncle or a character on television. In this way, they learn the gender signals appropriate for their sex. Regional, class and ethnic patterns of body behavior are also learned in childhood and persist throughout life. 36

Such patterns of masculine and feminine body behavior vary widely from one culture to another. In America, for example, women stand with their thighs together. Many walk with their pelvis tipped slightly forward and their upper arms close to their body. When they sit, they cross their legs at the knee or, if they are well past middle age, they may cross their ankles. American men hold their arms away from their body, often swinging them as they walk. They stand with their legs apart (an extreme example is the cowboy, with legs apart and thumbs tucked into his belt). When they sit, they put their feet on the floor with legs apart and, in some parts of the country, they cross their legs by putting one ankle on the other knee. 37

Leg behavior indicates sex, status and personality. It also indicates whether or not one is at ease or is showing respect or disrespect for the other person. Young Latin-American males avoid crossing their legs. In their world of *machismo,* the preferred position for young males when with one another (if there is no older dominant male present to whom they must show respect) is to sit on the base of their spine with their leg muscles relaxed and their feet wide apart. Their respect position is our military equivalent; spine straight, heels and ankles to- 38 gether—almost identical to that displayed by properly brought up young women in New England in the early part of this century.

American women who sit with their legs spread apart in the pres-   39
ence of males are *not* normally signaling a come-on—they are simply (and often unconsciously) sitting like men. Middle-class women in the presence of other women to whom they are very close may on occasion throw themselves down on a soft chair or sofa and let themselves go. This is a signal that nothing serious will be taken up. Males, on the other hand, lean back and prop their legs up on the nearest object.

The way we walk, similarly, indicates status, respect, mood and   40
ethnic or cultural affiliation. The many variants of the female walk are too well known to go into here, except to say that a man would have to be blind not to be turned on by the way some women walk—a fact that made Mae West rich before scientists ever studied these matters. To white Americans, some French middle-class males walk in a way that is both humorous and suspect. There is a bounce and looseness to the French walk, as though the parts of the body were somehow unrelated. Jacques Tati, the French movie actor, walks this way; so does the great mime, Marcel Marceau.

Blacks and whites in America—with the exception of middle- and   41
upper-middle-class professionals of both groups—move and walk very differently from each other. To the blacks, whites often seem incredibly stiff, almost mechanical in their movements. Black males, on the other hand, have a looseness and coordination that frequently makes whites a little uneasy; it's too different, too integrated, too alive, too male. Norman Mailer has said that squares walk from the shoulders, like bears, but blacks and hippies walk from the hips, like cats.

All over the world, people walk not only in their own characteristic   42
way but have walks that communicate the nature of their involvement with whatever it is they're doing. The purposeful walk of North Europeans is an important component of proper behavior on the job. Any male who has been in the military knows how essential it is to walk properly (which makes for a continuing source of tension between blacks and whites in the Service). The quick shuffle of servants in the Far East in the old days was a show of respect. On the island of Truk, when we last visited, the inhabitants even had a name for the respectful walk that one used when in the presence of a chief or when walking past a chief's house. The term was *sufan,* which meant to be humble and respectful.

The notion that people communicate volumes by their gestures,   43
facial expressions, posture and walk is not new; actors, dancers, writers and psychiatrists have long been aware of it. Only in recent years, however, have scientists begun to make systematic observations of

body motions. Ray L. Birdwhistell of the University of Pennsylvania is one of the pioneers in body-motion research and coined the term kinesics to describe this field. He developed an elaborate notation system to record both facial and body movements, using an approach similar to that of the linguist, who studies the basic elements of speech. Birdwhistell and other kinesicists such as Albert Sheflen, Adam Kendon and William Condon take movies of people interacting. They run the film over and over again, often at reduced speed for frame-by-frame analysis, so that they can observe even the slightest body movements not perceptible at normal interaction speeds. These movements are then recorded in notebooks for later analysis.

To appreciate the importance of nonverbal-communication sys-   44
tems, consider the unskilled inner-city black looking for a job. His handling of time and space alone is sufficiently different from the white middle-class pattern to create great misunderstandings on both sides. The black is told to appear for a job interview at a certain time. He arrives late. The white interviewer concludes from his tardy arrival that the black is irresponsible and not really interested in the job. What the interviewer doesn't know is that the black time system (often referred to by blacks as C. P. T.—colored people's time) isn't the same as that of whites. In the words of a black student who had been told to make an appointment to see his professor: "Man, you *must* be putting me on. I never had an appointment in my life."

The black job applicant, having arrived late for his interview, may   45
further antagonize the white interviewer by his posture and his eye behavior. Perhaps he slouches and avoids looking at the interviewer; to him, this is playing it cool. To the interviewer, however, he may well look shifty and sound uninterested. The interviewer has failed to notice the actual signs of interest and eagerness in the black's behavior, such as the subtle shift in the quality of the voice—a gentle and tentative excitement—an almost imperceptible change in the cast of the eyes and a relaxing of the jaw muscles.

Moreover, correct reading of black-white behavior is continually   46
complicated by the fact that both groups are comprised of individuals—some of whom try to accommodate and some of whom make it a point of pride *not* to accommodate. At present, this means that many Americans, when thrown into contact with one another, are in the precarious position of not knowing which pattern applies. Once identified and analyzed, nonverbal-communication systems can be taught, like a foreign language. Without this training, we respond to nonverbal communications in terms of our own culture; we read everyone's behavior as if it were our own, and thus we often misunderstand it.

Several years ago in New York City, there was a program for   47 sending children from predominantly black and Puerto Rican low-income neighborhoods to summer school in a white upper-class neighborhood on the East Side. One morning, a group of young black and Puerto Rican boys raced down the street, shouting and screaming and overturning garbage cans on their way to school. A doorman from an apartment building nearby chased them and cornered one of them inside a building. The boy drew a knife and attacked the doorman. This tragedy would not have occurred if the doorman had been familiar with the behavior of boys from low-income neighborhoods, where such antics are routine and socially acceptable and where pursuit would be expected to invite a violent response.

The language of behavior is extremely complex. Most of us are   48
lucky to have under control one subcultural system—the one that reflects our sex, class, generation and geographic region within the United States. Because of its complexity, efforts to isolate bits of nonverbal communication and generalize from them are in vain; you don't become an instant expert on people's behavior by watching them at cocktail parties. Body language isn't something that's independent of the person, something that can be donned and doffed like a suit of clothes.

Our research and that of our colleagues has shown that, far from   49
being a superficial form of communication that can be consciously manipulated, nonverbal-communication systems are interwoven into the fabric of the personality and, as sociologist Erving Goffman has demonstrated, into society itself. They are the warp and woof of daily interactions with others and they influence how one expresses oneself, how one experiences oneself as a man or a woman.

Nonverbal communications signal to members of your own group   50
what kind of person you are, how you feel about others, how you'll fit into and work in a group, whether you're assured or anxious, the degree to which you feel comfortable with the standards of your own culture, as well as deeply significant feelings about the self, including the state of your own psyche. For most of us, it's difficult to accept the reality of another's behavioral system. And, of course, none of us will ever become fully knowledgeable of the importance of every nonverbal signal. But as long as each of us realizes the power of these signals, this society's diversity can be a source of great strength rather than a further—and subtly powerful—source of divison.

QUESTIONS ON CONTENT

1. Describe the phenomenon the Halls call "pupillary reflex," and discuss any examples of it that you have noticed.

2. To what extent, according to the Halls, does ethnic background produce differences in nonverbal-communication behavior?

3. What do the Halls mean by the "invisible bubble of space" surrounding each of us? What factors may affect its size at any given time?

4. What are the four distances used by most white middle-class Americans in social and business situations? Describe the varying sensory inputs at each distance (auditory, olfactory, tactile, visual, and so forth).

5. What are "preening gestures"? Give some examples.

6. To illustrate many of the points that the Halls make in their essay, play a game, such as this one, that uses nonverbal communication. Divide players into small groups to act out situations involving body language—a tough cop ticketing a motorist (of either sex); one person trying to give directions to another but not succeeding; a man trying to be friendly with a woman (or vice versa) who really does not wish to be bothered but who also does not wish to be impolite. All the players should discuss each performance not on the basis of the dialogue but on the basis of how well the performers illustrate an awareness of body language. What conclusions can you draw about the relationship between body language and verbal language?

QUESTIONS ON RHETORIC

1. What is the function of the first four paragraphs. (Glossary: *Beginnings*)

2. Would you describe the diction of this essay as formal or informal? Support your conclusions with specific examples from the text. (Glossary: *Diction*)

3. The Halls use comparison and contrast as well as classification in this essay. Identify several examples of each rhetorical technique. (Glossary: *Comparison and Contrast, Division and Classification*)

4. The Halls start several of their paragraphs with questions. What do they achieve by doing so? (Glossary: *Rhetorical Questions*)

VOCABULARY

savors (1)	dilated (12)	inhibitions (28)
proximity (3)	vehemence (19)	volatile (30)
cordial (4)	melee (21)	precarious (46)
congruity (5)		

WRITING TOPICS

1. Using examples from your own experience, discuss the implications of the Halls's statement: "Once identified and analyzed, nonverbal-

communication systems can be taught, like a foreign language. Without this training, we respond to nonverbal communications in terms of our own culture; we read everyone's behavior as if it were our own, and thus we often misunderstand it."

2. Time is a very important ingredient in nonverbal communication, and Americans apparently place a high value on promptness. How important do you think time is? Are there occasions when it is acceptable or even polite to be late? Are Americans in your experience obsessed with time? Is your sense of time different from that of your parents?

3. How do you handle space? Do you have a strong sense of territoriality, always seeking out the same chair or table in certain situations? When people invade your space bubble, how do you feel? At what distances do you operate most comfortably? In what ways does an awareness of how you handle space help you to deal with it more effectively?

WRITING ASSIGNMENTS FOR "LANGUAGE AWARENESS"

1. Like Malcolm X, we can all tell of an experience that has been unusually significant for us. Think about your own experiences, identify one incident that has been especially important for you, and write an essay about it. In preparing to write, ask yourself such questions as these: Why is the incident important for me? What aspects of the incident might interest someone else? What details will help me re-create the incident in the most engaging way? How can my narrative of the incident be most effectively organized?

2. Norman Cousins, believes that people ought to be aware of their own langauge and the language that is used around them. How clear and precise is your writing? As a test of your skills, study the following diagrams:

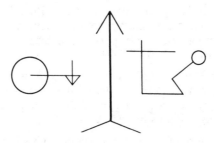

Next, produce a diagram of your own of comparable difficulty. Write a precise description of your diagram. Give your description (but not your diagram) to another member of your class, and ask that person to draw the figure you have described. Compare your original drawing with your classmate's drawing based on your description. Discuss the reasons for any discrepancies that exist.

3. It has often been said that language reveals the character of the person using it. Write an essay in which you analyze the character of a particular writer or speaker with whom you are familiar, based on his or her use of language.

4. Paul Roberts argues that "no understanding of the English language can be very satisfactory without a notion of the history of the language." What exactly does Roberts mean by "understanding"? Write an essay in which you substantiate or dispute his claim.

5. Collect a dozen printed advertisements with pictures which illustrate principles of body language. Limit your study to advertisements for one product (such as perfume, stockings, cars, cigarettes, and so

on). Write an essay in which you discuss the importance of body language in advertising.

NOTE: Suggested topics for research papers appear on p. 446.

NOTABLE QUOTATIONS

The following quotations are drawn from the essays in this section. They are presented as additional topics for classroom discussion or for writing assignments.

"I saw that the best thing I could do was get hold of a dictionary—to study, to learn some words." *Malcolm X* (11)

"Not every human being can play the violin, do calculus, jump high hurdles, or sail a canoe, no matter how excellent his teachers or how arduous his training—but every person constantly creates utterances never before spoken on earth." *Farb* (3)

"In 1500 English was a minor language, spoken by a few people on a small island. Now it is perhaps the greatest language of the world, spoken natively by over a quarter of a billion people and as a second language by many millions more." *Roberts* (44)

"Good writing, most of all, is clear writing. This is painstaking and often painful work. It requires time. It requires sustained and sequential thought." *Cousins* (11)

"Few of us realize how much we all depend on body movement in our conversation. . . ." *Hall* and *Hall* (6)

"How a person handles space in dating others is an obvious and very sensitive indicator of how he or she feels about the other person." *Hall* and *Hall* (33)

"Body language isn't something that's independent of the person, something that can be donned and doffed like a suit of clothes." *Hall* and *Hall* (48)

II

American English Today

Good English is that form of speech which is appropriate to the purpose of the speaker, true to the language as it is, and comfortable to speaker and listener. . . . It is never fixed, but changes with the organic life of the language.

Robert C. Pooley

The reading and writing skills of most Americans have never been remarkable, and the inability of the average high-school graduate to write three or four clear expository paragraphs has been the object of scornful criticism at least since the time of Mark Twain. . . . What makes the new illiteracy so dismaying is precisely the fact that writing ability among even the best-educated young people seems to have fallen so far so fast.

Merrill Sheils

Academic excellence cannot be achieved without first mastering Standard English—not black or any other kind of nonstandard English.

Banjamin H. Alexander

Did the powerful people who 'rule' America . . . 'get ahead' by speaking like characters in a Henry James novel? Did oilmen? Did Teamster presidents? I doubt it.

Ishmael Reed

A thing is not necessarily true because badly uttered, nor false because spoken magnificently.

St. Augustine

1
Language on the Skids

EDWIN NEWMAN

Edwin Newman, besides being a television newsman and commentator, is the author of Strictly Speaking *and* A Civil Tongue—*two very popular books that have established his reputation as an advocate of correct usage and a guardian of American English. In "Language on the Skids," Newman provides numerous examples of redundant, flabby, and self-important language. He believes the English language is being abused and argues for the responsible use of langauge.*

It is typical of the English spoken on this side of the Atlantic that enough is almost never enough. Cecil Smith, television critic of the Los Angeles *Times,* considered CBS's "Bicentennial Minutes" not merely unique but singularly unique. Sen. Abraham Ribicoff of Connecticut was worried not only about nuclear proliferation but about the spread of nuclear proliferation. And Reggie Jackson, the *New York Times* advised its readers, "stole second successfully," which is better than stealing it unsuccessfully. 1

All of this is redundancy, to which we have become addicted. A large part of our speech and writing is unnecessary and boring, which makes reading and conversation a chore. We slog through the repetitious, and tarry when we should be moving on. Redundancy triumphs. 2

One reason for our extravagant use of words is the feeling that an idea is more effective if it is repeated and reinforced. That is why Jimmy Carter once described the international situation as very dormant. (Those were the days!) It is why he said that the place where he would meet Leonid Brezhnev would depend not merely on a mutual decision but on "a mutual decision between us." You can't be too careful when dealing with the Russians. 3

Another cause is a failure to understand what words mean. The New York *Daily News* would not have said of a motion picture that it "extolled the evils of the advertising business" if it knew what extolled meant. The weather forecaster at the CBS station in Washington, D.C., would not have said, "Tomorrow afternoon, the temperature will gradually plummet. . . ." And what could have led the New Bed- 4 ford, Mass., *Standard Times* to run this headline: "Tie vote kills bottle bill, but not fatally"?

There is a third reason for our extravagant use of words—a desire 5
to make what is being done, however simple and routine it may be, sound grand and complicated. Thus, two newspapers in Nevada announce that they intend to put up a building. Do they call it a building? No. It is to be "a community-information center." The Postal Service issues statements about "sortation" of mail. Not sorting. Sortation. The Los Angeles City Teachers' Mathematics Association, at its Annual Recognition Dinner, schedules an associative hour rather than a cocktail hour. What does one do during an associative hour? Get acquainted? Not since computer language has descended on us. One interfaces on a personal basis. By the way, if any well-dressed women are present, it is possible that their dress reflects "Executive Wardrobe Engineering."

Why is such language used? Self-importance, of course, but also 6
because it serves as a fence that keeps others outside and respectful, or leads them to ignore what is going on inside because it is too much trouble to find out. So you may hear about "a horizontal analysis spanning the formal vertical departmental structure" intended to "identify multi-purpose citizen contacts requiring timely responses." Or you may hear of a California school district that closes schools not because there are fewer pupils than expected but because of "accelerated enrollment slippage."

This sort of language is increasingly characteristic of a society 7
where engaged couples are said to be in a commitment situation, and where an economist may refer to work as labor-force participation. In Boston, the Metropolitan District commission did not want to say, "Keep off the ice." It urged that "all persons terminate using any body of water under MDC control for any ice-related recreation." It could have been worse. It could have been ice-related recreation-oriented activity.

There is, of course, a technique involved, but it is easy to grasp. 8
Never say that a tank may spring a leak. Say there may be a "breach of containment." Never say of a product that people won't buy it. Say that it "met consumer resistance." In Knoxville, Tenn., a nurse won a product-naming contest with the suggestion that dust covers for medical equipment be called instead "sterility maintenance covers." That was worth $500 and a lunch at the Hyatt Regency Hotel.

I want to turn now to what I take to be the new pastime. It is 9
"izing." A reporter I know, covering a Presidential visit to Boston, asked the Secret Service where he could park his car. The Secret Service could not help. What should he do, then? "If I were you," the

Secret Service man replied, "I would put myself in a chauffeurized situation." The head of the United States Professional Tennis Association proposed "to focalize all major USPTA activities and programs
from a single site." Would he be the focalist? Some plastic surgeons,
advertising a customized approach, promise "wrinkles youthfulized."
This, apparently, leaves the patient with young wrinkles.

Sports broadcasters often have only a shaky grip on grammar and   10
on the connection between words and meaning. During one football
game, the announcer told viewers that because of the way some of the
boxes in the Superdome were placed, he could not visually see them.
This sort of thing is by no means confined to the sports world. For example, we have all heard about alleged victims. They have become
confused in some journalistic minds with intended victims, but intended victims are sometimes rendered as would-be victims, who apparently go out in the hope of being robbed.

An ironic thing is happening now. As we demand more and more   11
openness from those in public life—unwisely, it seems to me—our
language becomes more and more obscure, turgid, ponderous and
overblown. The candor expected of public officials about their health,
their money, their private lives is offset in public matters by language
that conceals more than it tells, and often conceals the fact that there is
little or nothing worth telling.

We ought to demand that our leaders speak better English, so that   12
we know what they are talking about and, incidentally, so that they do.
Some safety does lie in more sensible public attitudes, especially toward the public-relations and advertising techniques now widely used
by politicians. It lies also in independent reporting by those of us in the
news business, and in greater skepticism on the part of the public, and
in an unremitting puncturing of the overblown. In all of this, language
is crucial.

I have been told that my view is cranky and pedantic, that I want to   13
keep the language from growing, and to impose a standard and rigid
English. Far from it. Our language should be specific and concrete,
eloquent where possible, playful where possible, and personal so that
we don't all sound alike. Instead, high crimes and misdemeanors are
visited upon it, and those who commit them do not understand that the
crimes are crimes against themselves. The language belongs to all of
us. We have no more valuable possession.

QUESTIONS ON CONTENT

1. In his opening paragraph Newman gives three examples of our extravagant use of words: "singularly unique," "the spread of nuclear

proliferation," and "stole second successfully." Explain what the problem is in each case.

2. Newman believes that for most Americans "enough is almost never enough" (1). What does he see as the causes of our extravagance with words?

3. Why, according to Newman, do people use language that promotes self-importance? Is such usage ever appropriate or legitimate in your opinion? Explain.

4. What relationship does Newman see between society and the language used?

5. What does Newman believe we can do to correct the situation he describes?

6. In his final paragraph Newman admits that people sometimes find him "cranky and pedantic." What do you think? Are the language abuses that he cites really "high crimes and misdemeanors" against American English? Explain.

QUESTIONS ON RHETORIC

1. What is Newman's thesis in the essay? Where is it stated? (Glossary: *Thesis*)

2. What is the topic sentence in paragraph 4? How is it related to the other sentences in the paragraph? (Glossary: *Topic Sentence*)

3. How would you describe Newman's tone in this essay? (Glossary: *Tone*) Does he ever come across as "cranky and pedantic"?

4. Discuss Newman's use of irony in paragraph 8. (Glossary: *Irony*) What do you suppose was his intent?

5. Without his many examples, how persuasive would Newman's argument be? Did you think that he could have used more examples at any points in the essay? If so, where?

6. What purpose is served by the question that begins paragraph 6? (Glossary: *Rhetorical Question*)

VOCABULARY

unique (1)   extolled (4)   turgid (11)
redundancy (2)   plummet (4)   ponderous (11)

WRITING TOPICS

1. One area of language abuse that Newman discusses is sports. Carefully read the sports section of your local or school newspaper and/or listen to the broadcast of several sports events, collecting examples for

an essay on the language abuses of sports broadcasters and writers. Do you agree with Newman's assessment of their language?

2. Write an essay in which you discuss the redundant, highfalutin', and obscure language that you regularly encounter. Where in your experience is such language most common? What effect has this language abuse had on you?

2

Is There Really a Language Crisis?

HARVEY DANIELS

For the last ten or fifteen years writers like Edwin Newman have warned of the widespread corruption of our language and the demise of Standard English. Such language critics—or pop grammarians, as Harvey Daniels prefers to call them— complain that "jargon is rampant; the kids talk funny; politicians brutalize the language in their endless attempts to mislead us; bureaucrats pollute the environment with obfuscation and bluster; the verbal test scores of our schoolchildren are plunging; substandard dialects are often accepted or even encouraged in the schools; non-English speakers are infiltrating our cities; and no one in school or business can write a simple English sentence correctly." In the following chapter from his book Famous Last Words: The American Language Crisis Reconsidered, *Daniels takes issue with the "trivial obsessions" of the critics. He believes that much of their "scolding and fussing about language focuses on red-penciling the superficial niceties of written and spoken utterances, rather than on understanding where they come from and what they might mean."*

The deathwatch over American English has begun again. After all   1
the shocks and assaults of her long life, and after all of her glorious re-
coveries, the Mother Tongue now faces the final hour. Around the
bedside cluster the mourners: Edwin Newman, John Simon, Clifton
Fadiman, Tony Randall, and Ann Landers. In darkened ranks behind
stand somber professors of freshman composition, a few school board
members, a representative from the National Assessment of Educational Progress, and the entire usage panel of the *American Heritage
Dictionary.* Like all deaths, this one evokes in the bereaved the whole
range of human feeling: anger, frustration, denial, despair, confusion,
and grim humor. It has been a long, degenerative disease and not
pretty to watch.

Is there room for hope? Is it really, uh, terminal? The specialists   2
leave no room for miracles—the prognosis is firm. The obituaries have
been prepared and, in some cases, already published. Services will be
announced. Memorials are referred to the Educational Testing Service. *Requiescat in pace* American English.

Yet, curiously, the language clings to life. She even weakly speaks   3
from time to time, in delirium no doubt, for her words are in jargon,
cant, argot, doublespeak, and various substandard dialects. She splits
infinitives and dangles participles, and one of the watchers actually
thought he heard her begin a sentence with *hopefully.* How can one so
ill survive? It is torture to see this. It must end.

But it won't. If this is death in life, it is still the normal condition of   4
American English and of all other human languages. As compelling as
the medical metaphors may be, languages really are not very much
like people, healthy or sick, and make poor candidates for personification. The illnesses, the abuses, the wounds, the sufferings of a language
reside in the minds and hearts of its users, as do its glories, triumphs,
and eras of progress. Our language is an essentially neutral instrument
with which we communicate, more or less, and into which we pour an
abundance of feeling. It is our central cultural asset and our cherished
personal friend, but it is not, in many ways, what we think it is or
would like it to be.

But here is another story about death which I believe does tell us   5
something important about the present state of American English. In
Chicago, during the Christmas season of 1978, twenty-six Spanish-
speaking people were killed in a series of tragic fires. Many of them
perished because they could not understand the instructions that firemen shouted in English. When the city promptly instituted a program
to teach the firefighters a few emergency phrases in Spanish, a storm of
protest arose. "This is America," proclaimed the head of the Chicago
Firefighters Union, "let them speak English." A local newspaper columnist suggested, with presumably innocent irony: "Let's stop cater-
ing to the still-flickering nationalistic desires to perpetuate the Latin
heritage." The city's top-rated television newscaster used his bylined
editorial minute to inveigh against the Spanish-teaching program in
the firehouses.

An exasperated resident wrote to the letters column of the Chicago   6
Tribune: "I object to bilingual everything. It is a pretty low sort of person who wants to enjoy the benefits of this country while remaining
apart from it, hiding in an ethnic ghetto." Another letter writer huffed:
"What does it take to bring home to these stiff-necked Latinos that
when they move to a foreign country the least they can do is learn the
language? I, for one, am fed up with the ruination of the best country
in the world." Still another correspondent was even more succinct: "If
they can't understand two words—don't jump—they should go back
where they came from." And after my own brief article on the language controversy appeared, an angry firefighter's wife wrote me to
explain her husband's awful dilemma in being stationed in the Latino
community. "Why should he risk his life for nothing?" she wondered.

What does this story, which concerns speakers of Spanish, tell us   7
about the current state of English? It reminds us that our attitudes
about the speechways of other people are as much a part of the linguistic environment as nouns, verbs, and adjectives—and that today
these attitudes appear unusually harsh and unforgiving. In the Chicago controversy, some otherwise decent people were willing to
imply—and some plainly stated—that people who don't talk right can
damn well take their chances in a burning building. And while the underlying hostilities that give rise to such sentiments may not begin with
language, it is clear that we frequently use language as both a channel
and an excuse for expressing some of our deepest prejudices. Admit-
tedly, our unforgiving attitudes about certain kinds of language do not
often decide matters of life and death. Judging by the angry reaction to
the fire crisis in Chicago, it is a good thing that they don't.

It seems worth noting that this particular outpouring of linguistic   8
intolerance occurred in the midst of a period of more general concern
about the fate of the English language. For the last decade we have
been increasingly hearing about the sudden and widespread corruption of our native tongue. Standard English is supposedly becoming an
endangered species; jargon is rampant; the kids talk funny; politicians
brutalize the language in their endless attempts to mislead us; bureaucrats pollute the environment with obfuscation and bluster; the verbal
test scores of our schoolchildren are plunging; substandard dialects are
often accepted or even encouraged in the schools; non-English speakers are infiltrating our cities; and no one in school or business can write
a simple English sentence correctly.

We have been having a "literacy crisis"—a panic about the state of   9
our language in all of its uses, reading and writing and speaking. Predictions of linguistic doom have become a growth industry. *Time* magazine asks: "Can't Anyone Here Speak English?" while *Newsweek* explains "Why Johnny Can't Write." *TV Guide* warns of "The New
Illiteracy," *Saturday Review* bemoans "The Plight of the English Language," and even United Airline's *Mainliner Magazine* blusters
"Who's Been Messing Around with Our Mother Tongue?" Pop grammarians and language critics appear in every corner of the popular
media, relentlessly detailing the latest abuses of language and pillo-
rying individual abusers.

Blue-ribbon commissions are impaneled to study the declining   10
language skills of the young, and routinely prescribe strong doses of
"The Basics" as a remedy. Astute educational publishers crank out
old-fangled grammar books. English professors offer convoluted explanations of the crisis and its causes, most of which lay the blame on
public school English teachers. The *New York Times Magazine* adds

Spiro Agnew's former speechwriter to its roster as a weekly commentator "On Language." The president of the United States goes on record as encouraging the "back-to-basics" movement generally and the rebirth of grammar instruction in particular. Scores of books on illiteracy are published, but none outsells *Strictly Speaking*. Edwin Newman, house grammarian of the National Broadcasting Company had posed the question first, and apparently most frighteningly: "Will America be the death of English?" His answer was frightening too: "My mature, considered judgment is that it will."

It was in the midst of this ripening language panic that the Spanish 11 courses were begun in a few Chicago firehouses. The resulting controversy and debate would surely have happened anyway, since the expression of linguistic prejudice is one of humankind's most beloved amusements. But I also believe that the dispute was broadened, extended, and made more explicitly cruel by the prevailing climate of worry about the overall deterioration of American English.

The public had repeatedly been informed that the language was in 12 a mess, that it was time to draw the line, time to clean up the tongue, time to toughen our standards, time to quit coddling inadequate speakers. In Chicago, that line was drawn in no uncertain terms. Obviously, the connections between the "language crisis," with its mythical Mother Tongue writhing on her deathbed, and the all-too-real events of that recent Chicago winter are subtle and indirect.

Language is changing, yes. People "misuse" language constantly— 13 use it to lie, mislead, and conceal. Few of us write very well. Young people do talk differently from grownups. Our occupations do generate a lot of jargon. We do seem to swear more. I do not personally admire each of these phenomena. But reports of the death of the English language are greatly exaggerated.

English is not diseased, it has not been raped and ravaged, it is not 14 in peril. A language cannot, by its very nature, suffer in such ways. In fact, it cannot suffer at all. One of the sternest of the pop grammarians, Richard Mitchell, has said in one of his calmer moments:

> There is nothing wrong with English. We do not live in the twilight of a dying language. To say that our English is outmoded or corrupt makes as much sense as to say that multiplication has been outmoded by Texas Instruments and corrupted because we've all forgotten the times tables. You may say as often as you please that six times seven is forty-five, but arithmetic will not suffer.

Mitchell goes on to say that the real problem we face lies not in the language itself but in the ignorance and stupidity of its users. I agree, although my definition of ignorance and stupidity is quite different from his.

At least some of the ignorance from which we suffer is ignorance of   15
the history of language and the findings of linguistic research. History
shows us that language panics, some just as fierce as our present one,
are as familiar a feature of the human chronicle as wars. In fact, one of
the persistent characteristics of past crises has been the inevitable sense
that everything was fine until the moment at hand, 1965, or 1789, or
2500 B.C., when suddenly the language (be it American English, British English, or Sumerian) began the final plunge to oblivion. Looking
at the history of prior language crises gives us a reassuring perspective
for evaluating the current one.

But we need more than reassurance—we need facts, or at least the   16
closest thing to them, about the nature of language and how it works.
The study of linguistics, which has emerged only during the present
century, provides just such crucial information. The fact that the
sponsors of the language crisis almost unanimously condemn modern
linguistics suggests the irreconcilable difference between the critic's
and the linguist's views of language. The linguist's work is not to ridicule poor speakers and praise good ones; not to rank various languages
according to their supposed superiority in expressing literary or scientific concepts; not to defend the Mother Tongue from real or imagined
assaults. Instead, the linguist tries to understand and explain some of
the wonderfully complex mechanisms which allow human beings to
communicate with each other. This does not mean that linguists don't
have opinions about good and bad language, or even that some of
them won't cringe at a dangling *hopefully*. But their main business is
not evaluative but explanatory, not prescriptive but descriptive—an
orientation which is utterly alien to the work of the contemporary language critics.

Even if a review of the history of language and linguistic research   17
does tend to deflate our sense of crisis, this does not mean that the
widespread fear of linguistic corruption is meaningless. Far from it.
Something is indeed going on, and the wordsmiths of our society have
been able to spread their concern about it quite easily to people who
do not make their living by teaching, writing, or editing English. . . .

All this worry about a decline extends well beyond the speaking   18
and writing of American English. It represents a much wider concern
about the direction of our society, our culture, as a whole. We have
displaced (to use some jargon) much of our anxiety about current cultural changes into concern for the language which of necessity reflects
them. Today, as at certain other moments in the past, talking about
language has become a way of talking about ourselves, and about what
we mean by knowledge, learning, education, discipline, intelligence,
democracy, equality, patriotism, and truth.

But there are problems, serious ones. Language itself cannot be   19
asked to carry the weight of such grave issues alone. To the extent that
we assign our problems mainly to language, and explain them mostly
by reference to aspects of language, we often defeat our own purposes.
The critics, in this sense, are actually compounding the problems they
profess to solve. First, they are promulgating or reinforcing ideas
about language that are just plain wrong. If language is as important
as the critics unanimously claim, then we should at least try to tell the
truth about it, even if the facts run counter to our favorite prejudices.
Second, the ministrations of the critics, with their inaccurate notions
about the workings of language, threaten to bring back old—or to inspire new—teaching curricula and techniques that will hinder, rather
than enhance, our children's efforts to develop their reading and writing and speaking skills.

Third, the critics, ironically enough, often trivialize the study of   20
language. Through their steadfast preoccupation with form—with
spelling and punctuation and usage and adolescent jargon and bureaucratic bluster and political doublespeak—they deflect us from meaning. Of course we know that form and content are intimately related,
as the study of political propaganda reveals. Yet the real study of propaganda involves penetrating beyond the surface features to the message which is being sent, to the messages unsent, and to the purposes of
the senders. But much of the current scolding and fussing about language focuses on red-penciling the superficial niceties of written and
spoken utterances, rather than on understanding where they come
from and what they might mean.

For all their trivial obsessions, the critics do also offer a deeper,   21
more general message. As they advise us to strengthen our democracy
by cleaning up the language, they also encourage us to continue using
minor differences in language as ways of identifying, classifying,
avoiding, or punishing anyone whom we choose to consider our social
or intellectual inferior. And this is the gravest problem which the language crisis has given us: it has reinforced and occasionally glorified
some of the basest hatreds and flimsiest prejudices in our society.
Surely this unfortunate side effect has been mainly inadvertent—but
just as surely, it affects us all.

QUESTIONS ON CONTENT

1. What, according to Daniels, is the "normal condition" of American
English? Why isn't he concerned about all the so-called abuses cited
by language watchdogs and pop grammarians?

2. In paragraphs 5 and 6 Daniels relates the story of the 1978 fires in Chicago. What does this story have to do with the current state of English in the United States? Why does Daniels think that it is more than coincidence that the Chicago incident happened at the same time that there was growing public awareness of and concern about the decline of the English language?

3. What solutions have been offered for the "literacy crisis"? What is Daniels's attitude toward these solutions?

4. Daniels states that there are several irreconcilable differences between language critics and linguists. What exactly are these differences?

5. Daniels believes that the pop grammarians and language critics are "actually compounding the problems they profess to solve" (19). What reasons does he give for his opinion? Do you find yourself agreeing or disagreeing with Daniels?

6. What does Daniels think is the "gravest problem" that the current language crisis has strapped us with?

QUESTIONS ON RHETORIC

1. How would you characterize Daniels's writing: formal, informal, colloquial? How appropriate is his style to his subject and his argument?

2. How has Daniels organized his essay? You may find it helpful to make an outline of the essay so that you can see how the parts are related.

3. How would you characterize Daniels's tone in this essay? (Glossary: *Tone*) What is his attitude toward pop grammarians? toward the current language crisis? (Glossary: *Attitude*)

4. How does paragraph 13 function in the context of the essay?

5. Why do you think Daniels quotes Richard Mitchell in paragraph 14? Does he make effective use of the quotation? Why, or why not?

6. Why does Daniels find "medical metaphors" used to describe the language crisis generally unsatisfactory?

VOCABULARY

somber (1)	argot (3)	convoluted (10)
bereaved (1)	inveigh (5)	coddling (12)
prognosis (2)	succinct (6)	inadvertent (21)
cant (3)	obfuscation (8)	

WRITING TOPICS

1. After reading what both Newman ("Language on the Skids," p. 61) and Daniels have to say about the language crisis in America,

what is your position? Are you more in agreement with watchdog Newman or with linguist Daniels? Explain.

2. While you were in high school you were probably exposed to the "back to basics" movement. What exactly did "back to basics" mean in your area? How did it affect the curriculum? Did this approach adequately address students' language problems in writing, reading, and speaking?

3. Daniels believes that by insisting upon correctness, pop grammarians "encourage us to continue using minor differences in language as ways of identifying, classifying, avoiding, or punishing anyone whom we choose to consider our social or intellectual inferior" (21). Have you ever reacted to anyone negatively or positively on the basis of the English that he or she used, or have you ever been judged on that same basis? Write an essay in which you recount one such incident and discuss how language prejudiced opinion.

3

Black Children, Black Speech

DOROTHY Z. SEYMOUR

In this essay, linguist and long-time elementary-school reading teacher Dorothy Seymour discusses an important question facing present-day educators: On the basis of available evidence, how does one approach the conflict between the patterns of a nonstandard dialect, which the child learns either at home or from other children, and the equivalent patterns of Standard English? The issue, as you can well imagine, is highly controversial and emotional. Seymour first analyzes the distinguishing features of Black English and then considers the impact of Black English on schools in America, before making her case for a program of bidialectism. She believes that teachers and parents need to be informed about nonstandard language in order to implement such a program in our nation's schools.

"C'mon, man, les git goin'!" called the boy to his companion. "Dat 1
bell ringin'. It say, 'Git in rat now!' " He dashed into the school yard.

"Aw, f'get you," replied the other. "Whe' Richuh? Whe' da' muv- 2
vuh? He be goin' to schoo'."

"He in de' now, man!" was the answer as they went through the 3
door.

In the classroom they made for their desks and opened their books. 4
The name of the story they tried to read was "Come." It went:

> Come, Bill, come
> Come with me.
> Come and see this.
> See what is here.

The first boy poked the second. "Wha' da' wor'?"

"Da' wor' *is,* you dope." 5

"*Is?* Ain't no wor' *is.* You jivin' me? Wha' da' wor' mean?" 6

"Ah dunno. Jus' *is.* " 7

To a speaker of Standard English, this exchange is only vaguely 8
comprehensible. But it's normal speech for thousands of American

children. In addition it demonstrates one of our biggest educational problems: children whose speech style is so different from the writing style of their books that they have difficulty learning to read. These children speak Black English, a dialect characteristic of many inner-city Negroes. Their books are, of course, written in Standard English. To complicate matters, the speech they use is also socially stigmatized. Middle-class whites and Negroes alike scorn it as low-class poor people's talk.

Teachers sometimes make the situation worse with their attitudes toward Black English. Typically, they view the children's speech as "bad English" characterized by "lazy pronunciation," "poor grammar," and "short, jagged words." One result of this attitude is poor mental health on the part of the pupils. A child is quick to grasp the feeling that while school speech is "good," his own speech is "bad," and that by extension he himself is somehow inadequate and without value. Some children react to this feeling by withdrawing; they stop talking entirely. Others develop the attitude of "F'get you, honky." In either case, the psychological results are devastating and lead straight to the dropout route.

It is hard for most teachers and middle-class Negro parents to accept the idea that Black English is not just "sloppy talk" but a dialect with a form and structure of its own. Even some eminent black educators think of it as "bad English grammar" with "slurred consonants" (Professor Nick Aaron Ford of Morgan State College in Baltimore) and "ghettoese" (Dr. Kenneth B. Clark, the prominent educational psychologist).

Parents of Negro school children generally agree. Two researchers of Columbia University report that the adults they worked with in Harlem almost unanimously preferred that their children be taught Standard English in school.

But there is another point of view, one held in common by black militants and some white liberals. They urge that middle-class Negroes stop thinking of the inner-city dialect as something to be ashamed of and repudiated. Black author Claude Brown, for example, pushes this view.

Some modern linguists take a similar stance. They begin with the premise that no dialect is intrinsically "bad" or "good," and that a nonstandard speech style is not defective speech but different speech. More important, they have been able to show that Black English is far from being a careless way of speaking the Standard; instead, it is a rather rigidly-constructed set of speech patterns, with the same sort of specialization in sounds, structure, and vocabulary as any other dialect.

THE SOUNDS OF BLACK ENGLISH

Middle-class listeners who hear black inner-city speakers say "dis"   14
and "tin" for "this" and "thin" assume that the black speakers are just
being careless. Not at all; these differences are characteristic aspects of
the dialect. The original cause of such substitutions is generally a
carryover from one's original language or that of his immigrant parents. The interference from that carryover probably caused the substi-
tution of /d/ for the voiced *th* sound in *this,* and /t/ for the unvoiced *th*
sound in *thin.* (Linguists represent language sounds by putting letters
within slashes or brackets.) Most speakers of English don't realize that
the two *th* sounds of English are lacking in many other languages and
are difficult for most foreigners trying to learn English. Germans who
study English, for example, are surprised and confused about these
sounds because the only Germans who use them are the ones who lisp.
These two sounds are almost nonexistent in the West African languages which most black immigrants brought with them to America.

Similar substitutions used in Black English are /f/, a sound similar   15
to the unvoiced *th,* in medial word-position, as in *birfday* for *birthday,*
and in final word-position, as in *roof* for *Ruth* as well as /v/ for the
voiced *th* in medial position, as in *bruvver* for *brother.* These sound
substitutions are also typical of Gullah, the language of black speakers
in the Carolina Sea Island. Some of them are also heard in Caribbean
Creole.

Another characteristic of the sounds of Black English is the lack of   16
/l/ at the end of words, sometimes replaced by the sound /w/. This
makes words like *tool* sound like *too.* If /l/ occurs in the middle of a
Standard English word, in Black English it may be omitted entirely: "I
can hep you." This difference is probably caused by the instability and
sometimes interchangeability of /l/ and /r/ in West African languages.

One difference that is startling to middle-class speakers is the fact   17
that Black English words appear to leave off some consonant sounds at
the end of words. Like Italian, Japanese and West African words, they
are more likely to end in vowel sounds. Standard English *boot* is pronounced *boo* in Black English. *What is wha. Sure is sho. Your is yo.*
This kind of difference can make for confusion in the classroom. Dr.
Kenneth Goodman, a psycholinguist, tells of a black child whose
white teacher asked him to use *so* in a sentence—not "sew a dress" but
"the other *so.*" The sentence the child used was "I got a *so* on my leg."

A related feature of Black English is the tendency in many cases   18
not to use sequences of more than one final consonant sound. For example, *just* is pronounced *jus', past* is *pass, mend* sounds like *men* and

hold like *hole. Six* and *box* are pronounced *sick* and *bock.* Why should this be? Perhaps because West African languages, like Japanese, have almost no clusters of consonants in their speech. The Japanese, when importing a foreign word, handle a similar problem by inserting vowel sounds between every consonant, making *baseball* sound like *besu-boru.* West Africans probably made a simpler change, merely cutting a series of two consonant sounds down to one. Speakers of Gullah, one linguist found, have made the same kind of adaptation of Standard English.

Teachers of black children seldom understand the reason for these   19
differences in final sounds. They are apt to think that careless speech is the cause. Actually, black speakers aren't "leaving off" any sounds; how can you leave off something you never had in the first place?

Differences in vowel sounds are also characteristic of the nonstan-   20
dard language. Dr. Goodman reports that a black child asked his teacher how to spell rat. "R-a-t," she replied. But the boy responded "No ma'am, I don't mean rat mouse, I mean rat now." In Black English, *right* sounds like *rat.* A likely reason is that in West African languages, there are very few vowel sounds of the type heard in the word *right.* This type is common in English. It is called a glided or dipthongized vowel sound. A glided vowel sound is actually a close combination of two vowels; in the word *right* the two parts of the sound "eye" are actually "ah-ee." West African languages have no such long, two-part, changing vowel sounds; their vowels are generally shorter and more stable. This may be why in Black English, *time* sounds like *Tom, oil* like *all,* and *my* like *ma.*

LANGUAGE STRUCTURE

Black English differs from Standard English not only in its sounds but   21
also in its structure. The way the words are put together does not al-ways fit the description in English grammar books. The method of ex-pressing time, or tense, for example, differs in significant ways.

The verb *to be* is an important one in Standard English. It's used as   22
an auxiliary verb to indicate different tenses. But Black English speak-ers use it quite differently. Sometimes an inner-city Negro says "He coming"; other times he says "He be coming." These two sen-ences mean different things. To understand why, let's look at the tenses of West African languages; they correspond with those of Black English.

Many West African languages have a tense which is called the ha-   23
bitual. This tense is used to express action which is always occurring

and it is formed with a verb that is translated as *be*. "He be coming" means something like "He's always coming," "He usually comes," or "He's been coming."

In Standard English there is no regular grammatical construction 24 for such a tense. Black English speakers, in order to form the habitual tense in English, use the word *be* as an auxiliary: *He be doing it. My Momma be working. He be running.* The habitual tense is not the same as the present tense, which is constructed in Black English without any form of the verb *to be: He do it. My Momma working. He running.* (This means the action is occurring right now.)

There are other tense differences between Black English and Stan- 25 dard English. For example, the nonstandard speech does not use changes in grammar to indicate the past tense. A white person will ask, "What did your brother say?" and the black person will answer, "He say he coming." (The verb *say* is not changed to *said.*) "How did you get here?" "I walk." This style of talking about the past is paralleled in the Yoruba, Fante, Hausa, and Ewe languages of West Africa.

Expression of plurality is another difference. The way a black child 26 will talk of "them boy" or "two dog" makes some white listeners think Negroes don't know how to turn a singular word into a plural word. As a matter of fact, it isn't necessary to use an *s* to express plurality. In Chinese and Japanese, singular and plural are not generally distinguished by such inflections; plurality is conveyed in other ways. For example, in Chinese it's correct to say "There are three book on the table." This sentence already has two signals of the plural, *three* and *are;* why require a third? This same logic is the basis of plurals in most West African languages, where nouns are often identical in the plural and the singular. For example, in Ibo, one correctly says *those man,* and in both Ewe and Yoruba one says *they house.* American speakers of Gullah retain this style; it is correct in Gullah to say *five dog.*

Gender is another aspect of language structure where differences 27 can be found. Speakers of Standard English are often confused to find that the nonstandard vernacular often uses just one gender of pronoun, the masculine, and refers to women as well as men as *he* or *him.* "He a nice girl," even "Him a nice girl" are common. This usage probably stems from West African origins, too, as does the use of multiple negatives, such as "Nobody don't know it."

Vocabulary is the third aspect of a person's native speech that 28 could affect his learning of a new language. The strikingly different vocabulary often used in Negro Nonstandard English is probably the most obvious aspect of it to a casual white observer. But its vocabulary differences don't obscure its meaning the way different sounds and different structure often do.

Recently there has been much interest in the African origins of   29
words like *goober* (peanut), *cooter* (turtle), and *tote* (carry), as well as
others that are less certainly African, such as *to dig* (possibly from the
Wolof *degan,* "to understand"). Such expressions seem colorful rather
than low-class to many whites; they become assimilated faster than
their black originators do. English professors now use *dig* in their
scholarly articles, and current advertising has enthusiastically adopted
rap.

Is it really possible for old differences in sound, structure, and vo-   30
cabulary to persist from the West African languages of slave days into
present-day inner city Black English? Easily. Nothing else really explains such regularity of language habits, most of which persist among
black people in various parts of the Western Hemisphere. For a long
time scholars believed that certain speech forms used by Negroes were
merely leftovers from archaic English preserved in the speech of early
English settlers in America and copied by their slaves. But this theory
has been greatly weakened, largely as the result of the work of a black
linguist, Dr. Lorenzo Dow Turner of the University of Chicago. Dr.
Turner studied the speech of Gullah Negroes in the Sea Islands off the
Carolina coast and found so many traces of West African languages
that he thoroughly discredited the archaic-English theory.

When anyone learns a new language, it's usual to try speaking the   31
new language with the sounds and structure of the old. If a person's
first language does not happen to have a particular sound needed in
the language he is learning, he will tend to substitute a similar or related sound from his native language and use it to speak the new one.
When Frenchman Charles Boyer said "Zees ees my heart," and when
Latin American Carmen Miranda sang "Souse American way," they
were simply using sounds of their native languages in trying to pronounce sounds of English. West Africans must have done the same
thing when they first attempted English words. The tendency to retain
the structure of the native language is a strong one, too. That's why a
German learning English is likely to put his verb at the end: "May I a
glass beer have?" The vocabulary of one's original language may also
furnish some holdovers. Jewish immigrants did not stop using the
word *bagel* when they came to America; nor did Germans stop saying
sauerkraut.

Social and geographical isolation reinforces the tendencies to re-   32
tain old language habits. When one group is considered inferior, the
other group avoids it. For many years it was illegal to give any sort of
instruction to Negroes, and for slaves to try to speak like their masters
would have been unthinkable. Conflict of value systems doubtless re-
tards changes, too. As Frantz Fanon observed in *Black Skin, White*

Masks, those who take on white speech habits are suspect in the ghetto, because others believe they are trying to "act white." Dr. Kenneth Johnson, a black linguist, put it this way: "As long as disadvantaged black children live in segregated communities and most of their relationships are confined to those within their own subculture, they will not replace their functional nonstandard dialect with the nonfunctional standard dialect."

Linguists have made it clear that language systems that are different are not necessarily deficient. A judgment of deficiency can be made only in comparison with another language system. Let's turn the tables on Standard English for a moment and look at it from the West African point of view. From this angle, Standard English: (1) is lacking in certain language sounds, (2) has a couple of unnecessary language sounds for which others may serve as good substitutes, (3) doubles and drawls some of its vowel sounds in sequences that are unusual and difficult to imitate, (4) lacks a method of forming an important tense, (5) requires an unnecessary number of ways to indicate tense, plurality and gender, and (6) doesn't mark negatives sufficiently for the result to be a good strong negative statement.   33

Now whose language is deficient?   34

How would the adoption of this point of view help us? Say we accepted the evidence that Black English is not just a sloppy Standard but an organized language style which probably has developed many of its features on the basis of its West African heritage. What would we gain?   35

The psychological climate of the classroom might improve if teachers understood why many black students speak as they do. But we still have not reached a solution of the main problem. Does the discovery that Black English has pattern and structure mean that it should not be tampered with? Should children who speak Black English be excused from learning the Standard in school? Should they perhaps be given books in Black English to learn from?   36

Any such accommodation would surely result in a hardening of the new separatism being urged by some black militants. It would probably be applauded by such people as Roy Innis, Director of C.O.R.E., who is currently recommending dual autonomous education systems for white and black. And it might facilitate learning to read, since some experiments have indicated that materials written in Black English syntax aid problem readers from the inner city.   37

But determined resistance to the introduction of such printed materials into schools can be expected. To those who view inner-city speech as bad English, the appearance in print of sentences like "My mama, he work" can be as shocking and repellent as a four-letter word.   38

Middle-class Negro parents would probably mobilize against the move. Any stratagem that does not take into account such practicalities of the matter is probably doomed to failure. And besides, where would such a permissive policy on language get these children in the larger society, and in the long run? If they want to enter an integrated America they must be able to deal with it on its own terms. Even Professor Toni Cade of Rutgers, who doesn't want "ghetto accents" tampered with, advocates mastery of Standard English because, as she puts it, "if you want to get ahead in this country, you must master the language of the ruling class." This has always been true, wherever there has been a minority group.

The problem then appears to be one of giving these children the   39
ability to speak (and read) Standard English without denigrating the vernacular and those who use it, or even affecting the ability to use it. The only way to do this is to officially espouse bidialectism. The result would be the ability to use either dialect equally well—as Dr. Martin Luther King did—depending on the time, place, and circumstances. Pupils would have to learn enough about Standard English to use it when necessary, and teachers would have to learn enough about the inner-city dialect to understand and accept it for what it is—not just a "careless" version of Standard English but a different form of English that's appropriate in certain times and places.

Can we accomplish this? If we can't, the result will be continued   40
alienation of a large section of the population, continued dropout trouble with consequent loss of earning power and economic contribution to the nation, but most of all, loss of faith in America as a place where a minority people can at times continue to use those habits that remind them of their link with each other and with their past.

QUESTIONS ON CONTENT

1. How does Seymour define Black English?

2. What characteristics of Black English establish it as a distinct dialect rather than as improper usage of Standard English? How does Seymour account for the differences between Black English and Standard English?

3. Why does Seymour believe that Black children need facility with Standard English as well?

4. What distinction does Seymour make between a person's language being "different" and its being "defective"? In what ways is this distinction important to her argument?

5. In what ways, according to Seymour, is Standard English "deficient" when looked at from the West African point of view?

6. Why does Seymour advocate a program of bidialectism? What does she believe such a program will require of teachers, parents, and students?

QUESTIONS ON RHETORIC

1. What is Seymour's purpose in this essay? Does she seem to be more interested in explaining the issues to her readers or in persuading them to her point of view? (Glossary: *Purpose*) Do you think that she accomplishes her purpose? Why, or why not?

2. In what ways do the first seven paragraphs form an appropriate introduction for Seymour's essay? (Glossary: *Beginnings*)

3. Seymour presents her argument inductively; that is, she first introduces the problem, then examines and analyzes the evidence, and finally draws a conclusion based on her considered analysis. Is this organization effective given the nature of her topic? Could she have, for example, introduced her solution early in the essay? Why, or why not?

4. Seymour frequently cites authorities to strengthen her argument. What exactly is gained with each of these citations?

5. Seymour's essay includes a great deal of technical linguistic information about the sounds, structure, and vocabulary of Black English. Did you have any difficulties understanding her descriptions and explanations? Has Seymour done anything to accommodate readers without a linguistics background? If so, what? (Glossary: *Technical Language*)

6. How would you characterize Seymour's tone in this essay? (Glossary: *Tone*) Did you find it appropriate for her argument? Why, or why not?

7. Do you think paragraph 34 could be joined to paragraph 33? Why do you suppose Seymour chooses to make a separate, one-sentence paragraph?

8. In paragraphs 34–36 Seymour presents a series of questions. How do these questions function in the context of the essay? (Glossary: *Rhetorical Questions*)

VOCABULARY

stigmatized (8)	intrinsically (13)	stratagem (38)
devastating (9)	assimilated (29)	denigrating (39)
eminent (10)	autonomous (37)	vernacular (39)
repudiated (12)		

WRITING TOPICS

1. According to Seymour, linguists believe that when children become ashamed of their language, they become ashamed of themselves. Write an essay in which you first discuss how your attitude toward other people is affected by the way they speak. Second, discuss the nature of the relationship between one's use of language and one's feelings of self-worth. Be sure to describe any specific experiences that have made these relationships clear for you.

2. How important do you believe it is for individuals to understand the characteristics of nonstandard dialects like Black English? Write an essay in which you evaluate the possible advantages for individuals and for American society as a whole.

3. Many critics of bidialectism argue that while materials written in Black English syntax may facilitate learning for many inner-city children, they also make these children dependent on a dialect that excludes them from full participation in the American way of life. Where do you stand on the issue of bidialectism? Cite reasons to support your position.

4

The Country's Going
Through a Rough Spell

BOB GREENE

Have you ever been told that spelling is important and that you should work to improve yours? You're not alone if you have. Many people view this advice as just another manifestation of our national mania for correctness, but, with the current trend back to basics, spelling is again in the limelight. Bob Greene, a nationally syndicated newspaper columnist and author of the essay collection American Beat, *places a premium on good spelling, and in the following essay he explains why he believes it's so important.*

I'm in love with a wonderful girl. She's thirteen years old, she lives in   1
El Paso, Texas, and her name is Paige Pipkin. In an age of glamour girls and disco queens and Playmates of the Month, Miss Pipkin has the rarest of qualities. She can spell.

Last week Miss Pipkin correctly spelled the word *sarcophagus* and   2
thus won the 54th National Spelling Bee in Washington, D.C. She triumphed over a young man who misspelled the word *philippic,* and thus she finished first in the competition, which is sponsored each year by the Scripps-Howard Newspapers.

The idea of a National Spelling Bee seems somehow out of date,   3
but I think it's great. If you deal with the written word and you receive a lot of mail, then you know that people simply can't spell anymore. It is a skill that is becoming extinct in America—people apparently feel that they don't need to know how to do it, or that it is too hard to bother with.

When I go through the mail each day, I am constantly dismayed by   4
this trend. It is getting to the point where a letter with no misspelled words is the exception. The problem goes across the board—letters from students, letters from businessmen, letters from people in public life. Even the most prosperous executives have secretaries who can't spell. And—worst of all—I sometimes get letters from teachers, and even their letters are full of misspellings.

This may seem like a minor thing, but I don't think it is. If I know   5
that a person can't spell, then I have trouble trusting anything else

about him. If he can't even get the spelling of a word right, then why should I put any faith in his version of events, or his opinions? Obviously he is sloppy in his thinking if he can't even take the trouble to make certain of the spelling of the words he uses.

I fear I am in a minority here. I don't know if there have been any   6 official studies done on the problem, but just from personal observation I know that, in the last decade, the ability of people to spell has diminished rapidly. And yet you hardly ever hear it discussed.

I identify with Alexander Portnoy, the fictional protagonist of   7 Philip Roth's *Portnoy's Complaint,* on this issue. In the book, Portnoy meets a beautiful, loving, affectionate woman and immediately falls for her. But he soon makes a terrible discovery about her. He finds notes she has left for the cleaning lady, and sees that each note contains five or six misspellings. It dismays him. He wants to love her, but he knows that this awful flaw rules such a thing out. He could never truly be in love with a woman who can't even spell.

Say what you will about my writing. You may think it's lousy, it   8 may annoy you, it may even make you sick. But believe me on one thing. I am a hell of a speller. Ask any copy editor I've ever worked with. They will tell you. In the ten years I have been writing a newspaper column, I have misspelled no more than three words. And that's an outside estimate; to be truthful, I don't think I have misspelled any.

It's not such a great feat—all you have to do is look up the words   9 you aren't sure of. Today, for example, before I turn this column in to the copy desk, I will look up *protagonist,* which was used two paragraphs above this one. A simple enough step.

But most people aren't willing to take it. That's the worst thing   10 about the new inability of Americans to spell. If it just had to do with misspelled words, it would be one thing. But it is symbolic of an overall lack of discipline, a readiness not to care, a willingness to be second-rate. I know it may seem like a small thing to you, but it's really not. All the talk lately about the U.S. auto industry suffering because workmanship allegedly is inferior to workmanship in Japan—that's precisely the sort of thing that starts with a nation of people who can't even spell correctly.

And it's destined to get worse. In the television age, all print skills   11 are going to suffer, and spelling is going to be the first one to go. People are going to decide that knowing how to spell is an archaic discipline, and they are going to decide they can get along without it. And the worst thing is, they'll be able to—if enough people just can't spell, then businesses, by default, are going to have to employ them anyway, and try to look past this fault.

Which takes us back to Paige Pipkin, the thirteen-year-old spelling   12 champ from El Paso. For some reason, she has grown up believing that she must have enough pride in herself to be a perfect speller. It is difficult to imagine that she will ever fail in any important area of her life; you know instinctively that she is the kind of young woman who will succeed, because she cares about doing things right.

So congratulations to Miss Pipkin for winning the National Spelling Bee. If there were any justice in this world, they would have crowned her Miss America. 13

QUESTIONS ON CONTENT

1. Why does Greene think the idea of a National Spelling Bee is great? Do you agree with his comment that it seems somehow out of date?

2. How does Greene react to a person who can't spell? Do you think that his reaction is fair or justified? Why, or why not?

3. Greene admits that he is a good speller. How does he account for his own expertise?

4. What for Greene is "the worst thing about the new inability of Americans to spell" (10)? Does he seem to be stretching a point when he links bad spelling with the workmanship crisis in the auto industry? Why, or why not?

5. What is Greene's forecast for the future? Do you think that he is overly pessimistic? Why, or why not?

6. With the other members of your class, put together a list of fifteen to twenty words that people are likely to have trouble spelling. What does this list suggest about how you might improve your performance as a speller?

QUESTIONS ON RHETORIC

1. What is Greene's purpose in this essay? Is he mainly interested in criticizing the inability of Americans to spell or in celebrating Paige Pipkin's victory in the 54th National Spelling Bee? Explain.

2. Reread Greene's opening paragraph. How is it related to what follows? Is it an effective opening paragraph? (Glossary: *Beginnings*)

3. Greene appears to be defensive about the position he takes in this essay: "This may seem like a minor thing, . . ." (5); "I fear I am in a minority here." (6); "I identify with Alexander Portnoy, . . ." (7); and "Say what you will about my writing" (8). What, if anything, does he gain by pursuing this strategy?

4. How has Greene organized his essay? You may find it helpful to make a scratch outline of his major points to see the sequence of his ideas. (Glossary: *Organization*)

5. What kinds of transitional devices does Greene use to link the paragraphs in his essay? (Glossary: *Transitions*)

VOCABULARY

sarcophagus (2)   protagonist (7)
philippic (2)   symbolic (10)

WRITING TOPICS

1. Bob Greene states that "in the television age, all print skills are going to suffer, and spelling is going to be the first one to go" (11). How do you think spelling will fare in the age of computers and word processing? Will the need to spell well become obsolete? What can word processors do for the poor speller? What can't they do?

2.   How important is good spelling to you? Has your spelling ever caused you any embarrassing moments? How do you react to people who have trouble with spelling or constantly misspell your name, for example? Write a well-organized essay in which you summarize your beliefs about spelling.

3. Bob Greene believes that people like Paige Pipkin will succeed in life because "she cares about doing things right" (12). Write an essay in which you explain what it takes for a person to succeed today.

5
Caught Between Two Languages

RICHARD RODRIGUEZ

Speaking and writing English well are difficult enough for those brought up in the language; for those who were not, they can be complicated and even wounding experiences. Like millions of Americans, Richard Rodriguez learned English as a second language. He was born in 1944 in San Francisco, but his parents were from Mexico, and Spanish was the language spoken at home. As a child Rodriguez had a painful struggle to master what he calls his "public" language. In the following essay from Hunger of Memory, *Rodriguez relates the hardships and confusion of growing up in a world divided by two languages in order to argue forcefully against bilingual education in America.*

I remember to start with that day in Sacramento—a California now nearly thirty years past—when I first entered a classroom, able to understand some fifty stray English words.

The third of four children, I had been preceded to a neighborhood Roman Catholic school by an older brother and sister. But neither of them had revealed very much about their classroom experiences. Each afternoon they returned, as they left in the morning, always together, speaking in Spanish as they climbed the five steps of the porch. And their mysterious books, wrapped in shopping-bag paper, remained on the table next to the door, closed firmly behind them.

An accident of geography sent me to a school where all my classmates were white, many the children of doctors and lawyers and business executives. All my classmates certainly must have been uneasy on that first day of school—as most children are uneasy—to find themselves apart from their families in the first institution of their lives. But I was astonished.

The nun said, in a friendly but oddly impersonal voice, "Boys and girls, this is Richard Rodriguez." (I heard her sound out: *Rich-heard Road-ree-guess.*) It was the first time I had heard anyone name me in English. "Richard," the nun repeated more slowly, writing my name down in her black leather book. Quickly I turned to see my mother's face dissolve in a watery blur behind the pebbled glass door.

Many years later there is something called bilingual education—a scheme proposed in the late 1960s by Hispanic-American social activists, later endorsed by congressional vote. It is a program that seeks to permit non-English-speaking children, many from lower-class homes, to use their family language as the language of school. (Such is the goal its supporters announce.) I hear them and am forced to say no: It is not possible for a child—any child—ever to use his family's language in school. Not to understand this is to misunderstand the public uses of schooling and to trivialize the nature of intimate life—a family's "language."

Memory teaches me what I know of these matters; the boy reminds the adult. I was a bilingual child, a certain kind—socially disadvantaged—the son of working-class parents, both Mexican immigrants.

In the early years of my boyhood, my parents coped very well in America. My father had steady work. My mother managed at home. They were nobody's victims. Optimism and ambition led them to a house (our home) many blocks from the Mexican south side of town. We lived among *gringos* and only a block from the biggest, whitest houses. It never occurred to my parents that they couldn't live wherever they chose. Nor was the Sacramento of the fifties bent on teaching them a contrary lesson. My mother and father were more annoyed than intimidated by those two or three neighbors who tried initially to make us unwelcome. ("Keep your brats away from my sidewalk!") But despite all they achieved, perhaps because they had so much to achieve, any deep feeling of ease, the confidence of "belonging" in public was withheld from them both. They regarded the people at work, the faces in crowds, as very distant from us. They were the others, *los gringos*. That term was interchangeable in their speech with another, even more telling, *los americanos*.

I grew up in a house where the only regular guests were my relations. For one day, enormous families of relatives would visit and there would be so many people that the noise and the bodies would spill out to the backyard and front porch. Then, for weeks, no one came by. (It was usually a salesman who rang the doorbell.) Our house stood apart. A gaudy yellow in a row of white bungalows. We were the people with the noisy dog. The people who raised pigeons and chickens. We were the foreigners on the block. A few neighbors smiled and waved. We waved back. But no one in the family knew the names of the old couple who lived next door; until I was seven years old, I did not know the names of the kids who lived across the street.

In public, my father and mother spoke a hesitant, accented, not always grammatical English. And they would have to strain—their bodies tense—to catch the sense of what was rapidly said by *los gringos.* At home they spoke Spanish. The language of their Mexican past sounded in counterpoint to the English of public society. The words would come quickly, with ease. Conveyed through those sounds was the pleasing, soothing, consoling reminder of being at home.

During those years when I was first conscious of hearing, my mother and father addressed me only in Spanish; in Spanish I learned to reply. By contrast, English (inglés), rarely heard in the house, was the language I came to associate with *gringos.* I learned my first words of English overhearing my parents speak to strangers. At five years of age, I knew just enough English for my mother to trust me on errands to stores one block away. No more.   10

I was a listening child, careful to hear the very different sounds of Spanish and English. Wide-eyed with hearing, I'd listen to sounds more than words. First, there were English (*gringo*) sounds. So many words were still unknown that when the butcher or the lady at the drugstore said something to me, exotic polysyllabic sounds would bloom in the midst of their sentences. Often, the speech of people in public seemed to me very loud, booming with confidence. The man behind the counter would literally ask, "What can I do for you!" But by being so firm and so clear, the sound of his voice said that he was a *gringo;* he belonged in public society.   11

I would also hear then the high nasal notes of middle-class American speech. The air stirred with sound. Sometimes, even now, when I have been traveling abroad for several weeks, I will hear what I heard as a boy. In hotel lobbies or airports, in Turkey or Brazil, some Americans will pass, and suddenly I will hear it again—the high sound of American voices. For a few seconds I will hear it with pleasure, for it is now the sound of *my* society—a reminder of home. But inevitably—already on the flight headed for home—the sound fades with repetition. I will be unable to hear it anymore.   12

When I was a boy, things were different. The accent of *los gringos* was never pleasing nor was it hard to hear. Crowds at Safeway or at bus stops would be noisy with sound. And I would be forced to edge away from the chirping chatter above me.   13

I was unable to hear my own sounds, but I knew very well that I spoke English poorly. My words could not stretch far enough to form complete thoughts. And the words I did speak I didn't know well enough to make into distinct sounds. (Listeners would usually lower their heads, better to hear what I was trying to say.) But it was one thing for *me* to speak English with difficulty. It was more troubling for me to hear my parents speak in public; their high-whining vowels and   14 guttural consonants; their sentences that got stuck with "eh" and "ah" sounds; the confused syntax; the hesitant rhythm of sounds so different from the way *gringos* spoke. I'd notice, moreover, that my parents' voices were softer than those of *gringos* we'd meet.

I am tempted now to say that none of this mattered. In adulthood I   15 am embarrassed by childhood fears. And, in a way, it didn't matter very much that my parents could not speak English with ease. Their linguistic difficulties had no serious consequences. My mother and father made themselves understood at the county hospital clinic and at government offices. And yet, in another way, it mattered very much— it was unsettling to hear my parents struggle with English. Hearing them, I'd grow nervous, my clutching trust in their protection and power weakened.

There were many times like the night at a brightly lit gasoline sta-   16 tion (a blaring white memory) when I stood uneasily, hearing my father. He was talking to a teenaged attendant. I do not recall what they were saying, but I cannot forget the sounds my father made as he spoke. At one point his words slid together to form one word—sounds as confused as the threads of blue and green oil in the puddle next to my shoes. His voice rushed through what he had left to say. And, toward the end, reached falsetto notes, appealing to his listener's understanding. I looked away to the lights of passing automobiles. I tried not to hear anymore. But I heard only too well the calm, easy tones in the attendant's reply. Shortly afterward, walking toward home with my father, I shivered when he put his hand on my shoulder. The very first chance that I got, I evaded his grasp and ran on ahead into the dark, skipping with feigned boyish exuberance.

But then there was Spanish. *Español:* my family's language.   17 *Español:* the language that seemed to me a private language. I'd hear strangers on the radio and in the Mexican Catholic church across town speaking in Spanish, but I couldn't really believe that Spanish was a public language, like English. Spanish speakers, rather, seemed related to me, for I sensed that we shared—through our language—the experience of feeling apart from *los gringos*. It was thus a ghetto Spanish that I heard and I spoke. Like those whose lives are bound by a barrio, I was reminded by Spanish of my separateness from *los otros, los gringos* in power. But more intensely than for most barrio children—because I did not live in a barrio—Spanish seemed to me the language of home. (Most days it was only at home that I'd hear it.) It became the language of joyful return.

A family member would say something to me and I would feel   18 myself specially recognized. My parents would say something to me and I would feel embraced by the sounds of their words. Those sounds said: *I am speaking with ease in Spanish. I am addressing you in words I never use with* los gringos. *I recognize you as someone special, close, like no one outside. You belong with us. In the family.*

(Ricardo.)   19

At the age of five, six, well past the time when most other children   20
no longer easily notice the difference between sounds uttered at home
and words spoken in public, I had a different experience. I lived in a
world magically compounded of sounds. I remained a child longer
than most; I lingered too long, poised at the edge of language—often
frightened by the sounds of *los gringos,* delighted by the sounds of
Spanish at home. I shared with my family a language that was star-
tlingly different from that used in the great city around us.

For me there were none of the gradations between public and pri-   21
vate society so normal to a maturing child. Outside the house was
public society; inside the house was private. Just opening or closing the
screen door behind me was an important experience. I'd rarely leave
home all alone or without reluctance. Walking down the sidewalk,
under the canopy of tall trees, I'd warily notice the—suddenly—silent
neighborhood kids who stood warily watching me. Nervously, I'd arrive at the grocery store to hear there the sounds of the *gringo*—foreign
to me—reminding me that in this world so big, I was a foreigner. But
then I'd return. Walking back toward our house, climbing the steps
from the sidewalk, when the front door was open in summer, I'd hear
voices beyond the screen door talking in Spanish. For a second or two,
I'd stay, linger there, listening. Smiling, I'd hear my mother call out,
saying in Spanish (words): "Is that you, Richard?" All the while
her sounds would assure me: *You are home now; come closer; inside.
With us.*

"Sí," I'd reply.   22

Once more inside the house I would resume (assume) my place in   23
the family. The sounds would dim, grow harder to hear. Once more at
home, I would grow less aware of that fact. It required, however, no
more than the blurt of the doorbell to alert me to listen to sounds all
over again. The house would turn instantly still while my mother went
to the door. I'd hear her hard English sounds. I'd wait to hear her voice
return to soft-sounding Spanish, which assured me, as surely as did the
clicking tongue of the lock on the door, that the stranger was gone.

Plainly, it is not healthy to hear such sounds so often. It is not   24
healthy to distinguish public words from private sounds so easily. I remained cloistered by sounds, timid and shy in public, too dependent
on voices at home. And yet it needs to be emphasized: I was an extremely happy child at home. I remember many nights when my father
would come back from work, and I'd hear him call out to my mother
in Spanish, sounding relieved. In Spanish, he'd sound light and free
notes he never could manage in English. Some nights I'd jump up just

at hearing his voice. With *mis hermanos* I would come running into the room where he was with my mother. Our laughing (so deep was the pleasure!) became screaming. Like others who know the pain of public alienation, we transformed the knowledge of our public separateness and made it consoling—the reminder of intimacy. Excited, we joined our voices in a celebration of sounds. *We are speaking now the way we never speak out in public. We are alone—together,* voices sounded, surrounded to tell me. Some nights, no one seemed willing to loosen the hold sounds had on us. At dinner, we invented new words. (Ours sounded Spanish, but made sense only to us.) We pieced together new words by taking, say, an English verb and giving it Spanish endings. My mother's instructions at bedtime would be lacquered with mock-urgent tones. Or a word like *sí* would become, in several notes, able to convey added measures of feeling. Tongues explored the edges of words, especially the fat vowels. And we happily sounded that military drum roll, the twirling roar of the Spanish *r.* Family language: my family's sounds. The voices of my parents and sisters and brother. Their voices insisting: *You belong here. We are family members. Related. Special to one another. Listen!* Voices singing and sighing, rising, straining, then surging, teeming with pleasure that burst syllables into fragments of laughter. At times it seemed there was steady quiet only when, from another room, the rustling whispers of my parents faded and I moved closer to sleep.

Supporters of bilingual education today imply that students like 25 me miss a great deal by not being taught in their family's language. What they seem not to recognize is that, as a socially disadvantaged child, I consider Spanish to be a private language. What I needed to learn in school was that I had the right—and the obligation—to speak the public language of *los gingos.* The odd truth is that my first-grade classmates could have become bilingual, in the conventional sense of that word, more easily than I. Had they been taught (as upper-middle-class children are often taught early) a second language like Spanish or French, they could have regarded it simply as that: another public language. In my case such bilingualism could not have been so quickly achieved. What I did not believe was that I could speak a single public language.

Without question, it would have pleased me to hear my teachers 26 address me in Spanish when I entered the classroom. I would have felt much less afraid. I would have trusted them and responded with ease. But I would have delayed—for how long postponed?—having to learn the language of public society. I would have evaded—and for how long could I have afforded to delay?—learning the great lesson of school, that I had a public identity.

Fortunately, my teachers were unsentimental about their responsi- 27 bility. What they understood was that I needed to speak a public language. So their voices would search me out, asking me questions. Each time I'd hear them, I'd look up in surprise to see a nun's face frowning at me. I'd mumble, not really meaning to answer. The nun would persist, "Richard, stand up. Don't look at the floor. Speak up. Speak to the entire class, not just to me!" But I couldn't believe that the English langauge was mine to use. (In part, I did not want to believe it.) I continued to mumble. I resisted the teacher's demands. (Did I somehow expect that once I learned the public language my pleasing family life would be changed?) Silent, waiting for the bell to sound, I remained dazed, diffident, afraid.

Because I wrongly imagined that English was intrinsically a public   28
language and Spanish an intrinsically private one, I easily noted the difference between classroom language and the language of home. At school, words were directed to a general audience of listeners. ("Boys and girls.") Words were meaningfully ordered. And the point was not self-expression alone but to make oneself understood by many others. The teacher quizzed: "Boys and girls, why do we use that word in this sentence? Could we think of a better word to use there? Would the sentence change its meaning if the words were differently arranged? And wasn't there a better way of saying much the same thing?" (I couldn't say. I wouldn't try to say.)

Three months. Five. Half a year passed. Unsmiling, ever watchful,   29
my teachers noted my silence. They began to connect my behavior with the difficult progress my older sister and brother were making. Until one Saturday morning three nuns arrived at the house to talk to our parents. Stiffly, they sat on the blue living room sofa. From the doorway of another room, spying the visitors, I noted the incongruity—the clash of two worlds, the faces and voices of school intruding upon the familiar setting of home. I overheard one voice gently wondering. "Do your children speak only Spanish at home, Mrs. Rodriguez?" While another voice added, "That Richard especially seems so timid and shy."

That Rich-heard!   30

With great tact the visitors continued, "Is it possible for you and   31
your husband to encourage your children to practice their English when they are at home?" Of course, my parents complied. What would they not do for their children's well-being? And how could they have questioned the Church's authority which those women represented? In an instant, they agreed to give up the language (the sounds) that had revealed and accentuated our family's closeness. The moment after the visitors left, the change was observed. *"Ahora,* speak to us *en inglés,"* my father and mother united to tell us.

At first, it seemed a kind of game. After dinner each night, the family gathered to practice "our" English. (It was still then *inglés,* a language foreign to us, so we felt drawn as strangers to it.) Laughing, we would try to define words we could not pronounce. We played with strange English sounds, often over-anglicizing our pronunciations. And we filled the smiling gaps of our sentences with familiar Spanish sounds. But that was cheating, somebody shouted. Everyone laughed. In school, meanwhile, like my brother and sister, I was required to attend a daily tutoring session. I needed a full year of special attention. I also needed my teachers to keep my attention from straying in class by calling out, *Rich-heard*—their English voices slowly prying loose my ties to my other name, its three notes, *Ri-car-do.* Most of all I needed to hear my mother and father speak to me in a moment of seriousness in broken—suddenly heartbreaking—English. The scene was inevitable: One Saturday morning I entered the kitchen where my parents were talking in Spanish. I did not realize that they were talking in Spanish however until, at the moment they saw me, I heard their voices change to speak English. Those *gringo* sounds they uttered startled me. Pushed me away. In that moment of trivial misunderstanding and profound insight, I felt my throat twisted by unsounded grief. I turned quickly and left the room. But I had no place to escape to with Spanish. (The spell was broken.) My brother and sisters were speaking English in another part of the house. 32

Again and again in the days following, increasingly angry, I was obliged to hear my mother and father: "Speak to us *en inglés.*" (*Speak.*) Only then did I determine to learn classroom English. Weeks after, it happened: one day in school I raised my hand to volunteer an answer. I spoke out in a loud voice. And I did not think it remarkable when the entire class understood. That day, I moved very far from the disadvantaged child I had been only days earlier. The belief, the calming assurance that I belonged in public, had at last taken hold. 33

QUESTIONS ON CONTENT

1. What does Richard Rodriguez remember about his first day at school? Why was this experience particularly memorable?

2. What, according to Rodriguez, is the stated goal of the supporters of bilingual education? Why is Rodriguez opposed to such a program?

3. Rodriguez distinguishes between "public language" and "private language." What differences does he see?

4. What did Rodriguez feel when he heard his parents trying to speak English in public? What difficulties did Rodriguez himself have

while trying to learn English? How did his attitude toward the sounds of *los gringos* change over time?

5. What for Rodriguez was "the great lesson of school" (26)?

6. What changes occurred in the Rodriguez household after the three nuns from the Catholic school visited one Saturday morning? Why did they want to know what language was spoken in the home?

7. What does Rodriguez mean when he says, "The odd truth is that my first-grade classmates could have become bilingual, in the conventional sense of the word, more easily than I" (25)?

QUESTIONS ON RHETORIC

1. Why is Rodriguez particularly suited to speak on the question of bilingual education?

2. Rodriguez uses a highly personal narrative of his childhood to develop his argument against bilingual education. Did you find this strategy to be effective? Why, or why not?

3. What is the function of the first four paragraphs? How are they related to the essay as a whole?

4. Throughout the essay Rodriguez juxtaposes Spanish words (*los gringos, Ricardo, inglés*) with their English equivalents (the others, Richard, English). How does this device help him establish the separate worlds of his private language and the public language of society in general? How does he use it to show what changes take place as he grows older?

5. In paragraph 23 Rodriguez says, "Once more inside the house I would resume (assume) my place in the family." What does his use of the words "resume" and "assume" reveal about his struggle?

VOCABULARY

endorsed (5)	counterpoint (9)	canopy (21)
intimidated (7)	nasal (12)	diffident (27)
gaudy (8)	barrio (17)	

WRITING TOPICS

1. Think back to your early experiences with language. Did you have problems learning English? What were they? Do you find that you now have greater facility with language? How do you account for any changes?

2. Discuss your own experience learning a foreign language. What are the greatest stumbling blocks, and what are the most effective ways of overcoming them? Were your difficulties at all like those of Rodriguez?

3. Even though we may not have a second language spoken in the home like the Rodriguez family, we are all aware of the differences between the way we talk and write in public or at school and the way we talk at home or among close friends. Write an essay in which you analyze these differences and attempt to explain the reasons for them.

WRITING ASSIGNMENTS FOR "AMERICAN ENGLISH TODAY"

1. Write an essay in which you compare and contrast the views of the state of American English held by Edwin Newman and Bob Greene with those of Harvey Daniels.

2. The concept of "Standard English" has caused much misunderstanding and debate. For many Americans, "standard" implies that one variety of English is more correct or more functional than other varieties. Write an essay in which you attempt to define "Standard English" and to explain its power or mystique.

3. Bidialectism and bilingualism are highly controversial subjects. Pick one and then prepare a report that (a) presents the opposing views objectively, or (b) supports one particular view over the other. What sociologic and economic factors are important? What issues do not seem to be relevant? From an educational point of view, which argument do you think is strongest? Defend whatever position you take.

4. Each of the following items is normally discussed as a question of usage by usage guides and dictionaries. Consult three or four usage guides in the reference room of your library for information about each item. What advice does each guide offer? How does the advice given by one guide compare with that given by another? What conclusions can you draw about the usefulness of such usage guides?

    a. hopefully
    b. nauseous
    c. imply/infer
    d. contact (as a verb)
    e. ain't
    f. among/between
    g. enthuse
    h. irregardless
    i. lay/lie
    j. uninterested/disinterested

NOTE: Suggested topics for research papers appear on p. 446.

NOTABLE QUOTATIONS

The following quotations are drawn from the essays in this section. They are presented as additional topics for classroom discussion or for writing assignments.

"A large part of our speech and writing is unnecessary and boring, which makes reading and conversation a chore." *Newman* (2)

"Our language should be specific and concrete, eloquent where possible, playful where possible, and personal so that we don't all sound alike." *Newman* (13)

"The language belongs to all of us. We have no more valuable possession." *Newman* (13)

"Our language is an essentially neutral instrument with which we communicate, more or less, and into which we pour an abundance of feeling. It is our central cultural asset and our cherished personal friend, but it is not, in many ways, what we think it is or would like it to be." *Daniels* (4)

". . . Reports of the death of the English language are greatly exaggerated." *Daniels* (13)

"The problem then appears to be one of giving these children the ability to speak (and read) Standard English without denigrating the vernacular and those who use it, or even affecting the ability to use it. The only way to do this is to officially espouse bidialectism." *Seymour* (39)

"[Spelling] is a skill that is becoming extinct in America. . . ." *Greene* (3)

"For some reason, [Paige Pipkin] has grown up believing that she must have enough pride in herself to be a perfect speller. It is difficult to imagine that she will ever fail in any important area of her life; you know instinctively that she is the kind of young woman who will succeed, because she cares about doing things right." *Greene* (12)

"It is not possible for a child—any child—ever to use his family's language in school. Not to understand this is to misunderstand the public uses of schooling and to trivialize the nature of intimate life—a family's 'language.' " *Rodriguez* (5)

"What I needed to learn in school was that I had the right—and the obligation—to speak the public language of *los gringos.*" *Rodriguez* (25)

III

Language, Politics, and Propaganda

To concepts like suicide, homicide, and genocide, we should
add 'semanticide'—the murder of language. The deliberate (or
quasi-deliberate) misuse of language through hidden metaphor
and professional mystification, breaks the basic contract between people, namely the tacit agreement on the proper use of
words. Thus it is that the 'great' philosophers and politicians
whose aim was to control man, from Rousseau to Stalin and
Hitler, have preached and practiced semanticide; whereas those
who have tried to set man free to be his own master, from
Emerson to Kraus and Orwell, have preached and practiced respect for language.

Thomas Szasz

If language be not in accordance with the truth of things, affairs cannot be carried on to success.

Confucius

Our politics would be improved if our English were, and so
would other parts of our national life. If we were more careful
about what we say, and how, we might be more critical and less
gullible. Those for whom words have lost their value are likely
to find that ideas have also lost their value.

Edwin Newman

1
Selection, Slanting, and Charged Language

NEWMAN P. BIRK and
GENEVIEVE B. BIRK

The more we learn about language and how it works, the more abundantly clear it becomes that our language shapes our perceptions of the world. Because we all have the same set of physical organs for perceiving reality—eyes to see, ears to hear, noses to smell, tongues to taste, and skins to feel, reality should be the same for all of us. But we know that it isn't; and language, it seems, is the big difference. Our language, in effect, acts as a filter, heightening certain perceptions, dimming others, and totally voiding still others. In the following selection from their book Understanding and Using English, *Newman and Genevieve Birk discuss how we learn new things, how we put our knowledge into words, and how language can be manipulated to create particular impressions.*

A. THE PRINCIPLE OF SELECTION

Before it is expressed in words, our knowledge, both inside and out- 1
side, is influenced by the principle of selection. What we know or observe depends on what we notice; that is, what we select, consciously or
unconsciously, as worthy of notice or attention. As we observe, the
principle of selection determines which facts we take in.

Suppose, for example, that three people, a lumberjack, an artist, 2
and a tree surgeon, are examining a large tree in a forest. Since the tree
itself is a complicated object, the number of particulars or facts about
it that one could observe would be very great indeed. Which of these
facts a particular observer will notice will be a matter of selection, a
selection that is determined by his interests and purposes. A lumberjack might be interested in the best way to cut the tree down, cut it up
and transport it to the lumber mill. His interest would then determine
his principle of selection in observing and thinking about the tree. The
artist might consider painting a picture of the tree, and his purpose
would furnish his principle of selection. The tree surgeon's profes-

sional interest in the physical health of the tree might establish a principle of selection for him. If each man were now required to write an exhaustive, detailed report on every thing he observed about the tree, the facts supplied by each would differ, for each would report those facts that his particular principle of selection led him to notice.[1]

The principle of selection holds not only for the specific facts that people observe but also for the facts they remember. A student suddenly embarrassed may remember nothing of the next ten minutes of class discussion but may have a vivid recollection of the sensation of the blood mounting, as he blushed, up his face and into his ears. In both noticing and remembering, the principle of selection applies, and it is influenced not only by our special interest and point of view but by our whole mental state of the moment.

The principle of selection then serves as a kind of sieve or screen through which our knowledge passes before it becomes our knowledge. Since we can't notice everything about a complicated object or situation or action or state of our own consciousness, what we do notice is determined by whatever principle of selection is operating for us at the time we gain the knowledge.

It is important to remember that what is true of the way the principle of selection works for us is true also of the way it works for others. Even before we or other people put knowledge into words to express meaning, that knowledge has been screened or selected. Before an historian or an economist writes a book, or before a reporter writes a news article, the facts that each is to present have been sifted through the screen of a principle of selection. Before one person passes on knowledge to another, that knowledge has already been selected and shaped, intentionally or unintentionally, by the mind of the communicator.

B. THE PRINCIPLE OF SLANTING

When we put our knowledge into words, a second process of selection, the process of slanting, takes place. Just as there is something, a rather mysterious principle of selection, which chooses for us what we will notice, and what will then become our knowledge, there is also a principle which operates, with or without our awareness, to select certain facts and feelings from our store of knowledge, and to choose the

[1] Of course, all three observers would probably report a good many facts in common—the height of the tree, for example, and the size of the trunk. The point we wish to make is that each observer would give us a different impression of the tree because of the different principle of selection that guided his observation.

words and the emphasis that we shall use to communicate our meaning.[2] Slanting may be defined as the process of selecting (1) knowledge—factual and attitudinal; (2) words; and (3) emphasis, to achieve the intention of the communicator. Slanting is present in some degree in all communication: one may *slant for* (favorable slanting), *slant against* (unfavorable slanting), or *slant both ways* (balanced slanting). . . .

C. SLANTING BY USE OF EMPHASIS

Slanting by use of the devices of emphasis is unavoidable,[3] for emphasis is simply the giving of stress to subject matter, and so indicating what is important and what is less important. In speech, for example, if we say that Socrates was *a wise old man,* we can give several slightly different meanings, one by stressing *wise,* another by stressing *old,* another by giving equal stress to *wise* and *old,* and still another by giving chief stress to *man.* Each different stress gives a different slant (favorable or unfavorable or balanced) to the statement because it conveys a different attitude toward Socrates or a different judgment of him. Connectives and word order also slant by the emphasis they give: consider the difference in slanting or emphasis produced by *old but wise, old and wise, wise but old.* In writing, we cannot indicate subtle stresses on words as clearly as in speech, but we can achieve our emphasis and so can slant by the use of more complex patterns of word order, by choice of connectives, by underlining heavily stressed words, and by marks of punctuation that indicate short or long pauses and so give light or heavy emphasis. Question marks, quotation marks, and exclamation points can also contribute to slanting.[4] It is impossible either in speech or in writing to put two facts together without giving some slight emphasis or slant. For example, if we have in mind only two facts about a man, his awkwardness and his strength, we subtly slant those facts favorably or unfavorably in whatever way we may choose to join them:

[2] Notice that the "principle of selection" is at work as *we take in* knowledge, and that slanting occurs as *we express* our knowledge in words.

[3] When emphasis is present—and we can think of no instance in the use of language in which it is not—it necessarily influences the meaning by playing a part in the favorable, unfavorable, or balanced slant of the communicator. We are likely to emphasize by voice stress, even when we answer *yes* or *no* to simple questions.

[4] Consider the slanting achieved by punctuation in the following sentences: He called the Senator an honest man? *He* called the Senator an honest man? He called the Senator an honest man! He said one more such "honest" senator would corrupt the state.

More Favorable Slanting	Less Favorable Slanting
He is awkward and strong.	He is strong and awkward.
He is awkward but strong.	He is strong but awkward.
Although he is somewhat awkward, he is very strong.	He may be strong, but he's very awkward.

With more facts and in longer passages it is possible to maintain a delicate balance by alternating favorable emphasis and so producing a balanced effect.

All communication, then, is in some degree slanted by the *emphasis*   8
of the communicator.

D. SLANTING BY SELECTION OF FACTS

To illustrate the technique of slanting by selection of facts, we shall ex-   9
amine three passages of informative writing which achieve different
effects simply by the selection and emphasis of material. Each passage
is made up of true statements or facts about a dog, yet the reader is
given three different impressions. The first passage is an example of
objective writing or balanced slanting, the second is slanted unfavorably, and the third is slanted favorably.

1. Balanced Presentation

> Our dog, Toddy, sold to us a cocker, produces various reactions in various   10
> people. Those who come to the back door she usually growls and barks at
> (a milkman has said that he is afraid of her); those who come to the front
> door, she whines at and paws; also she tries to lick people's faces unless we
> have forestalled her by putting a newspaper in her mouth. (Some of our
> friends encourage these actions; others discourage them. Mrs. Firmly, one
> friend, slaps the dog with a newspaper and says, "I know how hard dogs
> are to train.") Toddy knows and responds to a number of words and
> phrases, and guests sometimes remark that she is a "very intelligent dog."
> She has fleas in the summer, and she sheds, at times copiously, the year
> round. Her blonde hairs are conspicuous when they are on people's cloth-
> ing or on rugs or furniture. Her color and her large brown eyes frequently
> produce favorable comment. An expert on cockers would say that her ears
> are too short and set too high and that she is at least six pounds too heavy.

The passage above is made up of facts, verifiable facts,[5] deliber-   11
ately selected and emphasized to produce a *balanced* impression. Of

---

[5] *Verifiable facts* are facts that can be checked and agreed upon and proved to be
true by people who wish to verify them. That a particular theme received a failing

course not all the facts about the dog have been given—to supply *all* the facts on any subject, even such a comparatively simple one, would be an almost impossible task. Both favorable and unfavorable facts are used, however, and an effort has been made to alternate favorable and unfavorable details so that neither will receive greater emphasis by position, proportion, or grammatical structure.

2. Facts Slanted Against

That dog put her paws on my white dress as soon as I came in the door, and she made so much noise that it was two minutes before she had quieted down enough for us to talk and hear each other. Then the gas man came and she did a great deal of barking. And her hairs are on the rug and on the furniture. If you wear a dark dress they stick to it like lint. When Mrs. Firmly came in, she actually hit the dog with a newspaper to make it stay down, and she made some remark about training dogs. I wish the Birks would take the hint or get rid of that noisy, short-eared, overweight "cocker" of theirs.   12

This unfavorably slanted version is based on the same facts, but now these facts have been selected and given a new emphasis. The speaker, using her selected facts to give her impression of the dog, is quite possibly unaware of her negative slanting.   13

Now for a favorably slanted version: 14

3. Facts Slanted For

What a lively and responsive dog! When I walked in the door, there she was with a newspaper in her mouth, whining and standing on her hind legs and wagging her tail all at the same time. And what an intelligent dog. If you suggest going for a walk, she will get her collar from the kitchen and hand it to you, and she brings Mrs. Birk's slippers whenever Mrs. Birk says she is "tired" or mentions slippers. At a command she catches balls, rolls over, "speaks," or stands on her hind feet and twirls around. She sits up and balances a piece of bread on her nose until she is told to take it; then she tosses it up and catches it. If you are eating something, she sits up in front of you and "begs" with those big dark brown eyes set in that light,   15

---

grade is a verifiable fact; one needs merely to see the theme with the grade on it. That the instructor should have failed the theme is not, strictly speaking, a verifiable fact, but a matter of opinion. That women on the average live longer than men is a verifiable fact; that they live better is a matter of opinion, *a value judgment.*

buff-colored face of hers. When I got up to go and told her I was leaving, she rolled her eyes at me and sat up like a squirrel. She certainly is a lively and intelligent dog.

Speaker 3, like Speaker 2, is selecting from the "facts" summarized 16 in balanced version 1, and is emphasizing his facts to communicate his impression.

All three passages are examples of *reporting* (i.e., consist only of 17 verifiable facts), yet they give three very different impressions of the same dog because of the different ways the speakers slanted the facts. Some people say that figures don't lie, and many people believe that if they have the "facts," they have the "truth." Yet if we carefully examine the ways of thought and language, we see that any knowledge that comes to us through words has been subjected to the double screening of the principle of selection and the slanting of language. . . .

Wise listeners and readers realize that the double screening that is 18 produced by the principle of selection and by slanting takes place even when people honestly try to report the facts as they know them. (Speakers 2 and 3, for instance, probably thought of themselves as simply giving information about a dog and were not deliberately trying to mislead.) Wise listeners and readers know too that deliberate manipulators of language, by mere selection and emphasis, can make their slanted facts appear to support almost any cause.

In arriving at opinions and values we cannot always be sure that 19 the facts that sift into our minds through language are representative and relevant and true. We need to remember that much of our information about politics, governmental activities, business conditions, and foreign affairs comes to us selected and slanted. More than we realize, our opinions on these matters may depend on what newspaper we read or what news commentator we listen to. Worth-while opinions call for knowledge of reliable facts and reasonable arguments for and against—and such opinions include beliefs about morality and truth and religion as well as about public affairs. Because complex subjects involve knowing and dealing with many facts on both sides, reliable judgments are at best difficult to arrive at. If we want to be fairminded, we must be willing to subject our opinions to continual testing by new knowledge, and must realize that after all they *are* opinions, more or less trustworthy. Their trustworthiness will depend on the representativeness of our facts, on the quality of our reasoning, and on the standard of values that we choose to apply.

We shall not give here a passage illustrating the unscrupulous 20 slanting of facts. Such a passage would also include irrelevant facts and false statements presented as facts, along with various subtle distortions of fact. Yet to the uninformed reader the passage would be indistinguishable from a passage intended to give a fair account. If two passages (2 and 3) of casual and unintentional slanting of facts about a dog can give such contradictory impressions of a simple subject, the reader can imagine what a skilled and designing manipulation of facts and statistics could do to mislead an uninformed reader about a really complex subject. An example of such manipulation might be the account of the United States that Soviet propaganda has supplied to the average Russian. Such propaganda, however, would go beyond the mere slanting of the facts: it would clothe the selected facts in charged words and would make use of the many other devices of slanting that appear in charged language.

E. SLANTING BY USE OF CHARGED WORDS

In the passages describing the dog Toddy, we were illustrating the   21
technique of slanting by the selection and emphasis of facts. Though the facts selected had to be expressed in words, the words chosen were as factual as possible, and it was the selection and emphasis of facts and not of words that was mainly responsible for the two distinctly different impressions of the dog. In the passages below we are demonstrating another way of slanting—by the use of charged words. This time the accounts are very similar in the facts they contain; the different impressions of the subject, Corlyn, are produced not by different facts but by the subtle selection of charged words.

The passages were written by a clever student who was told to   22
choose as his subject a person in action, and to write two descriptions, each using the "same facts." The instructions required that one description be slanted positively and the other negatively, so that the first would make the reader favorably inclined toward the person and the action, and the second would make him unfavorably inclined.

Here is the favorably charged description. Read it carefully and   23
form your opinion of the person before you go on to read the second description.

Corlyn

Corlyn paused at the entrance to the room and glanced about. A well-cut   24
black dress draped subtly about her slender form. Her long blonde hair gave her chiseled features the simple frame they required. She smiled an engaging smile as she accepted a cigarette from her escort. As he lit it for her she looked over the flame and into his eyes. Corlyn had that rare talent of making every male feel that he was the one man in the world.

She took his arm and they descended the steps into the room. She   25
walked with an effortless grace and spoke with equal ease. They each took

a cup of coffee and joined a group of friends near the fire. The flickering light danced across her face and lent an ethereal quality to her beauty. The good conversation, the crackling logs, and the stimulating coffee gave her a feeling of internal warmth. Her eyes danced with each leap of the flames.

Taken by itself this passage might seem just a description of an attractive girl. The favorable slanting by use of charged words has been done so skillfully that it is inconspicuous. Now we turn to the unfavorable slanted description of the "same" girl in the "same" actions: 26

Corlyn

Corlyn halted at the entrance to the room and looked around. A plain black dress hung on her thin frame. Her stringy bleached hair accentuated her harsh features. She smiled an inane smile as she took a cigarette from her escort. As he lit it for her she stared over the lighter and into his eyes. Corlyn had a habit of making every male feel that he was the last man on earth.   27

She grasped his arm and they walked down the steps and into the room. Her pace was fast and ungainly, as was her speech. They each reached for some coffee and broke into a group of acquaintances near the fire. The flickering light played across her face and revealed every flaw. The loud talk, the fire, and the coffee she had gulped down made her feel hot. Her eyes grew more red with each leap of the flames.   28

When the reader compares these two descriptions, he can see how charged words influence the reader's attitude. One needs to read the two descriptions several times to appreciate all the subtle differences between them. Words, some rather heavily charged, others innocent-looking but lightly charged, work together to carry to the reader a judgment of a person and a situation. If the reader had seen only the first description of Corlyn, he might well have thought that he had formed his "own judgment on the basis of the facts." And the examples just given only begin to suggest the techniques that may be used in heavily charged language. For one thing, the two descriptions of Corlyn contain no really good example of the use of charged abstractions; for another, the writer was obliged by the assignment to use the same set of facts and so could not slant by selecting his material.   29

F. SLANTING AND CHARGED LANGUAGE

... When slanting of facts, or words, or emphasis, or any combination of the three *significantly influences* feelings toward, or judgments about, a subject, the language used is charged language. ...   30

Of course communications vary in the amount of charge they carry   31
and in their effect on different people; what is very favorably charged
for one person may have little or no charge, or may even be adversely
charged, for others. It is sometimes hard to distinguish between
charged and uncharged expression. But it is safe to say that whenever
we wish to convey any kind of inner knowlege—feelings, attitudes,
judgments, values—we are obliged to convey that attitudinal meaning
through the medium of charged language; and when we wish to understand the inside knowledge of others, we have to interpret the
charged language that they choose, or are obliged to use. Charged language, then, is the natural and necessary medium for the communication of charged or attitudinal meaning. At times we have difficulty in
living with it, but we should have even greater difficulty in living without it.

Some of the difficulties in living with charged language are caused   32
by its use in dishonest propaganda, in some editorials, in many
political speeches, in most advertising, in certain kinds of effusive
salesmanship, and in blatantly insincere, or exaggerated, or sentimental expressions of emotion. Other difficulties are caused by the misunderstandings and misinterpretations that charged language produces.
A charged phrase misinterpreted in a love letter; a charged word spoken in haste or in anger; an acrimonious argument about religion or
politics or athletics or fraternities; the frustrating uncertainty produced
by the effort to understand the complex attitudinal meaning in a poem
or play or a short story—these troubles, all growing out of the use of
charged language, may give us the feeling that Robert Louis Stevenson
expressed when he said, "The battle goes sore against us to the going
down of the sun."

But however charged language is abused and whatever misunder-   33
standings it may cause, we still have to live with it—and even by it. It
shapes our attitudes and values even without our conscious knowledge; it gives purpose to, and guides, our actions; through it we establish and maintain relations with other people and by means of it we
exert our greatest influence on them. Without charged language, life
would be but half life. The relatively uncharged language of bare factual statement, though it serves its informative purpose well and is
much less open to abuse and to misunderstanding, can describe only
the bare land of factual knowledge; to communicate knowledge of the
turbulencies and the calms and the deep currents of the sea of inner
experience we must use charged language.

QUESTIONS ON CONTENT

1. What is the "principle of selection," and how does it work?

2. How is "slanting" different from the "principle of selection"? What devices can a writer or speaker use to slant knowledge?

3. Paragraph 7 is full of examples of slanting by use of emphasis. Explain how each example works.

4. What exactly are "charged words"? Demonstrate your understanding of charged language by picking good examples from the two descriptions of Corlyn. What are some of the difficulties in living with charged language?

5. Why does a given word—like *lilac, religion,* or *lady*—mean different things to different people?

6. What do the Birks mean when they say, "Without charged language, life would be but half life" (33)?

QUESTIONS ON RHETORIC

1. Did you find the examples about Toddy the dog and Corlyn particularly helpful? What would have been lost had the examples not been included? (Glossary: *Examples*)

2. What is the relationship between paragraphs 1 and 2?

3. How have the Birks organized their essay? Is the organizational pattern appropriate for the subject matter? Explain. (Glossary: *Organization*)

4. What is the Birks' purpose in this essay? Do they seem more intent on explaining or arguing their position? (Glossary: *Purpose*)

VOCABULARY

exhaustive (2)   attitudinal (6)   abstractions (29)
blushed (3)   verifiable (11)   turbulencies (33)
sieve (4)   inconspicuous (26)

WRITING TOPICS

1. Select an article about a current event from a newspaper or news magazine. Without changing the facts given, rewrite the article so that it makes a different impression on the reader. Hand in the original article, your rewritten version, and your comments about how each version should affect the reader.

2. Following the Birks' example of their dog Toddy, write three descriptions (one balanced, one slanted for, and one slanted against) of one of the following:

a. your room
b. your best friend
c. your favorite coffee cup
d. a rock star or other celebrity
e. your school's dining hall
f. a hamburger
g. sunglasses
h. your mother, your father, or a sibling
i. a video game
j. a book

3. The following news stories about a Little League World Series appeared in two very different newspapers. Carefully read each article, looking for slanting and charged language. Point out the "verifiable facts." How do you know?

LITTLE LEAGUE SERIES BARS FOREIGNERS

WILLIAMSPORT, PA., NOV. 11 (AP)—The Little League will confine future world series to teams from the continental United States.

This was announced today at the headquarters of the national baseball organization. The effect was to exclude Taiwan, which won the series for boys 8 to 12 years old in the last four years, causing protests in this country. Japan won the two previous years, and Monterrey, Mexico, took the series in 1957 and 1958. The last United States winner was Wayne, N.J., in 1970.

The league said its board of directors had acted after a review of the competition. It said the regional championship series would be continued in Canada, the Far East, Europe and Latin America, and the play-offs for senior (ages 13 to 15) or big league (16 to 18) programs would not be affected.

A spokesman cited travel costs for foreign entries and the nationalistic approach taken abroad as reasons for the change. He described the United States programs as regional in make-up.

Since the Little League expanded in 1957 to include teams outside the continental United States, 20 foreign teams have competed. There are 9,000 teams in the United States.

Robert H. Stirrat, vice president and public relations director, would only say:

"We are standing by the board's resolution and will offer no further details."

The world series will be played next Aug. 19 to 23 at Williamsport, the birthplace of Little League baseball. Only four teams—the United States regional champions—will be entered. There were eight when foreign teams competed.

The ruling eliminates from world series competition children of American servicemen stationed in Europe because, a spokesman said, they are considered "foreign."

The first world series was played in 1947.

Last Aug. 24 Taiwan wrapped up its fourth straight world series with a 12–1 victory in the final over Red Bluff, Calif. The run was the first allowed by the Taiwanese in 46 innings, so complete did they dominate the series.

The team was led by Lin Wen-hsiung, a 12-year-old, right-handed pitcher, who hit two home runs and hurled a two-hitter in the final, striking out 15 of the 21 batters he faced.

The game was shown throughout Taiwan on television via satellite at 3 A.M, but many fans there considered the outcome such a foregone conclusion that they elected to go to sleep rather than watch.

Nevertheless, there were bursts of firecrackers before dawn to celebrate the victory.

So proficient have Taiwanese youngsters become at baseball that they have dominated not only Little League competition, but also divisions for older boys.

This year a Taiwanese team captured the Senior Little League world championship in Gary, Ind., for the third straight time, and the island's Big League team won the title at Fort Lauderdale, Fla., in its first attempt.

LITTLE LEAGUE BANS FOREIGNERS

No More Chinese HRs

Little League Shrinks Map
Limits World Series After Taiwan Romp

After watching Taiwan dominate the Little League World Series at Williamsport, Pa., for four years, the American sponsors found a way yesterday to end that victory streak: they banned foreign entries.

The ban, obviously, will do away with the so-called Chinese home run, a phrase New Yorkers learned about when the upper deck hung out over the playing field at the defunct Polo Grounds where the foul lines were short and homers were plentiful.

Peter J. McGovern, chief executive officer and board chairman of the Little League, said that the series would be restricted to the four regional U.S. champions from now on.

Robert H. Stirrat, vice president and public relations director for the league, said that the organization "is not nationalistic in its point of view." Stirrat said the group feels Little League is basically a community program and it intends returning to the original concept.

"The board took a long view of the international aspects of the program and decided a reassessment of the World Series competition for children aged 12 and under had to be regarded," Stirrat said. "It was their decision to limit the series from here on to the United States."

Stirrat also emphasized the ban on foreign clubs involves only the Little League series at Williamsport. He added that the senior league (13–15) and big league (16–18) are not affected. Those championships will still be waged on an international basis.

"The senior division is the world's largest baseball program," Stirrat said. "But they are unaffected by the decision." The seniors' finale will be played at Gary, Ind., with the big league finals at Fort Lauderdale, Fla.

Japanese Led the Parade

League officials deny the latest ruling was an effort to exclude Taiwan or any other non-U.S. Squad. There are 9,000 little leagues in this country and since the Williamsport brass broadened its program in 1957 to include "outside" teams, 20 foreign clubs have competed.

An American team hasn't been the Little League champ since Wayne, N.J., in 1970. Since then, Japanese representatives won in 1968 and 1969, followed by Taiwan the past four years.

Regional championships will continue to be held in Canada, Latin America, Europe and the Far East, but those winners will not compete in Williamsport.

"The Little League is taken pretty much as a summertime activity for kids in the United States," Stirrat said, "and the World Series is sort of a natural finish of the season for them."

Now, with only four clubs contesting for the 1975 title, which will be decided Aug. 19–23 at Williamsport, Little League brass were undecided as to its new format. They must determine whether sudden-death or a double elimination series will be played.

In any event, the Little League World Series will be an all-American affair.

What kind of newspaper do you think each article appeared in? On what stylistic evidence did you base your decision? Does a knowledge of the kind of newspaper it appeared in help to explain the way in which it was written? In an essay compare and contrast the two reports and your evaluations of their use of slanting and charged language.

2
Politics and the English Language

GEORGE ORWELL

An essay usually becomes a classic because it makes an important statement about a subject with unusual effectiveness. Such is the case with this essay, written in the 1940s. Here George Orwell, author of 1984, discusses the condition of the English language and the ways in which he believes it has seriously deteriorated. He attributes this decline to political and economic causes. Orwell concludes by suggesting a number of remedies to help restore the language to a healthier state.

Most people who bother with the matter at all would admit that the English language is in a bad way, but it is generally assumed that we cannot by conscious action do anything about it. Our civilization is decadent and our language—so the argument runs—must inevitably share in the general collapse. It follows that any struggle against the abuse of language is a sentimental archaism, like preferring candles to electric light or hansom cabs to aeroplanes. Underneath this lies the half-conscious belief that language is a natural growth and not an instrument which we shape for our own purposes.

Now, it is clear that the decline of a language must ultimately have political and economic causes: it is not due simply to the bad influence of this or that individual writer. But an effect can become a cause, reinforcing the original cause and producing the same effect in an intensified form, and so on indefinitely. A man may take to drink because he feels himself to be a failure, and then fail all the more completely because he drinks. It is rather the same thing that is happening to the English language. It becomes ugly and inaccurate because our thoughts are foolish, but the slovenliness of our language makes it easier for us to have foolish thoughts. The point is that the process is reversible. Modern English, especially written English, is full of bad habits which spread by imitation and which can be avoided if one is willing to take the necessary trouble. If one gets rid of these habits one can think more clearly, and to think clearly is a necessary first step towards political regeneration: so that the fight against bad English is not frivolous and is not the exclusive concern of professional writers. I will come back to this presently, and I hope that by that time the meaning of what I have said here will have become clearer. Meanwhile here are five specimens of the English language as it is now habitually written.

These five passages have not been picked out because they are   3 especially bad—I could have quoted far worse if I had chosen—but because they illustrate various of the mental vices from which we now suffer. They are a little below the average, but are fairly representative samples. I number them so that I can refer back to them when necessary:

(1) I am not, indeed, sure whether it is not true to say that the Milton who once seemed not unlike a seventeenth-century Shelley had not become, out of an experience ever more bitter in each year, more alien [*sic*] to the founder of that Jesuit sect which nothing could induce him to tolerate.

Professor Harold Laski (Essay in *Freedom of Expression*)

(2) Above all, we cannot play ducks and drakes with a native battery of idioms which prescribes such egregious collocations of vocables as the Basic *put up with* for *tolerate* or *put at a loss* for *bewilder*.

Professor Lancelot Hogben (*Interglossa*)

(3) On the one side we have the free personality: by definition it is not neurotic, for it has neither conflict nor dream. Its desires, such as they are, are transparent, for they are just what institutional approval keeps in the forefront of consciousness; another institutional pattern would alter their number and intensity; there is little in them that is natural, irreducible, or culturally dangerous. But *on the other side,* the social bond itself is nothing but the mutual reflection of these self-secure integrities. Recall the definition of love. Is not this the very picture of a small academic? Where is there a place in this hall of mirrors for either personality or fraternity?

Essay on psychology in *Politics* (New York)

(4) All the "best people" from the gentlemen's clubs, and all the frantic fascist captains, united in common hatred of Socialism and bestial horror of the rising tide of the mass revolutionary movement, have turned to acts of provocation, to foul incendiarism, to medieval legends of poisoned wells, to legalize their own destruction of proletarian organizations, and rouse the agitated petty-bourgeoisie to chauvinistic fervor on behalf of the fight against the revolutionary way out of the crisis.

Communist pamphlet

(5) If a new spirit *is* to be infused into this old country, there is one thorny and contentious reform which must be tackled, and that is the humaniza-

tion and galvanization of the B.B.C. Timidity here will bespeak canker and atrophy of the soul. The heart of Britain may be sound and of strong beat, for instance, but the British lion's roar at present is like that of Bottom in Shakespeare's *Midsummer Night's Dream*—as gentle as any sucking dove. A virile new Britain cannot continue indefinitely to be traduced in the eyes or rather ears, of the world by the effete languors of Langham Place, brazenly masquerading as "standard English." When the voice of Britain is heard at nine o'clock, better far and infinitely less ludicrous to hear aitches honestly dropped than the present priggish, inflated, inhibited, school-ma'amish arch braying of blameless bashful mewing maidens!

Letter in *Tribune*

Each of these passages has faults of its own, but, quite apart from avoidable ugliness, two qualities are common to all of them. The first is staleness of imagery; the other is lack of precision. The writer either has a meaning and cannot express it, or he inadvertently says something else, or he is almost indifferent as to whether his words mean anything or not. This mixture of vagueness and sheer incompetence is the most marked characteristic of modern English prose, and especially of any kind of political writing. As soon as certain topics are raised, the concrete melts into the abstract and no one seems able to think of turns of speech that are not hackneyed: prose consists less and less of *words* chosen for the sake of their meaning, and more and more of *phrases* tacked together like the sections of a prefabricated henhouse. I list below, with notes and examples, various of the tricks by means of which the work of prose-construction is habitually dodged:

DYING METAPHORS. A newly invented metaphor assists thought by evoking a visual image, while on the other hand a metaphor which is technically "dead" (e.g., *iron resolution*) has in effect reverted to being an ordinary word and can generally be used without loss of vividness. But in between these two classes there is a huge dump of worn-out metaphors which have lost all evocative power and are merely used because they save people the trouble of inventing phrases for themselves. Examples are: *Ring the changes on, take up the cudgels for, toe the line, ride roughshod over, stand shoulder to shoulder with, play into the hands of, no axe to grind, grist to the mill, fishing in troubled waters, on the order of the day, Achilles' heel, swan song, hotbed.* Many of these are used without knowledge of their meaning (what is a "rift," for instance?), and incompatible metaphors are frequently mixed, a sure sign that the writer is not interested in what he is saying. Some metaphors now current have been twisted out of their original meaning without those who use them even being aware of the fact. For example, *toe the line* is sometimes written *tow the line.* Another example is the *hammer and the anvil,* now always used with the implication that the anvil gets the worst of it. In real life it is always the anvil that breaks the hammer, never the other way about: a writer who stopped to think what he was saying would be aware of this, and would avoid perverting the original phrase.

OPERATORS OR VERBAL FALSE LIMBS. These save the trouble of picking out appropriate verbs and nouns, and at the same time pad each sentence with extra syllables which give it an appearance of symmetry. Characteristic phrases are *render inoperative, militate against, make contact with, be subjected to, give rise to, give grounds for, have the effect of, play a leading part (role) in, make itself felt, take effect, exhibit a tendency to, serve the purpose of,* etc., etc. The keynote is the elimination of simple verbs. Instead of being a single word, such as *break, stop, spoil, mend, kill,* a verb becomes a *phrase,* made up of a noun or adjective tacked on to some general-purposes verb such as *prove, serve, form, play, render.* In addition, the passive voice is wherever possible used in preference to the active, and noun constructions are used instead of gerunds (*by examination of* instead of *by examining*). The range of verbs is further cut down by means of the *-ize* and *de-* formations, and the banal statements are given an appearance of profundity by means of the *not un-* formation. Simple conjunctions and prepositions are replaced by such phrases as *with respect to, having regard to, the fact that, by dint of, in view of, in the interests of, on the hypothesis that;* and the ends of sentences are saved from anticlimax by such resounding common-places as *greatly to be desired, cannot be left out of account, a development to be expected in the near future, deserving of serious consideration, brought to a satisfactory conclusion,* and so on and so forth. 6

PRETENTIOUS DICTION. Words like *phenomenon, element, individual* (as noun), *objective, categorical, effective, virtual, basic, primary, promote, constitute, exhibit, exploit, utilize, eliminate, liquidate,* are used to dress up simple statements and give an air of scientific impartiality to biased judgments. Adjectives like *epoch-making, epic, historic, unforgettable, triumphant, age-old, inevitable, inexorable, veritable,* are used to dignify the sordid processes of international politics, while writing that aims at glorifying war usually takes on an archaic color, its characteristic words being: *realm, throne, chariot, mailed fist, trident, sword, shield, buckler, banner, jackboot, clarion.* Foreign words and expressions such as *cul de sac, ancien régime, deus ex machina, mutatis mutandis, status quo, gleichschaltung, weltanschauung,* are used to give an air of culture 7 and elegance. Except for the useful abbreviations *i.e., e.g.,* and *etc.,* there is no real need for any of the hundreds of foreign phrases now current in English. Bad writers, and especially scientific, political and sociological writers, are nearly always haunted by the notion that Latin or Greek words are grander than Saxon ones, and unnecessary words like *expedite, ameliorate, predict, extraneous, deracinated, clandestine, subaqueous* and hundreds of others constantly gain ground from their Anglo-Saxon opposite numbers.[1] The jargon peculiar to Marxist writing (*hyena, hangman, cannibal, petty bourgeois, these gentry, lacquey, flunkey, mad dog, White Guard,* etc.) consists largely of words and phrases translated from Russian, German or French; but the normal way of coining a new word is to use a Latin or Greek root with the appropriate affix and, where necessary, the *-ize* formation. It is often easier to make up words of this kind (*deregionalize, impermissible, extramarital, non-fragmentary* and so forth) than to think up the English words that will cover one's meaning. The result, in general, is an increase in slovenliness and vagueness.

MEANINGLESS WORDS. In certain kinds of writing, particularly in art criticism and literary criticism, it is normal to come across long passages which are almost completely lacking in meaning.[2] Words like *romantic, plastic, values, human, dead, sentimental, natural, vitality,* as used in art criticism, are strictly meaningless, in the sense that they not only do not point to any discoverable object, but are hardly ever expected to do so by the reader. When one critic writes, "The outstanding feature of Mr. X's work is its living quality," while another writes, "The immediately striking thing about Mr. X's work is its peculiar deadness," the reader accepts this as a simple difference of opinion. If words like *black* and *white* were involved, instead of the jargon words *dead* and *living,* he would see at once that language was being used in an improper way. Many political words are similarly abused. The word *Fascism* has now no meaning except in so far as it signifies "something not desirable." The words *democracy, freedom, patriotic,*

8

[1] An interesting illustration of this is the way in which the English flower names which were in use till very recently are being ousted by Greek ones, *snapdragon* becoming *antirrhinum, forget-me-not* becoming *myosotis,* etc. It is hard to see any practical reason for this change of fashion: it is probably due to an instinctive turning-away from the more homely word and a vague feeling that the Greek word is scientific.

[2] Example: "Comfort's catholicity of perception and image, strangely Whitmanesque in range, almost the exact opposite in aesthetic compulsion, continues to evoke that trembling atmospheric accumulative hinting at a cruel, an inexorably serene timelessness.... Wrey Gardiner scores by aiming at simple bull's-eyes with precision. Only they are not so simple, and through this contented sadness runs more than the surface bittersweet of resignation." (*Poetry Quarterly*)

realistic, justice, have each of them several different meanings which cannot be reconciled with one another. In the case of a word like *democracy,* not only is there no agreed definition, but the attempt to make one is resisted from all sides. It is almost universally felt that when we call a country democratic we are praising it: consequently the defenders of every kind of regime claim that it is a democracy, and fear that they might have to stop using the word if it were tied down to any one meaning. Words of this kind are often used in a consciously dishonest way. That is, the person who uses them has his own private definition, but allows his hearer to think he means something quite different. Statements like, *Marshal Pétain was a true patriot, The Soviet Press is the freest in the world, The Catholic Church is opposed to persecution,* are almost always made with intent to deceive. Other words used in variable meanings, in most cases more or less dishonestly, are: *class, totalitarian, science, progressive, reactionary, bourgeois, equality.*

Now that I have made this catalogue of swindles and perversions,   9
let me give another example of the kind of writing that they lead to. This time it must of its nature be an imaginary one. I am going to translate a passage of good English into modern English of the worst sort. Here is a well-known verse from *Ecclesiastes:*

> I returned and saw under the sun, that the race is not to the swift, nor the battle to the strong, neither yet bread to the wise, nor yet riches to men of understanding, nor yet favour to men of skill; but time and chance happeneth to them all.

Here it is in modern English: 10

> Objective consideration of contemporary phenomena compels the conclusion that success or failure in competitive activities exhibits no tendency to be commensurate with innate capacity, but that a considerable element of the unpredictable must invariably be taken into account.

This is a parody, but a very gross one. Exhibit (3), above, for instance, contains several patches of the same kind of English. It will be seen that I have not made a full translation. The beginning and ending of the sentence follow the original meaning fairly closely, but in the middle the concrete illustrations—race, battle, bread—dissolve into the vague phrase "success or failure in competitive activities." This had to be so, because no modern writer of the kind I am discussing— no one capable of using phrases like "objective consideration of contemporary phenomena"—would ever tabulate his thoughts in that precise and detailed way. The whole tendency of modern prose is away from concreteness. Now analyse these two sentences a little more closely. The first contains forty-nine words but only sixty syllables, and all its words are those of everyday life. The second contains thirty-eight words of ninety syllables: eighteen of its words are from Latin roots, and one from Greek. The first sentence contains six vivid images, and only one phrase ("time and chance") that could be called vague. The second contains not a single fresh, arresting phrase, and in spite of its ninety syllables it gives only a shortened version of the meaning contained in the first. Yet without a doubt it is the second kind of sentence that is gaining ground in modern English. I do not want to exaggerate. This kind of writing is not yet universal, and outcrops of simplicity will occur here and there in the worst-written page. Still, if you or I were told to write a few lines on the uncertainty of human fortunes, we should probably come much nearer to my imaginary sentence than to the one from *Ecclesiastes.*

As I have tried to show, modern writing at its worst does not consist 12 in picking out words for the sake of their meaning and inventing images in order to make the meaning clearer. It consists in gumming together long strips of words which have already been set in order by someone else, and making the results presentable by sheer humbug. The attraction of this way of writing is that it is easy. It is easier—even quicker, once you have the habit—to say *In my opinion it is not an unjustifiable assumption that* than to say *I think.* If you use ready-made phrases, you not only don't have to hunt about for words; you also don't have to bother with the rhythms of your sentences, since these phrases are generally so arranged as to be more or less euphonious. When you are composing in a hurry—when you are dictating to a stenographer, for instance, or making a public speech—it is natural to fall into a pretentious, Latinized style. Tags like *a consideration which we should do well to bear in mind* or *a conclusion to which all of us would readily assent* will save many a sentence from coming down with a bump. By using stale metaphors, similes and idioms, you save much mental effort, at the cost of leaving your meaning vague, not only for your reader but for yourself. This is the significance of mixed metaphors. The sole aim of a metaphor is to call up a visual image. When these images clash—as in *The Fascist octopus has sung its swan song, the jackboot is thrown into the melting pot*—it can be taken as certain that the writer is not seeing a mental image of the objects he is naming; in other words he is not really thinking. Look again at the examples I gave at the beginning of this essay. Professor Laski (1) uses five negatives in fifty-three words. One of these is superfluous, making nonsense of the whole passage, and in addition there is the slip *alien* for akin, making further nonsense, and several avoidable pieces of clumsiness which increase the general vagueness. Professor Hogben (2) plays ducks and drakes with a battery which is able to write prescriptions, and, while disapproving of the everyday phrase *put up with,* is unwilling to look *egregious* up in the dictionary and see what it means; (3), if one takes an uncharitable attitude towards it, is simply meaningless: probably one could work out its intended meaning by reading the whole of the article in which it occurs. In (4), the writer knows more or less what he wants to say, but an accumulation of stale phrases chokes him like tea leaves blocking a sink. In (5), words and meaning have almost parted company. People who write in this manner usually have a general emotional meaning—they dislike one thing and want to express solidarity with another—but they are not interested in the detail of what they are saying. A scrupulous writer, in every sentence that he writes, will ask himself at least four questions, thus: What am I trying to say? What words will express it? What image or idiom will make it clearer? Is this image fresh enough to have an effect? And he will probably ask himself two more: Could I put it more shortly? Have I said anything that is avoidably ugly? But you are not obliged to go to all this trouble. You can shirk it by simply throwing your mind open and letting the ready-made phrases come crowding in. They will construct your sentences for you—even think your thoughts for you, to a certain extent—and at need they will perform the important service of partially concealing your meaning even from yourself. It is at this point that the special connection between politics and the debasement of language becomes clear.

In our time it is broadly true that political writing is bad writing. 13 Where it is not true, it will generally be found that the writer is some kind of rebel, expressing his private opinions and not a "party line." Orthodoxy, of whatever color, seems to demand a lifeless, imitative style. The political dialects to be found in pamphlets, leading articles, manifestos, White Papers and the speeches of under-secretaries do, of course, vary from party to party, but they are all alike in that one almost never finds in them a fresh, vivid, home-made turn of speech. When one watches some tired hack on the platform mechanically repeating the familiar phrases—*bestial atrocities, iron heel, bloodstained tyranny, free peoples of the world, stand shoulder to shoulder*—one often has a curious feeling that one is not watching a live human being but some kind of dummy: a feeling which suddenly becomes stronger at moments when the light catches the speaker's spectacles and turns them into blank discs which seem to have no eyes behind them. And this is not altogether fanciful. A speaker who uses that kind of phraseology has gone some distance towards turning himself into a machine. The appropriate noises are coming out of his larynx, but his brain is not involved as it would be if he were choosing his words for himself. If the speech he is making is one that he is accustomed to make over and over again, he may be almost unconscious of what he is saying, as one is when one utters the responses in church. And this reduced state of consciousness, if not indispensable, is at any rate favorable to political conformity.

In our time, political speech and writing are largely the defence of the indefensible. Things like the continuance of British rule in India, the Russian purges and deportations, the dropping of the atom bombs on Japan, can indeed be defended, but only by arguments which are too brutal for most people to face, and which do not square with the professed aims of political parties. Thus political language has to consist largely of euphemism, question-begging and sheer cloudy vagueness. Defenceless villages are bombarded from the air, the inhabitants driven out into the countryside, the cattle machine-gunned, the huts set on fire with incendiary bullets: this is called *pacification*. Millions of peasants are robbed of their farms and sent trudging along the roads with no more than they can carry: this is called *transfer of population* or *rectification of frontiers*. People are imprisoned for years without trial, or shot in the back of the neck or sent to die of scurvy in Arctic lumber camps: this is called *elimination of unreliable elements*. Such phraseology is needed if one wants to name things without calling up mental pictures of them. Consider for instance some comfortable English professor defending Russian totalitarianism. He cannot say outright, "I believe in killing off your opponents when you can get good results by doing so." Probably, therefore, he will say something like this:

> While freely conceding that the Soviet régime exhibits certain features which the humanitarian may be inclined to deplore, we must, I think, agree that a certain curtailment of the right to political opposition is an unavoidable concomitant of transitional periods, and that the rigors which the Russian people have been called upon to undergo have been amply justified in the sphere of concrete achievement.

The inflated style is itself a kind of euphemism. A mass of Latin words falls upon the facts like soft snow, blurring the outlines and covering up all the details.The great enemy of clear language is insincerity. When there is a gap between one's real and one's declared aims, one turns as it were instinctively to long words and exhausted idioms, like a cuttlefish squirting out ink. In our age there is no such thing as "keeping out of politics." All issues are political issues, and politics itself is a mass of lies, evasions, folly, hatred and schizophrenia. When the general atmosphere is bad, language must suffer. I should expect to find—this is a guess which I have not sufficient knowledge to verify— that the German, Russian and Italian languages have all deteriorated in the last ten or fifteen years, as a result of dictatorship.

But if thought corrupts language, language can also corrupt thought. A bad usage can spread by tradition and imitation, even among people who should and do know better. The debased language that I have been discussing is in some ways very convenient. Phrases like *a not unjustifiable assumption, leaves much to be desired, would serve no good purpose, a consideration which we should do well to bear in mind,* are a continuous temptation, a packet of aspirins always at one's elbow. Look back through this essay, and for certain you will find that I have again and again committed the very faults I am protesting against. By this morning's post I have received a pamphlet dealing with conditions in Germany. The author tells me that he "felt impelled" to write it. I open it at random, and here is almost the first sentence that I see: "[The Allies] have an opportunity not only of achieving a radical transformation of Germany's social and political structure in such a way as to avoid a nationalistic reaction in Germany itself, but at the same time of laying the foundations of a cooperative and unified Europe." You see, he "feels impelled" to write—feels, presumably, that he has something new to say—and yet his words, like cavalry horses answering the bugle, group themselves automatically into the familiar dreary pattern. The invasion of one's mind by ready-made phrases (*lay the foundations, achieve a radical transformation*) can only be prevented if one is constantly on guard against them, and every such phrase anaesthetizes a portion of one's brain.

I said earlier that the decadence of our language is probably curable. Those who deny this would argue, if they produced an argument at all, that language merely reflects existing social conditions, and that we cannot influence its development by any direct tinkering with words and constructions. So far as the general tone or spirit of a language goes, this may be true, but it is not true in detail. Silly words and expressions have often disappeared, not through any evolutionary process but owing to the conscious action of a minority. Two recent examples were *explore every avenue* and *leave no stone unturned,* which were killed by the jeers of a few journalists. There is a long list of fly-blown metaphors which could similarly be got rid of if enough people would interest themselves in the job; and it should also be possible to laugh the *not un-* formation out of existence,[3] to reduce the amount of Latin and Greek in the average sentence, to drive out foreign phrases and strayed scientific words, and, in general, to make pretentiousness unfashionable. But all these are minor points. The defence of the English language implies more than this, and perhaps it is best to start by saying what it does *not* imply.

To begin with, it has nothing to do with archaism, with the salvaging of obsolete words and turns of speech, or with the setting up of a

[3] One can cure oneself of the *not un-* formation by memorizing this sentence: *A not unblack dog was chasing a not unsmall rabbit across a not ungreen field.*

"standard English" which must never be departed from. On the contrary, it is especially concerned with the scrapping of every word or idiom which has outworn its usefulness. It has nothing to do with correct grammar and syntax, which are of no importance so long as one makes one's meaning clear, or with the avoidance of Americanisms, or with having what is called a "good prose style." On the other hand it is not concerned with fake simplicity and the attempt to make written English colloquial. Nor does it even imply in every case preferring the Saxon word to the Latin one, though it does imply using the fewest and shortest words that will cover one's meaning. What is above all needed is to let the meaning choose the word, and not the other way about. In prose, the worst thing one can do with words is to surrender to them. When you think of a concrete object, you think wordlessly, and then, if you want to describe the thing you have been visualizing you probaby hunt about till you find the exact words that seem to fit it. When you think of something abstract you are more inclined to use words from the start, and unless you make a conscious effort to prevent it, the existing dialect will come rushing in and do the job for you, at the expense of blurring or even changing your meaning. Probably it is better to put off using words as long as possible and get one's meaning as clear as one can through pictures or sensations. Afterwards one can choose—not simply *accept*—the phrases that will best cover the meaning, and then switch round and decide what impression one's words are likely to make on another person. This last effort of the mind cuts out all stale or mixed images, all prefabricated phrases, needless repetitions, and humbug and vagueness generally. But one can often be in doubt about the effect of a word or a phrase, and one needs rules that one can rely on when instinct fails. I think the following rules will cover most cases:

1. Never use a metaphor, simile, or other figure of speech which you are used to seeing in print.
2. Never use a long word where a short one will do.
3. If it is possible to cut a word out, always cut it out.
4. Never use the passive where you can use the active.
5. Never use a foreign phrase, a scientific word or a jargon word if you can think of an everyday English equivalent.
6. Break any of these rules sooner than say anything outright barbarous.

These rules sound elementary, and so they are, but they demand a deep change of attitude in anyone who has grown used to writing in the style now fashionable. One could keep all of them and still write bad English, but one could not write the kind of stuff that I quoted in those five specimens at the beginning of this article.

I have not here been considering the literary use of language, but   19 merely language as an instrument for expressing and not for conceal-ing or preventing thought. Stuart Chase and others have come near to claiming that all abstract words are meaningless, and have used this as a pretext for advocating a kind of political quietism. Since you don't know what Fascism is, how can you struggle against Fascism? One need not swallow such absurdities as this, but one ought to recognize that the present political chaos is connected with the decay of lan-guage, and that one can probably bring about some improvement by starting at the verbal end. If you simplify your English, you are freed from the worst follies of orthodoxy. You cannot speak any of the nec-essary dialects, and when you make a stupid remark its stupidity will be obvious, even to yourself. Political language—and with variations this is true of all political parties, from Conservatives to Anarchists—is designed to make lies sound truthful and murder respectable, and to give an appearance of solidity to pure wind. One cannot change this all in a moment, but one can at least change one's own habits, and from time to time one can even, if one jeers loudly enough, send some worn-out and useless phrase—some *jackboot, Achilles' heel, hotbed, melting pot, acid test, veritable inferno* or other lump of verbal refuse—into the dustbin where it belongs.

QUESTIONS ON CONTENT

1. In your own words, summarize Orwell's argument in this essay.

2. It is often said that "mixed metaphors" (for example, "politicians who have their heads in the sand are leading the country over the prec-ipice") are undesirable in either speech or writing because they are in-accurate. For Orwell, a mixed metaphor is symptomatic of a greater problem. What is that problem?

3. Reread paragraph 2 of the essay. What, according to Orwell, is the nature of cause-and-effect relationships?

4. Our world is becoming increasingly prefabricated. What does the concept of prefabrication have to do with Orwell's argument concern-ing the prevalance of the habitual and trite phrase?

5. Orwell states that he himself in this essay is guilty of some of the errors he is pointing out. Can you detect any of them?

6. According to Orwell, what are four important prewriting questions scrupulous writers ask themselves?

7. Orwell says that one of the evils of political language is "question-begging" (14). What does he mean? Why, according to Orwell, has po-litical language deteriorated? Do you agree with him that "the deca-dence of our language is probably curable" (17)? Explain.

QUESTIONS ON RHETORIC

1. Why does Orwell present the "five specimens of the English language as it is now habitually written" (2)? What use does he make of these five passages later in his essay?

2. Following are some of the metaphors and similes that Orwell uses in his essay. (Glossary: *Figures of Speech*) Explain how each one works and comment on its effectiveness.

   a. ... prose consists less ... of *words* chosen for the sake of their meaning, and more ... of *phrases* tacked together like the sections of a prefabricated hen-house (4).
   b. But in between these two classes there is a huge dump of worn-out metaphors which have lost all evocative power.... (5).
   c. ... the writer knows ... what he wants to say, but an accumulation of stale phrases chokes him like tea leaves blocking a sink (12).
   d. A mass of Latin words falls upon the facts like soft snow, blurring the outlines and covering up all the details (15).
   e. When there is a gap between one's real and one's declared aims, one turns ... instinctively to long words and exhausted idioms, like a cuttlefish squirting out ink (15).
   f. ... he ... feels, presumably, that he has something new to say—and yet his words, like cavalry horses answering the bugle, group themselves automatically into the familiar dreary pattern (16).

3. At the end of paragraph 4 Orwell speaks of "the tricks by means of which the work of prose-construction is habitually dodged," and he then goes on to classify them. Why is classification a useful rhetorical strategy in this situation? (Glossary: *Division and Classification*)

4. Point out several terms and concepts that Orwell defines in this essay. What is his purpose in defining them? How does he go about it in each instance? (Glossary: *Definition*)

5. In this essay Orwell moves from negative arguments to positive ones. Where does he make the transition from criticisms to proposals? What is the effect of his organizing the argument in this way?

6. Orwell describes many of the langauge abuses that he is criticizing as "habits" or "mental vices." Are these terms consistent with his thesis? Explain. (Glossary: *Diction*)

7. Orwell suggests that you should never use the passive voice when you can use the active voice. Consider the following example:

   Passive: It is expected that the welfare budget will be cut by Congress.
   Active: We expect Congress to cut the welfare budget.

Not only is the active version shorter, but it is more precise in that it properly emphasizes "Congress" as the doer of the action. Rewrite each of the following sentences in the active voice.

a. The line-drive single was hit by John.
b. Two eggs and one stick of butter should be added to the other ingredients.
c. Information of a confidential nature cannot be released by doctors.
d. Figures showing that the cost of living rose sharply during the past twelve months were released by the administration today.
e. It was decided that a meeting would be held on each Monday.

Are there any situations in which the passive voice is more appropriate than the active? Explain. What conclusions can you draw about the active and passive voices?

VOCABULARY

decadent (1)	impartiality (7)	scrupulous (12)
frivolous (2)	biased (7)	humanitarian (14)
inadvertently (4)	reconciled (8)	evolutionary (17)
implication (5)	pretentious (12)	

WRITING TOPICS

1. Write an essay in which you analyze the language in the following ad, which appeared in *Seventeen* magazine. What do you think Orwell's response to this would be?

SOME STRAIGHT TALK ABOUT SMOKING
FOR YOUNG PEOPLE

We're R.J. Reynolds Tobacco, and we're urging you not to smoke.

We're saying this because, throughout the world, smoking has always been an adult custom. And because today, even among adults, smoking is controversial.

Your first reaction might be to ignore this advice. Maybe you feel we're talking to you as if you were a child. And you probably don't think of yourself that way.

But just because you're no longer a child doesn't mean you're already an adult. And if you take up smoking just to prove you're not a kid, you're kidding yourself.

So please don't smoke. You'll have plenty of time as an adult to decide whether smoking is right for you.

That's about as straight as we can put it.

R.J. Reynolds Tobacco Company[1]

2. Gather five examples of recent American political English that you consider, in Orwell's words, "ugly and inaccurate." You should be able to find more than enough material in current newspapers, magazines, and books. Are the "tricks" used by today's writers the same as those used in Orwell's day? If not, what terms would you invent to describe the "new" tricks?

[1] © 1985 R.J. REYNOLDS TOBACCO CO.

3. As many of Orwell's examples suggest, language is sometimes used not to express but to conceal meaning. Is this true only of politics? Can you think of any situation in which you or others you know have been under pressure to say something, yet had nothing that you were ready or willing to say? What happened? Write an essay in which you first give some examples of the problem and then suggest ways of handling such situations honestly.

3

The Joys of Watergate

JIM QUINN

This essay from Jim Quinn's American Tongue and Cheek *is a direct attack on pop grammarians—including George Orwell, Edwin Newman, and William and Mary Morris—who believe that there is a connection between political and linguistic corruption. Edwin Newman, in particular, deplores the language used by those who were involved in the Watergate scandal during Nixon's second term and what he believes this language reveals about the condition of American life. Hogwash, says Quinn, sentimental humanism at its worst. In Quinn's view, all this criticism of political language ignores its essential linguistic vitality.*

One of the most sacred of all the sacred cows of pop grammar is its insistence that there is a connection between clear thinking and good grammar—that bad thinking, and especially bad political thinking, produces bad writing. This proposition was stated with much pop certitude in George Orwell's essay "Politics and the English Language." But it goes back even further, at least as far as 1927, when Ezra Pound wrote:

> The individual cannot think and communicate his thought, the governor cannot act effectively or frame his laws, without words, and the solidity and validity of these words is in the care of the damned and despised *literati.* When their work goes rotten—by that I do not mean when they express indecorous thoughts—but when their very medium, the very essence of their work, the application of the word to thing goes rotten, i.e., becomes slushy or inexact, or excessive or bloated, the whole machinery of social and of individual thought and order goes to pot.

This is brilliant pop grammar writing—the simple declaration of the connection is itself so well written that we believe it immediately. But it's not true.

And I can demonstrate that it's not true with a simple list of writers who never let their work go rotten, who were never slushy or inexact, or excessive or bloated: Ezra Pound, William Butler Yeats, T. S. Eliot, Wyndham Lewis . . . all of these writers had more or less open flirtations with fascism, which is arguably the most indecent form of social organization ever proposed. If good writing makes good politics, and bad politics makes bad language, how come the *Cantos* is such a great poem?

It is possible, buyers of language books being what they are, that   4 some readers are unduly sympathetic to fascism. In that case I have another list of great writers: W. H. Auden, Stephen Spender, Hugh MacDiarmid, Richard Wright, who have had more or less open flirtations with communism.

George Bernard Shaw went to the end of his life insisting that the   5 careers of Stalin, Mussolini, and Hitler—who he defended indiscriminately—demonstrated the failure of democracy as a viable form of government. So whether you are pro-left or pro-right in your personal politics, you have in Shaw a man who never wrote an inexact sentence—and never escaped a reputation for outrageous paradox.

If good thought made good writing, and good writing made good   6 thought, then Immanuel Kant, Hegel, and Ludwig Wittgenstein are not worth reading.

If good prose made great art, then Theodore Dreiser would be a   7 worse novelist than either Arthur Machen or Thorne Smith.

If it were not possible to lie in English, and to disguise your   8 thoughts, and put bad meanings in a better light, then we would have to have another language, because one of the functions of language is deceit. English does not belong to people with virtue, or people with talent, or people who can remember very clearly the difference between a gerund and a gerundive, or people who have succeeded in imitating the affected unregional accents and measured sentences of television announcers. English belongs to everybody—the liars, the fuzzy thinkers, the dishonest ad writer, the crooks, the presidents of the United States. . . .

THE JOYS OF WATERGATE—HOW YOU CAN LEARN TO STOP WORRYING AND LOVE THE LANGUAGE

The refusal to recognize that reprehensible people can and do   9 make good speakers and writers is in fact the most ignorant kind of sentimental humanism: it is just not true that people we agree with are more likely to be talented or intelligent than people we disagree with.

One of the best examples of the sentimental humanist style of pop   10 grammar criticism is Edwin Newman, who in *Strictly Speaking* goes on like this:

One of the things the Watergate hearings revealed was a poverty of ex-   11
pression, an inability to say anything in a striking way, an addiction to
language that was almost denatured. . . .

Watergate, in the course of revealing so much else about American   12
life, also revealed the sad state of the language; apparently form and substance are related. In Washington, as we learned from the White House
transcripts, a president may speak of kicking butts, call a problem a can of
worms, decide not to be in the position of basically hunkering down, anticipate something hitting the fan, propose to tough it through, sight
minefields down the road, see somebody playing hard ball, claim political
savvy, and wonder what stroke some of his associates have with others. He
may be told by members of his staff what is the bottom line, that a situation has cycled somewhat while another situation is a bullet biter, that a
lawyer has done some dove-tailing for him, that a lot of people have to
pull oars, and that another man was a ballplayer who carried tremendous
water for the President's cause.

It seems extraordinary that Newman can, on the same page, com-   13
plain about denatured language, and at the same time provide so
much compelling evidence that linguistic vitality is not limited to the
good guys, or to the friends of American freedom. What a wonderful
range of metaphor in that second paragraph! From carpentry (*dove-
tailing*) to Western novels (*bite the bullet*) to accounting (*bottom line*)
to massage parlor (*?have stroke with someone*), to sports (*play hard
ball, pull oars*) to laundromats (*?cycled* = a washer cycling into rinse)
to medical examinations (*?carry tremendous water for* = be prepared to
help out even in urinalysis) to war (*minefields*) to superb American inventions like *Let's kick ass, Don't open that can of worms* (=don't open
a new line of inquiry, because once the can is open the worms can
never be put back inside), and *when the shit hits the fan.*

Newman is not alone in his conviction that somehow the people he   14
dislikes talk worse than the people he likes. In the *Harper Dictionary,*
the Morrises reprint a letter from panelist Barry Bingham, Sr., a man
they call "one of the country's most literate journalists." (Bingham, not
to be outdone, calls the Morrises, "our most valued watchdogs of the
English language.") In his letter, Bingham complains about the "lame
and degenerate language" of the hearings. The Morrises agree that the
testimony and the tapes are "fraught with solecisms and sheer illitera-
cies," and they provide translations of expressions they doubt will survive "except as horrible examples of language torn asunder":

STROKE (translation: soothe or cajole a potential troublemaker). [Alas, the
masturbatory metaphorical sense of stroke is lost on the Morrises.]

GO THE HANGOUT ROAD (translation: tell the truth.) [Once again, this is a
faulty perception of this fascinating metaphor. *Let it all hang out* was pop-

ularized by football players, and to them it means roughly, *act like an animal.* Of course, let it all hang out also means *expose yourself*—possibly from an old joke of a guy in a factory walking around with his penis hanging out of his pants. Asked by the foreman why he doesn't button up, he replies, "You work me like a horse, I might as well walk around looking like one."]

LAUNDER THE MONEY (translation: pass illegal campaign contributions through foreign banks so that the donor's identity is hidden). [The Morrises at least understand what this metaphor means, but they seem unable to appreciate its aptness: to clean money would mean that something was done to it, to launder is to use a laundry: drop it off, and pick it up later when it has been cleaned for you. Neatly put.]

PLUMBER (translation: undercover political espionage agent). [Really, this is rewriting history. The Plumbers may have been espionage agents from the beginning, but they were formed to stop leaks. (Get it, William and Mary Morris? See, a leak is like a leak in a pipe.)]

But William and Mary Morris do not, of course, get it. They simply 15 know that the Watergate and presidential tapes were "revelations of corruption both political and linguistic."

Now it is a curiosity of pop grammarians that they are always dis- 16 covering the close connection between political and linguistic corruption—but it is always after the fact. Even Edwin Newman, determined to prove that bad language makes bad thought, suddenly comes to himself with a start, and writes:

> The argument for preciseness of language has limits, of course. I don't know whether grammarians were less taken in by, for example, the Gulf of Tonkin affair than other groups in the population.

Come to think of it, as a longtime antiwar marcher, I never remem- 17 ber seeing a contingent calling itself Copy Editors Against Genocide, or Proofreaders Demand an End to Linguistic Evasions like Body Count and Pacification Program.

I like to think about what those copy editors would have done to an 18 old friend of mine whom I will call M. J. Weed. I returned to Temple University, a large inner-city school in Philadelphia, in 1965. There was so little antiwar activity on campus that the administration (whose stupidity was actually astounding) decided to let the United States Army, as part of its recruiting program, put up an exhibit of captured Vietnamese weapons in the middle of the student union. The ten or fifteen people who were part of the antiwar groups on campus decided we had to do something—and what we did was set up a vigil in front of this display. A vigil was technically different than a sit-in—at least in a

Quaker city—but there was a problem about whether we would let other students see the display. There was much talk about censorship, and then M. J. to the rescue. I see him now: hair just beginning to reach his collar, Indian temple bells sewn along the seams of his jeans, a leather thong tied around his forehead, and an expression of laid-back innocence:

> Hey, man, everybody like listen to me a minute because we shouldn't stop anybody from seeing this like stuff, man. I been looking at it and looking—you know what I see? I see rifles. I see pistols. I see little sticks with the ends sharpened. I don't see, like tanks, like helicopters, machine guns, and B-52s. So they must not have them. I mean if they had them and since we're winning, we would show them, right? But you mean this is all that they got? And we keep on winning, but we never win? This is like . . . like the army and the air force fights the ghetto. And we still can't win? We should ask everybody who sees this, how come with all our like guns we're still having so much trouble with these little mothers? Could it be, man, that the whole country is on their side? Could it be, man, we are the invaders? War is a bummer anyway, you know? But this kind of war, where we got all the bombs and big guns and they got all the sticks . . . like wow . . . unfair, man, unfair. And this whole country, if we keep letting this go on, we're just building up the karma. . . .

I remember that I winced at M. J.'s language at the time, and I sus-   19
pect that I have cleaned it up—certainly dropped a couple *man*'s and *you know*'s; but as political analysis, it beat a lot of the editorials in papers like the *New York Times* and the Washington *Post.*

There is a possibility, of course, that I am wrong, and that it is only   20
nostalgia for the sixties that makes me think that the thinking of M. J. Weed was superior to that of the high-paid, hardworking, highly educated, and articulate men and women who write editorials for our major papers.

But I do not think so.   21

QUESTIONS ON CONTENT

1. What is Ezra Pound's point in the passage quoted in paragraph 1? Why doesn't Quinn agree with Pound? How does Quinn demonstrate that the point is simply not true?

2. Do you agree with Quinn that "one of the functions of language is deceit" (8)? Explain.

3. On what basis does Quinn criticize the passage from Edwin Newman's *Strictly Speaking?* What evidence of linguistic vitality does Quinn point to in the language of the Watergate participants?

4. What, according to Quinn, do the Morrises' translations of Watergate expressions reveal about them?

QUESTIONS ON RHETORIC

1. Explain how the first eight paragraphs work in the context of this essay. (Glossary: *Beginnings*)

2. What is Quinn's thesis, and where is it stated? (Glossary: *Thesis*)

3. In paragraphs 18–21, Quinn provides the example of his friend M. J. Weed. What is his purpose in concluding with this extended example?

4. Could paragraphs 20 and 21 be combined? Why do you suppose Quinn left them separate?

5. How would you characterize Quinn's tone in this essay? (Glossary: *Tone*) Is it appropriate for his subject and audience?

VOCABULARY

fascism (3)	affected (8)	asunder (14)
indiscriminately (5)	reprehensible (9)	contingent (17)
viable (5)	fraught (14)	vigil (18)
paradox (5)	solecisms (14)	laid-back (18)

WRITING TOPICS

1. Now that you have read George Orwell's "Politics and the English Language" (p. 116) and Jim Quinn's "The Joys of Watergate," what is your own position? Write an essay in which you argue for or against the connection between political and linguistic corruption. You might refer to examples of current political speech.

2. In paragraph 18, Quinn quotes M. J. Weed's speech. Carefully read the quotation. What is Weed saying? Now, rewrite the speech in correct Standard English. What is lost and what is gained in your rewrite?

3. If it is indeed true, as Quinn suggests, that scoundrels can and do make good speakers and writers, how does the American public protect itself? Or does it even need protection from lies and deceit? In an essay discuss the problems associated with public trust in political leadership.

4

Propaganda: How Not to Be Bamboozled

DONNA WOOLFOLK CROSS

While most people are against propaganda in principle, few people know exactly what it is and how it works. In the following essay, Donna Woolfolk Cross, who teaches at Onondaga Community College in New York, takes the mystery out of propaganda. Cross starts by providing a definition of propaganda. She then classifies the tricks of the propagandist into thirteen major categories and discusses each thoroughly. Her essay is chock-full of useful advice on how not to be manipulated by propaganda.

Propaganda. If an opinion poll were taken tomorrow, we can be sure that nearly everyone would be against it because it *sounds* so bad. When we say, "Oh, that's just propaganda," it means, to most people, "That's a pack of lies." But really, propaganda is simply a means of persuasion and so it can be put to work for good causes as well as bad—to persuade people to give to charity, for example, or to love their neighbors, or to stop polluting the environment. 1

For good or evil, propaganda pervades our daily lives, helping to shape our attitudes on a thousand subjects. Propaganda probably determines the brand of toothpaste you use, the movies you see, the candidates you elect when you get to the polls. Propaganda works by tricking us, by momentarily distracting the eye while the rabbit pops out from beneath the cloth. Propaganda works best with an uncritical audience. Joseph Goebbels, Propaganda Minister in Nazi Germany, once defined his work as "the conquest of the masses." The masses would not have been conquered, however, if they had known how to challenge and to question, how to make distinctions between propaganda and reasonable argument. 2

People are bamboozled mainly because they don't recognize propaganda when they see it. They need to be informed about the various devices that can be used to mislead and deceive—about the propagandist's overflowing bag of tricks. The following, then, are some common pitfalls for the unwary. 3

1. NAME-CALLING

As its title suggests, this device consists of labeling people or ideas with words of bad connotation, literally, "calling them names." Here the propagandist tries to arouse our contempt so we will dismiss the "bad name" person or idea without examining its merits.   4

Bad names have played a tremendously important role in the history of the world. They have ruined reputations and ended lives, sent people to prison and to war, and just generally made us mad at each other for centuries.   5

Name-calling can be used against policies, practices, beliefs and ideals, as well as against individuals, groups, races, nations. Name-calling is at work when we hear a candidate for office described as a "foolish idealist" or a "two-faced liar" or when an incumbent's policies are denounced as "reckless," "reactionary," or just plain "stupid." Some of the most effective names a public figure can be called are ones that may not denote anything specific: "Congresswoman Jane Doe is a *bleeding heart!*" (Did she vote for funds to help paraplegics?) or "The Senator is a *tool of Washington!*" (Did he happen to agree with the President?) Senator Yakalot uses name-calling when he denounces his opponent's "radical policies" and calls them (and him) "socialist," "pinko," and part of a "heartless plot." He also uses it when he calls small cars "puddle-jumpers," "can openers," and "motorized baby buggies."   6

The point here is that when the propagandist uses name-calling, he doesn't want us to think—merely to react, blindly, unquestioningly. So the best defense against being taken in by name-calling is to stop and ask, "Forgetting the bad name attached to it, what are the merits of the idea itself? What does this name really mean, anyway?"   7

2. GLITTERING GENERALITIES

Glittering generalities are really name-calling in reverse. Name-calling uses words with bad connotations; glittering generalities are words with good connotations—"virtue words," as the Institute for Propaganda Analysis has called them. The Institute explains that while name-calling tries to get us to *reject* and *condemn* someone or something without examining the evidence, glittering generalities try to get us to *accept* and *agree* without examining the evidence.   8

We believe in, fight for, live by "virtue words" which we feel deeply about: "justice," "motherhood," "the American way," "our Constitutional rights," "our Christian heritage." These sound good,   9 but when we examine them closely, they turn out to have no specific, definable meaning. They just make us feel good. Senator Yakalot uses glittering generalities when he says, "I stand for all that is good in America, for our American way and our American birthright." But what exactly *is* "good for America"? How can we define our "American birthright"? Just what parts of the American society and culture does "our American way" refer to?

We often make the mistake of assuming we are personally unaf-   10
fected by glittering generalities. The next time you find yourself assuming that, listen to a political candidate's speech on TV and see how often the use of glittering generalities elicits cheers and applause. That's the danger of propaganda; it *works.* Once again, our defense against it is to ask questions: Forgetting the virtue words attached to it, what are the merits of the idea itself? What does "Americanism" (or "freedom" or "truth") really *mean* here? . . .

Both name-calling and glittering generalities work by stirring our   11
emotions in the hope that this will cloud our thinking. Another approach that propaganda uses is to create a distraction, a "red herring," that will make people forget or ignore the real issues. There are several different kinds of "red herrings" that can be used to distract attention.

3. PLAIN FOLKS APPEAL

"Plain folks" is the device by which a speaker tries to win our confi-   12
dence and support by appearing to be a person like ourselves—"just one of the plain folks." The plain-folks appeal is at work when candidates go around shaking hands with factory workers, kissing babies in supermarkets, and sampling pasta with Italians, fried chicken with Southerners, bagels and blintzes with Jews. "Now I'm a businessman like yourselves" is a plain-folks appeal, as is "I've been a farm boy all my life." Senator Yakalot tries the plain-folks appeal when he says, "I'm just a small-town boy like you fine people." The use of such expressions once prompted Lyndon Johnson to quip, "Whenever I hear someone say, 'I'm just an old country lawyer,' the first thing I reach for is my wallet to make sure it's still there."

The irrelevancy of the plain-folks appeal is obvious: even if the   13
man *is* "one of us" (which may not be true at all), that doesn't mean that his ideas and programs are sound—or even that he honestly has our best interests at heart. As with glittering generalities, the danger here is that we may mistakenly assume we are immune to this appeal. But propagandists wouldn't use it unless it had been proved to work. You can protect yourself by asking, "Aside from his 'nice guy next

door' image, what does this man stand for? Are his ideas and his past record really supportive of my best interests?"

4. ARGUMENTUM AD POPULUM (STROKING)

Argumentum ad populum means "argument to the people" or "telling the people what they want to hear." The colloquial term from the Watergate era is "stroking," which conjures up pictures of small animals or children being stroked or soothed with compliments until they come to like the person doing the complimenting—and, by extension, his or her ideas.   14

We all like to hear nice things about ourselves and the group we belong to—we like to be liked—so it stands to reason that we will respond warmly to a person who tells us we are "hard-working taxpayers" or "the most generous, free-spirited nation in the world." Politicians tell farmers they are the "backbone of the American economy" and college students that they are the "leaders and policy makers of tomorrow." Commercial advertisers use stroking more insidiously by asking a question which invites a flattering answer: "What kind of a man reads *Playboy?*" (Does he really drive a Porsche and own $10,000 worth of sound equipment?) Senator Yakalot is stroking his audience when he calls them the "decent law-abiding citizens that are the great pulsing heart and the life blood of this, our beloved country," and when he repeatedly refers to them as "you fine people," "you wonderful folks."   15

Obviously, the intent here is to sidetrack us from thinking critically about the man and his ideas. Our own good qualities have nothing to do with the issue at hand. Ask yourself, "Apart from the nice things he has to say about me (and my church, my nation, my ethnic group, my neighbors), what does the candidate stand for? Are his or her ideas in my best interests?"   16

5. ARGUMENTUM AD HOMINEM

Argumentum ad hominem means "argument to the man" and that's exactly what it is. When a propagandist uses *argumentum ad hominem,* he wants to distract our attention from the issue under consideration with personal attacks on the people involved. For example, when Lincoln issued the Emancipation Proclamation, some people responded by calling him the "baboon." But Lincoln's long arms and awkward carriage had nothing to do with the merits of the Proclamation or the question of whether or not slavery should be abolished.   17

Today *argumentum ad hominem* is still widely used and very effective. You may or may not support the Equal Rights Amendment, but   18 you should be sure your judgment is based on the merits of the idea itself, and not the result of someone's denunciation of the people who support the ERA as "fanatics" or "lesbians" or "frustrated old maids." Senator Yakalot is using *argumentum ad hominem* when he dismisses the idea of using smaller automobiles with a reference to the personal appearance of one of its supporters, Congresswoman Doris Schlepp. Refuse to be waylaid by *argumentum ad hominem* and ask, "Do the personal qualities of the person being discussed have anything to do with the issue at hand? Leaving him or her aside, how good is the idea itself?"

6. TRANSFER (GUILT OR GLORY BY ASSOCIATION)

In *argumentum ad hominem,* an attempt is made to associate negative 19 aspects of a person's character or personal appearance with an issue or idea he supports. The transfer device uses this same process of association to make us accept or condemn a given person or idea.

A better name for the transfer device is guilt (or glory) by associa- 20 tion. In glory by association, the propagandist tries to transfer the positive feelings of something we love and respect to the group or idea he wants us to accept. "This bill for a new dam is in the best tradition of this country, the land of Lincoln, Jefferson, and Washington," is glory by association at work. Lincoln, Jefferson, and Washington were great leaders that most of us revere and respect, but they have no logical connection to the proposal under consideration—the bill to build a new dam. Senator Yakalot uses glory by association when he says full-sized cars "have always been as American as Mom's apple pie or a Sunday drive in the country."

The process works equally well in reverse, when guilt by associa- 21 tion is used to transfer our dislike or disapproval of one idea or group to some other idea or group that the propagandist wants us to reject and condemn. "John Doe says we need to make some changes in the way our government operates; well, that's exactly what the Ku Klux Klan has said, so there's a meeting of great minds!" That's guilt by association for you; there's no logical connection between John Doe and the Ku Klux Klan apart from the one the propagandist is trying to create in our minds. He wants to distract our attention from John Doe and get us thinking (and worrying) about the Ku Klux Klan and its politics of violence. (Of course, there are sometimes legitimate associations between the two things; if John Doe had been a *member* of the Ku Klux Klan, it would be reasonable and fair to draw a connection between the man and his group.) Senator Yakalot tries to trick his audience with guilt by association when he remarks that "the words 'Community' and 'Communism' look an awful lot alike!" He does it again when he mentions that Mr. Stu Pott "sports a Fidel Castro beard."

How can we learn to spot the transfer device and distinguish be-   22
tween fair and unfair associations? We can teach ourselves to *suspend judgment* until we have answered these questions: "Is there any legitimate connection between the idea under discussion and the thing it is associated with? Leaving the transfer device out of the picture, what are the merits of the idea by itself?"

7. BANDWAGON

Ever hear of the small, ratlike animal called the lemming? Lemmings   23
are arctic rodents with a very odd habit: periodically, for reasons no one entirely knows, they mass together in a large herd and commit suicide by rushing into deep water and drowning themselves. They all run in together, blindly, and not one of them ever seems to stop and ask, "*Why* am I doing this? Is this really what I want to do?" and thus save itself from destruction. Obviously, lemmings are driven to perform their strange mass suicide rites by common instinct. People choose to "follow the herd" for more complex reasons, yet we are still all too often the unwitting victims of the bandwagon appeal.

Essentially, the bandwagon urges us to support an action or an   24
opinion because it is popular—because "everyone else is doing it." This call to "get on the bandwagon" appeals to the strong desire in most of us to be one of the crowd, not to be left out or alone. Advertising makes extensive use of the bandwagon appeal ("join the Pepsi people"), but so do politicians ("Let us join together in this great cause"). Senator Yakalot uses the bandwagon appeal when he says that "More and more citizens are rallying to my cause every day," and asks his audience to "join them—and me—in our fight for America."

One of the ways we can see the bandwagon appeal at work is in the   25
overwhelming success of various fashions and trends which capture the interest (and the money) of thousands of people for a short time, then disappear suddenly and completely. For a year or two in the fifties, every child in North America wanted a coonskin cap so they could be like Davy Crockett; no one wanted to be left out. After that there was the hula-hoop craze that helped to dislocate the hips of thousands of Americans. More recently, what made millions of people rush out to buy their very own "pet rocks"?

The problem here is obvious: just because everyone's doing it   26
doesn't mean that *we* should too. Group approval does not prove that

something is true or is worth doing. Large numbers of people have supported actions we now condemn. Just a generation ago, Hitler and Mussolini rose to absolute and catastrophically repressive rule in two of the most sophisticated and cultured countries of Europe. When they came into power they were welled up by massive popular support from millions of people who didn't want to be "left out" at a great historical moment.

Once the mass begins to move—on the bandwagon—it becomes   27 harder and harder to perceive the leader *riding* the bandwagon. So don't be a lemming, rushing blindly on to destruction because "everyone else is doing it." Stop and ask, "Where is this bandwagon headed? Never mind about everybody else, is this what is best for *me*?". . .

As we have seen, propaganda can appeal to us by arousing our   28 emotions or distracting our attention from the real issues at hand. But there's a third way that propaganda can be put to work against us—by the use of faulty logic. This approach is really more insidious than the other two because it gives the appearance of reasonable, fair argument. It is only when we look more closely that the holes in the logical fiber show up. The following are some of the devices that make use of faulty logic to distort and mislead.

8. FAULTY CAUSE AND EFFECT

As the name suggests, this device sets up a cause-and-effect relation-   29 ship that may not be true. The Latin name for this logical fallacy is *post hoc ergo propter hoc,* which means "after this, therefore because of this." But just because one thing happened after another doesn't mean that one *caused* the other.

An example of false cause-and-effect reasoning is offered by the   30 story (probably invented) of the woman aboard the ship *Titanic.* She woke up from a nap and, feeling seasick, looked around for a call button to summon the steward to bring her some medication. She finally located a small button on one of the walls of her cabin and pushed it. A split second later, the *Titanic* grazed an iceberg in the terrible crash that was to send the entire ship to its destruction. The woman screamed and said, "Oh, God, what have I done? What have I done?" The humor of that anecdote comes from the absurdity of the woman's assumption that pushing the small red button resulted in the destruction of a ship weighing several hundred tons: "It happened after I pushed it, therefore it must be *because* I pushed it"—*post hoc ergo propter hoc* reasoning. There is, of course, no cause-and-effect relationship there.

The false cause-and-effect fallacy is used very often by political   31 candidates. "After I came to office, the rate of inflation dropped to 6 percent." But did the person do anything to cause the lower rate of inflation or was it the result of other conditions? Would the rate of inflation have dropped anyway, even if he hadn't come to office? Senator Yakalot uses false cause and effect when he says "our forefathers who made this country great never had free hot meal handouts! And look what they did for our country!" He does it again when he concludes that "driving full-sized cars means a better car safety record on our American roads today."

False cause-and-effect reasoning is terribly persuasive because it seems so logical. Its appeal is apparently to experience. We swallowed X product—and the headache went away. We elected Y official and unemployment went down. Many people think, "There *must* be a connection." But causality is an immensely complex phenomenon; you need a good deal of evidence to prove that an event that follows another in time was "therefore" caused by the first event.   32

Don't be taken in by false cause and effect; be sure to ask, "Is there enough evidence to prove that this cause led to that effect? Could there have been any *other* causes?"   33

9. FALSE ANALOGY

An analogy is a comparison between two ideas, events, or things. But comparisons can be fairly made only when the things being compared are alike in significant ways. When they are not, false analogy is the result.   34

A famous example of this is the old proverb "Don't change horses in the middle of a stream," often used as an analogy to convince voters not to change administrations in the middle of a war or other crisis. But the analogy is misleading because there are so many differences between the things compared. In what ways is a war or political crisis like a stream? Is the President or head of state really very much like a horse? And is a nation of millions of people comparable to a man trying to get across a stream? Analogy is false and unfair when it compares two things that have little in common and assumes that they are identical. Senator Yakalot tries to hoodwink his listeners with false analogy when he says, "Trying to take Americans out of the kind of cars they love is as undemocratic as trying to deprive them of the right to vote."   35

Of course, analogies can be drawn that are reasonable and fair. It would be reasonable, for example, to compare the results of busing in one small Southern city with the possible results in another, *if* the   36 towns have the same kind of history, population, and school policy. We can decide for ourselves whether an analogy is false or fair by asking, "Are the things being compared truly alike in significant ways? Do the differences between them affect the comparison?"

10. BEGGING THE QUESTION

Actually, the name of this device is rather misleading, because it does 37 not appear in the form of a question. Begging the question occurs when, in discussing a questionable or debatable point, a person assumes as already established the very point that he is trying to prove. For example, "No thinking citizen could approve such a completely unacceptable policy as this one." But isn't the question of whether or not the policy *is* acceptable the very point to be established? Senator Yakalot begs the question when he announces that his opponent's plan won't work "because it is unworkable."

We can protect ourselves against this kind of faulty logic by asking, 38 "What is assumed in this statement? Is the assumption reasonable, or does it need more proof?"

11. THE TWO EXTREMES FALLACY (FALSE DILEMMA)

Linguists have long noted that the English language tends to view reality in sets of two extremes or polar opposites. In English, things are 39 either black or white, tall or short, up or down, front or back, left or right, good or bad, guilty or not guilty. We can ask for a "straightforward yes-or-no answer" to a question, the understanding being that we will not accept or consider anything in between. In fact, reality cannot always be dissected along such strict lines. There may be (usually are) *more* than just two possibilities or extremes to consider. We are often told to "listen to both sides of the argument." But who's to say that every argument has only two sides? Can't there be a third—even a fourth or fifth—point of view?

The two-extremes fallacy is at work in this statement by Lenin, the 40 great Marxist leader: "You cannot eliminate *one* basic assumption, one substantial part of this philosophy of Marxism (it is as if it were a block of steel), without abandoning truth, without falling into the arms of bourgeois-reactionary falsehood." In other words, if we don't agree 100 percent with every premise of Marxism, we must be placed at the opposite end of the political-economic spectrum—for Lenin, "bourgeois-reactionary falsehood." If we are not entirely *with* him, we must be against him; those are the only two possibilities open to us. Of course, this is a logical fallacy; in real life there are any number of political positions one can maintain *between* the two extremes of Marxism and capitalism. Senator Yakalot uses the two-extremes fallacy in the same way as Lenin when he tells his audience that "in this world a man's either for private enterprise or he's for socialism."

One of the most famous examples of the two-extremes fallacy in   41
recent history is the slogan, "America: Love it or leave it," with its implicit suggestion that we either accept everything just as it is in America today without complaint—or get out. Again, it should be obvious that there is a whole range of action and belief between those two extremes.

Don't be duped; stop and ask, "Are those really the only two op-   42
tions I can choose from? Are there other alternatives not mentioned that deserve consideration?"

12. CARD STACKING

Some questions are so multifaceted and complex that no one can make   43
an intelligent decision about them without considering a wide variety of evidence. One selection of facts could make us feel one way and another selection could make us feel just the opposite. Card stacking is a device of propaganda which selects only the facts that support the propagandist's point of view, and ignores all the others. For example, a candidate could be made to look like a legislative dynamo if you say, "Representative McNerd introduced more new bills than any other member of the Congress," and neglect to mention that most of them were so preposterous that they were laughed off the floor.

Senator Yakalot engages in card stacking when he talks about the   44
proposal to use smaller cars. He talks only about jobs without mentioning the cost to the taxpayers or the very real—though still denied—threat of depletion of resources. He says he wants to help his countrymen keep their jobs, but doesn't mention that the corporations that offer the jobs will also make large profits. He praises the "American chrome industry," overlooking the fact that most chrome is imported. And so on.

The best protection against card stacking is to take the "Yes, but   45
. . ." attitude. This device of propaganda is not untrue, but then again it is not the *whole* truth. So ask yourself, "Is this person leaving something out that I should know about? Is there some other information that should be brought to bear on this question?" . . .

So far, we have considered three approaches that the propagandist   46 can use to influence our thinking: appealing to our emotions, distracting our attention, and misleading us with logic that may appear to be reasonable but is in fact faulty and deceiving. But there is a fourth approach that is probably the most common propaganda trick of them all.

13. TESTIMONIAL

The testimonial device consists in having some loved or respected person give a statement of support (testimonial) for a given product or idea. The problem is that the person being quoted may *not* be an expert in the field; in fact, he may know nothing at all about it. Using the name of a man who is skilled and famous in one field to give a testimonial for something in another field is unfair and unreasonable.   47

Senator Yakalot tries to mislead his audience with testimonial when he tells them that "full-sized cars have been praised by great Americans like John Wayne and Jack Jones, as well as by leading experts on car safety and comfort."   48

Testimonial is used extensively in TV ads, where it often appears in such bizarre forms as Joe Namath's endorsement of a pantyhose brand. Here, of course, the "authority" giving the testimonial not only is no expert about pantyhose, but obviously stands to gain something (money!) by making the testimonial.   49

When celebrities endorse a political candidate, they may not be making money by doing so, but we should still question whether they are in any better position to judge than we ourselves. Too often we are willing to let others we like or respect make our decisions *for us,* while we follow along acquiescently. And this is the purpose of testimonial—to get us to agree and accept *without* stopping to think. Be sure to ask, "Is there any reason to believe that this person (or organization or publication or whatever) has any more knowledge or information than I do on this subject? What does the idea amount to on is own merits, without the benefit of testimonial?"   50

The cornerstone of democratic society is reliance upon an informed and educated electorate. To be fully effective citizens we need to be able to challenge and to question wisely. A dangerous feeling of indifference toward our political processes exists today. We often abandon our right, our duty, to criticize and evaluate by dismissing *all* politicians as "crooked," *all* new bills and proposals as "just more government bureaucracy." But there are important distinctions to be made, and this kind of apathy can be fatal to democracy.   51

If we are to be led, let us not be led blindly, but critically, intelli-   52 gently, with our eyes open. If we are to continue to be a government "by the people," let us become informed about the methods and purposes of propaganda, so we can be the masters, not the slaves of our destiny.

QUESTIONS ON CONTENT

1. What is propaganda? Who uses propaganda? Why is it used?

2. Why does Cross feel that people should be informed about propaganda? What is her advice for dealing with it?

3. What is "begging the question"?

4. What, according to Cross, is the most common propaganda trick of them all? Provide some examples of it from your own experience.

5. Why does Cross feel that it is necessary for people in a democratic society to become informed about the methods and practices of propaganda?

QUESTIONS ON RHETORIC

1. Why is classification an appropriate organizational strategy for Cross to use in this essay? (Glossary: *Division and Classification*)

2. How does Cross organize the discussion of each propaganda device she includes in her essay?

3. What use does Cross make of examples in her essay? How effective do you find them? Explain. (Glossary: *Examples*)

4. In her discussion of the bandwagon appeal, Cross uses the analogy of the lemmings. How does this analogy work? Why is it not a "false analogy"? (Glossary: *Analogy*)

VOCABULARY

connotations (8)   colloquial (14)   spectrum (40)
elicits (10)   insidiously (15)

WRITING TOPICS

1. As Cross says in the beginning of her essay, propaganda "can be put to work for good causes as well as bad" (1). Using materials from the Red Cross, United Way, or some other public service organization, write an essay in which you discuss the propaganda used by such organ-

izations. How would you characterize their appeals? Do you ever find such propaganda objectionable? Does the end always justify the means?

2. Using the devices described by Cross, try a piece of propaganda yourself. You can attempt to persuade your classmates to (a) join a particular campus organization, (b) support, either spiritually or financially, a controversial movement or issue on campus, or (c) vote for one candidate and not another in a campus election.

WRITING ASSIGNMENTS FOR "LANGUAGE, POLITICS, AND PROPAGANDA"

1. Governments and the news media are prone to using euphemisms, misplaced technical jargon, stock phrases, and connotatively "loaded" words for propaganda purposes. Depending on your position, for example, a "terrorist" and a "freedom fighter" are two very different things. To refer to a group as "self-styled" or as "calling themselves . . ." or to world leaders as "intransigent," "belligerent," "stern," and "forceful" is to use language that embodies strong value judgments. Examine a recent newspaper or news magazine article on a current event for examples of "loaded" words. Then write an analysis of how the writer of the article has attempted to alter your attitudes through biased language.

2. We all have been affected by propaganda at some time in our lives. Think of an experience you have had when you were unwittingly manipulated by propaganda, and write an analysis of the propaganda devices used.

3. In his book *The Second Sin*, psychiatrist Thomas Szasz makes the following observations:

   a. The prevention of parenthood is called "planned parenthood."
   b. Policemen receive bribes; politicians receive campaign contributions.
   c. Homicide by physicians is called "euthanasia."
   d. Marijuana and heroin are sold by pushers; cigarettes and alcohol are sold by businessmen.
   e. Imprisonment by psychiatrists is called "mental hospitalization."

Using Szasz's observations or similar ones of your own, write an essay in which you discuss the way people manipulate words and meanings to suit their particular needs.

4. Using either Orwell's standards of good writing or Cross's list of propaganda devices, write an essay in which you analyze a newspaper editorial, a political speech, a public service advertisement, or a comparable example of contemporary political prose.

5. Orwell says, "As soon as certain topics are raised, the concrete melts into the abstract . . ." (4). One such topic has always been war. Compare the following two war prayers, the first from a Catholic missal and the second by Mark Twain:

> O Lord, graciously regard the sacrifice which we offer up: that it may deliver us from all the evil of war, and establish us under Thy sure protection. Through our Lord Jesus Christ, Thy Son, who liveth and reigneth with Thee in the unity of the Holy Ghost.

Oh Lord our God, help us to tear their soldiers to bloody shreds with our shells; help us to cover their smiling fields with their patriot dead; help us to lay waste their humble homes with a hurricane of fire; help us to wring the hearts of their unoffending widows with unavailing grief; help us to turn them out roofless with their little children to wander unfriended the wastes of their desolated land in rags and hunger and thirst. Lord, blast their hopes, blight their lives, protract their bitter pilgrimage, make heavy their steps, water their way with their tears. We ask it, in the spirit of love, of Him Who is the Source of Love, and who is the ever-faithful refuge and friend of all that are sore beset and seek his aid.

How would you characterize the very different effects of these two war prayers? Specifically, how do you account for the differences in effect?

6. Write an essay in which you compare and contrast a national tabloid newspaper (such as the *National Enquirer*) with your local newspaper. You may wish to consider one or more of the following:

   a. intended audience
   b. types of stories covered
   c. placement of stories
   d. formality or informality of writing
   e. amount of visual material
   f. amount and type of advertising

7. Choose an editorial dealing with a controversial issue. Assume that you have been offered equal space in the newspaper in which to present the opposing viewpoint. Write a rebuttal. Hand in both your rebuttal and the original editorial that stimulated it.

8. Write three paragraphs in which you describe the same incident, person, scene, or thing. In the first paragraph, use language that will produce a neutral impression; in the second, language that will produce a favorable impression; and in the third, language that will produce an unfavorable impression. Keep the factual content of each of your paragraphs constant; vary only the language.

9. Write an essay in which you use one of the following statements as your thesis:

Nobody wants to be dull. But if the alternative to dullness is dishonesty, it may be better to be dull.

                                       Walker Gibson

More than ever before in American politics, language is used not as an instrument for forming and expressing thought. It is used to prevent, confuse, and conceal thinking.

                                      Richard Gambino

NOTE: Suggested topics for research papers appear on p. 446.

NOTABLE QUOTATIONS

The following quotations are drawn from the essays in this section. They are presented as additional topics for classroom discussion or for writing assignments.

"We need to remember that much of our information about politics, governmental activities, business conditions, and foreign affairs comes to us selected and slanted. More than we realize, our opinions on these matters may depend on what newspaper we read or what news commentator we listen to." *Birk* and *Birk* (19)

"But however charged language is abused and whatever misunderstandings it may cause, we still have to live with it—and even by it. It shapes our attitudes and values even without our conscious knowledge; it gives purpose to, and guides, our actions; through it we establish and maintain relations with other people and by means of it we exert our greatest influence on them." *Birk* and *Birk* (33)

"Most people who bother with the matter at all would admit that the English language is in a bad way, but it is generally assumed that we cannot by conscious action do anything about it." *Orwell* (1)

"In our time, political speech and writing are largely the defence of the indefensible." *Orwell* (14)

"The inflated style is itself a kind of euphemism." *Orwell* (15)

"But if thought corrupts language, language can also corrupt thought." *Orwell* (16)

"The refusal to recognize that reprehensible people can and do make good speakers and writers is in fact the most ignorant kind of sentimental humanism. . . ." *Quinn* (9)

"Now it is a curiosity of pop grammarians that they are always discovering the close connection between political and linguistic corruption—but it is always after the fact." *Quinn* (16)

"For good or evil, propaganda pervades our daily lives, helping to shape our attitudes on a thousand subjects." *Cross* (2)

"If we are to continue to be a government 'by the people,' let us become informed about the methods and purposes of propaganda, so we can be the masters, not the slaves of our destiny." *Cross* (52)

IV

Words, Meanings, and Dictionaries

Good words are worth much, and cost little.

George Herbert

"When I use a word," Humpty Dumpty said in a rather scornful tone, "it means just what I choose it to mean—neither more nor less."
"The question is," said Alice, "whether you can make words mean so many different things."
"The question is," said Humpty Dumpty, "which is to be master—that's all."

Lewis Carroll

The difference between the almost right word and the right is really a large matter—'tis the difference between the lightning bug and the lightning.

Mark Twain

As sheer casual reading matter, I still find the English dictionary the most interesting book in our language.

Albert Jay Nock

1
The Power of Words

BERGEN EVANS

"Words are the tools for the job of saying what you want to say," writes the late Bergen Evans, an authority on the uses and abuses of the English language. With this sentence he introduces the central point of his article and emphasizes a major theme of Language Awareness: *the importance of the word. In this selection, Evans develops his analogy of words as tools and discusses the importance of an effective vocabulary.*

Words are the tools for the job of saying what you want to say. And what you want to say are your thoughts and feelings, your desires and your dislikes, your hopes and your fears, your business and your pleasure—almost everything, indeed, that makes up *you*. Except for our vegetablelike growth and our animallike impulses, almost all that we are is related to our use of words. Man has been defined as a tool-using animal, but his most important tool, the one that distinguishes him from all other animals, is his speech.

As with other tools, the number and variety of the words we know should meet all our needs. Not that any man has ever had a vocabulary exactly fitted to his every need at all times. The greatest writers—those who have shown the rest of us how *in*adequate our own command of words is—have agonized over their verbal shortcomings. But we can approach our needs. The more words we know, the closer we can come to expressing precisely what we want to.

We can, for instance, give clear instructions, and reduce misunderstandings. If we say, "See that he does it," we should make sure that the person spoken to knows what he is to do when he *sees*, that it is clear to him who *he* is and what *it* is and what must be accomplished to *do* it.

Some of history's great disasters have been caused by misunderstood directions. The heroic but futile charge of the Light Brigade at

155

Balaclava in the Crimean War is a striking example. "Someone had blundered," Tennyson wrote. That was true, and the blunder consisted of the confusion over one word, which meant one thing to the person speaking but another to the persons spoken to.

The brigade was ordered to charge "the guns." The man who gave   5
the order was on a hilltop and had in mind a small battery which was very plain to him but was concealed from the soldiers in the valley by a slight rise. The only guns *they* could see were the main Russian batteries at the far end of the valley. Therefore they assumed that "the guns" referred to the batteries *they* saw. The command seemed utter madness, but it was a command and the leader of the brigade, after filing a protest, carried it out.

Fortunately, most misunderstandings don't have such disastrous   6
consequences. But the continual confusion about such general terms as *thing, deal, it, fix,* and the like, certainly can be frustrating. Taken as a whole, the exasperation, humiliation, disappointment and quarreling caused by misunderstandings probably produce a thousand times the misery and suffering that the Light Brigade endured.

So the wise man, who wants peace of mind, and the efficient man,   7
who wants to get on with the job, will take the trouble to use specific terms instead of doubtful ones.

Besides clarity, a large vocabulary provides variety. And that is   8
useful; it is the basis for discrimination, since it provides a larger number of tools to choose from. A hammer won't do when a file is called for. Furthermore a large and varied vocabulary makes the speaker or writer more interesting. It allows him to avoid the dullness of repetition and to provoke attention. The interesting man is much more likely to be persuasive than the dull one. Dull people bore us. We don't listen to them. We hear them, but with a secret distaste. Instead of listening to them, we think only about getting away from them. Therefore a varied vocabulary is very useful for winning others to our point of view.

Thomas Wolfe reveled in words with more glory and gusto than   9
perhaps any man since Shakespeare or Rabelais. On seeing a shabby little man lying dead on a subway bench, Wolfe was struck with the thought of the dull and miserable existence such a man must have had because of the sterility of his speech. "Poor, dismal, ugly, sterile, shabby little man," Wolfe wrote in his essay, "Death the Proud Brother," "with your little scrabble of harsh oaths, and cries, and stale constricted words, your pitiful little designs and feeble purposes. . . . Joy, glory, and magnificence were here for you upon this earth, but you scrabbled along the pavements rattling a few stale words like gravel in your throat, and would have none of them."

When Caliban, the half-human monster in Shakespeare's last play,   10
The Tempest, furiously denies that he owes any gratitude to his master,
the magician Prospero, he demands to know what Prospero has ever
done for him. The magician passes over all the many benefits he has
conferred on the wretched creature, to stress only one: he has taught
him to speak.

> *I . . . took pains to make thee speak.*
> *When thou didst not, savage,*
> *Know thine own meaning, but wouldst gabble like*
> *A thing most brutish, I endow'd thy purposes*
> *With words that made them known.*

The simple fact is that we all begin as Calibans—and do not know   11
even our own purposes until we endow them with words. We do not,
indeed, know ourselves. The pleasure you will feel as you develop your
vocabulary is not solely the pleasure that comes with increased power;
it is also the greater pleasure that comes with increased knowledge,
especially of yourself. You will begin to appreciate expression as an art
and to feel not only the advantage of commanding words but the satisfaction. You will notice that this or that phrase which someone utters
in your hearing or which you see in the newspapers is very good.

And you will be pleased that it *is* good, just as you are pleased to   12
see a forward pass completed, or a long putt holed, or a dance step
gracefully executed. For words are to the mind what such actions are
to the body.

You will see that the rightness of a well-chosen word is not merely   13
a source of pleasure; it may provoke the most serious consequences or
avoid the gravest danger. When, for example, America and Russia
confronted each other during the Cuban crisis in 1962, and the world
hovered for a few days on the brink of disaster, the use of the word
quarantine instead of *blockade* was extremely important. A *blockade* is
an act of war. No one knew quite what a *quarantine* meant, under the
circumstances. But the very use of the word indicated that, while we
were determined to protect ourselves, we wanted to avoid war. It was
all a part of giving Russia some possibility of saving face. We wanted
her missiles and planes out of Cuba and were prepared to fight even a
nuclear war to get them out. But we certainly preferred to have them
removed peacefully. We did not want to back Russia into a corner
from which there could have been no escape except by violence.

Thus the use of *quarantine,* a purposefully vague word, was part of   14
our strategy. Furthermore, it had other advantages over *blockade.* It is
commonly associated with a restriction imposed by all civilized nations on people with certain communicable diseases to prevent them

from spreading their disease throughout the community. It is a public health measure which, for all the inconvenience that it may impose on the afflicted individual, serves the public welfare. Thus, whereas a blockade would have been an announcement that we were proceeding aggressively to further our own interests, regardless of the rights of others, quarantine suggested a concern for the general welfare. In addition, it suggested that what was going on in Cuba was a dangerous disease which might spread.

So, as you develop a larger vocabulary you will be increasingly aware of what is going on. You will enjoy what you read more. New pleasures will be opened to you.   15

You will understand more. Difficult books whose meaning has been uncertain will become readable. The great poets who have enlarged our experience, the philosophers who have shaped our thoughts, the historians who have sought for patterns in the human story, the essayists whose observations have delighted men for centuries—all these and more will be available to you. And in sharing their thoughts your own world will expand. This particular benefit of an increased vocabulary is dramatically apparent in the strides that children make in comprehension as they progress in their use of language. Increased learning increases the child's word stock and the increased word stock makes learning easier. The National Conference on Research in English says "a child's ability to read, to speak, to write, and to think is inevitably conditioned by his vocabulary."   16

This goes for an adult too. Words cannot be separated from ideas. They interact. The words we use are so associated with our experiences and what the experiences mean to us that they cannot be separated. The idea comes up from our subconscious clothed in words. It can't come any other way.   17

We don't know how words are stored in our minds, but there does seem to be a sort of filing system. The filing system appears to be controlled by a perverse if not downright wacky filing clerk. Everyone has tried to remember a word and been unable to. Sometimes it is a common word, one that we *know* we know. Yet it won't come when we want it. It can be almost a form of torture trying to recall it, but no amount of fuming or fretting helps. Then suddenly, usually some time later when it is no longer useful to us, it will come to mind readily. When we are searching for one of these words—often for a person's name—we will come up with other words or names that we know are close to but not exactly the one we want. This is curious in itself. For if we can't remember the word we want, how do we know the other word is very much like it? It's as though the filing clerk had seen the word we actually wanted or was even holding it in his hand but wouldn't give it to us.   18

Often we know that the unacceptable word has the same sound or 19
begins with the same letter as the word we can't remember. And when
we finally recall the word we wanted, we find this is so. It seems as
though our mental filing systems were arranged alphabetically and
cross-indexed for similarity of internal sound. If we are well-read, we
can call up a host of synonyms (words that mean the same thing) for
many words, which suggests more crossfiling. Furthermore, words
have subtle and complex associations. The speech and writing of some
people who have sustained brain injuries or suffered strokes indicate a
curious kind of damage. Some injured people seem to lose all proper
names, some all adjectives, and many mix up capitals and small
letters. This indicates that the interlocking connections of words in our
minds are more complex than we can imagine. The chances are that
the most spectacular computer is a simple gadget compared to the
human mind.

For our purposes, our ignorance of how this intricate filing system 20
works does not matter. What matters to a person trying to enlarge his
vocabulary is the many connections among the words he knows. Once
we master a word, it is connected in our mind with scores of other
words in what appears to be an infinite number of relationships and
shades of meaning. A new word does not drop as a single addition into
our word stock. Each new word learned enlarges a whole complex of
thinking and is itself enlarged in meaning and significance.

A vocabulary is a tool which one uses in formulating the important 21
questions of life, the questions which must be asked before they can be
answered. To a large extent, vocabulary shapes all the decisions we
make. Most decisions, of course, are shaped by our emotions, by circumstances, and by the forces which may hold us back or urge us on.
These circumstances and forces are largely beyond our control. But
our speech is a sort of searchlight that helps us to see these things more
clearly and to see ourselves in relation to them. At least it helps us call
things by their right names.

To a great extent our speech affects our judgments. We don't al- 22
ways—sometimes we can't—distinguish between words and things. A
slogan, for example, especially if it rhymes, or is alliterative (that is,
has a number of words that begin with the same sound), or has a
strong rhythm, will move us to action. It convinces us that the action is
necessary. "Motorists wise Simonize" is far more effective in promoting sales than "Simonize, wise motorists" or "Wise motorists, Simonize" would have been. It's the witchery of rhythm, one of the most
subtle and dangerous of unseen forces that move and muddle our
minds. Seduced by "Fifty-four forty or fight," our great-grandfathers
almost went to war in 1844. And there are historians who trace much
of the misery of the modern world to the fascination that Grant's

"Unconditional surrender" held for four generations of Americans.

Certainly anyone who develops the valuable habit of examining   23
his own prejudices will find that many of them are, at bottom, verbal.
A situation automatically calls forth a single word. The word is bathed
in emotion. So whenever the situation is repeated, it produces the same
emotional response. There is no effort to be rational, to see what is actually going on. The word triggers the response. But the more words
one has at his command, the greater the possibility that he may be his
own master. It takes words to free us from words. Removing an emotionally charged word from a phrase and substituting a neutral synonym often gives us an insight that nothing else can.

Speech is the means of relating our separate experiences and emo-   24
tions, of combining them, reliving them and, as far as we can, understanding them. If we did not have the words *justice, equal, radiation*—
and a thousand others like them—our minds and our whole lives
would be much narrower. Each new word of this kind increases the
scope of thought and adds its bit to humanity. Once we have the word,
of course, it seems natural and it is an effort to imagine being without it.

Consider that remarkable British phrase which Lord Broughton   25
invented during the reign of George IV (1820–1830): "His Majesty's
opposition." Political parties rose in seventeenth-century England
during a period of limited civil war and they behaved as if parliamen-
tary victories were military ones. When one party gained power it immediately proceeded to impeach the leaders of the other party, demanding their very heads. But after a hundred and fifty years of peace
and prosperity, men's tempers began to cool. A sense of fairness compelled them to grant their neighbor the right to a different opinion and
even to grant that men who opposed them might still be loyal and
honorable. But the atmosphere Lord Broughton described had to precede his phrase, just as the invention of the wheel had to precede the
medieval concept of Fortune's wheel.

Once uttered, the phrase helped to further the idea it described.   26
Men saw that criticism of an administration can be as much a part of
good government as the government itself and that a man was not necessarily a traitor because he disagreed with the party in power.

Many studies have established the fact that there is a high correla-   27
tion between vocabulary and intelligence and that the ability to increase one's vocabulary throughout life is a sure reflection of intellectual progress.

It is hard to stretch a small vocabulary to make it do all the things   28
that intelligent people require of words. It's like trying to plan a series
of menus from the limited resources of a poverty-stricken, war-torn

country compared to planning such a series in a prosperous, stable country. Words are one of our chief means of adjusting to all the situations of life. The better control we have over words, the more successful our adjustment is likely to be.

QUESTIONS ON CONTENT

1. According to Evans, how can a large vocabulary help you? Explain.

2. What, according to Evans, is the cause for misunderstandings between people? How can the chances of misunderstanding be reduced?

3. What does Evans believe is the relationship between vocabulary and intelligence?

4. Explain how a large vocabulary increases one's awareness of what is going on.

5. Many newspapers carry regular "vocabulary building" columns, and the *Reader's Digest* has had for years a section called "It Pays to Increase Your Word Power." What does the continuing popularity of these features suggest about the attitude of many Americans toward language?

6. Evans says, "The words we use are so associated with our experiences and what the experiences mean to us that they cannot be separated" (17). What associations do the following words have for you as a result of your own experiences?

    dinner
    money
    Thanksgiving
    fear
    success

Compare your associations with those of your classmates.

QUESTIONS ON RHETORIC

1. What is Evans's thesis, and where is it stated? (Glossary: *Thesis*)

2. Consider the central analogy of Evans's essay: words as a tool. How effective is the analogy? What other extended analogy does Evans use? (Glossary: *Analogy*)

3. What is the purpose of Evans's reference to Caliban, a character in Shakespeare's *The Tempest?*

4. What technique does Evans use to support his generalization that "the rightness of a well-chosen word is not merely a source of pleasure; it may provoke the most serious consequences or avoid the gravest danger" (13)? (Glossary: *Examples*)

5. How would you describe the author's tone? Would you say that the author's tone is formal, conversational, preachy, chatty, or informal? (Glossary: *Tone*)

VOCABULARY

futile (4)	inevitably (16)	intricate (20)
exasperation (6)	subconscious (17)	muddle (22)
communicable (14)	perverse (18)	correlation (27)

WRITING TOPICS

1. Evans makes the point that words must be defined for communication to be effective. As a writer you will often need to define, and the more precise your definitions, the more clearly you will communicate. One way of defining a term is to place it in a class of similar items and then to show how it is different from the other items in that class. For example,

Word	Class	Characteristics
a *watch*	is a *mechanical device*	*for telling time and is usually carried or worn*
semantics	is an *area of linguistics*	*concerned with the study of the meaning of words*

Certainly such definitions are not complete, and one could write an entire paragraph, essay, or book to define these terms more fully. This process, however, is useful for getting started in both thinking and writing.

Place each of the following terms in a class, and then write a statement differentiating each term:

paper clip
pamphlet
anxiety
freedom

Now write a brief essay in which you fully define one of the above terms, or one of your own choosing.

2. Evans argues that an impoverished vocabulary certainly limits one's perceptions of the world and ability to deal with it. Using examples from your own personal experiences, discuss how your vocabulary has affected you—has it ever made you feel restricted or at a disadvantage, or has it ever given you the feeling that you were in charge, in complete control of the situation? You might wish to consider your work in a particular job or area of academic study.

3. Most of us while we were growing up heard from our parents and teachers that it was important to have a large vocabulary. Is it difficult

to acquire a large vocabulary? Why hasn't "vocabulary-building" become a regular part of the public school curriculum, or if it has, what have been the results? What exactly is involved in increasing your vocabulary—memorizing, practice, writing, reading, speaking, all of the above?

2

Vogue Words
Are Trific, Right?

WILLIAM SAFIRE

William Safire is a journalist, speech writer, novelist, and commentator on the English language. In the following essay, which first appeared in Safire's "On Language" column in the New York Times Magazine, *he examines an interesting language phenomenon—vogue words. Each year it seems certain words come into being and sweep the country. While they're with us, these words are the rage; to use them is to be "with-it." But then, just like a storm, most of them pass away.*

Vogue words are bits of language that slip into American speech, are   1
disseminated far and wide by television talk shows, and make a person
appear with-it. Many of the words run a flulike course and disappear,
leaving memories of semantic headaches and fevered articulation.
Others, like "détente," are formally banished by Presidential fiat. Here
is my first annual vogue-word watch, compiled with the help of a few
lexicographical colleagues around the country.

VOGUES FROM ALL OVER

Is a word merely for the nonce, or worth including in a dictionary?   2
Some stalwart vogues seem to be establishing themselves as permanent
features of the language. Among businessmen, "net net" has already
faded, but *bottom line* (the "final accounting" or "essence") is spreading. Among youthful linguists, "way to go" has faded, "no way" is bor-
derline, but the familiar *into*—as "he's into slang"—is putting down
roots, and lexicographer David Guralnik thinks it may get into non-
nonce status.

"Getting it together," picked up by lemminglike copywriters for   3
commercials, has been dropped by the coiners who originate these
phrases; "mellow," which went the opposite route, is also on the wane,
as is "laid back," which might originally have had a sexual connota-

tion but more likely springs from reclining seats on motorcycles. "Heavy," a 40s word for "villain," became a 60s word for "depressing" but is sinking. *Off the wall,* on the other hand—which comes from the squash court and means "unexpected" or "veering crazily"—shows signs of life.

"That bums me out" has already given way to "that cracks me up," and the jazzman's "suss it out" (figure it out) doesn't seem to figure. The disgusted "yecchy," with its comic-strip origins, fades, but the equally disgusted *gross* (ugly, objectionable, and sometimes used admiringly) shows staying power. (To many, a "gross national product" is a derogation of the country's goods.)

TELEVISIONESE

The use of the phrase *has learned* to mean "found out" has been growing. "CBS has learned" does three things: (1) removes the need for *sourcing* (a journalism vogue word for identifying the person responsible for a story), (2) gives the impression of being the first to know and to tell the viewer and (3) plugs the network. The report is given as a certainty—much more solid than "reliable sources say"—but conceals, or covers up, the fact that nobody is willing to stand behind the message except the medium.

Private person is the *sine qua non* of soap operas and daytime talk shows. Nobody is an introvert any more; hermits no longer exist; damnable publicity-shunners have drifted from the scene—today, anybody who will not grant an interview is a "very private person."

Bleep has become a usable word-substitute, from the sound made when a word is excised from a tape. Columnist Herb Caen has popularized this as a euphemism, lexicographer Peter Tamony reports—as in: "That's no bullbleep."

TESTIMONY TALK

From the land of "to the best of my knowledge" comes the verb of perjury-avoiding fuzziness: *indicate.* Under cross-examination, nobody ever "said" or "told me" or even "suggested"—rather, they "indicated." *To indicate,* which used to mean "to point to," as "he indicated they went thataway," has now become a cover-up word for "he may have told me this, but if he says no, then maybe I was mistaken." The use of "indicate" indicates guilt.

Cover-up was originally used to describe a specific obstruction of justice. Now this compound word is used to describe a compounded felony. Of the recent vogue words, "cover-up," still too young to lose its hyphen, also stands a good chance of making it into the dictionary, just after the entry for *cover story,* a C.I.A.-ism whose cover appears to have been blown.

ADJECTIVAL JIVE

Long ago, it was "hep," then it changed to "hip," then, in the 60s, "cool" took hold; now, perhaps from a sanguine view of cool, comes *cold-blooded,* to convey in-group approval.   10

If a woman is "sexy" she is over 30 and not to be trusted. The replacement is *foxy,* a "counter word" with plenty of connotation but no denotation. (While *lady* has been replaced by "woman" or "person" in liberated discourse, it has taken over the place formerly held by "girl friend." "She's my lady," claims the former "fella," now the *dude.*)   11

Turning a noun into an adjective is the vogue among fun couples, but the vogue word fades fast: "dynamite" (sometimes pronounced "dyn-o-*mite,*" as on the "Good Times" television show), was last year's favorite modifier, as in "Those are dynamite boots," which is being replaced by *killer,* as in "That's a killer whip."   12

CAMP FOLLOWING

"Camp" means "so banal as to be perversely sophisticated." It began as "establishing a camp," which was what the veterans of the Civil War called their reunions, then became a word to define any meeting of an insiders' group, and was taken up by homosexuals to mean the daring use in public of previously private ways.   13

The fashionable-by-being-unfashionable idea has several modern off-shoots, not synonymous but related: *kinky, funky,* and *glitzy.*   14

"Kinky," from the Scandinavian "kink," or curl, bend, or twist, became popularized in the United States as "kinky hair," and was applied in the past decade to young fashion, as "offbeat, deliberately bizzare." The word has moved to the sexy, or foxy, world, and now tumbles out of its pornucopia: "Kinky" means perverse or twisted, usually cruel, sex, and the word has held on long enough to merit serious lexicographic attention.   15

"Funky" has traveled a happier road. Originally a jazz term referring to the smell of cigar smoke, the word bottomed out in meaning as "old cigars, old and decrepit surroundings, just plain old." (Louis   16

Armstrong often referred to "Funky Butt Hall, where I first heard Buddy Bolden play.") Later, as "old" became desirable, "funky" gained its current meaning of "nostalgic," or sweetly memorable, if cornball. (Some of those old cigars were Havanas.)

"Glitzy," often used to describe *"kitsch"* (which is unconscious in 17 its tastelessness) comes directly from the German *"glitzen,"* and means "sparkling," or dazzlingly meretricious.

In sum, "kinky" has curled away from "funky" in meaning, leav- 18 ing funkiness next to glitziness, though that may be a glitzening generality.

RIGHT?

Where funkiness is next to glitziness, trendiness is surely next to godli- 19 ness, and nowhere is that better illustrated than in the interrogative reassurance.

In the early 70s, the grunted "y'know?" studded the speech of 20 every teen ager. Put it this way: "I was walking—y'know?—down the street—y'know?—and I ran into this splivvy dude, y'know?" Youth responds quickly to ridicule (adults move slowly, which is why "viable" and "meaningful" linger on) and when others began saying "No, I don't know," "y'know?" began its disappearance.

However, the need for constant verbal reassurance remained. 21 Many people believe they are not being listened to, or believe their listeners do not believe in them as a source of communication. Thus, *right* has emerged, not as something that makes might, but as a word that makes a speaker feel secure, and usually as part of a historical present tense: "Now I'm taking this walk—right?—down the street—right?—minding my own business—right?"

TRIFIC

Finally, the adjective-as-encouragement-to-continue. In some dis- 22 courses, encouragement is direct: "keep talking" became "I dig" which became "lay it on me" and now crosses its transcendental *t*'s with *keep it flowing.*

In most current speech, however, a single adjective is preferred. In 23 the 30s, this was "fine-'n-dandy." In the 50s, "super" made the grade; in the 60s "fantastic" became a word used not to express amazement, but understanding; and in the early 70s, "beautiful"—usually murmured, head nodding as if in mutual meditation—became the most frequently used word of approval and reassurance. "I found a fish, y'know?" "Beautiful."

Today, the adjective-as-encouragement has become *terrific*, sometimes pronounced with two syllables, "trific." The root meaning—as that which causes one to "wriggle in fear"—changed to "tremble with enthusiasm": after a brief vogue in the early 60s, "terrific" has returned with a rush. "I found a fish—right?" "Trific." Often, the word is repeated, just as "beautiful" used to be: "Now we're sitting around here at The Times—right? and we get this idea—right? for a piece on the way people talk today—right?" "Trific, trific. . . ." 24

QUESTIONS ON CONTENT

1. What, for Safire, is a vogue word? Where does he define the term?

2. Why don't vogue words stay in vogue? Is there any way of predicting which vogue words will become a permanent part of the language?

3. What's the difference, if any, between vogue words and slang? You may find it helpful to look at Stuart Berg Flexner's "Preface to the *Dictionary of American Slang*" on pp. 180–190.

4. Why, according to Safire, did the word *right* emerge as a vogue word? Do you agree. Why, or why not?

QUESTIONS ON RHETORIC

1. What is Safire's purpose in this essay? (Glossary: *Purpose*)

2. What function or functions are served by the many examples that Safire uses in this essay? (Glossary: *Examples*)

3. What is Safire's tone in this essay? What leads you to your conclusion? (Glossary: *Tone*)

4. What purpose do Safire's subheadings serve? Are they in any way related to his overall organizational pattern?

VOCABULARY

disseminated (1)	lexicographer (2)	meretricious (17)
fiat (1)	derogation (4)	interrogative (19)
nonce (2)	sanguine (10)	

WRITING TOPICS

1. Safire wrote his essay in 1976. How many of the vogue words that he discusses have "run a flulike course and disappeared"? How many are still being used? Write an essay in which you speculate about the

reasons why certain words have established "themselves as permanent features of the language."

2. What are the vogue words on your campus this year? Write an essay in which you discuss the vogue words as well as the people who use them. What do people seem to gain from using vogue words?

3

Differences in Vocabulary

ROGER W. SHUY

Most of us take the words that we use in everyday speech and writing for granted. Little do we realize what our vocabulary can reveal about each of us—our age, sex, education, occupation, and geographical and cultural origins. In the following selection from Discovering American Dialects, *Roger W. Shuy discusses, with many examples, the words we use. He also provides a shortened version of the vocabulary questionnaire used by fieldworkers to collect data for the various regional linguistic atlases, so that we can see how our vocabulary compares with that of people from other regions.*

Words are interesting to almost everyone. Through his vocabulary a   1
person may reveal facts about his age, his sex, his education, his occupation, and his geographical and cultural origins. Our first reaction
may be to imagine that all speakers of English use the same words.
Nothing could be further from the truth; our language contains a vast
number of synonyms to show different shades of meaning or reveal as
much of our inner feelings as we want to. Some of these vocabulary
choices are made deliberately. We use other words, however, without
really knowing that our vocabulary is influenced by our audience.

AGE

Certain words tell how old we are. For example, many people refer to   2
an electric refrigerator as an *ice box* despite the fact that in most parts
of our country ice boxes have not been in common use for many years.
Older natives of some Northern dialect areas still may call a frying pan
a *spider,* a term which remained in the vocabulary of the older generation long after the removal of the four legs which gave the descriptive
title. Frying pans no longer look like four-legged spiders, but the name
remains fixed in the vocabulary of certain people.

SEX

Our vocabulary may also identify whether we are male or female.   3
Most high school boys, for example, are not likely to use *lovely, peachy, darling,* and many words ending in *-ie.* Adult males are not apt to know or use very many words concerned with fabrics, color shadings, sewing, or women's styles. Women of all ages are not likely to use the specialized vocabulary of sports, automobile repair, or plumbing.*

EDUCATION

A person also reveals his educational background through his choice   4
of words. It is no secret that learning the specialized vocabulary of psychology, electronics, or fishing is necessary before one becomes fully accepted as an "insider," and before he can fully participate in these areas. Much of what a student learns about a course in school is shown in his handling of the vocabulary of the subject. It is also true, however, that a person's choice of words is not nearly as revealing of education as his grammar and pronunciations are.

OCCUPATION

The specialized vocabulary of occupational groups also appears in   5
everyday language. Truck drivers, secretaries, tirebuilders, sailors, farmers, and members in many other occupations use such words. Linguists who interview people for *The Linguistic Atlas of the United States and Canada* have found that the calls to certain animals, for example, illustrate what might be called farm vocabulary, particularly for the older generation of farmers (city dwellers obviously have no particular way of calling sheep or cows from pasture). Even within farming areas, furthermore, vocabulary will reveal specialization. Recent Illinois language studies showed that a male sheep was known as a *buck* only to farmers who had at some time raised sheep.

ORIGINS

It is common knowledge that certain words indicate where we are   6
from. Northerners use *pail* for a kind of metal container which Mid-

* Editors' note: Writing in 1967, Shuy could not have foreseen the many social changes that have occurred in the United States that necessitate some restriction of his generalizations in this area.

landers refer to as a *bucket*. *Pits* are inside cherries and peaches of
Northerners; *seeds* are found by some Midlanders. It is amusing to
some people, furthermore, that as a general rule horses are said to
whinny or *whinner* in Northern dialect areas, whereas they *nicker* in
some of the Midland parts of our country.

Customs are also revealed in our vocabulary. The *county seat* is   7
relatively unknown in rural New England, where local government is
handled at the town meeting.

The special names for various ethnic or national groups, whether   8
joking or derogatory, are an indication of the settlement patterns of an
area. If a person has the terms *Dago, Kraut,* or *Polack* in his active vocabulary, it is quite likely that he lives among or near Italians, Germans, or Polish people. Sometimes the nickname of a specific immigrant group becomes generalized to include most or all newcomers.
Such a case was . . . noted in Summit County, Ohio, where some natives refer to almost all nationality groups as *Hunkies,* regardless of
whether or not they come from Hungary. That this practice has been
with us for many years is shown in a comment by Theodore Roosevelt
that anything foreign was referred to as *Dutch*. One nineteenth-century politician even referred to Italian paintings as "Dutch daubs from
Italy."

VOCABULARY FIELDWORK

To show some of the ways a speaker's vocabulary may reveal his age,   9
sex, occupation, or regional and cultural origins, let us do a dialect vocabulary project as it might be done by a linguist (called a fieldworker
in this case) who interviews people (called informants) for the *Linguistic Atlas.*

The *Atlas* fieldworker gathers his information in face-to-face inter-   10
views. He may supplement his interview data, however, with questionnaires such as the one which follows. Sometimes these questionnaires are mailed; sometimes the fieldworker distributes them
personally. Whatever method of distribution is used, one thing is certain: The questionnaires have been extremely helpful, reliable, and accurate indications of vocabulary in use.

A CHECKLIST OF REGIONAL EXPRESSIONS

Directions

1. Please put a circle around the word or words in each group which you
   ordinarily use (don't circle words you have heard—just those you actually use).

2. If the word you ordinarily use is not listed in the group, please write it in the space by the item.
3. If you never use any word in the group, because you never need to refer to the thing described, do not mark the word.

Example:
Center of a peach: pit, seed, ⟨stone⟩ kernel, heart

Household

1. *to put a single room of the house in order:* clean up, do up, redd up, ridd up, straighten up, tidy up, put to rights, slick up
2. *paper container for groceries, etc.:* bag, poke, sack, toot
3. *device found on outside of the house or in yard or garden:* faucet, spicket, spigot, hydrant, tap
4. *window covering on rollers:* blinds, curtains, roller shades, shades, window blinds, window shades
5. *large open metal container for scrub water:* pail, bucket
6. *of peas:* to hull, to podd, to shell, to shuck
7. *web hanging from ceiling of a room:* cobweb, dust web, spider's web, web
8. *metal utensil for frying:* creeper, fryer, frying pan, fry pan, skillet, spider
9. *over a sink:* faucet, hydrant, spicket, spigot, tap
10. *overlapping horizontal boards on outside of house:* clapboards, siding, weatherboards, weatherboarding
11. *large porch with roof:* gallery, piazza, porch, portico, stoop, veranda
12. *small porch, often with no roof:* deck, platform, porch, portico, step, steps, stoop, veranda, piazza
13. *devices at edges of roof to carry off rain:* eaves, eaves spouts, eaves-troughs, gutters, rain troughs, spouting, spouts, water gutter
14. *rubber or plastic utensil for scraping dough or icing from a mixing bowl:* scraper, spatula, kidcheater, bowl scraper
15. *vehicle for small baby:* baby buggy, baby cab, baby carriage, baby coach
16. *to ——— the baby (in such a vehicle):* ride, roll, wheel, push, walk, stroll
17. *furry stuff which collects under beds and on closet floors:* dust, bunnies, dust kittens, lint balls, pussies

Family

18. *family word for father:* dad, daddy, father, pa, papa, pappy, paw, pop
19. *family word for mother:* ma, mama, mammy, maw, mom, mommer, mommy, mother

20. *immediate family:* my family, my folks, my parents, my people, my relatives, my relations, my kin, my kinfolks
21. *others related by blood:* my family, my folks, my kind, my kinfolks, my people, my relation, my relatives, my relations, my kin
22. of a child: favors (*his mother*), features, looks like, resembles, takes after, is the spitting image of
23. *of children:* brought up, fetched up, raised, reared
24. *the baby* moves on all fours *across the floor:* crawls, creeps

Automotive

25. *place in front of driver where instruments are:* dash, dashboard, instrument panel, panel, crash panel
26. *automobile device for making the car go faster:* accelerator, gas, gas pedal, pedal, throttle
27. *place where flashlight and maps may be kept:* glove compartment, compartment, shelf, cabinet
28. *automobile with two doors:* tudor, coupe, two-door
29. *the car needs ————:* a grease job, greased, lubrication, a lube job, to be greased, to be lubed, greasing, servicing, to be serviced
30. *large truck with trailer attached:* truck, truck and trailer, semi, rig, trailer-truck

Urban

31. *new limited access road:* turnpike, toll road, freeway, parkway, pay road, tollway, thruway, expressway
32. *service and eating areas on no. 31:* service stop, service area, oasis, rest area
33. *grass strip in the center of a divided road:* median, center strip, separator, divider, barrier, grass strip, boulevard
34. *place where fire engines are kept:* fire hall, fire house, fire station
35. *place where scheduled airlines operate:* airport, port, terminal, air terminal (by proper name), air field, field
36. *place where train stops:* station, railway station, depot, train stop, train station, railroad station
37. *place where firemen attach hose:* fire hydrant, fire plug, plug, hydrant, water tap
38. *grass strip between sidewalk and street:* berm, boulevard, boulevard strip, parking, parking strip, parkway, sidewalk plot, tree lawn, neutral ground, devil strip, tree bank, city strip
39. *call to hail a taxi:* taxi!, cab!, cabbie!, hack!, hey!, (wave arm), (whistle)
40. *policeman:* cop, policeman, copper, fuzz, dick, officer, bull

41. *the road is:* slick, slippery
42. *place where packaged groceries can be purchased:* grocery store, general store, supermarket, store, delicatessen, grocery, market, food market, food store, supermart
43. *a piece of pavement between two houses on a city block:* gangway, walk, path, sidewalk
44. *place where you watch technicolor features in a car:* drive-in, drive-in movie, outdoor movie, outdoor theater, open-air movie, open-air theater, passion pit

Nature

45. *animal with strong odor:* polecat, skunk, woodspussy, wood-pussy
46. *small, squirrel-like animal that runs along the ground:* chipmunk, grinnie, ground squirrel
47. *worm used for bait in fishing:* angledog, angleworm, bait worm, eace worm, earthworm, eelworm, fish bait, fishing worm, fishworm, mudworm, rainworm, redworm
48. *larger worm:* dew worm, night crawler, night walker, (Georgia) wriggler, town worm
49. *dog of no special kind or breed:* common dog, cur, cur dog, fice, feist, mongrel, no-count, scrub, heinz, sooner, mixed dog, mutt
50. *insect that glows at night:* fire bug, firefly, flow worm, june bug, lightning bug, candle bug
51. *large winged insect seen around water:* darning needle, devil's darning needle, dragon fly, ear-sewer, mosquito hawk, sewing needle, snake doctor, snake feeder, sewing bug
52. *freshwater shellfish with claws; swims backward:* crab, craw, crawdad(die), crawfish, crayfish
53. *center of cherry:* pit, seed, stone, kernel, heart
54. *center of a peach:* pit, seed, stone, kernel, heart
55. *hard inner cover of a walnut:* hull, husk, shell, shuck
56. *green outer cover of a walnut:* hull, husk, shell, shuck
57. *bunch of trees growing in open country (particularly on a hill):* motte, clump, grove, bluff
58. *web found outdoors:* cobweb, dew web, spider nest, spider's nest, spider web, web
59. *tree that produces sugar and syrup:* hard maple, rock maple, sugar maple, sugar tree, maple tree, candy tree, sweet maple

Foods

60. *melon with yellow or orange insides:* muskmelon, melon, mushmelon, lope, cantaloup, mussmellon

61. *a spreadable luncheon meat made of liver:* liver sausage, braun-schweiger, liverwurst
62. *a carbonated drink:* pop, soda, soda pop, tonic, soft drink
63. *a glass containing ice cream and root beer:* a float, a root beer float, a black cow, a Boston cooler
64. *dish of cooked fruit eaten at the end of a meal:* fruit, sauce, dessert, compote
65. *peach whose meat sticks to seed:* cling, cling peach, clingstone, cling-stone peach, hard peach, plum-peach, press peach
66. *food eaten between regular meals:* a bite, lunch, a piece, piece meal, a snack, a mug-up, munch, nash, nosh
67. *corn served on cob:* corn-on-the-cob, garden corn, green corn, mutton corn, roasting ears, sugar corn, sweet corn
68. *beans eaten in pods:* green beans, sallet beans, snap beans, snaps, string beans, beans
69. *edible tops of turnips, beets, etc.:* greens, salad, salat
70. *a white lumpy cheese:* clabber cheese, cottage cheese, curd cheese, curd(s), dutch cheese, home-made cheese, pot cheese, smear-case, cream cheese
71. *round, flat confection with hole in center, made with baking powder:* crull, cruller, doughnut, fatcake, fried cake, cake doughnut, raised doughnut
72. *bread made of corn meal:* cornbread, corn dodger(s), cornpone, hoe cake(s), johnnycake, pone bread
73. *cooked meat juices poured over meat, potatoes, or bread:* gravy, sop, sauce, drippings
74. *ground beef in a bun:* hamburg, hamburger, burger
75. *large sandwich designed to be a meal in itself:* hero, submarine, hoagy, grinder, poor-boy

Games

76. *children's cry at halloween time:* trick or treat!, tricks or treats!, beg-gar's night!, help the poor!, Halloween!, give or receive!
77. *fast moving amusement park ride (on tracks):* coaster, roller coaster, rolly-coaster, shoot-the-chutes, the ride of doom
78. *call to players to return because a new player wants to join:* allie-allie-in-free, allie-allie-oxen free, allie-allie-ocean free, bee-bee bumble bee, everybody in free, newcomer-newcomer!
79. *call to passerby to return a ball to the playground:* little help!, ball!, hey!, yo!, ball up!
80. *to coast on sled lying down flat:* belly-booster, belly-bump, belly-bumper, belly-bunker, belly-bunt, belly-bust, belly buster, belly-down, belly-flop, belly-flopper, belly-grinder, belly-gut, belly-gutter, belly-kachug, belly-kachuck, belly-whack, belly-whop, belly-whop-per, belly-slam, belly-smacker

81. *to hit the water when diving:* belly-flop, belly-flopper, belly-bust, belly-buster
82. *to stop a game you call:* time!, time out!, times!, pax!, fins!

School

83. *to be absent from school:* bag school, bolt, cook jack, lay out, lie out, play hookey, play truant, run out of school, skip class, skip school, slip off from school, ditch, flick, flake school, blow school
84. *where swings and play areas are:* schoolyard, playground, school ground, yard, grounds
85. *holds small objects together:* rubber band, rubber binder, elastic binder, gum band, elastic band
86. *drinking fountain:* cooler, water cooler, bubbler, fountain, drinking fountain
87. *the amount of books you can carry in both arms:* armful, armload, load, turn

Clothing

88. *short knee-length outer garment worn by men:* shorts, bermuda shorts, bermudas, walking shorts, knee (length) pants, pants, knee-knockers
89. *short knee-length outer garment worn by women:* shorts, bermudas, walking shorts, pants
90. *outer garment of a heavy material worn by males as they work:* levis, overalls, dungarees, jeans, blue jeans, pants
91. *garment worn by women at the seashore:* swimsuit, swimming suit, bathing suit
92. *garment worn by men at the seashore:* swimsuit, swimming suit, bathing suit, swimming trunks, trunks, bathing trunks, swimming shorts

Miscellaneous

93. *a time of day:* quarter before eleven, quarter of eleven, quarter till eleven, quarter to eleven, 10:45
94. *someone from the country:* backwoodsman, clodhopper, country gentleman, country jake, countryman, hayseed, hick, hoosier, hillbilly, jackpine savage, mossback, mountain-boomer, pumpkinhusker, railsplitter, cracker, redneck, rube, sharecropper, stump farmer, swamp angel, yahoo, yokel, sodbuster
95. *someone who won't change his mind is:* bull-headed, contrary, headstrong, ornery, otsny, owly, pig-headed, set, sot, stubborn, mulish, muley

96. *when a girl stops seeing a boyfriend she is said to:* give him the air, give him the bounce, give him the cold shoulder, give him the mitten, jilt him, kick him, throw him over, turn him down, shoot him down, give him the gate, brush him off, turn him off, break up with him
97. *become ill:* be taken sick, get sick, take sick, be taken ill, come down
98. *become ill with a cold:* catch a cold, catch cold, get a cold, take cold, take a cold, come down with a cold
99. *sick ———:* at his stomach, in his stomach, on his stomach, to his stomach, of his stomach, with his stomach
100. *I ——— you're right:* reckon, guess, figger, figure, suspect, imagine

The preceding vocabulary questionnaire, frequently called a   11
checklist, is only suggestive of what might be asked for in a particular community. Of the hundred items in ten general fields, you may find some questions more interesting and useful to study than others. Furthermore, you may add other words to this list, or you may find other answers to questions listed here.

QUESTIONS ON CONTENT

1. Using your own specific examples, discuss how vocabulary can reveal facts about your age, sex, education, occupation, and geographical and cultural origins.

2. In light of the many social changes that have occurred in the United States in the last fifteen or twenty years, are Shuy's generalizations about words that may identify a person's sex (3) at all valid? Explain.

3. Would you agree with Shuy's statement that "a person's choice of words is not nearly as revealing of education as his grammar and pronunciations are" (4)? What examples can you give to support your position?

4. Complete the vocabulary questionnaire on pp. 172–178. Compare your responses with those of other members of the class. What patterns can you detect in your responses? How do you account for any deviations from the patterns?

QUESTIONS ON RHETORIC

1. What is Shuy's thesis, and where is it stated? (Glossary: *Thesis*)

2. Identify the topic sentences in paragraphs 2 through 8. (Glossary: *Topic Sentence*) Explain how Shuy supports and develops each one. (Glossary: *Examples*)

3. How would you characterize Shuy's intended audience? (Glossary: *Audience*) What in the essay led you to this conclusion? Explain.

VOCABULARY

cultural (1)   dialect (2)   ethnic (8)

synonyms (1)   apt (3)

WRITING TOPICS

1. Using examples from your own educational experience, write an essay in which you agree or disagree with Shuy's belief that "much of what a student learns about a course in school is shown in his handling of the vocabulary of the subject" (4).

2. Shuy cites the examples of *ice box* and *refrigerator* and of *spider* and *frying pan* to illustrate differences in vocabulary from one generation to another. Write an essay in which you discuss words that your parents or grandparents use that you do not and the words that you use in their place. How do you account for the individual differences?

4

Preface to the *Dictionary of American Slang*

STUART BERG FLEXNER

When a fellow student asks you if you have any bread *or* cabbage, *he is most likely interested in money and not something to eat. We all use slang, and no discussion of words would be complete without a look at it. In his preface to the* Dictionary of American Slang *(1960), Stuart Berg Flexner examines the nature and function of slang. He explains the origins of slang, its cultural subgroups, the dominant imagery of our slang expressions, and their place in American usage.*

American slang, as used in the title of this dictionary, is the body of   1
words and expressions frequently used by or intelligible to a rather large portion of the general American public, but not accepted as good, formal usage by the majority. No word can be called slang simply because of its etymological history; its source, its spelling, and its meaning in a larger sense do *not* make it slang. Slang is best defined by a dictionary that points out who uses slang and what "flavor" it conveys. . . .

The English language has several levels of vocabulary: 2

Standard usage comprises those words and expressions used, un-   3
derstood, and accepted by a majority of our citizens under any circumstances or degree of formality. Such words are well defined and their most accepted spellings and pronunciations are given in our standard dictionaries. In standard speech one might say: *Sir, you speak English well.*

Colloquialisms are familiar words and idioms used in informal   4
speech and writing, but not considered explicit or formal enough for polite conversation or business correspondence. Unlike slang, however, colloquialisms are used and understood by nearly everyone in the United States. The use of slang conveys the suggestion that the speaker and the listener enjoy a special "fraternity," but the use of colloquialisms emphasizes only the informality and familiarity of a gen-

180

eral social situation. Almost all idiomatic expressions, for example, could be labeled colloquial. Colloquially, one might say: *Friend, you talk plain and hit the nail right on the head.*

Dialects are the words, idioms, pronunciations, and speech habits   5 peculiar to specific geographical locations. A dialecticism is a regionalism or localism. In popular use "dialect" has come to mean the words, foreign accents, or speech patterns associated with any ethnic group. In Southern dialect one might say: *Cousin, y'all talk mighty fine.* In ethnic-immigrant "dialects" one might say: *Paisano, you speak good the English,* or *Landsman, your English is plenty all right already.*

Cant, jargon, and *argot* are the words and expressions peculiar to   6 special segments of the population. *Cant* is the conversational, familiar idiom used and generally understood only by members of a specific occupation, trade, profession, sect, class, age group, interest group, or other subgroup of our culture. *Jargon* is the technical or even secret vocabulary of such a subgroup; jargon is "shop talk." *Argot* is both the cant and the jargon of any professional criminal group. In such usages one might say, respectively: *CQ-CQ-CQ . . . the tone of your transmission is good; You are free of anxieties related to interpersonal communication;* or *Duchess, let's have a bowl of chalk.*

Slang is generally defined above. In slang one might say: *Buster,*   7 *your line is the cat's pajamas,* or *Doll, you come on with the straight jazz, real cool like.*

Each of these levels of language, save standard usage is more com-   8 mon in speech than in writing, and slang as a whole is no exception. Thus, very few slang words and expressions (hence very few of the entries in this dictionary) appear in standard dictionaries.

American slang tries for a quick, easy, personal mode of speech. It   9 comes mostly from cant, jargon, and argot words and expressions whose popularity has increased until a large number of the general public uses or understands them. Much of this slang retains a basic characteristic of its origin: it is *fully* intelligible only to initiates.

Slang may be represented pictorially as the more popular portion   10 of the cant, jargon, and argot from many subgroups (only a few of the subgroups are shown on page 182). The shaded areas represent only general overlapping between groups.

Eventually, some slang passes into standard speech; other slang   11 flourishes for a time with varying popularity and then is forgotten; finally, some slang is never fully accepted nor completely forgotten. *O.K., jazz* (music), and *A-bomb* were recently considered slang, but they are now standard usages. *Bluebelly, Lucifer,* and *the bee's knees* have faded from popular use. *Bones* (dice) and *beat it* seem destined to

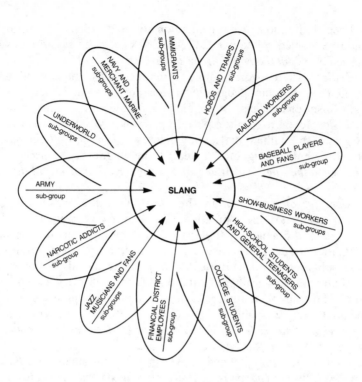

remain slang forever: Chaucer used the first and Shakespeare used the second.

It is impossible for any living vocabulary to be static. Most new 12 slang words and usages evolve quite naturally: they result from specific situations. New objects, ideas, or happenings, for example, require new words to describe them. Each generation also seems to need some new words to describe the same old things.

Railroaders (who were probably the first American subgroup to 13 have a nationwide cant and jargon) thought *jerk water town* was ideally descriptive of a community that others called a *one-horse town*. The changes from *one-horse town* and *don't spare the horses* to a *wide place in the road* and *step on it* were natural and necessary when the automobile replaced the horse. The automobile also produced such new words and new meanings (some of them highly specialized) as *gas buggy, jalopy, bent eight, Chevvie, convertible,* and *lube.* Like most major innovations, the automobile affected our social history and introduced or encouraged *dusters, hitch hikers, road hogs, joint hopping, necking, chicken* (the game), *car coats,* and *suburbia.*

The automobile is only one obvious example. Language always re- 14 sponds to new concepts and developments with new words.

Consider the following: 15
wars: *redcoats, minutemen, bluebelly, over there, doughboy, gold brick, jeep.*
mass immigrations: *Bohunk, greenhorn, shillalagh, voodoo, pizzeria.*
science and technology: *'gin, side-wheeler, wash-and-wear, fringe area, fall-out.*
turbulent eras: *Redskin, maverick, speak, Chicago pineapple, free love, fink, breadline.*
evolution in the styles of eating: *applesauce, clambake, luncheonette, hot dog, coffee and.*
dress: *Mother Hubbard, bustle, shimmy, sailor, Long Johns, zoot suit, Ivy League.*
housing: *lean-to, bundling board, chuckhouse, W.C., railroad flat, split-level, sectional.*
music: *cakewalk, bandwagon, fish music, long hair, rock.*
personality: *Yankee, alligator, flapper, sheik, hepcat, B.M.O.C., beetle, beat.*
new modes of transportation: *stage, pinto, jitney, kayducer, hot shot, jet jockey.*
new modes of entertainment: *barnstormer, two-a-day, clown alley, talkies, d.j., Spectacular.*
changing attitudes toward sex: *painted woman, fast, broad, wolf, jail-bait, sixty-nine.*
human motivations: *boy crazy, gold-digger, money-mad, Momism, Oedipus complex, do-gooder, sick.*
personal relationships: *bunky, kids, old lady, steady, ex, gruesome two-some, John.*
work and workers: *clod buster, scab, pencil pusher, white collar, graveyard shift, company man.*
politics: *Tory, do-nothing, mug-wump, third party, brain trust, fellow tra-veler, Veep.*
and even hair styles: *bun, rat, peroxide blonde, Italian cut, pony tail, D.A.*

Those social groups that first confront a new object, cope with a 16
new situation, or work with a new concept devise and use new words
long before the population at large does. The larger, more imaginative,
and useful a group's vocabulary, the more likely it is to contribute
slang. To generate slang, a group must either be very large and in constant contact with the dominant culture or be small, closely knit, and
removed enough from the dominant culture to evolve an extensive,
highly personal, and vivid vocabulary. Teenagers are an example of a
large sub-group contributing many words. Criminals, carnival workers, and hoboes are examples of the smaller groups. The smaller
groups, because their vocabulary is personal and vivid, contribute to
our general slang out of proportion to their size.

Whether the United States has more slang words than any other 17
country (in proportion to number of people, area, or the number of
words in the standard vocabulary) I do not know. Certainly the

French and the Spanish enjoy extremely large slang vocabularies. Americans, however, do use their general slang more than any other people.

American slang reflects the kind of people who create and use it. Its   18
diversity and popularity are in part due to the imagination, self-confidence, and optimism of our people. Its vitality is in further part due to our guarantee of free speech and to our lack of a national academy of language or of any "official" attempt to purify our speech. Americans are restless and frequently move from region to region and from job to job. This hopeful wanderlust, from the time of the pioneers through our westward expansion to modern mobility, has helped spread regional and group terms until they have become general slang. Such restlessness has created constantly new situations which provoke new words. Except for a few Eastern industrial areas and some rural regions in the South and West, America just doesn't look or sound "lived in." We often act and speak as if we were simply visiting and observing. What should be an ordinary experience seems new, unique, or colorful to us, worthy of words and forceful speech. People do not "settle down" in their jobs, towns, or vocabularies.

Nor do we "settle down" intellectually, spiritually, or emotionally.   19
We have few religious, regional, family, class, psychological, or philosophical roots. We don't believe in roots, we believe in teamwork. Our strong loyalties, then, are directed to those social groups—or subgroups as they are often called—with which we are momentarily identified. This ever-changing "membership" helps to promote and spread slang.

But even within each sub-group only a few new words are gen-   20
erally accepted. Most cant and jargon are local and temporary. What persist are the exceptionally apt and useful cant and jargon terms. These become part of the permanent, personal vocabulary of the group members, giving prestige to the users by proving their acceptance and status in the group. Group members then spread some of this more honored cant and jargon in the dominant culture. If the word is also useful to nongroup members, it is on its way to becoming slang. Once new words are introduced into the dominant culture, via television, radio, movies, or newspapers, the rapid movement of individuals and rapid communication between individuals and groups spread the new word very quickly.

For example, consider the son of an Italian immigrant living in   21
New York City. He speaks Italian at home. Among neighborhood youths of similar background he uses many Italian expressions because he finds them always on the tip of his tongue and because they give him a sense of solidarity with his group. He may join a street gang, and after school and during vacations work in a factory. After

leaving high school, he joins the navy; then he works for a year seeing the country as a carnival worker. He returns to New York, becomes a longshoreman, marries a girl with a German background, and becomes a boxing fan. He uses Italian and German borrowings, some teen-age street-gang terms, a few factory terms, slang with a navy origin, and carnival, dockworker's, and boxing words. He spreads words from each group to all other groups he belongs to. His Italian parents will learn and use a few street-gang, factory, navy, carnival, dockworker's, and boxing terms; his German in-laws will learn some Italian words from his parents; his navy friends will begin to use some of his Italian expressions; his carnival friends a few navy words; his co-workers on the docks some carnival terms, in addition to all the rest; and his social friends, with whom he may usually talk boxing and dock work, will be interested in and learn some of his Italian and carnival terms. His speech may be considered very "slangy" and picturesque because he has belonged to unusual, colorful sub-groups.

On the other hand, a man born into a Midwestern, middle-class, Protestant family whose ancestors came to the United States in the eighteenth century might carry with him popular high-school terms. At high school he had an interest in hot rods and rock-and-roll. He may have served two years in the army, then gone to an Ivy League college where he became an adept bridge player and an enthusiast of cool music. He may then have become a sales executive and developed a liking for golf. This second man, no more usual or unusual than the first, will know cant and jargon terms of teen-age high-school use, hot-rods, rock-and-roll, Ivy League schools, cool jazz, army life, and some golf player's and bridge player's terms. He knows further a few slang expressions from his parents (members of the Jazz Age of the 1920s), from listening to television programs, seeing both American and British movies, reading popular literature, and from frequent meetings with people having completely different backgrounds. When he uses cool terms on the golf course, college expressions at home, business words at the bridge table, when he refers to whiskey or drunkenness by a few words he learned from his parents, curses his next-door neighbor in a few choice army terms—then he too is popularizing slang.

It is, then, clear that three cultural conditions especially contribute to the creation of a large slang vocabulary: (1) hospitality to or acceptance of new objects, situations, and concepts; (2) existence of a large number of diversified sub-groups; (3) democratic mingling between these sub-groups and the dominant culture. Primitive peoples have little if any slang because their life is restricted by ritual; they develop few new concepts; and there are no sub-groups that mingle with the dominant culture. (Primitive sub-groups, such as medicine men or magic men, have their own vocabularies; but such groups do not mix with the dominant culture and their jargon can never become slang because it is secret or sacred.)

But what, after all, are the advantages that slang possesses which   24
make it useful? Though our choice of any specific word may usually be made from habit, we sometimes consciously select a slang word because we believe that it communicates more quickly and easily, and more personally, than does a standard word. Sometimes we resort to slang because there is no one standard word to use. In the 1940s *WAC, cold war,* and *cool* (music) could not be expressed quickly by any standard synonyms. Such words often become standard quickly, as have the first two. We also use slang because it often is more forceful, vivid, and expressive than are standard usages. Slang usually avoids the sentimentality and formality that older words often assume. Taking a girl to a *dance* may seem sentimental, may convey a degree of formal, emotional interest in the girl, and has overtones of fancy balls, fox trots, best suits, and corsages. At times it is more fun to go to a *hop.* To be *busted* or without a *hog* in one's *jeans* is not only more vivid and forceful than being penniless or without funds, it is also a more optimistic state. A *mouthpiece* (or *legal beagle*), *pencil pusher, sawbones, boneyard, bottle washer* or a course in *biochem* is more vivid and forceful than a lawyer, clerk, doctor, cemetery, laboratory assistant, or a course in biochemistry—and is much more real and less formidable than a legal counsel, junior executive, surgeon, necropolis (or memorial park), laboratory technician, or a course in biological chemistry. . . .

We often use slang *fad* words as a bad habit because they are close   25
to the tip of our tongue. Most of us apply several favorite but vague words to any of several somewhat similar situations; this saves us the time and effort of thinking and speaking precisely. At other times we purposely choose a word because it is vague, because it does not commit us too strongly to what we are saying. For example, if a friend has been praising a woman, we can reply "she's *the bee's knees*" or "she's a real *chick,*" which can mean that we consider her very modern, intelligent, pert, and understanding—or can mean that we think she is one of many nondescript, somewhat confused, followers of popular fads. We can also tell our friend that a book we both have recently read is *the cat's pajamas* or *the greatest.* These expressions imply that we liked the book for exactly the same reasons that our friend did, without having to state what these reasons were and thus taking the chance of ruining our rapport.

In our language we are constantly recreating our image in our own   26
minds and in the minds of others. Part of this image, as mentioned above, is created by using sub-group cant and jargon in the dominant

society; part of it is created by our choice of both standard and slang words. A sub-group vocabulary shows that we have a group to which we "belong" and in which we are "somebody"—outsiders had better respect us. Slang is used to show others (and to remind ourselves of) our biographical, mental, and psychological background; to show our social, economic, geographical, national, racial, religious, educational, occupational, and group interests, memberships, and patriotisms. One of the easiest and quickest ways to do this is by using counter-words. These are automatic, often one-word responses of like or dislike, of acceptance or rejection. They are used to counter the remarks, or even the presence, of others. Many of our fad words and many student and quasi-intellectual slang words are counter-words. For liking: *beat, the cat's pajamas, drooly, gas, George, the greatest, keen, nice, reet, smooth, super, way out,* etc. For rejection of an outsider (implying incompetence to belong to our group): *boob, creep, dope, drip, droop, goof, jerk, kookie, sap, simp, square, weird,* etc. Such automatic counters are overused, almost meaningless, and are a substitute for thought. But they achieve one of the main purposes of speech: quickly and automatically they express our own sub-group and personal criteria. Counter-words are often fad words creating a common bond of self-defense. All the rejecting counters listed above could refer to a moron, an extreme introvert, a birdwatcher, or a genius. The counters merely say that the person is rejected—he does not belong to the group. In uttering the counter we don't care what the person is; we are pledging our own group loyalty, affirming our identity, and expressing our satisfaction at being accepted. . . .

The relation between a sub-group's psychology and its cant and jargon is interesting, and the relation between an individual's vocabulary and psychological personality is even more so. Slang can be one of the most revealing things about a person, because our own personal slang vocabulary contains many words used by choice, words which we use to create our own image, words which we find personally appealing and evocative—as opposed to our frequent use of standard words merely from early teaching and habit. Whether a man calls his wife *baby, doll, honey, the little woman, the Mrs.,* or *my old lady* certainly reveals much about him. What words one uses to refer to a mother (*Mom, old lady*), friend (*buddy, bunkie, old man*), the bathroom (*can, John, little boy's room*), parts of the body and sex acts (*boobies, gigi, hard, laid, score*), being tired (*all in, beat*), being drunk (*clobbered, high, lit up like a Christmas tree, paralyzed*), and the like, reveal much about a person and his motivations.

The basic metaphors, at any rate, for all levels of language depend on the five senses. Thus *rough, smooth, touch; prune, sour puss, sweet; fishy, p.u., rotten egg; blow, loud; blue, red, square.* In slang, many metaphors refer to touch (including the sense of heat and cold) and to taste.

Food is probably our most popular slang image. Food from the   29
farm, kitchen, or table, and its shape, color, and taste suggest many
slang metaphors. This is because food can appeal to taste, smell, sight,
and touch, four of our five senses; because food is a major, universal
image to all people, all sub-groups; because men work to provide it
and women devote much time to buying and preparing it; because
food is before our eyes three times every day.

Many standard food words mean money in nonstandard use: 30
cabbage, kale, lettuce. Many apply to parts of the body: *cabbage
head, cauliflower ear, meat hooks, nuts, plates of meat.* Many food words
refer to people: *apple, cold fish, Frog, fruitcake, honey, sweetie pie.*
Others refer to general situations and attitudes: to *brew* a plot, to
receive a *chewing out,* to find oneself *in a pickle* or something *not
kosher,* to be unable to *swallow* another's story, to ask *what's cooking?*
Many drunk words also have food images: *boiled, fried, pickled;*
and so do many words for nonsense: *applesauce, banana oil, spinach.*
Many standard food words also have sexual meanings in slang. The
many food words for money, parts of the body, people, and sex reveal that food means much more to us than mere nourishment.
When a *good egg brings home the bacon* to his *honey,* or when a
string bean of a *sugar daddy* takes his *piece* of *barbecue* to get *fried*
with his hard-earned *kale,* food images have gone a long way from
the farm, kitchen, and table.

Sex has contributed comparatively few words to modern slang, but   31
these are among our most frequently used. The use of sex words to
refer to sex in polite society and as metaphors in other fields is increasing. Sex metaphors are common for the same conscious reasons
that food metaphors are. Sex appeals to, and can be used to apply to,
most of the five senses. It is common to all persons in all sub-groups,
and so we are aware of it continually.

Slang words for sexual attraction and for a variety of sexual acts,   32
positions, and relationships are more common than standard words.
Standard non-taboo words referring to sex are so scarce or remote and
scientific that slang is often used in referring to the most romantic, the
most obscene, and the most humorous sexual situations. Slang is so
universally used in sexual communication that when "a man meets a
maid" it is best for all concerned that they know slang. Slang words for
sex carry little emotional connotation; they express naked desire or
mechanical acts, devices, and positions. They are often blunt, cynical
and "tough."

The subconscious relating of sex and food is also apparent from   33
reading this dictionary. Many words with primary, standard meanings

of food have sexual slang meanings. The body, parts of the body, and descriptions of each, often call food terms into use: *banana, bread, cheese cake, cherry, jelly roll, meat,* etc. Beloved, or simply sexually attractive, people are also often called by food names: *cookie, cup of tea, honey, peach, quail, tomato,* etc. This primary relation between sex and food depends on the fact that they are man's two major sensuous experiences. They are shared by all personalities and all sub-groups and they appeal to the same senses—thus there is bound to be some overlapping in words and imagery. However, there are too many standard food words having sexual meanings in slang for these conscious reasons to suffice. Sex and food seem to be related in our subconscious.

Also of special interest is the number of slang expressions relating   34
sex and cheating. Used metaphorically, many sex words have secondary meanings of being cheated, deceived, swindled, or taken advantage of, and several words whose primary meaning is cheating or deceiving have further specific sexual meanings: *cheating, fucked, make, royal screwing, score, turn a trick,* etc. As expressed in slang, sex is a trick somehow, a deception, a way to cheat and deceive us. To curse someone we can say *fuck you* or *screw you,* which expresses a wish to deprive him of his good luck, his success, perhaps even his potency as a man. Sex is also associated with confusion, exhausting tasks, and disaster: *ball buster, screwed up, snafu,* etc. It seems clear, therefore, that, in slang, success and sexual energy are related or, to put it more accurately, that thwarted sexual energy will somehow result in personal disaster.

Language is a social symbol. The rise of the middle class coincided   35
with the period of great dictionary makers, theoretical grammarians, and the "correct usage" dogma. The new middle class gave authority to the dictionaries and grammarians in return for "correct usage" rules that helped solidify their social position. Today, newspaper ads still implore us to take mail-order courses in order to "learn to speak like a college graduate," and some misguided English instructors still give a good speaking ability as the primary reason for higher education.

The gap between "correct usage" and modern practice widens each   36
day. Are there valid theoretical rules for speaking good English, or should "observed usage" be the main consideration? Standard words do not necessarily make for precise, forceful, or useful speech. On the other hand, "observed usage" can never promise logic and clarity. Today, we have come to depend on "observed usage," just as eighteenth- and nineteenth-century social climbers depended on "correct usage," for social acceptance.

Because it is not standard, formal, or acceptable under all conditions, slang is usually considered vulgar, impolite, or boorish. As this   37 dictionary shows, however, the vast majority of slang words and expressions are neither taboo, vulgar, derogatory, nor offensive in meaning, sound, or image. There is no reason to avoid any useful, explicit word merely because it is labeled "slang." . . .

Remember that "slang" actually does not exist as an entity except   38 in the minds of those of us who study the language. People express themselves and are seldom aware that they are usuing the artificial divisions of "slang" or "standard." First and forever, language is language, an attempt at communication and self-expression. The fact that some words or expressions are labeled "slang" while others are labeled "jargon" or said to be "from the Anglo-Saxon" is of little value except to scholars. Thus this dictionary is a legitimate addition to standard dictionaries, defining many words just as meaningful as and often more succinct, useful, and popular than many words in standard dictionaries.

QUESTIONS ON CONTENT

1. What distinctions does Flexner make in discussing the terms *argot, slang, colloquialism, cant, jargon,* and *dialect?*

2. How, according to Flexner, is slang created? Why does some slang pass into standard speech, while other slang disappears?

3. What does Flexner believe are the three cultural conditions that contribute to the formation of a large slang vocabulary?

4. Why is food imagery so prevalent in slang usage? What other images does Flexner mention? Can you think of any others not included by Flexner?

5. Make a list of the areas of American life that are now contributing to the corpus of American slang. Discuss some of these areas (e.g., television videos, computers, health and fitness, rock music, drugs, etc.) and the slang associated with them. You might also consider the general areas Flexner lists in paragraph 15.

6. Why does Flexner think more dictionaries don't deal with slang terms?

QUESTIONS ON RHETORIC

1. How does Flexner define *slang?* Do his examples help you understand the nature and function of slang? Explain.

2. What is Flexner's purpose in this essay? (Glossary: *Purpose*) How successful do you think he is in achieving his purpose?

3. What is the relationship between paragraphs 21 and 22 and paragraph 20?

4. Identify any passages where Flexner uses process analysis in his discussion of slang. Why is this mode appropriate in these instances? (Glossary: *Process Analysis*)

VOCABULARY

etymological (1)	synonyms (24)	evocative (27)
idioms (4)	pert (25)	derogatory (37)
mode (9)	rapport (25)	succinct (38)
wanderlust (18)		

WRITING TOPICS

1. Compare and contrast the slang that you used in high school with the slang that you now use in college. Try to explain why you no longer use some slang terms, why some were carried over from high school, and why you adopted new terms after arriving at college.

2. As Flexner points out, slang is very important to subgroups in America. Identify a subgroup that you belong to, and write an essay in which you discuss the group's slang terms and the value or function that this language has for the group.

3. Choose several slang terms that are currently in wide usage. Investigate or speculate about their origins and how they have spread. In an essay use these terms as examples to describe the process of how slang evolves in contemporary culture.

5
How Dictionaries Are Made

S. I. HAYAKAWA

S. I. Hayakawa is one of this country's leading semanticists. In this excerpt from his Language in Thought and Action, *Hayakawa explains the process of how a dictionary is made in order to dispel certain myths about dictionaries and their use.*

It is widely believed that every word has a correct meaning, that we learn these meanings principally from teachers and grammarians (except that most of the time we don't bother to, so that we ordinarily speak "sloppy English"), and that dictionaries and grammars are the supreme authority in matters of meaning and usage. Few people ask by what authority the writers of dictionaries and grammars say what they say. I once got into a dispute with an Englishwoman over the pronunciation of a word and offered to look it up in the dictionary. The Englishwoman said firmly, "What for? I am English. I was born and brought up in England. The way I speak *is* English." Such self-assurance about one's own language is not uncommon among the English. In the United States, however, anyone who is willing to quarrel with the dictionary is regarded as either eccentric or mad.

Let us see how dictionaries are made and how the editors arrive at definitions. What follows applies, incidentally, only to those dictionary offices where first-hand, original research goes on—not those in which editors simply copy existing dictionaries. The task of writing a dictionary begins with reading vast amounts of the literature of the period or subject that the dictionary is to cover. As the editors read, they copy on cards every interesting or rare word, every unusual or peculiar occurrence of a common word, a large number of common words in their ordinary uses, and also the sentences in which each of these words appear, thus:

> pail
> The dairy *pails* bring home increase of milk
>
> Keats, *Endymion* I, 44–45

192

That is to say, the context of each word is collected, along with the   3
word itself. For a really big job of dictionary-writing, such as the *Oxford English Dictionary* (usually bound in about twenty-five volumes),
millions of such cards are collected, and the task of editing occupies
decades. As the cards are collected, they are alphabetized and sorted.
When the sorting is completed, there will be for each word anywhere
from two or three to several hundred illustrative quotations, each on
its card.

To define a word, then, the dictionary-editor places before him the   4
stack of cards illustrating that word; each of the cards represents an
actual use of the word by a writer of some literary or historical importance. He reads the cards carefully, discards some, rereads the rest, and
divides up the stack according to what he thinks are the several senses
of the word. Finally, he writes his definitions, following the hard-and-
fast rule that each definition *must* be based on what the quotations in
front of him reveal about the meaning of the word. The editor cannot
be influenced by what *he* thinks a given word *ought* to mean. He must
work according to the cards or not at all.

The writing of a dictionary, therefore, is not a task of setting up au-   5
thoritative statements about the "true meanings" of words, but a task
of *recording,* to the best of one's ability, what various words *have meant*
to authors in the distant or immediate past. *The writer of a dictionary is
a historian, not a lawgiver.* If, for example, we had been writing a dictionary in 1890, or even as late as 1919, we could have said that the
word "broadcast" means "to scatter" (seed, for example), but we could
not have decreed that from 1921 on, the most common meaning of the
word should become "to disseminate audible messages, etc., by radio
transmission." To regard the dictionary as an "authority," therefore, is
to credit the dictionary-writer with gifts of prophecy which neither he
nor anyone else possesses. In choosing our words when we speak or
write, we can be *guided* by the historical record afforded us by the dictionary, but we cannot be *bound* by it, because new situations, new experiences, new inventions, new feelings are always compelling us to
give new uses to old words. Looking under a "hood," we should ordinarily have found, five hundred years ago, a monk; today, we find a
motorcar engine.

QUESTIONS ON CONTENT

1. In paragraphs 2–4 Hayakawa explains how dictionaries are made.
What are the major steps involved in this process?

2. What are some of the commonly held myths about dictionaries that Hayakawa points to? Is it still true in the United States that "anyone who is willing to quarrel with the dictionary is regarded as either eccentric or mad" (1)?

3. What is Hayakawa's point in showing the changes that have occurred in the meaning of *broadcast?* Make a list of some other words whose meanings have changed.

4. Why does Hayakawa consider dictionary-makers as "historians" and not as "lawgivers"?

5. Look up the word *hood* in your desk dictionary or in *Webster's Third New International Dictionary.* What new meanings do you find?

QUESTIONS ON RHETORIC

1. What is Hayakawa's thesis in this essay? Where is it stated? (Glossary: *Thesis*)

2. What is his purpose for writing this essay? (Glossary: *Purpose*)

3. What type of process analysis is used in this essay? Would another type of process analysis be appropriate? Why, or why not? (Glossary: *Process Analysis*)

4. Hayakawa uses examples to clarify points discussed in his essay. Cite the ones he uses in paragraphs 1, 2, and 5, and point to the generalization that each supports. Why do you suppose Hayakawa uses a visual example in paragraph 2?

VOCABULARY

eccentric (1)   authoritative (5)   prophecy (5)
context (3)   disseminate (5)

WRITING TOPICS

1. If you were compiling a dictionary and had before you only the following quotations, what definition would you write for the word *lasto?* Do not try to find a one-word synonym; write a ten- to twenty-word definition:

   a. A lasto is sometimes difficult to clean.
   b. Mary put too much food into her lasto and it overflowed.
   c. A knife will do many of the jobs that a lasto will do, but the knife cannot do them as efficiently.
   d. The blades on a lasto must be bent for it to work well.
   e. Some lastos have only three speeds; others have as many as ten.

2. There are many different kinds of dictionaries published today. Dictionaries of foreign languages, artists, slang, psychology, and music are only a few. Consult the reference section of your library and list the different dictionaries it contains. Write an essay in which you briefly describe the various types (or categories) of dictionaries that you found.

3. Much of the controversy surrounding the making of dictionaries has centered on the role of the lexicographer or dictionary-maker. Is this person an historian or a lawgiver? Write an essay in which you define the words *prescriptive* and *descriptive* and show how these terms relate to the debate over the "decline" of American English. You may wish to do some reading about the controversy sparked by the publication of *Webster's Third New International Dictionary* in 1961.

4. Take a slang word that is currently used at your school and, using the method Hayakawa describes, define the word. Present your work in an essay of definition.

WRITING ASSIGNMENTS FOR "WORDS, MEANINGS, AND DICTIONARIES"

1. Ludwig Wittgenstein's statement "The limits of my language are the limits of my world" is often quoted. Write an essay in which you show how a person's vocabulary either limits or expands his or her world. Be sure to use examples to illustrate your points.

2. A worthwhile and enjoyable project for the class as a whole is a dictionary debate. Each of three or four groups is asked to become familiar with one of the various recently published desk dictionaries. In turn, individual members of each group are responsible for knowing about particular aspects of their dictionary (e.g., number of entries, usage labels, adequacy of etymology, illustrations, information about synonyms and antonyms, front matter, encyclopedic information, and appendices). It is probably a good idea for all the groups to consider the treatment of a particular word (e.g., *fun*). After the necessary research is completed, the groups meet and debate the merits of their dictionaries. Care should be taken to avoid comparisons between abridged and unabridged dictionaries. Finally, write a report of the merits of your particular dictionary.

3. Using Roger Shuy's "Checklist of Regional Expressions," survey your class, your dorm, or another well-defined group. Be sure to have each of your informants give you his or her name, age, hometown, and summer employment. Tabulate your results. Do any local or regional patterns emerge? Do you find any other patterns (e.g., systematic differences by age, sex, or occupation)? Write an essay in which you report your results.

4. Either as a class project or individually, compile a lexicon of slang used on your campus. Care should be taken in defining words so as to include the variety of usages observed. Before starting this project, you should reread Hayakawa's brief essay "How Dictionaries Are Made."

5. Many slang terms used on college campuses today are carried over from other subgroups of American slang, and so the question of how to define collegiate slang has become a difficult one. One area of slang that is unique to the college setting, however, consists of the familiar and somtimes facetious names that students give their courses. Some names collected at the University of Vermont include:

Con Law: Constitutional Law
Stones and Bones: Introductory Anthropology
Confusion: Chinese Religion and Thought
Edge of Night: Medieval European Civilization

Compile a list of slang names for courses on your campus. Analyze your collection. Do you see any patterns in the way slang names were formed (shortened forms, rhyming pairs, initials, etc.)? Do the names that you found on your campus suggest something about students' attitudes toward higher education in general? Write an essay detailing your findings.

6. The following words have interesting etymologies: *algebra, anaesthetic, bedlam, caucus, chapel, lord,* and *zest.* Look at their entries in the *Oxford English Dictionary,* and then write a brief summary of what you find out about each word. (If you have difficulty understanding the abbreviations and designations in the *OED,* consult the front sections called "General Explanations" and "List of Abbreviations."

NOTE: Suggested topics for research papers appeared on p. 446.

NOTABLE QUOTATIONS

The following quotations are drawn from the essays in this section. They are presented as additional topics for classroom discussion or for writing assignments.

"Man has been defined as a tool-using animal, but his most important tool, one that distinguishes him from all other animals, is his speech." *Evans* (1)

"A vocabulary is a tool which one uses in formulating the important questions of life, the questions which must be asked before they can be answered." *Evans* (21)

"Words are one of our chief means of adjusting to all the situations of life." *Evans* (28)

"Many of the [vogue] words run a flulike course and disappear, leaving memories of semantic headaches and fevered articulation." *Safire* (1)

" 'CBS has learned' does three things: (1) removes the need for *sourcing* (a journalism vogue word for identifying the person responsible for a story), (2) gives the impression of being the first to know and to tell the viewer and (3) plugs the network." *Safire* (5)

"Our language contains a vast number of synonyms to show different shades of meaning or reveal as much of our inner feelings as we want to." *Shuy* (1)

"Customs are also revealed in our vocabulary." *Shuy* (7)

"It is impossible for any living vocabulary to be static." *Flexner* (12)

"American slang reflects the kind of people who create and use it." *Flexner* (18)

"In the United States . . . anyone who is willing to quarrel with the dictionary is regarded as either eccentric or mad." *Hayakawa* (1)

V

Advertising and Language

As advertising blather becomes the nation's normal idiom, language becomes printed noise.

George F. Will

The great ads, when they do occur, truly enrich our daily lives, our language, our visual perception of things—and confer a new dimension on our very culture.

George Lois

Even though advertisements represent some of the most expensive and calculated acts of composition in America, the audiences they are directed to seldom attend to them analytically. . . . The public generally reacts to advertisements exactly the way advertising agencies would like them to—as consumers, not critics.

Donald McQuade and Robert Atwan

You can tell the ideals of a nation by its advertisements.

Norman Douglas

1

Bugs Bunny Says They're Yummy

DAWN ANN KURTH

In 1972, eleven-year-old Dawn Ann Kurth, a fifth-grader at Meadowlane Elementary School in Melbourne, Florida, was a surprise witness at a Senate subcommittee hearing on television advertising. She believes that TV commercials, especially those shown during the cartoons on Saturday mornings, take unfair advantage of children. Kurth does not argue for the banning of such advertising; instead, she calls for companies to produce constructive, truthful commercials. The following is a transcript of her testimony to the committee.

Mr. Chairman:

My name is Dawn Ann Kurth. I am 11 years old and in the fifth grade at Meadowlane Elementary School in Melbourne, Florida. This year I was one of the 36 students chosen by the teachers out of 20,000 5th-through-8th graders to do a project in the Talented Student Program in Brevard County. We were allowed to choose a project in any field we wanted. It was difficult to decide. There seem to be so many problems in the world today. What could I do?

A small family crisis solved my problem. My sister Martha, who is 7, had asked my mother to buy a box of Post Raisin Bran so that she could get the free record that was on the back of the box. It had been advertised several times on Saturday morning cartoon shows. My mother bought the cereal, and we all (there are four children in our family) helped Martha eat it so she could get the record. It was after the cereal was eaten and she had the record that the crisis occurred. There was no way the record would work.

Martha was very upset and began crying and I was angry too. It just didn't seem right to me that something could be shown on TV that worked fine and people were listening and dancing to the record and when you bought the cereal, instead of laughing and dancing, we were crying and angry. Then I realized that perhaps here was a problem I could so something about or, if I couldn't change things, at least I

201

could make others aware of deceptive advertising practices to children.

To begin my project I decided to keep a record of the number of 4
commercials shown on typical Saturday morning TV shows. There
were 25 commercial messages during one hour, from 8 to 9 A.M., not
counting ads for shows coming up or public service ads. I found there
were only 10 to 12 commercials during shows my parents like to watch.
For the first time, I really began to think about what the commercials
were saying. I had always listened before and many times asked my
mother to buy certain products I had seen advertised, but now I was
listening and really thinking about what was being said. Millions of
kids are being told:

"Make friends with Kool-Aid. Kool-Aid makes good friends."   5

"People who love kids have to buy Fritos."   6

"Hershey chocolate makes milk taste like a chocolate bar." Why   7
should milk taste like a chocolate bar anyway?

"Cheerios make you feel groovy all day long." I eat them some-   8
times and I don't feel any different.

"Libby frozen dinners have fun in them." Nothing is said about the   9
food in them.

"Cocoa Krispies taste like a chocolate milk shake only they are   10
crunchy."

"Lucky Charms are magically delicious with sweet surprises in-   11
side." Those sweet surprises are marshmallow candy.

I think the commercials I just mentioned are examples of deceptive   12
advertising practices.

Another type of commercial advertises a free bonus gift if you buy   13
a certain product. The whole commercial tells about the bonus gift and
says nothing about the product they want you to buy. Many times, as
in the case of the record, the bonus gift appears to be worthless junk or
isn't in the package. I wrote to the TV networks and found it costs
about $4,000 for a 30-second commercial. Many of those ads appeared
four times in each hour. I wonder why any company would spend
$15,000 or $20,000 an hour to advertise worthless junk.

The ads that I have mentioned I consider deceptive. However, I've   14
found others I feel are dangerous.

Bugs Bunny vitamin ads say their vitamins "taste yummy" and   15
taste good.

Chocolate Zestabs say their product is "delicious" and compare   16
taking it with eating a chocolate cookie.

If my mother were to buy those vitamins, and my little sister got to   17
the bottles, I'm sure she would eat them just as if they were candy.

I do not know a lot about nutrition, but I do know that my mother   18
tries to keep our family from eating so many sweets. She says they are
bad for our teeth. Our dentist says so too. If they are bad, why are

companies allowed to make children want them by advertising on TV? Almost all of the ads I have seen during children's programs are for candy, or sugar-coated cereal, or even sugar-coated cereal with candy in it.

I know people who make these commercials are not bad. I know 19 the commercials pay for TV shows and I like to watch TV. I just think that it would be as easy to produce a good commercial as a bad one. If there is nothing good that can be said about a product that is the truth, perhaps the product should not be sold to kids on TV in the first place.

I do not know all the ways to write a good commercial, but I think 20 commercials would be good if they taught kids something that was true. They could teach about good health, and also about where food is grown. If my 3-year-old sister can learn to sing, "It takes two hands to handle a whopper 'cause the burgers are better at Burger King," from a commercial, couldn't a commercial also teach her to recognize the letters of the alphabet, numbers, and colors? I am sure that people who write commercials are much smarter than I and they should be able to think of many ways to write a commercial that tells the truth about a product without telling kids they should eat it because it is sweeter or "shaped like fun" (what shape *is* fun, anyway?) or because Tony Tiger says so.

I also think kids should not be bribed to buy a product by com- 21 mercials telling of the wonderful free bonus gift inside.

I think kids should not be told to eat a certain product because a 22 well-known hero does. If this is a reason to eat something, then, when a well-known person uses drugs, should kids try drugs for the same reason?

Last of all, I think vitamin companies should never, never be al- 23 lowed to advertise their product as being delicious, yummy, or in any way make children think they are candy. Perhaps these commercials could teach children the dangers of taking drugs or teach children that, if they do find a bottle of pills, or if the medicine closet is open, they should run and tell a grown-up, and never, never eat the medicine.

I want to thank the Committee for letting me appear. When I leave 24 Washington, the thing that I will remember for the rest of my life is that some people *do* care what kids think. I know I could have led a protest about commercials through our shopping center and people would have laughed at me or thought I needed a good spanking or wondered what kind of parents I had that would let me run around in the streets protesting. I decided to gather my information and write letters to anyone I thought would listen. Many of them didn't listen, but some did. That is why I am here today. Because some people cared about what I thought. I hope now that I can tell every kid in America that when they see a wrong, they shouldn't just try to forget about it and hope it will go away. They should begin to do what they can to change it.

People will listen. I know, because you're here listening to me.   25

QUESTIONS ON CONTENT

1. Why do you think there are more than twice as many commercial messages during children's shows as during shows intended for adults?

2. Kurth feels that the ads for Kool-Aid, Fritos, Hershey chocolate, Cheerios, Libby frozen dinners, Cocoa Krispies, and Lucky Charms are "examples of deceptive advertising practices" (12). What exactly is deceptive about each ad?

3. What ads does Kurth feel are dangerous? Why?

4. If, as Kurth says, "it would be as easy to produce a good commercial as a bad one" (19), why are there not more good ads on television?

5. What solutions, if any, does Kurth offer for the problem of deceptive and dangerous ads aimed at children?

QUESTIONS ON RHETORIC

1. The writer prepared this statement to be read at a Senate subcommittee hearing in Washington. How does the style of the statement identify it as a speech rather than an essay?

2. What was Kurth's purpose in pursuing a project on advertisements directed at children, and where does she state her purpose? (Glossary: *Purpose*)

3. Why does the writer narrate the incident about Martha and the Post Raisin Bran record? (Glossary: *Narration*)

4. How has Kurth organized her argument? Make a scratch outline of her main points. (Glossary: *Organization*)

5. Where is the writer's argument summarized? What is the function of the last two paragraphs?

6. Did you find Kurth's argument convincing? Why, or why not?

VOCABULARY

deceptive (12)   nutrition (18)
bonus (13)   bribed (21)

WRITING TOPICS

1. You are preparing for a school vacation, and you are short of cash. You have decided to sell some of your possessions. Write an ad for the

dorm bulletin board or school newspaper (seventy-five-word limit) that will bring you the best possible price for one of the following: stereo amp, guitar, bicycle, skis, '64 Ford.

2. Next Saturday morning watch several hours of television, paying particular attention to commercials for children's foods, vitamins, and toys. Write an essay in which you analyze these advertisements. What changes have occurred since Kurth did her study in 1972?

2

Weasel Words:
God's Little Helpers

PAUL STEVENS

Commercials are a very real part of our daily lives. As a television critic reported in TV Guide, *the show "came on at 11 A.M. and was interrupted as follows: at 11:03 for two 30-second spots, at 11:12 for four 30s, at 11:18 for a one-minute network promo, 11:26 for two 30s and at 11:28 for a close-out with nearly a minute more of network blurbs and two 30s and a 10-second spot." In his book, I Can Sell You Anything, Paul Stevens, a writer of television commercials, catalogues the often overlooked language devices that play such a big role in successful advertising. Advertisers really don't have to substantiate their claims since they can make the consumer hear things that aren't being said. As consumers, we need to understand what's really being said in the ads we read.*

Advertising has power, all right. And advertising works, all right. 1
And what it really boils down to is that advertising works because you
believe it. You're the one who believes Josephine the Plumber really
knows about stains. You're the one who believes Winston tastes good
like a cigarette should. You're the one who believes Plymouth is coming through. The real question is, why do you believe all these things?
And the answer is, because you don't yet understand how advertising
makes you believe. You don't understand what to believe, or even how
to believe advertising. Well, if you're ready to learn how to separate
the wheat from the chaff, if you're ready to learn how to make advertising work *for* you, if you're ready to learn how to stop being a sucker,
then you're ready to go to work.

First of all, you know what a weasel is, right? It's a small, slimy ani- 2
mal that eats small birds and other animals, and is especially fond of
devouring vermin. Now, consider for a moment the kind of winning
personality he must have. I mean, what kind of a guy would get his
jollies eating rats and mice? Would you invite him to a party? Take
him home to meet your mother? This is one of the slyest and most
cunning of all creatures; sneaky, slippery, and thoroughly obnoxious.

And so it is with great and warm personal regard for these attributes that we humbly award this King of All Devious the honor of bestowing his name upon our golden sword: the weasel word.

A weasel word is "a word used in order to evade or retreat from a   3
direct or forthright statement or position" (Webster). In other words, if we can't say it, we'll weasel it. And, in fact, a weasel word has become more than just an evasion or retreat. We've trained our weasels. They can do anything. They can make you hear things that aren't being said, accept as truths things that have only been implied, and believe things that have only been suggested. Come to think of it, not only do we have our weasels trained, but they, in turn, have got you trained. When *you* hear a weasel word, you automatically hear the implication. Not the real meaning, but the meaning *it* wants *you* to hear. So if you're ready for a little reeducation, let's take a good look under a strong light at the two kinds of weasel words.

WORDS THAT MEAN THINGS THEY REALLY DON'T MEAN

Help

That's it. "Help." It means "aid" or "assist." Nothing more. Yet,   4
"help" is the one single word which, in all the annals of advertising, has done the most to say something that couldn't be said. Because "help" is the great qualifier; once you say it, you can say almost anything after it. In short, "help" has helped help us the most.

> Helps keep you young
> Helps prevent cavities
> Help keep your house germ-free

"Help" qualifies everything. You've never heard anyone say, "This   5
product will keep you young," or "This toothpaste will positively prevent cavities for all time." Obviously, we can't say anything like that, because there aren't any products like that made. But by adding that one little word, "help," in front, we can use the strongest language possible afterward. And the most fascinating part of it is, you are immune to the word. You literally don't hear the word "help." You only hear what comes after it. And why not? That's strong language, and likely to be much more important to you than the silly little word at the front end.

I would guess that 75 percent of all advertising uses the word   6
"help." Think, for a minute, about how many times each day you hear these phrases:

Helps stop . . .
Helps prevent . . .
Helps fight . . .
Helps overcome . . .
Helps you feel . . .
Helps you look . . .

I could go on and on, but so could you. Just as a simple exercise, call it homework if you wish, tonight when you plop down in front of the boob tube for your customary three and a half hours of violence and/or situation comedies, take a pad and pencil, and keep score. See if you can count how many times the word "help" comes up during the commercials. Instead of going to the bathroom during the pause before Marcus Welby operates, or raiding the refrigerator prior to witnessing the Mod Squad wipe out a nest of dope pushers, stick with it. Count the "helps," and discover just how dirty a four-letter word can be.

Like

Coming in second, but only losing by a nose, is the word "like," 7 used in comparison. Watch:

It's like getting one bar free
Cleans like a white tornado
It's like taking a trip to Portugal

Okay. "Like" is a qualifier, and is used in much the same way as 8 "help." But "like" is also a comparative element, with a very specific purpose; we use "like" to get you to stop thinking about the product per se, and to get you thinking about something that is bigger or better or different from the product we're selling. In other words, we can make you believe that the product is more than it is by likening it to something else.

Take a look at that first phrase, straight out of recent Ivory Soap 9 advertising. On the surface of it, they tell you that four bars of Ivory cost about the same as three bars of most other soaps. So, if you're going to spend a certain amount of money on soap, you can buy four bars instead of three. Therefore, it's like getting one bar free. Now, the question you have to ask yourself is, "Why the weasel? Why do they say 'like'? Why don't they just come out and say, 'You get one bar free'?" The answer is, of course, that for one reason or another, you really don't. Here are two possible reasons. One: sure, you get four bars, but in terms of the actual amount of soap that you get, it may very well be the same as in three bars of another brand. Remember, Ivory has a lot of air in it—that's what makes it float. And air takes up room. Room that could otherwise be occupied by more soap. So, in terms of pure product, the amount of actual soap in four bars of Ivory may be only as much as the actual amount of soap in three bars of most others. That's why we can't—or won't—come out with a straightforward declaration such as, "You get 25 percent more soap," or "Buy three bars, and get the fourth one free."

Reason number two: the actual cost and value of the product. Did   10 it ever occur to you that Ivory may simply be a cheaper soap to make and, therefore, a cheaper soap to sell? After all, it doesn't have any perfume or hexachlorophene, or other additives that can raise the cost of manufacturing. It's plain, simple, cheap soap, and so it can be sold for less money while still maintaining a profit margin as great as more expensive soaps. By way of illustrating this, suppose you were trying to decide whether to buy a Mercedes-Benz or a Ford. Let's say the Mercedes cost $7,000, and the Ford $3,500. Now the Ford salesman comes up to you with this deal: as long as you're considering spending $7,000 on a car, buy my Ford for $7,000 and I'll give you a second Ford, free! Well, the same principle can apply to Ivory: as long as you're considering spending 35 cents on soap, buy my cheaper soap, and I'll give you more of it.

I'm sure there are other reasons why Ivory uses the weasel "like."   11 Perhaps you've thought of one or two yourself. That's good. You're starting to think.

Now, what about that wonderful white tornado? Ajax pulled that   12 one out of the hat some eight years ago, and you're still buying it. It's a classic example of the use of the word "like" in which we can force you to think, not about the product itself, but about something bigger, more exciting, certainly more powerful than a bottle of fancy ammonia. The word "like" is used here as a transfer word, which gets you away from the obvious—the odious job of getting down on your hands and knees and scrubbing your kitchen floor—and into the world of fantasy, where we can imply that this little bottle of miracles will supply all the elbow grease you need. Isn't that the name of the game? The whirlwind activity of the tornado replacing the whirlwind motion of your arm? Think about the swirling of the tornado, and all the work it will save you. Think about the power of that devastating windstorm; able to lift houses, overturn cars, and now, pick the dirt up off your floor. And we get the license to do it simply by using the word "like."

It's a copywriter's dream, because we don't have to substantiate   13 anything. When we compare our product to "another leading brand," we'd better be able to prove what we say. But how can you compare ammonia to a windstorm? It's ludicrous. It can't be done. The whole statement is so ridiculous it couldn't be challenged by the government or the networks. So it went on the air, and it worked. Because the little word "like" let us take you out of the world of reality, and into your own fantasies.

Speaking of fantasies, how about the trip to Portugal? Mateus Rosé   14
is actually trying to tell you that you will be transported clear across the Atlantic Ocean merely by sipping their wine. "Oh, come on," you say. "You don't expect me to believe that." Actually, we don't expect you to believe it. But we do expect you to get our meaning. This is called "romancing the product," and it is made possible by the dear little "like." In this case, we deliberately bring attention to the word, and we ask you to join us in setting reality aside for a moment. We take your hand and gently lead you down the path of moonlit nights, graceful dancers, and mysterious women. Are we saying that these things are all contained inside our wine? Of course not. But what we mean is, our wine is part of all this, and with a little help from "like," we'll get you to feel that way, too. So don't think of us as a bunch of peasants squashing a bunch of grapes. As a matter of fact, don't think of us at all. Feel with us.

"Like" is a virus that kills. You'd better get immune to it.   15

Other Weasels

"Help" and "like" are the two weasels so powerful that they can stand   16
on their own. There are countless other words, not quite so potent, but equally effective when used in conjunction with our two basic weasels, or with each other. Let me show you a few.

VIRTUAL *or* VIRTUALLY. How many times have you responded to an ad   17
that said:

> Virtually trouble-free . . .
> Virtually foolproof . . .
> Virtually never needs service . . .

Ever remember what "virtual" means? It means "in essence or effect, but not in fact." Important—"but not in fact." Yet today the word "virtually" is interpreted by you as meaning "almost or just about the same as. . . ." Well, gang, it just isn't true. "Not," in fact, means not, in fact. I was scanning, rather longingly I must confess, through the brochure Chevrolet publishes for its Corvette, and I came to this phrase:

"The seats in the 1972 Corvette are virtually handmade." They had me, for a minute. I almost took the bait of that lovely little weasel. I almost decided that those seats were just about completely handmade. And then I remembered. Those seats were not, *in fact,* handmade. Remember, "virtually" means "not, in fact," or you will, in fact, get sold down the river.

ACTS *or* WORKS. These two action words are rarely used alone, and are generally accompanied by "like." They need help to work, mostly because they are verbs, but their implied meaning is deadly, nonetheless. Here are the key phrases: 18

> Acts like ...
> Acts against ...
> Works like ...
> Works against ...
> Works to prevent (or help prevent) ...

You see what happens? "Acts" or "works" brings an action to the product that might not otherwise be there. When we say that a certain cough syrup "acts on the cough control center," the implication is that the syrup goes to this mysterious organ and immediately makes it better. But the implication here far exceeds what the truthful promise should be. An act is simply a deed. So the claim "acts on" simply means it performs a deed on. What that deed is, we may never know.

The rule of thumb is this: if we can't say "cures" or "fixes" or use any other positive word, we'll nail you with "acts like" or "works against," and get you thinking about something else. Don't.   19

CAN BE. This is for comparison, and what we do is to find an announcer who can really make it sound positive. But keep your ears open. "Crest can be of significant value when used in...," etc., is indicative of an ideal situation, and most of us don't live in ideal situations.   20

UP TO. Here's another way of expressing an ideal situation. Remember the cigarette that said it was aged, or "cured for up to eight long, lazy weeks"? Well, that could, and should, be interpreted as meaning that the tobaccos used were cured anywhere from one hour to eight weeks. We like to glamorize the ideal situation; it's up to you to bring it back to reality.   21

AS MUCH AS. More of the same. "As much as 20 percent greater mileage" with our gasoline again promises the ideal, but qualifies it.   22

REFRESHES, COMFORTS, TACKLES, FIGHTS, COMES ON. Just a handful   23
of the same action weasels, in the same category as "acts" and
"works," though not as frequently used. The way to complete the
thought here is to ask the simple question, "How?" Usually, you won't
get an answer. That's because, usually, the weasel will run and hide.

FEEL *or* THE FEEL OF. This is the first of our subjective weasels. When   24
we deal with a subjective word, it is simply a matter of opinion. In our
opinion, Naugahyde has the feel of real leather. So we can say it. And,
indeed, if you were to touch leather, and then touch Naugahyde, you
may very well agree with us. But that doesn't mean it is real leather,
only that it feels the same. The best way to handle subjective weasels is
to complete the thought yourself, by simply saying, "But it isn't." At
least that way you can remain grounded in reality.

THE LOOK OF *or* LOOKS LIKE. "Look" is the same as "feel," our subjec-   25
tive opinion. Did you ever walk into a Woolworth's and see those
$29.95 masterpieces hanging in their "Art Gallery"? "The look of a
real oil painting," it will say. "But it isn't," you will now reply. And
probably be $29.95 richer for it.

WORDS THAT HAVE NO SPECIFIC MEANING

If you have kids, then you have all kinds of breakfast cereals in the   26
house. When I was a kid, it was Rice Krispies, the breakfast cereal that
went snap, crackle, and pop. (One hell of a claim for a product that is
supposed to offer nutritional benefits.) Or Wheaties, the breakfast of
champions, whatever that means. Nowadays, we're forced to a con-
frontation with Quisp, Quake, Lucky-Stars, Cocoa-Puffs, Clunkers,
Blooies, Snarkles and Razzmatazz. And they all have one thing in
common: they're all "fortified." Some are simply "fortified with vitamins," while others are specifically "fortified with vitamin D," or some
other letter. But what does it all mean?
    "Fortified" means "added on to." But "fortified," like so many   27
other weasel words of indefinite meaning, simply doesn't tell us
enough. If, for instance, a cereal were to contain one unit of vitamin D,
and the manufacturers added some chemical which would produce
two units of vitamin D, they could then claim that the cereal was "fortified with twice as much vitamin D." So what? It would still be about
as nutritional as sawdust.
    The point is, weasel words with no specific meaning don't tell us   28
enough, but we have come to accept them as factual statements closely

associated with something good that has been done to the product. Here's another example.

Enriched

We use this one when we have a product that starts out with nothing. 29 You mostly find it in bread, where the bleaching process combined with the chemicals used as preservatives renders the loaves totally void of anything but filler. So the manufacturer puts a couple of drops of vitamins into the batter, and presto! It's enriched. Sounds great when you say it. Looks great when you read it. But what you have to determine is, is it really great? Figure out what information is missing, and then try to supply that information. The odds are, you won't. Even the breakfast cereals that are playing it straight, like Kellogg's Special K, leave something to be desired. They tell you what vitamins you get, and how much of each in one serving. The catch is, what constitutes a serving? They say, one ounce. So now you have to whip out your baby scale and weigh one serving. Do you have an idea how much that is? Maybe you do. Maybe you don't care. Okay, so you polish off this mound of dried stuff, and now what? You have ostensibly received the minimum, repeat, minimum dosage of certain vitamins for the day. One day. And you still have to go find the vitamins you didn't get. Try looking it up on a box of frozen peas. Bet you won't find it. But do be alert to "fortified" and "enriched." Asking the right questions will prove beneficial.

Did you buy that last sentence? Too bad, because I weaseled you, 30 with the word "beneficial." Think about it.

Flavor *and* Taste

These are two totally subjective words that allow us to claim mar- 31 velous things about products that are edible. Every cigarette in the world has claimed the best taste. Every supermarket has advertised the most flavorful meat. And let's not forget "aroma," a subdivision of this category. Wouldn't you like to have a nickel for every time a room freshener (a weasel in itself) told you it would make your home "smell fresh as all outdoors"? Well, they can say it, because smell, like taste and flavor, is a subjective thing. And, incidentally, there are no less than three weasels in that phrase. "Smell" is the first. Then, there's "as" (a substitute for the ever-popular "like"), and, finally, "fresh," which, in context, is a subjective comparison, rather than the primary definition of "new."

Now we can use an unlimited number of combinations of these   32
weasels for added impact. "Fresher-smelling clothes." "Fresher-tast-
ing tobacco." "Tastes like grandma used to make." Unfortunately,
there's no sure way of bringing these weasels down to size, simply because you can't define them accurately. Trying to ascertain the meaning of "taste" in any context is like trying to push a rope up a hill. All
you can do is be aware that these words are subjective, and represent
only one opinion—usually that of the manufacturer.

Style *and* Good Looks

Anyone for buying a new car? Okay, which is the one with the good   33
looks? The smart new styling? What's that you say? All of them? Well,
you're right. Because this is another group of subjective opinions. And
it is the subjective and collective opinion of both Detroit and Madison
Avenue that the following cars have "bold new styling": Buick Ri-
viera, Plymouth Satellite, Dodge Monaco, Mercury Brougham, and
you can fill in the spaces for the rest. Subjectively, you have to decide
on which bold new styling is, indeed, bold new styling. Then, you
might spend a minute or two trying to determine what's going on
under that styling. The rest I leave to Ralph Nader.

Different, Special, *and* Exclusive

To be different, you have to be not the same as. Here, you must rely on   34
your own good judgment and common sense. Exclusive formulas and
special combinations of ingredients are coming at you every day, in
every way. You must constantly assure yourself that, basically, all
products in any given category are the same. So when you hear "special," "exclusive," or "different," you have to establish two things: on
what basis are they different, and is that difference an important one?
Let me give you a hypothetical example.

All so-called "permanent" antifreeze is basically the same. It is   35
made from a liquid known as ethylene glycol, which has two amazing
properties: It has a lower freezing point than water, and a higher boiling point than water. It does not break down (lose its properties), nor
will it boil away. And every permanent antifreeze starts with it as a
base. Also, just about every antifreeze has now got antileak ingredients, as well as antirust and anticorrosion ingredients. Now, let's
suppose that, in formulating the product, one of the companies comes
up with a solution that is pink in color, as opposed to all the others,
which are blue. Presto—an exclusivity claim. "Nothing else looks like

it, nothing else performs like it." Or how about, "Look at ours, and look at anyone else's. You can see the difference our exclusive formula makes." Granted, I'm exaggerating. But did I prove a point?

A Few More Goodies

At Phillips 66, it's performance that counts   36
Wisk puts its strength where the dirt is
At Bird's Eye, we've got quality in our corner
Delicious and long-lasting, too

Very quickly now, let's deflate those four lines. First, what the hell does "performance" mean? It means that this product will do what any other product in its category will do. Kind of a backhanded reassurance that this gasoline will function properly in your car. That's it, and nothing more. To perform means to function at a standard consistent with the rest of the industry. All products in a category are basically the same.

Second line: What does "strength" or "strong" mean? Does it mean   37
"not weak"? Or "superior in power"? No, it means consistent with the norms of the business. You can bet your first-born that if Wisk were superior in power to other detergents, they'd be saying it, loud and clear. So strength is merely a description of a property inherent in all similar products in its class. If you really want to poke a pin in a bubble, substitute the word "ingredients" for the word "strength." That'll do it every time.

Third line: The old "quality" claim, and you fell for it. "Quality" is   38
not a comparison. In order to do that, we'd have to say, "We've got better quality in our corner than any other frozen food." Quality relates only to the subjective opinion that Bird's Eye has of its own products, and to which it is entitled. The word "quality" is what we call a "parity" statement; that is, it tells you that it is as good as any other. Want a substitute? Try "equals," meaning "the same as."

Fourth line: How delicious is delicious? About the same as good-   39
tasting is good-tasting, or fresher-smelling is fresher-smelling. A subjective opinion regarding taste, which you can either accept or reject. More fun, though, is "long-lasting." You might want to consider writing a note to Mr. Wrigley, inquiring as to the standard length of time which a piece of gum is supposed to last. Surely there must be a guideline covering it. The longest lasting piece of gum I ever encountered lasted just over four hours, which is the amount of time it took me to get it off the sole of my shoe. Try expressing the line this way: "It has a definite taste, and you may chew it as long as you wish." Does that place it in perspective?

There are two other aspects of weasel words that I should mention   40
here. The first one represents the pinnacle of the copywriter's craft,
and I call it the "Weasel of Omission." Let me demonstrate:

Of America's best-tasting gums, Trident is sugar-free.

Disregard, for a moment, the obvious subjective weasel "best-tast-   41
ing." Look again at the line. Something has been left out. Omitted very
deliberately. Do you know what that word is? The word that's missing
is the word "only," which should come right before the name of the
product. But it doesn't. It's gone. Left out. And the question is, why?
The answer is, the government wouldn't let them. You see, they start
out by making a subjective judgment, that their gum is among the
best-tasting. That's fine, as far as it goes. That's their opinion, but it is
also the opinion of every other maker of sugar-free gum that his product is also among the best-tasting. And, since both of their opinions
must be regarded as having equal value, neither one is allowed the superiority claim, which is what the word "only" would do. So Trident
left it out. But the sentence is so brilliantly constructed, the word
"only" is so heavily implied, that most people hear it, even though it
hasn't been said. That's the Weasel of Omission. Constructing a set of
words that forces you to a conclusion that otherwise could not have
been drawn. Be on the lookout for what isn't said, and try to fill the
gaps realistically.

The other aspect of weasels is the use of all those great, groovy,   42
swinging, wonderful, fantastic, exciting and fun-filled words known as
adjectives. Your eyes, ears, mind, and soul have been bombarded by
adjectives for so long that you are probably numb to most of them by
now. If I were to give you a list of adjectives to look out for it, it would
require the next five hundred pages, and it wouldn't do any good, anyway. More important is to bear in mind what adjectives do, and then
to be able to sweep them aside and distinguish only the facts.

An adjective modifies a noun, and is generally used to denote the   43
quality or a quality of the thing named. And that's our grammar lesson
for today. Realistically, an adjective enhances or makes more of the
product being discussed. It's the difference between "Come visit Copenhagen," and "Come visit beautiful Copenhagen." Adjectives are
used so freely these days that we feel almost naked, robbed, if we don't
get at least a couple. Try speaking without adjectives. Try describing
something; you can't do it. The words are too stark, too bare-boned,
too factual. And that's the key to judging advertising. There is a direct,
inverse proportion between the number of adjectives and the number
of facts. To put it succinctly, the more adjectives we use, the less we
have to say.

You can almost make a scale, based on that simple mathematical   44
premise. At one end you have cosmetics, soft drinks, cigarettes, products that have little or nothing of any value to say. So we get them all
dressed up with lavish word and thought images, and present you with
thirty or sixty seconds of adjectival puffery. The other end of the scale
is much harder to find. Usually, it will be occupied by a new product
that is truly new or different. . . . Our craving for adjectives has become
so overriding that we simply cannot listen to what is known as "nuts
and bolts" advertising. The rest falls somewhere in the middle; a combination of adjectives, weasels, and semitruths. All I can tell you is, try
to brush the description aside, and see what's really at the bottom.

SUMMARY

A weasel word is a word that's used to imply a meaning that cannot be   45
truthfully stated. Some weasels imply meanings that are not the same
as their actual definition, such as "help," "like," or "fortified." They
can act as qualifiers and/or comparatives. Other weasels, such as
"taste" and "flavor," have no definite meanings, and are simply subjective opinions offered by the manufacturer. A weasel of omission is
one that implies a claim so strongly that it forces you to supply the
bogus fact. Adjectives are weasels used to convey feelings and emotions to a greater extent than the product itself can.

In dealing with weasels, you must strip away the innuendos and try   46
to ascertain the facts, if any. To do this, you need to ask questions such
as: How? Why? How many? How much? Stick to basic definitions of
words. Look them up if you have to. Then, apply the strict definition to
the text of the advertisement or commercial. "Like" means similar to,
but not the same as. "Virtually" means the same in essence, but not in
fact.

Above all, never underestimate the devious qualities of a weasel.   47
Weasels twist and turn and hide in dark shadows. You must come to
grips with them, or advertising will rule you forever.

My advice to you is: Beware of weasels. They are nasty and un-   48
trainable, and they attack pocketbooks.

QUESTIONS ON CONTENT

1. What are "weasel words"? Why do advertisers find them useful?
Why is it important for the average American to know about weasel
words?

2. What does Stevens mean by "qualifiers"?

3. Why has Stevens chosen the weasel to describe certain types of advertising language; that is, what characteristics does a weasel have that make this association appropriate? Explain.

4. Stevens uses the ad for Mateus Rosé as an example of what he calls "romancing the product." What other examples can you think of? Explain how each one works.

5. Weasel words help make advertising the fine art of deception. In weasels like "fortified" and "enriched," the advertisers try to convince us they give us something "extra." Is this true? What happens in the process of bleaching flour for "white" bread?

6. What does Stevens say we should do to protect ourselves from the dangers of deceptive language in ads?

QUESTIONS ON RHETORIC

1. What is the function of the questions Stevens asks in paragraph 2?

2. How does Stevens organize his classification of weasel words? What is the purpose of the classification? (Glossary: *Division and Classification*) Does his classification help you understand weasel words and how they are used?

3. Advertisers often create similes, direct comparisons using *like* or *as:* "Ajax cleans *like* a white tornado." What, according to Stevens, is the advertisers' intent in using the simile? Outside of the advertising world, similes are not normally used to deceive. What value do similes have for you as a student of composition? (Glossary: *Figures of Speech*)

4. Stevens has consciously adopted an informal style in this essay; he wishes to create the impression that he is talking to you, his reader. What devices does Stevens use to establish this informal style? How does his choice of words contribute to this informality?

5. The last four paragraphs serve as the conclusion to Stevens's essay. How effective did you find it? Did he seem to repeat too much from the essay itself, or do you think there was a reason for his doing this?

VOCABULARY

obnoxious (2)	ludicrous (13)	hypothetical (34)
odious (12)	edible (31)	perspective (39)
substantiate (13)	ascertain (32)	succinctly (43)

WRITING TOPICS

1. Using the phrase "adjectival puffery," Stevens claims that "our craving for adjectives has become so overriding that we simply cannot listen to what is known as 'nuts and bolts' advertising" (44). Examine several written advertisements with a substantial amount of text for

examples of adjectival puffery, weasel words, and semitruths. Is Stevens's claim valid? In an essay describe your findings.

2. As Stevens suggests, "tonight when you plop down in front of the boob tube for your customary three and a half hours of violence and/or situation comedies, take a pad and pencil, and keep score" (6). List the weasels that come up during the commercials. Compare your list with those made by others in your class. Write an essay in which you analyze your reactions to the TV commercials now that you are aware of weasel words.

3. Imagine that you are responsible for preparing the first ad for a new product. Let the product be whatever you wish—a car, a soft drink, disposable paper socks, anything—and let it have whatever features you like. How would you advertise it? Write an ad that will *sell* your product. The ad could be for a newspaper or magazine, or it could be the script for a 60-second spot on TV. The important thing is to write *persuasive* copy.

3
How to Write Potent Copy

DAVID OGILVY

No one knows better the persuasive and manipulative powers of words than the professional advertiser, and David Ogilvy is a giant in the field. His highly successful ad campaigns for Rolls-Royce, Sears, Hathaway shirts, and Pepperidge Farm show his genius and great craftsmanship in using words to stimulate consumer interest. In the following selection from his classic book Confessions of an Advertising Man, *Ogilvy stresses the importance of an ad's headline and discusses its relationship to body copy. The specific advice that he gives is intended not only to help us to write effective advertisements, but also to help us analyze how and why certain ads work.*

HEADLINES

The headline is the most important element in most advertisements. It is the telegram which decides the reader whether to read the copy.

On the average, five times as many people read the headline as read the body copy. When you have written your headline, you have spent eighty cents out of your dollar.

If you haven't done some selling in your headline, you have wasted 80 percent of your client's money. The wickedest of all sins is to run an advertisement *without* a headline. Such headless wonders are still to be found; I don't envy the copywriter who submits one to me.

A change of headline can make a difference of ten to one in sales. I never write fewer than sixteen headlines for a single advertisement, and I observe certain guides in writing them:

1. The headline is the "ticket on the meat." Use it to flag down the readers who are prospects for the kind of product you are advertising. If you are selling a remedy for bladder weakness, display the words *"Bladder Weakness"* in your headline; they catch the eye of everyone who suffers from this inconvenience. If you want *mothers* to read your advertisement, display *"Mothers"* in your headline. And so on.

Conversely, do not say anything in your headline which is likely to   6
exclude any readers who might be prospects for your product. Thus, if
you are advertising a product which can be used equally well by men
and women, don't slant your headline at women alone; it would
frighten men away.

2. Every headline should appeal to the reader's *self-interest.* It   7
should promise her a benefit, as in my headline for Helena Rubinstein's Hormone Cream: "How Women over 35 Can Look Younger."

3. Always try to inject *news* into your headlines, because the con-   8
sumer is always on the lookout for new products, or new ways to use
an old product, or new improvements in an old product.

The two most powerful words you can use in a headline are "Free"   9
and "New." You can seldom use "Free," but you can almost always
use "New"—if you try hard enough.

4. Other words and phrases which work wonders are "How To,"   10
"Suddenly," "Now," "Announcing," "Introducing," "It's Here." "Just
Arrived," "Important Development," "Improvement," "Amazing,"
"Sensational," "Remarkable," "Revolutionary," "Startling," "Mira-
cle," "Magic," "Offer," "Quick," "Easy," "Wanted," "Challenge,"
"Advice to," "The Truth About," "Compare," "Bargain," "Hurry,"
"Last Chance."

Don't turn up your nose at these clichés. They may be shopworn,   11
but they work. That is why you see them turn up so often in the headlines of mail-order advertisers and others who can measure the results
of their advertisements.

Headlines can be strengthened by the inclusion of *emotional* words,   12
like "Darling," "Love," "Fear," "Proud," "Friend," and "Baby." One
of the most provocative advertisements which has come out of our
agency showed a girl in a bathtub, talking to her lover on the telephone. The headline. *Darling, I'm having the most extraordinary experience . . . I'm head over heels in DOVE.*

5. Five times as many people read the headline as read the body   13
copy, so it is important that these glancers should at least be told what
brand is being advertised. That is why you should always include the
brand name in your headlines.

6. Include your selling promise in your headline. This requires   14
long headlines. When the New York University School of Retailing
ran headline tests with the cooperation of a big department store, they
found that headlines of ten words or longer, containing news and
information, consistently sold more merchandise than short headlines.

Headlines containing six to twelve words pull more coupon returns   15
than short headlines, and there is no significant difference between the
readership of twelve-word headlines and the readership of three-word

headlines. The best headline I ever wrote contained *eighteen* words: *At Sixty Miles an Hour the Loudest Noise in the New Rolls-Royce comes from the electric clock.*[1]

7. People are more likely to read your body copy if your headline   16
arouses their curiosity; so you should end your headline with a lure to
read on.

8. Some copywriters write *tricky* headlines—puns, literary allu-   17
sions, and other obscurities. This is a sin.

In the average newspaper your headline has to compete for atten-   18
tion with 350 others. Research has shown that readers travel so fast
through this jungle that they don't stop to decipher the meaning of
obscure headlines. Your headline must *telegraph* what you want to
say, and it must telegraph it in plain language. Don't play games with
the reader.

In 1960 the *Times Literary Supplement* attacked the whimsical tra-   19
dition in British advertising, calling it "self-indulgent—a kind of middle-class private joke, apparently designed to amuse the advertiser and
his client." Amen.

9. Research shows that it is dangerous to use *negatives* in head-   20
lines. If, for example, you write "Our Salt Contains No Arsenic,"
many readers will miss the negative and go away with the impression
that you wrote "Our Salt Contains Arsenic."

10. Avoid *blind* headlines—the kind which mean nothing unless   21
you read the body copy underneath them; most people *don't.*

BODY COPY

When you sit down to write your body copy, pretend that you are   22
talking to the woman on your right at a dinner party. She has asked
you, "I am thinking of buying a new car. Which would you recommend?" Write your copy as if you were answering that question.

1. Don't beat about the bush—go straight to the point. Avoid   23
analogies of the "just as, so too" variety. Dr. Gallup has demonstrated
that these two-stage arguments are generally misunderstood.

2. Avoid superlatives, generalizations, and platitudes. Be specific   24
and factual. Be enthusiastic, friendly, and memorable. Don't be a bore.
Tell the truth, but make the truth fascinating.

How long should your copy be? It depends on the product. If you   25
are advertising chewing gum, there isn't much to tell, so make your

[1] When the chief engineer at the Rolls-Royce factory read this, he shook his head
sadly and said, "It is time we did something about that damned clock."

copy short. If, on the other hand, you are advertising a product which has a great many different qualities to recommend it, write long copy: the more you tell, the more you sell.

There is a universal belief in lay circles that people won't read long copy. Nothing could be farther from the truth. Claude Hopkins once wrote five pages of solid text for Schlitz beer. In a few months, Schlitz moved up from fifth place to first. I once wrote a page of solid text for Good Luck Margarine, with most gratifying results. 26

Research shows that readership falls off rapidly up to fifty words of copy, but drops very little between fifty and 500 words. In my first Rolls-Royce advertisement I used 719 words—piling one fascinating fact on another. In the last paragraph I wrote, "People who feel diffident about driving a Rolls-Royce can buy a Bentley." Judging from the number of motorists who picked up the word "diffident" and bandied it about, I concluded that the advertisement was thoroughly read. In the next one I used 1,400 words. 27

Every advertisement should be a *complete* sales pitch for your product. It is unrealistic to assume that consumers will read a *series* of advertisements for the same product. You should shoot the works in every advertisement, on the assumption that it is the only chance you will ever have to sell your product to the reader—*now or never.* 28

Says Dr. Charles Edwards of the graduate School of Retailing at New York University, "The more facts you tell, the more you sell. An advertisement's chance for success invariably increases as the number of pertinent merchandise facts included in the advertisement increases." 29

In my first advertisement for Puerto Rico's Operation Bootstrap, I used 961 words, and persuaded Beardsley Ruml to sign them. Fourteen thousand readers clipped the coupon from this advertisement, and scores of them later established factories in Puerto Rico. The greatest professional satisfaction I have yet had is to see the prosperity in Puerto Rican communities which had lived on the edge of starvation for four hundred years before I wrote my advertisement. If I had confined myself to a few vacuous generalities, nothing would have happened. 30

We have even been able to get people to read long copy about gasoline. One of our Shell advertisements contained 617 words, and 22 percent of male readers read more than half of them. 31

Vic Schwab tells the story of Max Hart (of Hart, Schaffner & Marx) and his advertising manager, George L. Dyer, arguing about long copy. Dyer said, "I'll bet you ten dollars I can write a newspaper page of solid type and you'd read every word of it." 32

Hart scoffed at the idea. "I don't have to write a line of it to prove 33 my point," Dyer replied. "I'll only tell you the headline: 'This page is all about Max Hart.'"

Advertisers who put coupons in their advertisements *know* that short copy doesn't sell. In split-run tests, long copy invariably outsells short copy.   34

Do I hear someone say that no copywriter can write long advertisements unless his media department gives him big spaces to work with? This question should not arise, because the copywriter should be consulted before planning the media schedule.   35

3. You should always include testimonials in your copy. The reader finds it easier to believe the endorsement of a fellow consumer than the puffery of an anonymous copywriter. Says Jim Young, one of the best copywriters alive today, "Every type of advertiser has the same problem; namely to be believed. The mail-order man knows nothing so potent for this purpose as the testimonial, yet the general advertiser seldom uses it."   36

Testimonials from celebrities get remarkably high readership, and if they are honestly written they still do not seem to provoke incredulity. The better known the celebrity, the more readers you will attract. We have featured Queen Elizabeth and Winston Churchill in "Come to Britain" advertisements, and we were able to persuade Mrs. Roosevelt to make television commercials for Good Luck Margarine. When we advertised charge accounts for Sears, Roebuck, we reproduced the credit card of Ted Williams, "recently traded by Boston to Sears."   37

Sometimes you can cast your entire copy in the form of a testimonial. My first advertisement for Austin cars took the form of a letter from an "anonymous diplomat" who was sending his son to Groton with money he had saved driving an Austin—a well-aimed combination of snobbery and economy. Alas, a perspicacious *Time* editor guessed that I was the anonymous diplomat, and asked the headmaster of Groton to comment. Dr. Crocker was so cross that I decided to send my son to Hotchkiss.   38

4. Another profitable gambit is to give the reader helpful advice, or service. It hooks about 75 percent more readers than copy which deals entirely with the product.   39

One of our Rinso advertisements told housewives how to remove stains. It was better read (Starch) and better remembered (Gallup) than any detergent advertisement in history. Unfortunately, however, it forgot to feature Rinso's main selling promise—that Rinso washes whiter; for this reason it should never have run.[2]   40

[2] The photograph showed several different kinds of stain—lipstick, coffee, shoe polish, blood, and so forth. The blood was my own; I am the only copywriter who has ever *bled* for his client.

5. I have never admired the *belles lettres* school of advertising,   41
which reached its pompous peak in Theodore F. MacMann's famous
advertisement for Cadillac, "The Penalty of Leadership," and Ned
Jordan's classic, "Somewhere West of Laramie." Forty years ago the
business community seems to have been impressed by these pieces of
purple prose, but I have always thought them absurd; they did not give
the reader a single *fact*. I share Claude Hopkins's view that "fine writing is a distinct disadvantage. So is unique literary style. They take attention away from the subject."

6. Avoid bombast. Raymond Rubicam's famous slogan for   42
Squibb, "The priceless ingredient of every product is the honor and integrity of its maker," reminds me of my father's advice: when a company boasts about its integrity, or a woman about her virtue, avoid the
former and cultivate the latter.

7. Unless you have some special reason to be solemn and preten-   43
tious, write your copy in the colloquial language which your customers
use in everyday conversation. I have never acquired a sufficiently good
ear for vernacular American to write it, but I admire copywriters who
can pull it off, as in this unpublished pearl from a dairy farmer:

> *Carnation Milk is the best in the land,*
> *Here I sit with a can in my hand.*
> *No tits to pull, no hay to pitch,*
> *Just punch a hole in the son-of-a-bitch.*

It is a mistake to use highfalutin language when you advertise to   44
uneducated people. I once used the word *"Obsolete"* in a headline,
only to discover that 43 percent of housewives had no idea what it
meant. In another headline, I used the word "ineffable," only to discover that I didn't know what it meant myself.

However, many copywriters of my vintage err on the side of un-   45
derestimating the educational level of the population. Philip Hauser,
head of the Sociology Department at the University of Chicago, draws
attention to the changes which are taking place:

> The increasing exposure of the population to formal schooling . . . can be
> expected to effect important changes in . . . the style of advertising. . . .
> Messages aimed at the "average" American on the assumption that he has
> had less than a grade school education are likely to find themselves with a
> declining or disappearing clientele.[3]

Meanwhile, all copywriters should read Dr. Rudolph Flesch's *Art*   46
of Plain Talk. It will persuade them to use short words, short sentences,
short paragraphs, and highly *personal* copy.

---

[3] *Scientific American* (October 1962).

Aldous Huxley, who once tried his hand at writing advertisements, 47
concluded that "any trace of literariness in an advertisement is fatal to
its success. Advertisement writers may not be lyrical, or obscure, or in
any way esoteric. They must be universally intelligible. A good advertisement has this in common with drama and oratory, that it must be
immediately comprehensible and directly moving."[4]

8. Resist the temptation to write the kind of copy which wins 48
awards. I am always gratified when I win an award, but most of the
campaigns which produce *results* never win awards, because they don't
draw attention to themselves.

The juries that bestow awards are never given enough information 49
about the *results* of the advertisements they are called upon to judge.
In the absence of such information, they rely on their opinions, which
are always warped toward the highbrow.

9. Good copywriters have always resisted the temptation to *enter-* 50
tain. Their achievement lies in the number of new products they get off
to a flying start. In a class by himself stands Claude Hopkins, who is to
advertising what Escoffier is to cooking. By today's standards, Hopkins
was an unscrupulous barbarian, but technically he was the supreme
master. Next I would place Raymond Rubicam, George Cecil, and
James Webb Young, all of whom lacked Hopkins's ruthless salesmanship, but made up for it by their honesty, by the broader range of their
work, and by their ability to write civilized copy when the occasion required it. Next I would place John Caples, the mail-order specialist
from whom I have learned much.

These giants wrote their advertisements for newspapers and maga- 51
zines. It is still too early to identify the best writers for television.

QUESTIONS ON CONTENT

1. Why does Ogilvy believe that an ad's headline is so important?

2. Explain the power of "free" and "new." What are some of the other
words and phrases that work wonders mentioned by Ogilvy? Can you
add any words or phrases to his list?

3. What, according to Ogilvy, are the key points to keep in mind when
composing a headline for an advertisement? What recommendations
does he offer for body copy?

4. How long does Ogilvy think an ad's copy should be? Does the market research back him up on this point? Do you think his advice is as
valid today as it was in 1963? Explain.

[4] *Essays Old And New* (Harper & Brothers, 1927). Charles Lamb and Byron also
wrote advertisements. So did Bernard Shaw, Hemingway, Marquand, Sherwood
Anderson, and Faulkner—none of them with any degree of success.

5. Ogilvy believes that one of the greatest sins a copywriter can commit is to be a bore. He tells copywriters to "tell the truth, but make the truth fascinating." What advice does Ogilvy offer to help novice copywriters avoid being boring?

QUESTIONS ON RHETORIC

1. For what audience did Ogilvy write his essay? (Glossary: *Audience*)

2. Ogilvy believes that unless there are extenuating circumstances, the tone of an ad's copy should be conversational. What is Ogilvy's tone in this essay? (Glossary: *Tone*) Point to specific aspects of his writing that led you to this conclusion. Is his tone appropriate for his subject and his audience?

3. In paragraph 46, Ogilvy recommends Dr. Rudolph Flesch's book *Art of Plain Talk* to all copywriters. Has Flesch's book influenced Ogilvy? Explain.

4. This essay is sprinkled with examples from Ogilvy's own advertising work. Do these examples serve the same function as "testimonials"? Explain.

VOCABULARY

prospects (5)	testimonials (36)	vintage (45)
inject (8)	puffery (36)	esoteric (47)
provocative (12)	incredulity (37)	bestow (49)
glancers (13)	bombast (42)	warped (49)
whimsical (19)	pretentious (43)	unscrupulous (50)
bandied (27)	ineffable (44)	

WRITING TOPICS

1. Collect five or six different headlines from advertisements in magazines, and examine them according to Ogilvy's guidelines for headline writing. Write an essay in which you discuss the headlines' adherence to Ogilvy's suggestions and their effectiveness as headlines.

2. Ogilvy does not approve of copywriters who produce "tricky" headlines, headlines with puns, literary allusions, and other obscurities. Although Ogilvy does not approve of the practice, such ads sometimes work and work well. Collect several headlines that make use of a "trick," and write an essay in which you argue for or against their use.

3. Using Ogilvy's directions, write the headline and body copy of an advertisement for a product of your choice. You might consider one of the following:

    shampoo
    airline

fruit
car
jeans
soft drink
computer
jogging shoes

4. Many advertisements on television today—especially ones like those for Wendy's, Ryder Trucks, and Federal Express—entertain the viewer as they promote various products and services. Yet Ogilvy has said, "Good copywriters have always resisted the temptation to *entertain*" (50). Are ads that entertain apt to be less successful? If so, why? Write an essay in which you clearly state your position on the issue of entertainment and support it with examples from your own experience.

4

It's Natural! It's Organic! Or Is It?

CONSUMERS UNION

"Natural" and "organic" are two advertising buzz words of the 1980s, products of the health and fitness movement that is sweeping the country. But these two words have the Consumers Union worried because products labeled "natural" and/or "organic" often don't deliver what customers expect. In the following essay, the Consumers Union, a nonprofit organization that provides "consumers with information and counsel on consumer goods and services," examines the words "natural" and "organic" and how they are being used by advertisers. To educate consumers, the Union classifies a number of the deceptive advertising techniques used by manufacturers and advertising agencies.

"No artificial flavors or colors!" reads the Nabisco advertisement in *Progressive Grocer,* a grocery trade magazine. "And research shows that's exactly what consumers are eager to buy."

The ad, promoting Nabisco's *Sesame Wheats* as "a natural whole wheat cracker," might raise a few eyebrows among thoughtful consumers of Nabisco's *Wheat Thins* and *Cheese Nips,* which contain artificial colors, or of its *Ginger Snaps* and *Oreo Cookies,* which have artificial flavors. But Nabisco has not suddenly become a champion of "natural" foods. Like other giants of the food industry, the company is merely keeping its eye on what will produce a profit.

Nabisco's trade ad, which was headlined "A Natural for Profits," is simply a routine effort by a food processor to capitalize on the concerns that consumers have about the safety of the food they buy.

Supermarket shelves are being flooded with "natural" products, some of them containing a long list of chemical additives. And some products that never did contain additives have suddenly sprouted "natural" or "no preservative" labels. Along with the new formulations and labels have come higher prices, since the food industry has realized that consumers are willing to pay more for products they think are especially healthful.

The mass merchandising of "natural" foods is a spillover onto su-   5
permarket shelves of a phenomenon once confined to health-food
stores, as major food manufacturers enter what was once the exclusive
territory of small entrepreneurs. Health-food stores were the first to
foster and capitalize on the growing consumer interest in nutrition and
are still thriving. Along with honey-sweetened snacks, "natural" vitamins, and other "natural" food products, the health-food stores frequently feature "organic" foods.

Like the new merchandise in supermarkets, the products sold at   6
health-food stores carry the implication that they're somehow better
for you—safer or more nutritious. In this report, we'll examine that
premise, looking at both "natural" foods, which are widely sold, and
"organic" foods, which are sold primarily at health-food stores. While
the terms "natural" and "organic" are often used loosely, "organic"
generally refers to the way food is grown (without pesticides or chemical fertilizers) and "natural" to the character of the ingredients (no
preservatives or artificial additives) and to the fact that the food product has undergone minimal processing.

Langendorf Natural Lemon Flavored Creme Pie contains no cream.   7
It does contain sodium propionate, certified food colors, sodium benzoate, and vegetable gum.

That's natural?   8

Yes indeed, says L.A. Cushman, Jr., chairman of American Bak-   9
eries Co., the Chicago firm that owns Langendorf. The word "natural," he explains, modifies "lemon flavored," and the pie contains oil
from lemon rinds. "The lemon flavor," Cushman states "comes from
the natural lemon flavor as opposed to artificial lemon flavor, assuming there is such a thing as artificial lemon flavor."

Welcome to the world of natural foods.   10

You can eat your "natural" way from one end of the supermarket   11
to the other. Make yourself a sandwich of *Kraft Cracker Barrel Natural Cheddar Cheese* on *Better Way Natural Whole Grain Wheat Nugget
Bread* spread with *Autumn Natural Margarine.* Wash it down with *Anheuser-Busch Natural Light Beer* or *Rich-Life Natural Orange Nutri-
Pop.* Snack on any number of brands of "natural" potato chips and
"natural" candy bars. And don't exclude your pet: Feed your dog
Gravy Train Dog Food With Natural Beef Flavor or, if it's a puppy, try
Blue Mountain Natural Style Puppy Food.

The "natural" bandwagon doesn't end at the kitchen. You can   12
bathe in *Batherapy Natural Mineral Bath* (sodium sesquicarbonate,
isopropyl myristate, fragrance, D & C Green No. 5, D & C Yellow No.
10 among its ingredients), using *Queen Helene "All-Natural" Amino
Peptide Shampoo* (propylene glycol, hydroxyethyl cellulose, methyl-

paraben, D & C Red No. 3, D & C Brown No. 1) and *Organic Aid Natural Clear Soaps*. Then, if you're so inclined, you can apply *Naturade Conditioning Mascara with Natural Protein* (stearic acid, PVP, butylene glycol, sorbitan sesquioleate, triethanolamine, imidazolidinyl urea, methylparaben, propylparaben).

At its ridiculous extreme, the "natural" ploy extends to furniture, cigarettes, denture adhesives, and shoes.   13

The word "natural" does not have to be synonymous with "ripoff." Over the years, the safety of many food additives has been questioned. And a consumer who reads labels carefully can in fact find some foods in supermarkets that have been processed without additives.   14

But the word "natural" does not guarantee that. All too often, as the above examples indicate, the word is used more as a key to higher profits. Often, it implies a health benefit that does not really exist.   15

Co-op News, the publication of the Berkeley Co-op, the nation's largest consumer-cooperative store chain, reported on "two fifteen-ounce cans of tomato sauce, available side-by-side" at one of its stores. One sauce, called *Health Valley*, claimed on its label to have "no citric acid, no sugars, no preservatives, no artificial colors or flavors." There were none of those ingredients in the Co-op's house brand, either, but their absence was hardly worth noting on the label, since canned tomato sauce almost never contains artificial colors or flavors and doesn't need preservatives after being heated in the canning process. The visible difference between the two products was price, not ingredients. The *Health Valley* tomato sauce was selling for 85 cents; the Co-op house brand, for only 29 cents.   16

One supermarket industry consultant estimates that 7 percent of all processed food products now sold are touted as "natural." And that could be just the beginning. A Federal Trade Commission report noted that 63 percent of people polled in a survey agreed with the statement, "Natural foods are more nutritious than other foods." Thirty-nine percent said they regularly buy food because it is "natural," and 47 percent said they were willing to pay 10 percent more for a food that is "natural."   17

According to those who have studied the trend, the consumer's desire for "natural" foods goes beyond the fear of specific chemicals. "There is a mistrust of technology," says Howard Moskowitz, a taste researcher and consultant to the food industry. "There is a movement afoot to return to simplicity in all aspects of life." A spokeswoman for Lever Bros., one of the nation's major food merchandisers, adds: " 'Natural' is a psychological thing of everyone wanting to get out of the industrial world."   18

Because consumers are acting out of such vague, undefined feel-   19 ings, they aren't sure what they should be getting when they buy a product labeled "natural." William Wittenberg, president of Grandma's Food Inc., comments: "Manufacturers and marketers are making an attempt to appeal to a consumer who feels he should be eating something natural, but doesn't know why. I think the marketers of the country in effect mirror back to the people what they want to hear. People have to look to themselves for their own protection." Grandma's makes a *Whole Grain Date Filled Fruit 'n Oatmeal Bar* labeled "naturally Good Flavor." The ingredients include "artificial flavor."

"Natural" foods are not necessarily preferable nor, as we have   20
seen, necessarily natural.

Consider "natural" potato chips. They are often cut thick from un-   21
peeled potatoes, packaged without preservatives in heavy foil bags with fancy lettering, and sold at a premium price. Sometimes, such chips include "sea salt," a product whose advantage over conventional "land" salt has not been demonstrated. The packaging is intended to give the impression that "natural" potato chips are less of a junk food than regular chips. But nutritionally there is no difference. Both are made from the same food, the potato, and both have been processed so that they are high in salt and in calories.

Sometimes the "natural" products may have ingredients you'd pre-   22
fer to avoid. *Quaker 100% Natural* cereal, for example, contains 24 percent sugars, a high percentage, considering it's not promoted as a sugared cereal. (*Kellogg's Corn Flakes* has 7.8 percent sugar.) Many similar "natural" granola-type cereals have oil added, giving them a much higher fat content than conventional cereals.

Taste researcher Moskowitz notes that food processors are "trying   23
to signal to the consumer a sensory impact that can be called natural." Two of the most popular signals, says Moskowitz, are honey and coconut. But honey is just another sugar, with no significant nutrients other than calories, and coconut is especially high in saturated fats.

While many processed foods are less nutritious than their fresh   24
counterparts, processing can sometimes help foods: Freezing preserves nutrients that could be lost if fresh foods are not consumed quickly; pasteurization kills potentially dangerous bacteria in milk. Some additives are also both safe and useful. Sorbic acid, for instance, prevents the growth of potentially harmful molds in cheese and other products, and sodium benzoate has been used for more than 70 years to prevent the growth of microorganisms in acidic foods.

"Preservative" has become a dirty word, to judge from the number   25
of "no preservative" labels on food products. Calcium propionate might sound terrible on a bread label, but this mildew-retarding substance occurs naturally in both raisins and Swiss cheese. "Bread with-

out preservatives could well cost you more than bread with them," says Vernal S. Packard Jr., a University of Minnesota nutrition professor. "Without preservatives, the bread gets stale faster; it may go moldy with the production of hazardous aflatoxin. And already we in the United States return [to producers] 100 million pounds of bread each year—this in a world nagged by hunger and malnutrition."

Nor are all "natural" substances safe. Sassafras tea was banned by 26
the U.S. Food and Drug Administration several years ago because it contains safrole, which has produced liver cancer in laboratory animals. Kelp, a seaweed that is becoming increasingly fashionable as a dietary supplement, can have a high arsenic content. Aflatoxin, produced by a mold that can grow on improperly stored peanuts, corn, and grains, is a known carcinogen.

To complicate matters, our palates have become attuned to many 27
unnatural tastes. "We don't have receptors on our tongues that signal "natural," says taste researcher Moskowitz. He points out, for instance, that a panel of consumers would almost certainly reject a natural lemonade "in favor of a lemonade scientifically designed to taste natural. If you put real lemon, sugar, and water together, people would reject it as harsh. They are used to flavors developed by flavor houses." Similarly, Moskowitz points out, many consumers say that for health reasons they prefer less salty food—but the results of various taste tests have contradicted this, too.

In the midst of all this confusion, it's not surprising that the food 28
industry is having a promotional field day. Companies are using various tactics to convince the consumer that a food product is "natural"—and hence preferable. Here are some of the most common:

THE INDETERMINATE MODIFIER. Use a string of adjectives and claim 29
that "natural" modifies only the next adjective in line, not the product itself. Take *Pillsbury Natural Chocolate Flavored Chocolate Chip Cookies.* Many a buyer might be surprised to learn from the fine print that these cookies contain artificial flavor, as well as the chemical antioxidant BHA. But Pillsbury doesn't bat an eyelash at this. "We're not trying to mislead anybody," says a company representative, explaining that the word "natural" modifies only "chocolate flavored," while the artificial flavoring is vanilla. Then why not call the product "Chocolate Chip Cookies with Natural Chocolate Flavoring"? "From a labeling point of view, we're trying to use a limited amount of space" was the answer.

INNOCENCE BY ASSOCIATION. Put nature on your side. *Life Cinnamon* 30
Flavor High Protein Cereal, a Quaker Oats Co. product, contains BHA and artificial color, among other things. How could the company

imply the cereal was "natural" and still be truthful? One series of *Life* boxes solves the problem neatly. The back panel has an instructional lesson for children entitled "Nature." The box uses the word "Nature" four times and "natural" once—but never actually to describe the cereal inside. Other products surround themselves with a "natural" aura by picturing outdoor or farm scenes on their packages.

THE "PRINTER'S ERROR." From time to time, readers send us food   31
wrappers making a "natural" claim directly contradicted by the ingredients list. We have, for example, received a batch of individually wrapped *Devonsheer* crackers with a big red label saying: "A Natural Product, no preservatives." The ingredients list includes "calcium propionate (to retard spoilage)."

How could a manufacturer defend that? "At a given printing, the   32
printer was instructed to remove 'no preservatives, natural product' when we changed ingredients, but he didn't do it," says Curtis Marshall, vice president for operations at Devonsheer Melba Corp.

THE BEST DEFENSE. Don't defend yourself; attack the competition.   33
Sometimes the use of the word "natural" is, well, just plain unnatural. Take the battle that has been brewing between the nation's two largest beer makers, Miller Brewing Co. and Anheuser-Busch. The latter's product, *Anheuser-Busch Natural Light Beer,* has been the object of considerable derision by Miller.

Miller wants the word "natural" dropped from Anheuser-Busch's   34
advertisements because beers are "highly processed, complex products, made with chemical additives and other components not in their natural form."

Anheuser-Busch has responded only with some digs at Miller,   35
charging Miller with using artificial foam stabilizer and adding an industrial enzyme instead of natural malt to reduce the caloric content of its *Miller Lite* beer.

No victor has yet emerged from the great beer war, but the industry   36
is obviously getting edgy.

"Other brewers say it's time for the two companies to shut up," the   37
Wall Street Journal reported. "One thing they [the other brewers] are worried about, says William T. Elliot, president of C. Schmidt & Sons, a Philadelphia brewery, is all the fuss over ingredients. Publicity about that issue is disclosing to beer drinkers that their suds include sulfuric acid, calcium sulfate, alginic acid, or amyloglucosidase."

THE NEGATIVE PITCH. Point out in big letters on the label that the prod-   38
uct doesn't contain something it wouldn't contain anyway. The "no

artificial preservatives" label stuck on a jar of jam or jelly is true and always has been—since sugar is all the preservative jams and jellies need. Canned goods, likewise, are preserved in their manufacture—by the heat of the canning process. Then there is the "no cholesterol" claim of vegetable oils, margarines, and even (in a radio commercial) canned pineapple. Those are also true, but beside the point, since cholesterol is found only in animal products.

What can be done about such all-but-deceptive practices? One 39 might suggest that the word "natural" is so vague as to be inherently deceptive, and therefore should not be available for promotional use. Indeed, the FTC staff suggested precisely that a few years ago but later backed away from the idea. The California legislature last year passed a weak bill defining the word "organic," but decided that political realities argued against tackling the word "natural."

"If we had included the word 'natural' in the bill, it most likely 40 would not have gotten out of the legislature," says one legislative staff member. "When you've got large economic interests in certain areas, the tendency is to guard those interests very carefully."

Under the revised FTC staff proposal, which had not been acted on 41 by the full commission as we went to press, the word "natural" can be used if the product has undergone only minimal processing and doesn't have artificial ingredients. That would eliminate the outright frauds, as well as the labeling of such products as Lever Bros.' *Autumn Natural Margarine,* which obviously has been highly processed from its original vegetable-oil state. But the FTC proposal might run into difficulty in defining exactly what "minimal processing" means. And it would also allow some deceptive implications. For instance, a product containing honey might be called "natural," while a food with refined sugar might not, thus implying that honey is superior to other sugars, which it is not.

A law incorporating similar regulations went into effect in Maine 42 at the beginning of this year. If a product is to be labeled "natural" and sold in Maine, it must have undergone only minimal processing and have no additives, preservatives, or refined additions such as white flour and sugar.

So far, according to John Michael, the state legislator who spon- 43 sored the bill, food companies have largely ignored the law, but he expects the state to start issuing warnings this summer.

QUESTIONS ON CONTENT

1. Why are Americans eager to purchase "natural" foods? Are foods that carry the label *natural* a ripoff? Explain.

MADE OF THE FINEST FIBER

If you're like most people who eat right, you probably give high fiber high priority.

And like most people, when you think of fiber, you probably automatically think of bran cereals.

Well, there's another good source of dietary fiber you should know about. Delicious Campbell's® Bean with Bacon Soup.

In fact, Campbell's has four soups that are high in fiber.

And you can see from the chart that follows exactly how each one measures up to bran cereals.

So now when you think of fiber, you don't have to think about

FIBER IN A SUGGESTED SERVING			
CAMPBELL'S SOUP		**BRAN CEREALS**	
Bean with Bacon	9g	100% Brans	11g
Split Pea with Ham	6g	40% Brans	6g
Green Pea	5g	Raisin Brans	5g
Low Sodium Green Pea	7g	Others	5–10g
This comparison includes soluble and insoluble fiber			

having it just at breakfast.

Instead, you can do your body good any time during the day. With a hot, hearty bowl of one of these Campbell's Soups.

You just might feel better for it—right to the very fiber of your being.

CAMPBELL'S SOUP IS GOOD FOOD

Campbell's has a full line of low sodium soups for those people who are on a salt-restricted diet or have a concern about sodium.

2. Why are more manufacturers getting into the natural-food business? Why do they use the term *natural* in their products' names and in advertising for these products?

3. What relationship, if any, exists between natural and nutritious?

4. Many people believe that the processing of foods is necessarily bad. What, according to the Consumers Union, are some benefits of processing?

5. How, according to taste researcher Howard Moskowitz, have consumers' tastes complicated the issue of natural and artificial flavors?

6. What are the various tactics that companies use to convince potential consumers that their products are "natural"? How does each tactic work?

7. What regulations does Consumers Union believe ought to be imposed on current "all-but-deceptive" advertising practices?

8. The latest buzz word of the "health-food" market is *fiber*. Analyze the Campbell's ad on page 236. How do you suppose the Consumers Union would respond?

QUESTIONS ON RHETORIC

1. What is Consumers Union's purpose in this essay? (Glossary: *Purpose*)

2. In paragraph 6 Consumers Union defines both *natural* and *organic*. Why is it necessary for them to give these definitions?

3. The writers use examples both to illustrate and to support their generalizations about the use of the words *natural* and *organic* in the advertisements. How effective did you find these examples? Which ones seemed to work best? Why?

4. How is this essay organized? You may find it helpful to make a scratch outline of the essay so that you can see the overall structure.

VOCABULARY

trade (1)	bandwagon (12)	palates (27)
foster (5)	ploy (13)	derision (33)
implication (6)	touted (17)	
premise (6)	carcinogen (26)	

WRITING TOPICS

1. What for you are the connotations of the words *natural* and *organic?* Do you believe, as some have claimed, that these words are inherently deceptive? Write an essay in which you argue for or against the banning of these words from advertising.

2. Collect five or six print advertisements that use the word *natural*, and analyze each one carefully. Which of the Consumers Union's

"tactics of deception" do they employ? What benefits are implied in each ad? Do you think the advertisers are trying to deceive you? Write an essay in which you present your analysis and state your conclusions.

3. Spend some time in your local supermarket looking at the messages printed on a variety of products. Do you find other words that manufacturers and advertisers are using in much the same way they use *natural* and *organic?* Write an essay in which you discuss your findings.

5
Tell Me, Pretty Billboard

NOEL PERRIN

Noel Perrin is a New Yorker by birth and has spent much of his life teaching at Dartmouth College, yet he is most widely known for his essays on the difficulties and rewards of country living. These country pieces, which he calls "essays of a sometime farmer," have been collected in First Person Rural *and* Second Person Rural. *Perrin's interest in ordinary things and his professional concern with language come together in "Tell Me, Pretty Billboard." Which of us hasn't sometimes wanted to talk back to the unhearing pitchman on a television or radio commercial? Perrin goes even further; in this essay he not only talks to signs and packages but gets them to talk back to him.*

D runks talk to lamp posts. Little girls in Victorian novels talk to 1
imaginary playmates. I talk to the writing on packages and signs.

It, of course, has been talking to me ever since I learned to read, 2
but it is only recently that I have started answering. Most of my life I
have been a good consumer, like any other American, keeping my
mouth shut and my ears open. Quietly I pushed my cart down supermarket aisles, listening to the mechanical music and being influenced
by point-of-sale displays. Quietly I relaxed at home, watching tele-
shapes that couldn't see me, and hearing electronic voices that I could
turn off but not answer. It was all perfectly normal and perfectly one-
way. Never was I disturbed by my lack of I-thou relationships with
vending machines, or by the fact that though a girl on a poster could
stir me, there was no hope of my stirring her.

About a year ago, though, I suddenly found myself wanting to ask 3
a cigarette machine in Burlington, Vermont, why it charged more for
cigarettes than the human beings in the drug store across the street.
Hardly two weeks later I had an overwhelming urge to tell an electronic voice in my living room that the "nei" of "neither" may have
been pronounced "nigh" by the Electors of Hanover even after they
moved to England and began speaking the king's English, but the right
way to say it is still "knee." Naturally I couldn't do either.

The urge grew, though, and before I knew it I found myself writing 4 one letter to the company that owned the vending machine—you can sometimes find the address on the side—and another to the network that employed the rexophile announcer.

I promptly got answers from both, but the answers didn't tell me much, except that public relations is a growing field. Both might have been composed by the same man who handles correspondence for my congressman. (I had happened to send him a thoughtful letter about Far Eastern policy that same month.) All three replies had a kind of customized form-letter quality that I assume is designed to give people like me the illusion that we have gotten through when we haven't, except as statistics, or what the network probably calls feedback. The congressman said he valued my opinion, and would keep it in mind. The network said it was delighted to hear from me, and its dictionary approved both the pronunciations I mentioned. The vending machine company said vending machines were very expensive, and tobacco taxes very high. It also said that as I was obviously a thoughtful person, it was sending me a questionnaire to fill out on what kinds of products I would like to see available in vending machines, and a quarter for my trouble.

It was at this point that I turned to fantasy. If dialogue with the economy has to be an illusion, I decided, it might as well be illusion of my own making. The answers would be more interesting. Since then I have been holding frequent conversations with billboards and taped messages and directions on razor-blade packages, and life is bearable again.

I'll give an example. There is a highway sign I sometimes pass in Connecticut which asserts that there are eight friendly inns on a body of water called Lake Waramaug and urges me to stay at one of them. In mere reality it would be difficult to ask that sign how friendliness can be offered as a commodity, like clean towels or room service. For the dweller in fantasy it's a snap. The last time by I had a chat with it which went something like this:

ME: Hello, you friendly sign.

SIGN: (*friendlily*) Hello-alo. That's a nice car you're driving, Mister. I like you. Why don't you take your next left and come on to Lake Waramaug?

ME: Maybe I will. Are all eight of the inns really friendly?

SIGN: Are they? Why, Mister, you don't know what friendship means till you've stayed at Lake Waramaug.

ME: (*suddenly, at 39, struck by doubts*) By gosh, you're right. I don't know. What does friendship mean?

SIGN: At our inns, it means that everybody from the bellhop to the manager is sincerely glad to see you, that we have a relaxed, friendly atmosphere. . . .

ME: Hold it. You can't define a word in terms of itself.   14

SIGN: Oops. I mean a relaxed, *casual* atmosphere where every-   15
thing's very informal, where the bartender smiles as he mixes you a martini, where, well, where everybody from the bellhop to the manager is sincerely glad to see you.

ME: That's great! I love big welcomes. We'll all be real friends,   16
right?

SIGN: (*after a second's hesitation*) Sure. Every guest is a friend.   17

ME: Sign, this is the best news I've had in a long time. It just hap-   18
pens that I'm dead tired, dead broke, and very hungry. A clean bed and a good dinner are just what I need. Which of my new friends shall I stay with?

SIGN: (*icy cold*) Listen, buddy, if you're looking for charity, why   19
don't you try the Traveler's Aid?

ME: When I've got sincere friends all around Lake Waramaug?   20
Why should I?

SIGN: Okay, I walked into that one. So they're not your real friends.   21

ME: But they're still sincerely glad to see me?   22

SIGN: Well, yes, sure. What I meant was that provided you can pay   23
your bill, everybody from the bellhop to the manager feels sin-
cerely glad to see you, whether they personally like you or not; and any employee that can't feel that way gets fired. Fair enough?

ME: You mean you have to be a hypocrite to work at Lake Wara-   24
maug?

SIGN: Look, I'm just a sign, and I'm ten miles back on the road as it   25
is. Why don't you go talk to the man that wrote me?

But I don't do that. Instead I drive on up to Vermont. A few miles   26
from home I stop to buy some groceries. (I was lying when I told the sign I was broke. Unlike hotel keepers, I'm naturally insincere.) The first thing I buy is a package of garden-fresh frozen vegetables.

ME: What does garden-fresh mean, Package?   27

PACKAGE: Just what it says. What's nicer and fresher than a gar-   28
den? (*strikes an attitude*)
> A garden is a lovesome thing, Got wot!
> Rose plot . . .

ME: Listen, I like gardens, too. I just want to know what garden-   29
fresh means on a package of frozen peas.

PACKAGE: If I have to spell it out, it means the peas inside me are as   30
fresh as if you'd gone into your own vegetable garden and picked them right off the pea vines, ten minutes before dinner.

ME: When were the peas inside you picked?   31

PACKAGE: Oh, about six months ago. But they've been *frozen,* Mis-   32
ter. They could just as well have been picked today.

ME: Were they frozen ten minutes after being picked?   33

PACKAGE: It was the same day. We rush them from the fields to the   34
plant. . . .

ME: Ten minutes?   35

PACKAGE: All right, if you're going to be literal about it, the peas   36
inside me are as fresh as if you'd gone into your own vegetable
garden and picked them right off the pea vines within twelve hours
before dinner.

ME: And there has been no deterioration at all during the six   37
months?

PACKAGE: I said they were frozen.   38

ME: Biochemical change ceases entirely when peas are frozen?   39

PACKAGE: It goes a lot slower.   40

ME: But it does occur?   41

PACKAGE: Look, if you don't like frozen foods, grow your own   42
damn peas. *I* don't care.

ME: You are going to answer the question?   43

PACKAGE: (*in a fury*) Sure, there's a little deterioration. But it's well   44
within Department of Agriculture Standards, and. . . .

But at this point the woman at the check-out counter shoves   45
the package in a freezer bag, and I drive on home. My next conversation takes place about a month later, when I'm back in New York,
about to get a cup of coffee out of an automatic machine. There are no
less than five choices, with a button to push for each. I can have
black, sugar only, cream only, sugar and cream or sugar and extra
cream.

ME: Excuse me, but I was wondering why cream is spelled c-r-e-m-e?   46

MACHINE: Perfectly good spelling. The French use it, you know.   47
Voulez-vous un café-créme?

ME: *Oui. Avec sucre.* But why French in New York City?   48

MACHINE: I didn't say it *was* French. I said the French use that   49
spelling. As a matter of fact, it has something to do with trademarks.

ME: I don't follow.   50

MACHINE: Come on, you haven't grown up in America without   51
knowing about trademarks. No company can get exclusive rights to
a word unless they figure out a new spelling. That's why there are
so many. You don't think serious business executives *like* to name
their stuff Wonda Winda or Tas-tee Bitz, do you?

ME: Do you have exclusive rights to c-r-e-m-e? I could swear I'd 52
seen that on some kind of make-up my wife uses.

MACHINE: Sure. That's so your wife won't think her make-up has 53
cream from cows in it. It means a creamy or cream-type prepara-
tion.

ME: But you do mean cream from cows, don't you? 54

MACHINE: I mean it's fresh-made hot coffee, served twenty-four 55
hours a day, which is quite a miracle, when you come to think
of it.

ME: Cream from cows? 56

MACHINE: So it's from soybeans. You know there's a considerable 57
body of medical opinion that thinks cream from cows is pretty dangerous stuff. Bad for the heart. You ought to be down on your
knees thanking me.

ME: (*still upright*) I also know about that study of Irish twin broth- 58
ers, where one brother stayed in Ireland and the other came to the
United States. The ones back home used more butter and cream,
but the margarine-eaters over here had more heart attacks. What
about that?

MACHINE: Easy. There's lots more stresses in American life. 59

ME: And therefore I've got to drink soybean juice in my coffee? 60
Well, why not say plainly that's what you serve, and why? Maybe
you'd pull the trade from the dairy restaurants.

MACHINE: Mister, you think we got room for health lectures on the 61
panel above a lousy pushbutton? C-r-e-m-e fits on the panel,
everybody knows what it means, everybody's happy.

ME: But. . . . 62

MACHINE: (*going right on*) What else could we do? You've got to 63
think about customer recognition. Say we put your phrase—"soybean juice," was it?—on the panel. Does it sound like something to
go in coffee? Or does it confuse the hell out of everybody? Or
maybe you want we should put "soy sauce"? Listen, the stoops we
get would be coming with plates and silverware, looking for the
chow mein.

ME: But. . . . 64

MACHINE: And if we put "Cream substitute made from soybeans— 65
better for you," I ask you, how are we going to get it all on?

ME: But what I've been trying to say is that space is plainly not the 66
whole problem. You've got room to help the customer recognize.
Look at your own panel. I see "White Cross Dairy." There, right
above the c-r-e-m-e. What about that?

MACHINE: (*blushing bright scarlet*) It's not very big type. 67

ME: Interesting phrase, though. 68

MACHINE: Don't say it, I know what you're thinking. To some ex- 69 tent you have to compromise to succeed in business, and that's a fact.

ME: By the way, what's your sugar made of?   70

MACHINE: Sorry, Mister. You'll have to ask the Food and Drug   71
Administration. I just went out of order.

QUESTIONS ON CONTENT

1. What is Perrin's point about advertising in this essay? What makes you say so?

2. What, according to Perrin, was lacking in the three replies that he received to his letters? Why was it lacking?

3. Why does Perrin decide to turn to fantasy? Does fantasy help him?

4. What is the problem that Perrin sees on the billboard for "eight friendly inns" on Lake Waramaug (7)? on the package of "garden-fresh frozen vegetables" (26)? on the choice buttons of the automatic coffee machine (45)? Explain what's involved in each instance.

5. Why might business marketing executives want to invent catchy names for their products? What reason does the coffee vending machine give? What are the trademarks for?

6. Why does the coffee machine blush when Perrin points out the label "White Cross Dairy" on the panel above its buttons?

QUESTIONS ON RHETORIC

1. What advantages does Perrin gain by writing his essay as a series of imaginary dialogues? How else might he have presented his material?

2. Identify the transitional devices that Perrin uses to link his first seven paragraphs and explain how each one works. (Glossary: *Transitions*)

3. Identify particular lines in the fantasy dialogues that reveal Perrin is an English Professor and not just an average or typical consumer. Are most people as sensitive to details and nuances of language as Perrin is?

4. How does Perrin's tone in the fantasy dialogues compare with the tone of the sign, the package, and the machine? In what way does Perrin's tone continue that of the opening paragraph? (Glossary: *Tone*) Does Perrin's tone affect your reading of his criticisms? Explain your response by citing passages from the essay.

VOCABULARY

Victorian (1)   rexophile (4)
commodity (7)   trademarks (49)

WRITING TOPICS

1. Are there any ads today that you find especially irritating? What do you find wrong with each of them? Choose one and rewrite it to make it less objectionable—but no less interesting and effective.

2. Using Perrin's essay as a model, write a fantasy dialogue with a sign, a package, or a machine of your choice. Make sure that your dialogue exposes the problem that you have with the particular item you selected.

3. In paragraph 5, Perrin says that all the replies to his correspondence had a "kind of customized form-letter quality." Have you ever received such letters? How do you feel about them? Why do you suppose that companies and public figures use them? Do the advantages outweigh the disadvantages?

6
Intensify/Downplay

HUGH RANK

Hugh Rank, professor of literature at Governors State University in Park Forest, Illinois, is a member of the Committee on Public Doublespeak (National Council of Teachers of English). His schema "Intensify/Downplay" was developed to help people deal with public persuasion. As Rank explains, "INTENSIFY/DOWNPLAY is a pattern useful to analyze communication, persuasion, and propaganda. All people intensify *(commonly by* repetition, association, composition) *and* downplay *(commonly by* omission, diversion, confusion) *as they communicate in words, gestures, numbers, etc. But, 'professional persuaders' have more training, technology, money, and media access than the average citizen. Individuals can better cope with organized persuasion by recognizing the common ways* how *communication is intensified or downplayed, and by considering* who *is saying* what *to* whom, *with what* intent *and what* result."

The Committee on Public Doublespeak gave Rank's schema the George Orwell Award for 1976. The following is a schematic set of questions that Rank developed, based on his "Intensify/Downplay" schema, to help you analyze advertisements on radio and television and in newspapers and magazines.

INTENSIFY

Repetition

How often have you seen the ad? On TV? In print? Do you recognize the **brand name? trademark? logo? company? package?** What key words or images repeated within ad? Any repetition patterns *(alliteration, anaphora, rhyme)* used? Any **slogan?** Can you hum or sing the **musical theme** or **jingle?** How long has this ad been running? How old were you when you first heard it? (For information on frequency, duration, and costs of ad campaigns, see *Advertising Age.)*

Association

What **"good things"** - already loved or desired by the intended audience - are associated with the product? Any links with basic needs *(food, activity, sex, security)?* With an appeal to save or gain money? With desire for certitude or outside approval (from *religion, science,* or the *"best," "most,"* or *"average" people)?* With desire for a sense of space *(neighborhood, nation, nature)?* With desire for love and belonging *(intimacy, family, groups)?* With other human desires *(esteem, play, generosity, curiosity, creativity, completion)?* Are **"bad things"** - things already hated or feared - stressed, as in a **"scare-and-sell"** ad? Are *problems* presented, with products as *solutions?* Are the speakers (models, endorsers) **authority figures:** people you respect, admire? Or **friend figures:** people you'd like as friends, identify with, or would like to be?

Composition

Look for the basic strategy of "the pitch": Hi . . . TRUST ME . . . YOU NEED . . . HURRY . . . BUY. What are the **attention-getting (HI)** words, images, devices? What are the **confidence-building (TRUST ME)** techniques: words, images, smiles, endorsers, brand names? Is the main **desire-stimulation (YOU NEED)** appeal focused on our benefit-seeking *to get* or *to keep* a "good," or *to avoid* or *to get rid of* a "bad"? Are you the **"target audience"?** If not, who is? Are you part of an unintended audience ? When and where did the ads appear? Are **product claims** made for: *superiority, quantity, beauty, efficiency, scarcity, novelty, stability, reliability, simplicity, utility, rapidity,* or *safety?* Are any **"added values"** suggested or implied by using any of the association techniques (see above)? Is there any **urgency-stressing (HURRY)** by words, movement, pace? Or is a "soft sell" conditioning for *later* purchase? Are there specific **response-triggering** words **(BUY)**: to buy, to do, to call? Or is it conditioning (image building or public relations) to make us *"feel good"* about the company, to get favorable public opinion on *its* side *(against government regulations. laws, taxes)?* **Persuaders seek some kind of response!**

based on Hugh Rank's INTENSIFY/DOWNPLAY schema:

Omission

What "bad" aspects, disadvantages, drawbacks, hazards, have been **omitted** from the ad? Are there some unspoken assumptions? An unsaid story? Are some things implied or suggested, but not explicitly stated? Are there concealed problems concerning the **maker,** the **materials,** the **design,** the **use,** or the **purpose of the product? Are there any unwanted or harmful side effects:** *unsafe, unhealthy, uneconomical, inefficient, unneeded*? Does any **"disclosure law"** exist (or is needed) requiring public warning about a concealed hazard? In the ad, what gets less time, less attention, smaller print? *(Most ads are true, but incomplete.)*

Diversion

What benefits (low cost, high speed, etc.) get high priority in the ad's claim and promises? Are these **your** priorities? Significant, important to you? Is there any **"bait-and-switch"**? *(Ad stresses low cost, but the actual seller switches buyer's priority to high quality.)* Does ad divert focus from **key issues,** important things *(e.g., nutrition, health, safety)*? Does ad focus on **side-issues,** unmeaningful trivia *(common in parity products)*? Does ad divert attention from your other choices, other options: buy something else, use less, use less often, rent, borrow, share, do without? *(Ads need not show other choices, but you should know them.)*

Confusion

Are the words clear or ambiguous? Specific or vague? Are claims and promises absolute, or are there qualifying words *("may help," "some")*? Is the claim measurable? Or is it **"puffery"**? *(Laws permit most "sellers's talk" of such general praise and subjective opinions.)* Are the words common, understandable, familiar? Uncommon? Jargon? Any parts difficult to "translate" or explain to others? Are analogies clear? Are comparisons within the same kind? Are examples related? Typical? Adequate? Enough examples? Any contradictions? Inconsistencies? Errors? Are there frequent changes, variations, revisions *(in size, price, options, extras, contents, packaging)*? Is it too complex: too much, too many? Disorganized? Incoherent? Unsorted? Any confusing statistics? Numbers? Do you know exact costs? Benefits? Risks? Are **your own goals,** priorities, and desires clear or vague? Fixed or shifting? Simple or complex? *(Confusion can also exist within us as well as within an ad. If any confusion exists: slow down, take care.)*

DOWNPLAY

QUESTIONS ON CONTENT

1. What does Rank mean by "professional persuaders"?

2. What are the three ways persuaders intensify? Explain with examples how each way works.

3. What are the three ways persuaders downplay? Explain with examples how each way works.

4. Is it possible for someone to intensify and downplay at the same time? Explain.

QUESTIONS ON RHETORIC

1. Why did Rank develop his "Intensify/Downplay" schema? (Glossary: *Purpose*)

2. How has he used classification to achieve his purpose? (Glossary: *Division and Classification*)

VOCABULARY

logo	assumptions
slogan	explicitly
certitude	analogies

WRITING TOPICS

1. Study the ads that appear on pp. 250–253 (or other ads, if your instructor wishes). Find examples of intensifying and of downplaying in each. In a brief essay, describe your findings.

2. Real estate advertisements are often deliberately designed to manipulate potential buyers. For example, one language analyst noted that in his home town "adorable" meant "small," "eat-in kitchen" meant "no dining room," "handyman's special" meant "portion of building still standing," "by appointment only" meant "expensive," and "starter home" meant "cheap." Analyze the language used in the real estate advertisements in your local newspaper. Does the real estate that one company offers sound better to you than that offered by another company?

The ones to watch wear the one to watch.

Today's trendsetters don't have time for the ordinary.
Perhaps that's why so many of them are wearing the watch that will
shape the future of time: the Rado Diastar® "Anatom®."
The watch has been molded to anatomically fit the wrist,
unlike any you've worn before. The scratchproof sapphire crystal
and titanium carbide case top are among the hardest substances on
earth. So, as time goes by, your Anatom will continue to look like new.
Style-setters in Europe have been choosing Rado for more than 20
years. In fact, more Swiss buy Rado than any other quality Swiss watch.
Try one on. Feel it curve around your wrist. And discover what a
difference it makes when your watch doesn't have to go
through life with a straight face.
Available in a variety of styles at fine jewelry and selected
department stores. From $850. For free color brochure, contact:
Rado Watch Co., Inc., 1140 Avenue of the Americas,
New York, NY 10036, (212) 575-0920.

RADO
The one to watch.

Swiss Made

See Reader Service Card after page 172.

The idea that one could do something with money besides make it and spend it didn't seriously occur to me until two years ago. I'd just come out of a divorce (no alimony) and realized I might be responsible for <u>myself</u> the rest of my life! Well, from that moment on I began to save. From a not spectacular salary, I've now got an IRA, several shares of "safe" stocks, a few <u>not</u> so safe ones, plus (almost) the down-payment on a condo. My favorite magazine says making money grow is just as intriguing as making anything <u>else</u> grow and they give me helpful advice. I love that magazine. I guess you could say I'm That COSMOPOLITAN Girl.

© 1985, The Hearst Corporation

Photographed by Francesco Scavullo

One of my most satisfying relationships is with a magazine.

COSMOPOLITAN®

A PUBLICATION OF THE HEARST CORPORATION

"BETWEEN MY BREAKFAST AND THE WALL STREET JOURNAL, I GET ALL MY DAILY REQUIREMENTS."

WILLIAM D. SMITHBURG, CHAIRMAN & CEO, QUAKER OATS COMPANY

"To start my day, I need a good, balanced breakfast. But to start my business day, I need my copy of The Wall Street Journal.

"The Journal gives me all the business information and background I need. It's a reservoir of facts, figures and interpretations that keeps me thoroughly informed about the latest developments in every area of business. And being a daily paper devoted to business, The Journal does this better than any other source I know of.

"Reading business magazines once a week would do me as much good as eating breakfast once a week. And the quantity of business information other daily papers give me is a small portion by comparison. So every morning I read The Wall Street Journal.

"That way, when I get my daily business information, I'm sure to get a full serving."

THE WALL STREET JOURNAL.
All the business news you need. When you need it.

Subscribe today, call 800-345-8540 except Hawaii or Alaska. PA 800-662-5180. Or write: 200 Burnett Rd., Chicopee, MA 01021.

WRITING ASSIGNMENTS FOR "ADVERTISING AND LANGUAGE"

1. Have you ever been victimized by the language of advertising? Write an account of the incident. Be sure to analyze and describe how language was used to manipulate you.

2. Think of a product that you have used but that has failed to live up to advertising claims. Write and send a letter to the company explaining why you feel its advertisements have been misleading.

3. You have just been hired by a local real estate firm as an advertising copywriter. Your first assignment is to describe this house:

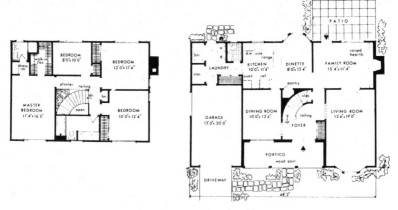

4. Many advertisers seem to believe that by manipulating language they can make any product appeal to consumers. Here is how a very common item might be made to appear desirable by means of advertising:

New! Convenient!
Strike-Ups

The latest scientific advance for smokers since the cigarette lighter. Inexpensive and lightweight, you'll never want to be caught without Strike-Ups.

Why tolerate heavy, expensive cigarette lighters? Why run the risk of soiling your clothes with dangerous lighter fluid? Why be hassled by the technicalities of replacing flints? Why be embarrassed by a lighter that fails when it means everything to you?

Strike-Ups Has a Better Way

Lightweight, 100% reliable, Strike-Ups gives 20, that's right 20, or more lights. Each booklet has its own handy striking surface, right where you need it—up front. A striking surface so large you'll be able to get quick and easy lights even in the darkest places. Strike-Ups comes with a handsome decorator cover. An added feature, at no extra cost, is the plain white surface inside the cover, useful for phone numbers or doodling.

Once you use Strike-Ups, you'll agree, as many Americans have, that you simply can't do without them.

Ask for Strike-Ups at All Stores Where
Quality Smoking Accessories Are Sold.

Write an advertisement for any one of the items listed below; use as many of the advertising tricks or persuasive techniques as you can in order to sell your product.

paper clips
dental floss
toothpicks
rubber bands
salt shakers
staples
bottle caps

5. As more and more of our basic material needs are satisfied, the advertisers must create and push new "needs" so the buying process on which our consumer culture is based can continue. Many of these new "needs" are created by exploitative appeals to values we all cherish or even hold sacred. For example, the Gino's fast-food chain used the word *freedom* to sell its food: "Freedom of Choice—French Fries or Onion Rings." The word *love* is another highly exploited device of advertisers.

Jerry Rubin once said, "How can I say 'I love you' when 'Cars love Shell'?" Here are some other examples:

"Canada Dry tastes like love."

"Hello. I'm Catherine Denueve. When somebody loves me, I'm always surprised. But I don't want to be told. I prefer gestures. Like—Chanel No. 5."

Olympic Gold Medal winner Mark Spitz: "You know what's a great feeling? Giving someone you love a gift. The Schick Flexamatic is a great gift."

A beautiful woman in a trench coat stands alone in the fog on a waterfront. She says, "I like men. Even when they're unkind to me. But men are men. They need love. They need understanding. And they need English Leather."

A good-looking man says, "I know what girls need. They need love. And love's a little color." A girl appears and the man starts applying makeup to her face. The announcer says, "Love's a Little Color isn't makeup. It's only a little color."

"Love is being a nurse. Learn all about professional nursing by writing to. . . ."

In each of these ads, a product is being sold by using the affective connotations of the word *love*—in other words, the word *love* (which ought to be sacred) is being exploited for profits.

Collect additional examples of the word *love* being used for commercial or promotional purposes. Write an essay in which you discuss the ways the word is being used as well as the possible effects on its meaning that this widespread usage may have.

6. Some people believe that advertising performs a useful service to consumers, and that most consumers know enough not to be taken in by half-truths and exaggerations. Do you agree? Why, or why not? If you agree, what benefits do we receive either directly or indirectly from advertising? Write an essay in which you clearly support your position on this issue.

7. Businessmen are very conscious of the connotations of the names they give their products. Automobile manufacturers draw heavily on animal names—Impala, Pinto, Cougar, Mustang, Thunderbird, Jaguar, Cricket, Skylark, and Charger—to suggest the strength, size, and speed of the various models. If an automobile can be named Cobra, why not Rattler or Sidewinder? Make up a brand name with unappealing connotations, and write an advertisement of a paragraph or two for the product—for instance, the Buick Buffalo, Weasel, or Ostrich.

8. Many product names are chosen because of their connotative or suggestive values. For example, the name *Tide* for the detergent suggests the power of the ocean tides and the rhythmic surge of cleansing waters, the name *Pride* for the wax suggests how the user will feel after using the product. Write an essay in which you discuss how the connotations of the brand names in one of the following categories en-

hance the appeal of the various products: cosmetics, deodorants, candy, paint, car batteries, motorcycles, fast-food sandwiches, and so on.

NOTE: Suggested topics for research papers appear on p. 446.

NOTABLE QUOTATIONS

The following quotations are drawn from the articles in this section. They are presented as additional topics for classroom discussion or for writing assignments.

"I had always listened before and many times asked my mother to buy certain products I had seen advertised, but now I was listening and really thinking about what was being said." *Kurth* (4)

"If there is nothing good that can be said about a product that is the truth, perhaps the product should not be sold to kids on TV in the first place." *Kurth* (19)

"Adjectives are used so freely these days that we feel almost naked, robbed, if we don't get at least a couple." *Stevens* (43)

"There is a direct, inverse proportion between the number of adjectives and the number of facts [in advertising]." *Stevens* (43)

"If you haven't done some selling in your headline, you have wasted 80 percent of your client's money." *Ogilvy* (3)

"There is a universal belief in lay circles that people won't read long copy. Nothing could be farther from the truth." *Ogilvy* (26)

"Good copywriters have always resisted the temptation to *entertain*." *Ogilvy* (50)

"Because consumers are acting out of such vague, undefined feelings, they aren't sure what they should be getting when they buy a product labeled 'natural.' " *Consumers Union* (19)

" 'Preservative' has become a dirty word, to judge from the number of 'no preservative' labels on food products." *Consumers Union* (25)

"Most of my life I have been a good consumer, like any other American, keeping my mouth shut and my ears open." *Perrin* (2)

"Individuals can better cope with organized persuasion by recognizing the common ways *how* communication is intensified or downplayed, and by considering *who is saying what to whom, with what intent and what result.*" *Rank* (headnote)

VI
Prejudice and Stereotypes

Effective war propaganda means painting the enemy as something other than human. That way I can hate him. That is why racial and religious epithets are so evil. To call somebody a nigger or a kike or a spic or wop is to rob a human being of his humanity. It is a form of hate, a form of murder.

Charles Osgood

If our language is perhaps an insidious cause for the perpetuation of racism, can it not also become the vehicle which propels us out of the mire of prejudice and hatred?

John A. Black

Our identities, who and what we are or think we are, how others see and define us, are greatly affected by language. The power of language to affect identity is reflected in the fact that language has been used again and again to define and dehumanize individuals or groups of individuals into submission.

Haig A. Bosmajian

1
The Language of Prejudice

GORDON ALLPORT

In this selection from The Nature of Prejudice, *Gordon Allport examines the connection between language and prejudice. Language plays a major role in the development and continuation of prejudice because human thinking is intimately linked to language. Allport identifies and explains some of the specific ways in which language, often very subtly and inadvertently, induces and shapes prejudice. Of particular interest to Allport are the labels—Jew, reactionary, jock, cripple—that we use to categorize people. Unfortunately, such labels tend to magnify one attribute while masking many other perhaps equally important ones.*

Without words we should scarcely be able to form categories at all. A dog perhaps forms rudimentary generalizations, such as small-boys-are-to-be avoided—but this concept runs its course on the conditioned reflex level, and does not become the object of thought as such. In order to hold a generalization in mind for reflection and recall, for identification and for action, we need to fix it in words. Without words our world would be, as William James said, an "empirical sand-heap." 1

NOUNS THAT CUT SLICES

In the empirical world of human beings there are some two and a half billion grains of sand corresponding to our category "the human race." We cannot possibly deal with so many separate entities in our thought, nor can we individualize even among the hundreds whom we encounter in our daily round. We must group them, form clusters. We welcome, therefore, the names that help us to perform the clustering. 2

The most important property of a noun is that it brings many grains of sand into a single pail, disregarding the fact that the same grains might have fitted just as appropriately into another pail. To state the matter technically, a noun *abstracts* from a concrete reality some one feature and assembles different concrete realities only with respect to this one feature. The very act of classifying forces us to 3 overlook all other features, many of which might offer a sounder basis than the rubric we select. Irving Lee gives the following example:

> I knew a man who had lost the use of both eyes. He was called a "blind man." He could also be called an expert typist, a conscientious worker, a good student, a careful listener, a man who wanted a job. But he couldn't get a job in the department store order room where employees sat and typed orders which came over the telephone. The personnel man was impatient to get the interview over. "But you're a blind man," he kept saying, and one could almost feel his silent assumption that somehow the incapacity in one aspect made the man incapable in every other. So blinded by the label was the interviewer that he could not be persuaded to look beyond it.

Some labels, such as "blind man," are exceedingly salient and powerful. They tend to prevent alternative classification, or even cross-classification. Ethnic labels are often of this type, particularly if they refer to some highly visible feature, e.g., Negro, Oriental. They resemble the labels that point to some outstanding incapacity—*feeble-minded, cripple, blind man.* Let us call such symbols "labels of primary potency." These symbols act like shrieking sirens, deafening us to all finer discriminations that we might otherwise perceive. Even though the blindness of one man and the darkness of pigmentation of another may be defining attributes for some purposes, they are irrelevant and "noisy" for others.   4

Most people are unaware of this basic law of language—that every label applied to a given person refers properly only to one aspect of his nature. You may correctly say that a certain man is *human, a philanthropist, a Chinese, a physician, an athlete.* A given person may be all of these; but the chances are that *Chinese* stands out in your mind as the symbol of primary potency. Yet neither this nor any other classificatory label can refer to the whole of a man's nature. (Only his proper name can do so.)   5

Thus each label we use, especially those of primary potency, distracts our attention from concrete reality. The living, breathing, complex individual—the ultimate unit of human nature—is lost to sight. As in the figure, the label magnifies one attribute out of all proportion to its true significance, and masks other important attributes of the individual. . . .   6

LABELS OF PRIMARY POTENCY

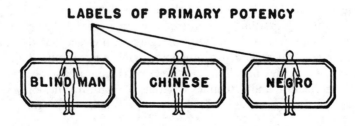

A category, once formed with the aid of a symbol of primary potency, tends to attract more attributes than it should. The category labeled *Chinese* comes to signify not only ethnic membership but also reticence, impassivity, poverty, treachery. To be sure, . . . there may be genuine ethnic-linked traits, making for a certain *probability* that the member of an ethnic stock may have these attributes. But our cognitive process is not cautious. The labeled category, as we have seen, includes indiscriminately the defining attribute, probable attributes, and wholly fanciful, nonexistent attributes.   7

Even proper names—which ought to invite us to look at the individual person—may act like symbols of primary potency, especially if they arouse ethnic associations. Mr. Greenberg is a person, but since his name is Jewish, it activates in the hearer his entire category of Jews-as-a-whole. An ingenious experiment performed by Razran shows this point clearly, and at the same time demonstrates how a proper name, acting like an ethnic symbol, may bring with it an avalanche of stereotypes.   8

Thirty photographs of college girls were shown on a screen to 150 students. The subjects rated the girls on a scale from one to five for *beauty, intelligence, character, ambition, general likability.* Two months later the same subjects were asked to rate the same photographs (and fifteen additional ones introduced to complicate the memory factor). This time five of the original photographs were given Jewish surnames (Cohen, Kantor, etc.), five Italian (Valenti, etc.), and five Irish (O'Brien, etc); and the remaining girls were given names chosen from the signers of the Declaration of Independence and from the Social Register (Davis, Adams, Clark, etc.).

When Jewish names were attached to photographs there occurred the following changes in ratings:
  decrease in liking
  decrease in character
  decrease in beauty
  increase in intelligence
  increase in ambition
For those photographs given Italian names there occurred:
  decrease in liking
  decrease in character
  decrease in beauty
  decrease in intelligence
Thus a mere proper name leads to prejudgments of personal attributes. The individual is fitted to the prejudice ethnic category, and not judged in his own right.

While the Irish names also brought about depreciated judgment, the depreciation was not as great as in the case of the Jews and Italians. The falling of likability of the "Jewish girls" was twice as great as for "Italians" and five times as great as for "Irish." We note, however, that the "Jewish" photographs caused higher ratings in *intelligence* and in *ambition*. Not all stereotypes of out-groups are unfavorable.

The anthropologist, Margaret Mead, has suggested that labels of   9
primary potency lose some of their force when they are changed from nouns into adjectives. To speak of a Negro soldier, a Catholic teacher, or a Jewish artist calls attention to the fact that some other group classifications are just as legitimate as the racial or religious. If George Johnson is spoken of not only as a Negro but also as a *soldier,* we have at least two attributes to know him by, and two are more accurate than one. To depict him truly as an individual, of course, we should have to name many more attributes. It is a useful suggestion that we designate ethnic and religious membership where possible with *adjectives* rather than *nouns*.

EMOTIONALLY TONED LABELS

Many categories have two kinds of labels—one less emotional and one   10
more emotional. Ask yourself how you feel, and what thoughts you have, when you read the words *school teacher,* and then *school marm*. Certainly the second phrase calls up something more strict, more ridiculous, more disagreeable than the former. Here are four innocent letters: m-a-r-m. But they make us shudder a bit, laugh a bit, and scorn a bit. They call up an image of a spare, humorless, irritable old maid. They do not tell us that she is an individual human being with sorrows and troubles of her own. They force her instantly into a rejective category.

In the ethnic sphere even plain labels such as Negro, Italian, Jew,   11
Catholic, Irish-American, French-Canadian may have emotional tone for a reason that we shall soon explain. But they all have their higher key equivalents: nigger, wop, kike, papist, harp, canuck. When these labels are employed we can be almost certain that the speaker *intends* not only to characterize the person's membership, but also to disparage and reject him.

Quite apart from the insulting intent that lies behind the use of   12
certain labels, there is also an inherent ("physiognomic") handicap in many terms designating ethnic membership. For example, the proper names characteristic of certain ethnic memberships strike us as absurd. (We compare them, of course, with what is familiar and therefore "right.") Chinese names are short and silly; Polish names intrinsically difficult and outlandish. Unfamiliar dialects strike us as ludicrous. Foreign dress (which, of course, is a visual ethnic symbol) seems unnecessarily queer.

But of all these "physiognomic" handicaps the reference to color, clearly implied in certain symbols, is the greatest. The word Negro comes from the Latin *niger* meaning black. In point of fact, no Negro has a black complexion, but by comparison with other blonder stocks, he has come to be known as a "black man." Unfortunately *black* in the English language is a word having a preponderance of sinister connotations: the outlook is black, blackball, blackguard, black-hearted, black death, blacklist, blackmail, Black Hand. In his novel *Moby Dick,* Herman Melville considers at length the remarkably morbid connotations of black and the remarkably virtuous connotations of white.   13

Nor is the ominous flavor of black confined to the English language. A cross-cultural study reveals that the semantic significance of black is more or less universally the same. Among certain Siberian tribes, members of a privileged clan call themselves "white bones," and refer to all others as "black bones." Even among Uganda Negroes there is some evidence for a white god at the apex of the theocratic hierarchy; certain it is that a white cloth, signifying purity, is used to ward off evil spirits and disease.   14

There is thus an implied value-judgment in the very concept of *white race* and *black race.* One might also study the numerous unpleasant connotations of *yellow,* and their possible bearing on our conception of the people of the Orient.   15

Such reasoning should not be carried too far, since there are undoubtedly, in various contexts, pleasant associations with both black and yellow. Black velvet is agreeable, so too are chocolate and coffee. Yellow tulips are well liked; the sun and moon are radiantly yellow. Yet it is true that "color" words are used with chauvinistic overtones more than most people realize. There is certainly condescension indicated in many familiar phrases: dark as a nigger's pocket, darktown strutters, white hope (a term originated when a white contender was sought against the Negro heavyweight champion, Jack Johnson), the white man's burden, the yellow peril, black boy. Scores of everyday phrases are stamped with the flavor of prejudice, whether the user knows it or not.   16

We spoke of the fact that even the most proper and sedate labels for minority groups sometimes seem to exude a negative flavor. In many contexts and situations the very terms *French-Canadian, Mexican,* or *Jew,* correct and nonmalicious though they are, sound a bit opprobrious. The reason is that they are labels of social deviants. Especially in a culture where uniformity is prized, the name of *any* deviant carries with it *ipso facto* a negative value-judgment. Words like *insane, alcoholic, pervert* are presumably neutral designations of a human condition, but they are more: they are finger-pointing at a deviance.   17

Minority groups are deviants, and for this reason, from the very outset, the most innocent labels in many situations imply a shading of disrepute. When we wish to highlight the deviance and denigrate it still further we use words of a higher emotional key: crackpot, soak, pansy, greaser, Okie, nigger, harp, kike.

Members of minority groups are often understandably sensitive to names given them. Not only do they object to deliberately insulting epithets, but sometimes see evil intent where none exists. Often the word Negro is spelled with a small *n*, occasionally as a studied insult, more often from ignorance. (The term is not cognate with white, which is not capitalized, but rather with Caucasian, which is.) Terms like "mulatto," or "octoroon" cause hard feeling because of the condescension with which they have often been used in the past. Sex differentiations are objectionable, since they seem doubly to emphasize ethnic difference: why speak of Jewess and not of Protestantess, or of Negress and not of whitess? Similar overemphasis is implied in the terms like Chinamen or Scotchman; why not American man? Grounds for misunderstanding lie in the fact that minority group members are sensitive to such shadings, while majority members may employ them unthinkingly. 18

THE COMMUNIST LABEL

Until we label an out-group it does not clearly exist in our minds. Take the curiously vague situation that we often meet when a person wishes to locate responsibility on the shoulders of some out-group whose nature he cannot specify. In such a case he usually employs the pronoun "they" without an antecedent. "Why don't they make these sidewalks wider?" "I hear they are going to build a factory in this town and hire a lot of foreigners." "I won't pay this tax bill; they can just whistle for their money." If asked "who?" the speaker is likely to grow confused and embarrassed. The common use of the orphaned pronoun *they* teaches us that people often want and need to designate out-groups (usually for the purpose of venting hostility) even when they have no clear conception of the out-group in question. And so long as the target of wrath remains vague and ill-defined specific prejudice cannot crystallize around it. To have enemies we need labels. 19

Until relatively recently—strange as it may seem—there was no agreed-upon symbol for *communist*. The word, of course, existed but it had no special emotional connotation, and did not designate a public enemy. Even when, after World War I, there was a growing feeling of economic and social menace in this country, there was no agreement as to the actual source of the menace. 20

A content analysis of the Boston *Herald* for the year 1920 turned   21
up the following list of labels. Each was used in a content implying
some threat. Hysteria had overspread the country, as it did after World
War II. Someone must be responsible for the postwar malaise, rising
prices, uncertainty. There must be a villain. But in 1920 the villain was
impartially designated by reporters and editorial writers with the following symbols:

> alien, agitator, anarchist, apostle of bomb and torch, Bolshevik, commu-
> nist, communist laborite, conspirator, emissary of false promise, extremist,
> foreigner, hyphenated-American, incendiary, IWW, parlor anarchist, par-
> lor pink, parlor socialist, plotter, radical, red, revolutionary, Russian agi-
> tator, socialist, Soviet, syndicalist, traitor, undesirable.

From this excited array we note that the *need* for an enemy (some-   22
one to serve as a focus for discontent and jitters) was considerably
more apparent than the precise *identity* of the enemy. At any rate,
there was no clearly agreed upon label. Perhaps partly for this reason
the hysteria abated. Since no clear category of "communism" existed
there was no true focus for the hostility.

But following World War II this collection of vaguely interchange-   23
able labels became fewer in number and more commonly agreed
upon. The out-group menace came to be designated almost always as
communist or *red*. In 1920 the threat, lacking a clear label, was vague;
after 1945 both symbol and thing became more definite. Not that people knew precisely what they meant when they said "communist," but
with the aid of the term they were at least able to point consistently to
something that inspired fear. The term developed the power of signifying menace and led to various repressive measures against anyone to
whom the label was rightly or wrongly attached.

Logically, the label should apply to specifiable defining attributes,   24
such as members of the Communist Party, or people whose allegiance
is with the Russian system, or followers, historically, of Karl Max. But
the label came in for far more extensive use.

What seems to have happened is approximately as follows. Having   25
suffered through a period of war and being acutely aware of devastating revolutions abroad, it is natural that most people should be upset,
dreading to lose their possessions, annoyed by high taxes, seeing customary moral and religious values threatened, and dreading worse disasters to come. Seeking an explanation for this unrest, a single identifiable enemy is wanted. It is not enough to designate "Russia" or some
other distant land. Nor is it satisfactory to fix blame on "changing social conditions." What is needed is a human agent near at hand: someone in Washington, someone in our schools, in our factories, in our
neighborhood. If we *feel* an immediate threat, we reason, there must

be a near-lying danger. It is, we conclude, communism, not only in Russia but also in America, at our doorstep, in our government, in our churches, in our colleges, in our neighborhood.

Are we saying that hostility toward communism is prejudice? Not necessarily. There are certainly phases of the dispute wherein realistic social conflict is involved. American values (e.g., respect for the person) and totalitarian values as represented in Soviet practice are intrinsically at odds. A realistic opposition in some form will occur. Prejudice enters only when the defining attributes of "communist" grow imprecise, when anyone who favors any form of social change is called a communist. People who fear social change are the ones most likely to affix the label to any persons or practices that seem to them threatening. 26

For them the category is undifferentiated. It includes books, movies, preachers, teachers who utter what for them are uncongenial thoughts. If evil befalls—perhaps forest fires or a factory explosion—it is due to communist saboteurs. The category becomes monopolistic, covering almost anything that is uncongenial. On the floor of the House of Representatives in 1946, Representative Rankin called James Roosevelt a communist. Congressman Outland replied with psychological acumen, "Apparently everyone who disagrees with Mr. Rankin is a communist." 27

When differentiated thinking is at a low ebb—as it is in times of social crises—there is a magnification of two-valued logic. Things are perceived as either inside or outside a moral order. What is outside is likely to be called "communist." Correspondingly—and here is where damage is done—whatever is called communist (however erroneously) is immediately cast outside the moral order. 28

This associative mechanism places enormous power in the hands of a demagogue. For several years Senator McCarthy managed to discredit many citizens who thought differently from himself by the simple device of calling them communist. Few people were able to see through this trick and many reputations were ruined. But the famous senator has no monopoly on the device. As reported in the Boston *Herald* on November 1, 1946, Representative Joseph Martin, Republican leader in the House, ended his election campaign against his Democratic opponent by saying, "The people will vote tomorrow between chaos, confusion, bankruptcy, state socialism or communism, and the preservation of our American life, with all its freedom and its opportunities." Such an array of emotional labels placed his opponent outside the accepted moral order. Martin was re-elected. . . . 29

Not everyone, of course, is taken in. Demagogy, when it goes too far, meets with ridicule. Elizabeth Dilling's book, *The Red Network,* 30 was so exaggerated in its two-valued logic that it was shrugged off by many people with a smile. One reader remarked, "Apparently if you step off the sidewalk with your left foot you're a communist." But it is not easy in times of social strain and hysteria to keep one's balance, and to resist the tendency of a verbal symbol to manufacture large and fanciful categories of prejudiced thinking.

VERBAL REALISM AND SYMBOL PHOBIA

Most individuals rebel at being labeled, especially if the label is un-   31
complimentary. Very few are willing to be called *fascistic, socialistic,* or *anti-Semitic.* Unsavory labels may apply to others; but not to us.

An illustration of the craving that people have to attach favorable   32
symbols to themselves is seen in the community where white people banded together to force out a Negro family that had moved in. They called themselves "Neighborly Endeavor" and chose as their motto the Golden Rule. One of the first acts of this symbol-sanctified band was to sue the man who sold property to Negroes. They then flooded the house which another Negro couple planned to occupy. Such were the acts performed under the banner of the Golden Rule.

Studies made by Stagner and Hartmann show that a person's polit-   33
ical attitudes may in fact entitle him to be called a fascist or a socialist, and yet he will emphatically repudiate the unsavory label, and fail to endorse any movement or candidate that overtly accepts them. In short, there is a *symbol phobia* that corresponds to *symbol realism.* We are more inclined to the former when we ourselves are concerned, though we are much less critical when epithets of "fascist," "communist," "blind man," "school marm" are applied to others.

When symbols provoke strong emotions they are sometimes re-   34
garded no longer as symbols, but as actual things. The expressions "son of a bitch" and "liar" are in our culture frequently regarded as "fighting words." Softer and more subtle expressions of contempt may be accepted. But in these particular cases, the epithet itself must be "taken back." We certainly do not change our opponent's attitude by making him take back a word, but it seems somehow important that the word itself be eradicated.

Such verbal realism may reach extreme length.   35

The City Council of Cambridge, Massachusetts, unanimously passed a resolution (December, 1939) making it illegal "to possess, harbor, seques-ter, introduce or transport, within the city limits, any book, map, maga-zine, newspaper, pamphlet, handbill or circular containing the words Lenin or Leningrad."

Such naiveté in confusing language with reality is hard to comprehend unless we recall that word-magic plays an appreciable part in human thinking. The following examples, like the one preceding, are taken from Hayakawa.

> The Malagasy soldier must eschew kidneys, because in the Malagasy language the word for kidney is the same as that for "shot"; so shot he would certainly be if he ate a kidney.

> In May, 1937, a state senator of New York bitterly opposed a bill for the control of syphilis because "the innocence of children might be corrupted by a widespread use of the term. . . . This particular word creates a shudder in every decent woman and decent man."

This tendency to reify words underscores the close cohesion that   36 exists between category and symbol. Just the mention of "communist," "Negro," "Jew," "England," "Democrats," will send some people into a panic of fear or a frenzy of anger. Who can say whether it is the word or the thing that annoys them? The label is an intrinsic part of any monopolistic category. Hence to liberate a person from ethnic or political prejudice it is necessary at the same time to liberate him from *word fetishism*. This fact is well known to students of general semantics who tell us that prejudice is due in large part to verbal realism and to symbol phobia. Therefore any program for the reduction of prejudice must include a large measure of semantic therapy.

QUESTIONS ON CONTENT

1. Allport quotes William James's statement that without words our lives would be an "empirical sand-heap" (1). What did James mean by the phrase? What are the implications of a world in which we could not determine categories?

2. Nouns or names provide an essential service in making categorization possible. Yet, according to Allport, nouns are also words that "cut slices." What does he mean by "cut slices"? What is inherently unfair about nouns?

3. What does Allport mean by the "orphaned pronoun *they*" (19)? Why is it used so often?

4. What are "labels of primary potency" (4)? Why are they so important? Can and should we avoid the use of such labels?

5. Why may "labels of primary potency lose some of their force when they are changed from nouns into adjectives" (9)? Do you agree that "it is a useful suggestion that we designate ethnic and religious membership where possible with *adjectives* rather than with *nouns*" (9)? Why, or why not?

6. Allport wrote "The Language of Prejudice" in the early 1950s. Does this help explain why he devotes paragraphs 19–30 to a discussion of the label *communist?* How do Americans react to the label *communist* today?

7. What do the terms *reify* (36), *verbal realism* (35), *symbol phobia* (33), *word fetishism* (36), and *symbol realism* (33) mean? Why does Allport believe that "any program for the reduction of prejudice must include a large measure of semantic therapy" (36)?

QUESTIONS ON RHETORIC

1. What is Allport's thesis, and where is it stated? (Glossary: *Thesis*)

2. The first three paragraphs of Allport's essay become progressively concrete. Explain how these paragraphs logically narrow our focus to the noun and how it functions. (Glossary: *Concrete/Abstract*)

3. Allport includes six fairly lengthy quotations in his essay. What is the function of each one? Do you think each quotation is effective? Why, or why not? (Glossary: *Examples*)

4. In paragraph 17, identify the topic sentence. What method is used to develop the paragraph? (Glossary: *Topic Sentence* and *Examples*)

VOCABULARY

rudimentary (1)	sinister (13)	array (29)
ethnic (4)	morbid (13)	cohesion (36)
inherent (12)	sedate (17)	intrinsic (36)
ludicrous (12)		

WRITING TOPICS

1. Read the following newspaper article. Write an essay in which you attack or defend the UN recommendations.

UN GROUP URGES DROPPING OF WORDS WITH RACIST TINGE

In an effort to combat racial prejudice, a group of United Nations experts is urging sweeping revision of the terminology used by teachers, mass media and others dealing with race.

Words such as *Negro, primitive, savage, backward, colored, bushman* and *uncivilized* would be banned as either "contemptuous, unjust or inadequate." They were described as aftereffects of colonialism.

The report said that the terms were "so charged with emotive potential that their use, with or without conscious pejorative intent, to describe or characterize certain ethnic, social or religious groups, generally provoked an adverse reaction on the part of these groups."

The report said further that even the term *race* should be used with particular care since its scientific validity was debatable and that it "often served to perpetuate prejudice." The experts suggested that the word *tribe* should be used as sparingly as possible, since most of the "population groups" referred to by this term have long since ceased to be tribes or are losing their tribal character. A *native* should be called *inhabitant,* the group advised, and instead of *paganism* the words *animists, Moslems, Brahmans* and other precise words should be used. The word *savanna* is preferable to *jungle,* and the new countries should be described as *developing* rather than *underdeveloped,* the experts said.

2. Make an extensive list of the labels that have been or could be applied to you. Write an essay in which you discuss the labels that you find "truly offensive," those you can "live with," and those that you "like to be associated with." Explain your reasons for putting labels in each of these categories.

2
Words with Built-in Judgments

S. I. HAYAKAWA

In Language in Thought and Action, *from which the following selection is taken, general semanticist S. I. Hayakawa explores the complex relationships that exist between reality and the language we use to describe it. He explains the power that some words—especially those associated with "race, religion, political heresy, and economic dissent"— have to evoke strong emotional responses and how an awareness of this power can help one both to stir up traditional prejudices and unintentionally to give offense.*

The fact that some words arouse both informative and affective connotations simultaneously gives a special complexity to discussions involving religious, racial, national, and political groups. To many people, the word "communist" means simultaneously "one who believes in communism" (informative connotations) *and* "one whose ideals and purposes are altogether repellent" (affective connotations). Words applying to occupations of which one disapproves ("pickpocket," "racketeer," "prostitute"), like those applying to believers in philosophies of which one may disapprove ("atheist," "heretic," "materialist," "Holy Roller," "radical," "liberal"), likewise often communicate *simultaneously* a fact and a judgment on the fact.

In some parts of the southwestern United States there is strong prejudice against Mexicans, both immigrant and American-born. The strength of this prejudice is indirectly revealed by the fact that newspapers and polite people have stopped using the word "Mexican" altogether, using the expression "Spanish-speaking person" instead. "Mexican" has been used with contemptuous connotations for so long that it has become, in the opinion of many people in the region, unsuitable for polite conversation. In some circles, the word is reserved for lower-class Mexicans, while the "politer" term is used for the upper class. There are also terms, such as "chicano" and "Latino," that

Mexican-American and Spanish-speaking groups have chosen to describe themselves.

In dealing with subjects about which strong feelings exist, we are   3
compelled to talk in roundabout terms if we wish to avoid traditional prejudices, which hinder clear thinking. Hence we have not only such terms as "Spanish-speaking persons" but also, in other contexts, "problem drinkers" instead of "drunkards," and "Hansen's disease" instead of "leprosy."

These verbal stratagems are necessitated by the strong affective   4
connotations as well as by the often misleading implications of their blunter alternatives; they are not merely a matter of giving things fancy names in order to fool people, as the simple-minded often believe. Because the old names are "loaded," they dictate traditional patterns of behavior toward those to whom they are applied. When everybody "knew" what to do about "little hoodlums," they threw them in jail and "treated 'em rough." Once in jail, little hoodlums showed a marked tendency to grow up into big hoodlums. When thoughtful people began to observe such facts, they started rethinking the problem, using different terminologies. What is the best way of describing these troubled and troublesome youths? Shall they be described as "defectives" or "psychopathic personalities"? Or as "maladjusted" or "neurotic"? Shall we say they are "deprived," "disadvantaged," "frustrated," or "socially displaced"? Shall we say they are "troubled by problems of identity"? Are they in need of "confinement," "punishment," "treatment," "education," or "rehabilitation"? It is through trying out many, many possible terms such as these that new ways of dealing with the problem are discovered and devised.

The meaning of words, as we have observed, changes from speaker   5
to speaker and from context to context. The words "Japs" and "niggers," for instance, although often used both as a designation and an insult, are sometimes used with no intent to offend. In some classes of society and in some geographical areas, there are people who know no other words for Japanese, and in other areas there are people who know no other words for Blacks. Ignorance of regional and class differences of dialect often results in feelings being needlessly hurt. Those who believe that the meaning of a word is *in the word* often fail to understand this simple point of differences in usage. For example, an elderly Japanese woman of my acquaintance used to squirm at the mention of the word "Jap," even when used in an innocuous or complimentary context. "Whenever I hear the word," she used to say, "I feel dirty all over."

The word "nigger" has a similar effect on most Blacks. A distinguished Black sociologist tells of an incident in his adolescence when   6 he was hitchhiking far from home in regions where Blacks are hardly ever seen. He was befriended by an extremely kindly white couple who fed him and gave him a place to sleep in their home. However, they kept calling him "little nigger"—a fact which upset him profoundly, even while he was grateful for their kindness. He finally got up courage to ask the man not to call him by that "insulting term."

"Who's insultin' you, son?" said the man.
"You are, sir—that name you're always calling me."
"What name?"
"Uh . . . you know."
"I ain't callin' you no names, son."
"I mean your calling me 'nigger.' "
"Well, what's insultin' about that? You are a nigger, ain't you?"

As the sociologist says now in telling the story, "I couldn't think of an answer then, and I'm not sure I can now." 7

In case the sociologist reads this book, we are happy to provide him with an answer, although it may be twenty-five years late. He might have said to his benefactor, "Sir, in the part of the country I come from, white people who treat colored people with respect call them Blacks, while those who wish to show their contempt for colored people call them niggers. I hope the latter is not your intention." And the man might have replied, had he been kindly in thought as he was in deed, "Well, you don't say! Sorry I hurt your feelings, son, but I didn't know." And that would have been that. Many black people now have rejected the term "Negro" as itself an insulting term and prefer to be called Blacks or Afro-Americans. Some "hip" terms that they use for themselves are "moulenjam," "splib," "member," "blood," and "boots." 8

Blacks, having for a long time been victims of unfair persecution because of race, are often even more sensitive about racial appellations than the Japanese woman previously mentioned. It need hardly be said that Blacks suffer from the confusion or informative and affective connotations just as often as white people—or Japanese. Such Blacks, and those white sympathizers with their cause who are equally naive in linguistic matters, tend to feel that the entire colored "race" is vilified whenever and wherever the word "nigger" occurs. They bristle even when it occurs in such expressions as "niggertoe" (the name of an herb; also a dialect term for Brazil nut), "niggerhead" (a type of chewing tobacco), "niggerfish" (a kind of fish found in West Indian and Floridan waters)—and even the word "niggardly" (of Scandinavian origin, unrelated, of course, to "Negro") has to be avoided before some audiences. 9

Such easily offended people sometimes send delegations to visit 10 dictionary offices to demand that the word "nigger" be excluded from future editions, being unaware that dictionaries . . . perform a historical, rather than legislative, function. To try to reduce racial discrimination by getting dictionaries to stop including the word "nigger" is like trying to cut down the birth rate by shutting down the office of the county register of births. When racial discrimination against Blacks is done away with, the word will either disappear or else lose its present connotations. By losing its present connotations, we mean, first, that people who need to insult their fellow men will have found more interesting grounds on which to base their insults and, second, that people who are called "niggers" will no longer fly off the handle any more than a person from New England does at being called a "Yankee."

One other curious fact needs to be recorded about words applied to   11
such hotly debated issues as race, religion, political heresy, and economic dissent. Every reader is acquainted with certain people who, according to their own flattering descriptions of themselves, "believe in being frank" and like to "tell it like [sic] it is." By "telling it like it is," they usually mean calling anything or anyone by the term which has the strongest and most disagreeable affective connotations. Why people should pin medals on themselves for "candor" for performing this nasty feat has often puzzled me. Sometimes it is necessary to violate verbal taboos as an aid to clearer thinking, but more often "calling a spade a spade" is to provide our minds with a greased runway down which we may slide back into old *and discredited* patterns of evaluation and behavior.

QUESTIONS ON CONTENT

1. What is the distinction Hayakawa draws between "informative connotations" and "affective connotations"?

2. Why, according to Hayakawa, have many people in the American Southwest stopped using the term "Mexican"?

3. How can names, as Hayakawa asserts, "dictate traditional patterns of behavior toward those to whom they are applied" (4)?

4. On what basis does Hayakawa argue that "verbal stratagems" (4) are often a necessity?

5. Why is it important to realize that the meanings of words may change "from speaker to speaker and from context to context" (5)? Explain how the Black sociologist's story in paragraph 6 serves to illustrate this point.

6. In what ways are Hayakawa's "words with built-in judgments" similar to Allport's "labels of primary potency" (Allport, paragraph 4)?

QUESTIONS ON RHETORIC

1. Most of the paragraphs in Hayakawa's essay are organized in the same way. Explain how they are organized, paying particular attention to the topic sentences. (Glossary: *Topic Sentence* and *Examples*)

2. What technique does Hayakawa use to define both informative and affective connotations? (Glossary: *Definition*) Did you find his definitions clear and easy to understand? Why, or why not?

3. Discuss Hayakawa's use of transitions between paragraphs. What transitions does he use? What effect does each transition have? (Glossary: *Transitions*)

4. How effective is the metaphor of the "greased runway" in the final paragraph? Explain. (Glossary: *Figures of Speech*)

VOCABULARY

simultaneously (1)	psychopathic (4)	benefactor (8)
repellent (1)	rehabilitation (4)	dissent (11)
contemptuous (2)	innocuous (5)	candor (11

WRITING TOPICS

1. Hawakawa lists a number of terms (*pickpocket, racketeer, prostitute, atheist, heretic, materialist, Holy Roller, radical, liberal, Mexican, drunkard, leprosy, hoodlums, Japs, niggers*) that evoke simultaneously both affective connotations and informative connotations. Think of at least three other terms that also do this. Write an essay in which you explain the affective and informative connotations of each term.

2. Using examples from your own experiences, write an essay in which you show that it is better "to talk in roundabout terms if we wish to avoid traditional prejudices, which hinder clear thinking" (3). Can you think of any situations in which it would be "necessary to violate verbal taboos as an aid to clearer thinking" (11)?

3
Does Language Libel the Left-Handed?

ENGLISH HIGHLIGHTS

Not all objections to prejudicial language are as loud and persistent as those made by many racial and ethnic groups in the United States. Some seem almost lighthearted, though an undercurrent of seriousness runs through the amusing examples of language that discriminates against left-handed people given in the following brief article. We should not forget that for many centuries "left" and "evil" have been linked and that left-handedness was even thought to be more common among criminals and the insane. The associations persist even today.

Have you ever noticed how language seems to discriminate against left-handed people? The left-handed sometimes complain that every device from doorknobs to kitchen sinks is designed for right-handed people. Left-handers might well object also to the implications of designating the socially inept as "gauche" ("left" in French), the evil as "sinister" ("left" in Latin), and barbed flattery as a "left-handed compliment." 1

On the other hand, the skillful worker is "adroit" (French *à droit,* "to the right") and "dexterous" (from Latin *dexter,* "right" or "right hand"). The boss depends on the worker who is his "right-hand man." Who ever heard of anyone's having a "left-hand man"? When Stonewall Jackson was severely wounded, didn't General Lee say, "He has lost his left arm. I have lost my right arm"? 2

If a young lady complains after a dance that her partner had "two left feet," she is immediately understood to mean that he was impossibly awkward. Still, she may try to stay on the "right side" of him, so she will not lack for partners another time. For popularity many a girl will dance with a "gawky" (original meaning, "left" or "left-handed") boy occasionally. 3

Many successful athletes have been both left-handed and extremely well coordinated. No one in his "right mind" would deny that Sandy Koufax was a great baseball player. Nor has the sports world a 4 corner on famous left-handers. Other "lefties" were Alexander the Great, Charlemagne, Leonardo da Vinci, and Holbein.

Yet, undeterred by the facts, we go right on with our canards. 5 When a person becomes very mixed up indeed, we may say that he is "way out in left field," in contrast to "right-minded" individuals, whom everyone recognizes as "right as rain."

These aspersions on the one out of twenty—the estimated number 6 of left-handed people in the world—have been cast far too long for there to be much hope of stopping them. It's enough to make a maligned left-hander send the next unsuspecting right-hander he meets to the store for a "left-handed monkey wrench."

QUESTIONS ON CONTENT

1. Speculate about the origins of the derogatory connotations associated with "left." You may wish to consult an unabridged or historical dictionary such as *Webster's Third New International Dictionary* or the *Oxford English Dictionary.*

2. Do you think that language really discriminates against left-handed people? How do the words and phrases cited in this article affect your attitude toward left-handed people?

3. Does the writer see any solution to the problem? Do you agree? Why, or why not?

4. Can you think of any examples of "left-handed" idioms that have been omitted?

QUESTIONS ON RHETORIC

1. What is the writer's purpose in this essay? (Glossary: *Purpose*)

2. The essay starts with a question. Is this an effective beginning? Explain. (Glossary: *Beginnings/Endings*)

3. What function do the examples of the positive characteristics of "right" and the examples of the famous left-handers serve in the context of the essay? (Glossary: *Examples*)

4. Describe the transitional techniques that the writer uses to gain coherence between paragraphs. (Glossary: *Transitions*)

5. What is the writer's tone in this essay? (Glossary: *Tone*)

VOCABULARY

inept (1)	undeterred (5)	aspersions (6)
barbed (1)	canards (5)	

WRITING TOPICS

1. Using this essay as a model, write an essay in which you talk about language that seems to discriminate against one of the following: old people, poor people, handicapped people, mentally or physically ill people.

2. Write an essay in which you explore the following thesis: "Our identities, who and what we are or think we are, how others see and define us, are greatly affected by language" (Haig Bosmajian).

4

What to Call an American of Hispanic Descent

TOMAS GUILLEN

Each year thousands of Spanish-speaking people immigrate to the United States from Cuba, Mexico, Puerto Rico, Honduras, the Dominican Republic, and elsewhere. Too often our white-dominant society stands ready to define them, to impose labels that are offensive, even prejudicial. Tomas Guillen and other Americans of Hispanic descent know the importance of self-identification, the value of finding a label that properly defines them and maintains the distinct cultural identity of the group. In the following essay, Guillen focuses on the problems that Americans of Hispanic descent have had in agreeing upon such a label.

You can call me Hispano or you can call me Chicano or you can call me Hispanic-American or you can call me Mexican or you can call me Mexican-American or you can call me Spanish-surnamed American or you can call me Latino or. . . .

Finding a person to identify with all of the above appellations would be as difficult as climbing Mount St. Helens with a plate of beans balanced on your head. As many have learned the hard way, it can be unhealthy using the wrong term. You cannot call a Mexican a Chicano. And although all Chicanos are said to be Mexican-Americans, not all Mexican-Americans are Chicanos.

For years, attempts have been made to line up Americans of Mexican descent behind one appellation. Success would help end confusion and would, more importantly, create an image of cohesiveness in the face of economic and political struggles. Attempts have failed.

For one, ethnic groups do not often name themselves. Take the Pima Indians in Arizona. *Pima* is a word of negation. *Ootham* is the tribe's name.

Also, a significant number of the millions of Americans of Mexican descent—concentrated in California, Arizona, New Mexico, Colorado and Texas—have found any term unacceptable.

More recently, various individuals and groups throughout the country have been promoting the term "Hispanic." They want the term because they feel it includes all Spanish speakers and persons of Mexican descent, including Cubans, South and Central Americans and Puerto Ricans. "It's becoming more acceptable and we use it mostly for purposes of unifying various Hispanic groups to promote their interests in the national and state legislative bodies," says Rep. Edward R. Roybal, D.-Calif., chairman of the Congressional Hispanic Caucus and president of the National Association of Latino Elected and Appointed Officials.

Ironically, the organizations apply different terms: "Hispanic" and "Latino." Why not the term "Latino?" It has a romantic flow that's appealing. Although "Latino" is widely used today, Roybal says no because Italians and Portuguese also can claim to be Latinos by virtue of speaking a romance language.   7

LULAC—League of United Latino American Citizens—bills itself as "the oldest and largest Hispanic organization in the U.S." It was established in 1929 in Texas. "We like to use the word Hispanic . . . it encompasses everybody," says Juan F. Aguilera, chief executive officer of LULAC. The group's name includes the term "Latino" and there are no plans to change it, although Aguilera says his group is promoting the term "Hispanic." "Latino" is in the name because it was fashionable back then, says Aguilera.   8

Reymundo Marin is a forty-three-year-old University of Washington professor of Chicano literature. He doubts that "Hispanic" or "Latino" will catch on. Efforts to put Americans of Mexican descent and Cubans and Puerto Ricans under one appellation is "promoting the melting-pot theory," he says. He feels Cubans and Puerto Ricans—and some Americans of Mexican descent—do not want to be mixed under one name. He specifically says use of "Latino" would connote that the population is from Latin America. It's a "misuse and it doesn't convey we were born here (in the U.S.)," he says.   9

Marin lashes out at LULAC for not using the term "Mexican" in its name when it started, a period when there was widespread discrimination against Mexicans. He feels the organization should have been LUMAC—League of United Mexican American Citizens—and the euphemism Latino should not have been used.   10

Actually, Hispano may not be that desirable for a national name. One school of thought has it that the ancient Greeks named Spain "Hesperia." A Latinized form evolved: "Hispana." One interpretation is that "Hesperia" meant "land of the rabbits."   11

Marin prefers to be called Chicano.   12

The term "Chicano" itself was an attempt at self-identification by Americans of Mexican descent, more commonly called Mexican-Americans. Chicanos still hope the term will gain wider use.   13

The origin of the term "Chicano" is traced to two schools of   14
thought, both plausible even though difficult to establish.

The first view is that Chicano stems from what the Aztecs called   15
themselves—Mexicans—but they pronounced it with a "sh" sound instead of "x." After the word "Mexico" was introduced to the Aztecs,
they combined "Mexicas" with Mexico to form *Meshicanos.* It was
later hyphenated to *Me-shi-canos.* The *Me,* later dropped, left *Shicanos*
and through time the "sh" became "ch"—hence Chicanos.

The second view is that Chicano is a combination of two words,   16
chico (small) and Mexicano. The belief is that Anglo-Saxons referred
to anyone of Mexican ancestry as Pancho, Pepé or Chico. The word
Chico was then coupled with Mexicano to form Chicano.

Chicano today is not commonly used in Mexico. And although the   17
term may have originated with the Aztecs or through Anglo-Saxon
generalization, Chicano now stands for something new. Chicanos are
individuals of Mexican ancestry who live in North American society
and are demanding recognition as first-class citizens. Chicanos demand the political and social rights promised their ancestors after the
Mexican-American War in 1848. Chicanos want to retain their culture,
especially their language, and through their struggle for political, social and economic equality, Chicanos evolved expecting their new appellation to become the national expression.

Chicanos resent the label "Mexican-American," which they feel   18
was imposed on them by the "gringo" or white-dominant society.
(Gringo is an offensive slang term used by some Mexican-Americans
to refer to Anglos. Gringo is similar to "greaser," which is used by
some Anglos to refer to Americans of Mexican descent.)

Conservative members of the Mexican-American community often   19
refuse to accept the term Chicano because of the persons who initially
identified with the term. It was the militants who first used the term.
And many Mexicans refused to associate with militants.

Adding to the Chicanos' problems are two main groups within the   20
Mexican-American community that despise being called Chicanos
and at times denounce those who identify with the term.

The first group consists of Mexican-Americans who do not associ-   21
ate with other Mexicans and who disown most aspects of the Mexican
culture. Members of this group generally speak English most of the
time, which for them symbolizes prestige. These persons are called
"coconuts" by other Mexican-Americans: They are brown on the outside and white inside. Coconut is used by Mexican-Americans as
"Oreo" is used by blacks and "banana" by Orientals. Within this
group are Mexican-Americans who for many years have said they are
Hispanic-Americans. This practice was called "passing" in the 1930s
and early 1940s. By calling themselves Hispanic-Americans, they

disregarded their Indian ancestry in order to become more acceptable in the dominant Anglo society.

The second group that scorns "Chicano" consists of persons of 22 Mexican descent who have never identified with North American society and who identify with the appellation "Mexican." Members of this group almost always will associate with Mexico's customs. First-generation Mexicans who immigrate to the U.S. think along the lines of not identifying with either North American culture or with U.S.-born Mexicans. This resistance has stifled recognition of the term Chicano as the national self-identifying expression.

The term Chicano might have first been used by trouble-making 23 militants or persons with vulgar expressions, but now counselors, teachers and some politicians of Mexican descent identify with the term. Chicanos have been the ones who have been pushing for jobs and political positions for those of Mexican descent living in the U.S. Marin puts it this way: "Chicanos are the philosophers and politicians. It is the intellectual movement by students. We are questioning everything."

In any event, the search by various groups and individuals for a 24 self-identifying name goes on. And the various appellations with which certain persons identify probably always will exist because of the varying cultural and political backgrounds—more so with a constant influx of persons who simply want to be called "Mexicans."

"Hispano" or "Latino" are probably the safest terms to use, espe- 25 cially in a large gathering of persons of Mexican descent. But it probably would be wiser to simply ask a person what they prefer to be called. Of course, many persons feel there would be no need to look for self-identifying expressions if everyone could simply say: "I'm an American."

QUESTIONS ON CONTENT

1. Why have attempts been made to find a single name for Americans of Mexican descent? What is the problem with the terms "Hispanic" and "Latino"?

2. What group uses the term "Chicano"? What are the two explanations that Guillen gives of the word's origin?

3. Why do Chicanos resent the label "Mexican-American"? What two groups despise being called Chicanos? Explain why each group resents the label.

4. What is a "coconut"? An "oreo"? A "banana"?

5. Is the term "Chicano" likely to be recognized as the "national self-identifying expression"? Why, or why not?

6. In the end what is Guillen's advice about addressing a person of Hispanic descent? Is this a satisfactory solution to the problem? Why, or why not?

7. What name are you most likely to use when referring to Americans of Hispanic descent? Why?

QUESTIONS ON RHETORIC

1. In what ways is the opening paragraph an effective beginning? (Glossary: *Beginnings*)

2. What is Guillen's purpose in this essay? Does he seem to be more interested in explaining the situation or arguing for a position? (Glossary: *Purpose*)

3. Paragraph 12 is a one-sentence paragraph. Explain how it functions in the context of the essay.

4. Explain how Guillen has organized his essay. You may find it helpful to make a scratch outline of his major points. (Glossary: *Organization*)

VOCABULARY

appellations (2)	connote (9)	prestige (21)
cohesiveness (3)	gringo (18)	influx (24)
ironically (7)		

WRITING TOPICS

1. Guillen states that "ethnic groups do not often name themselves" (4) and gives the example of the Pima Indians in Arizona to illustrate what he means. Do you belong to a group that has been named by outsiders? Or, have you named yourselves? Write an essay in which you discuss the importance of "self-identification" and the problems associated with names others give us.

2. American slang is loaded with derogatory terms for various racial, ethnic, or religious groups. Guillen points to "gringo" which is used by Mexican-Americans to refer to Anglos and "greaser" which is used by Anglos to refer to Americans of Mexican descent as examples of such slang. Write an essay in which you describe the slang labels that are used in your area, and then attempt to explain why they are used.

3. Although Guillen does not make an issue of it, we cannot forget that he is talking in part about Spanish-speaking immigrants: language has something to do with the discrimination they encounter. Do those who speak Standard English suffer less from discrimination and prejudice? Explain. You may find it helpful to read Richard Rodriquez's essay "Caught Between Two Languages" (pp. 88–97) before you start writing.

5

Dictionaries and Ethnic Sensibilities

ROBERT BURCHFIELD

As the chief editor of the Oxford English Dictionary *at Oxford University Press in England, Robert Burchfield is very familiar with the sensitive problems facing the modern lexicographer or dictionary maker. Burchfield strongly believes that it is the duty of lexicographers to record the ways in which people actually use words, and controversy arises when it comes to words that carry negative associations for a race, ethnic group, or nation. In the following essay, Burchfield gives us an historical perspective on an issue that is not likely to go away.*

At the beginning of *Macbeth*, a bleeding sergeant describes how brave Macbeth killed the "merciless" rebel, Macdonwald: "he unseamed him from the nave to th' chaps," that is, from the navel to the jaws, "and fixed his head upon our battlements." It may seem a far cry from the rebellious "kerns and gallow-glasses" of Macdonwald to the persevering scholarship involved in dictionary editing, but the connection will be made clear as I proceed.

The head some want to display on the battlements is that of a dictionary, or of its publishers, and, especially, any dictionary that records a meaning that is unacceptable or at best unwelcome to the person or group on the warpath. The ferocity of such assaults is almost unbelievable except as a by-product of what Professor Trevor-Roper calls the twentieth-century "epidemic fury of ideological belief." Key words are *Jew, Palestinian, Arab, Pakistan, Turk, Asiatic, Muhammadan,* and *Negro,* and there are others.

It is impossible to discover exactly when the battle cry was first heard, but certainly by the 1920s a pattern of protest existed. In the *Jewish Chronicle* of 24 October 1924, a leading article expressed "no small gratification" that, in deference to complaints that had been published in the *Jewish Chronicle,* the delegates of the Clarendon Press had decided that the "sinister meaning" attached to the word *Jew* (that is, the meaning "unscrupulous usurer or bargainer," and the corre-

1

2

3

sponding verb meaning "to cheat, overreach") should be labelled to make it clear that it was a derogatory use. The *Jewish Chronicle* had maintained that users of the *Pocket Oxford Dictionary* would conclude that "every Jew is essentially the sort of person thus described." Mr. R. W. Chapman, who at that time was the head of the section of OUP which publishes dictionaries, replied that "it is no part of the duty of a lexicographer to pass judgment on the justice or propriety of current usage." The editor of the *Pocket Oxford Dictionary,* the legendary H. W. Fowler, in a letter to Chapman declared:

> The dictionary-maker has to record what people say, not what he thinks they can politely say: how will you draw the line between this insult to a nation and such others as "Dutch courage," "French leave," "Punic faith," "the Huns," "a nation of shopkeepers," and hundreds more? The real question is not whether a phrase is rude, but whether it is current.

The *Pocket Oxford* and other Oxford dictionaries, and dictionaries   4
elsewhere, labelled the "sinister meaning" of the word *Jew* "derogatory," "opprobrious," or the like, and an uneasy peace was established. But not for long. Some other "sinister" meanings in the *Pocket Oxford* were pointed out. "*Turk:* Member of the Ottoman race; unmanageable child." "*Tartar:* native of Tartary (etc.); intractable person or awkward customer." "*Jesuit:* member of Society of Jesus (etc.); deceitful person."

Fowler felt that he was being incited, as he said, "to assume an au-   5
tocratic control of the language and put to death all the words and phrases that do not enjoy our approval." He maintained that the *POD* was not keeping the incriminated senses alive but that, unfortunately, they were not in danger of dying. In a letter to Kenneth Sisam in September 1924, he insisted: "I should like to repeat that I have neither religious, political, nor social antipathy to Jews"—nor, by implication, to Turks, Tartars, or Jesuits. The episode passed, but was not forgotten. The *Jewish Chronicle* at that time appeared to be satisfied by an assurance that the unfavorable senses would be labelled as such. They did not ask for, far less demand, the exclusion of the disapproved meanings.

In the United States in the 1920s, a parallel protest movement   6
aimed at the compulsory capitalization of the initial letter of the word *Negro* and the abandonment, except among black inhabitants of the States, of the word *nigger.* Again, dictionaries were among the main targets, and here, too, the lexicographers replied that if writers, including the editors of newspapers, used a capital initial for *Negro,* they would themselves be happy to include this form in their dictionaries, and to give it priority if it became the dominant form in print.

A half-century later, it is easy to see that the lexicographers had   7
"scotch'd the snake, not killed it." Resentment smoldered away in certain quarters, and the issues were brought out into the open again after
the 1939–1945 war. But this time there was a difference. Dictionaries
remained a prime target, but the protesters brought new assault techniques to bear, especially the threat of sanctions if the lexicographers
did not come to heel. Now, dictionary editors, judged by the standards
of the broad world, are a soft target. With little personal experience of
the broil that forms the daily experience of, for example, politicians,
newspaper editors, and psychiatrists, editors of dictionaries tend to be
too unworldly and too disdainfully scholarly to recognize the severity
of an assault made on them. What is this assault and what form does it
take? Quite simply, it is a concerted attempt by various pressure
groups to force dictionary editors to give up recording the factual un-
pleasantnesses of our times and to abandon the tradition of setting
down the language as it is actually used, however disagreeable, regret-
table, or uncongenial the use.

Two definitions in the *Concise Oxford Dictionary,* one in the early   8
fifties and the other in 1976, exacerbated things. One concerned the
word *Pakistan,* and the other, the word *Palestinian.* The editor of the
Concise Oxford Dictionary unwisely entered the word *Pakistan* in his
dictionary in 1951—unwisely, because names of countries as such do
not qualify for an entry in Oxford dictionaries—and defined it as "a
separate Moslem State in India, Moslem autonomy; (from 1947) the
independent Moslem Dominion in India."

It lay apparently unnoticed until 1959, when somebody must have   9
pointed it out. The Pakistanis, understandably, were outraged, and
called for a ban on the *COD* in Pakistan and for all unsold copies in
Pakistan to be confiscated. The OUP admitted that the definition was
"tactless" and "locally irritating," but pointed out that the intention
had been to show that Pakistan was in the familiar, triangular section
of territory which had always been called India on maps and in geography books. No political motive was in question. The Karachi police
raided bookstalls in the city and seized 215 copies of the fourth edition
of the *COD.* They also raided the Karachi office of the OUP, and
seized the only copy of the dictionary on the premises, which was, in
fact, the typist's copy. Copies in government offices were comman-
deered by the police, and apparently hundreds of copies were collected
from public offices, schools, and colleges.

After high-level discussion, the Pakistan government decided to lift   10
its ban on the *COD* in November 1959, after receiving an undertaking
by the OUP to issue a correction slip for insertion in all copies of *COD*
sold in Pakistan, and to enter a new definition in the next impression
of the dictionary. Later, a more permanent solution was found when

the word *Pakistan* was dropped from the main-line Oxford dictionaries altogether, as a proper name with no other meanings. It remains in the semi-encyclopedic *Oxford Illustrated Dictionary,* where it is defined as "Muslim State in SE Asia, formed in 1947 from regions where Muslims predominated."

This was a striking example of the serious consequences arising   11 from a simple error of judgment by a lexicographer. There were other minor skirmishes, for example, when it was noticed that the definition of the word *American* in some of the Oxford dictionaries failed to allow for the existence of black Americans and of Latin Americans. The dictionary editors gladly revised the definitions and brought them up to date with a minimum of fuss and with no heat generated on either side.

However, the problem of the word *Jew* kept returning in an in-   12 creasingly dramatic way. Some correspondents contrasted the derogatory definitions of *Jew* with the colloquial senses of the word *Christian. Christian* is defined as "a human being, as distinguished from a brute," for example, in Shaftesbury (1714): "The very word Christian is, in common language, us'd for Man, in opposition to Brute-beast." It is also recorded with the colloquial sense, "a decent, respectable, or presentable person," as in Dickens (1844): "You must take your passage like a Christian; at least as like a Christian as a fore-cabin passenger can."

One correspondent, in 1956, said that she was concerned with the   13 way in which stereotypes about groups of people became formulated, and she argued that the preservation of derogatory definitions in dictionaries did nothing to prevent the persistence of such stereotypes. Others drew attention to the cultural and scholarly achievements of Jews, for example, that thirty-eight Nobel prizes had been awarded to Jews by 1960. A representative of the American Conference of Businessmen came to the OED Department in Oxford in March 1966, and he and I discussed the problem amicably. "Men of good will," he said, "should unite to do everything possible not to give any appearance of acceptance to unfavorable applications of the word *Jew* if they exist." If they exist? But we knew from our quotation files that unfavorable applications of the word *Jew* did and do exist, both in speech and in print, deplorable though they are. All I could do was to repeat the familiar lexicographical arguments. It is the duty of lexicographers to record actual usage, as shown by collected examples, not to express moral approval or disapproval of usage; dictionaries cannot be regulative in matters of social, political, and religious attitudes; there is no question of any animus on the part of the lexicographers against the Jews, or the Arabs, or anyone else.

In 1969, a Jewish businessman from Salford came on the scene   14 and claimed that the definitions of *Jew* were "abusive and insulting and reflected a deplorable attitude toward Jewry." He turned the screw more forcibly by releasing the text of his letters to the national newspapers, who by now realized that the matter was an issue of public controversy. He also wrote to politicians, church leaders, including the chief rabbi and the archbishop of Canterbury, to the commissioner of police, and to other instruments of the church and state.

In 1972, this Salford businessman brought an action against the   15
Clarendon Press, claiming that the secondary definitions of the word *Jew* were "derogatory, defamatory, and deplorable." He lost the case in the High Court in July 1973. Mr. Justice Goff held that, in law, the plaintiff had no maintainable cause of action because he could not, as required by English law, show that the offending words in the dictionary entries "referred to him personally or were capable of being understood by others as referring to him."

The next episode occurred on the other side of the world. Toward   16
the end of 1976, Mr. Al Grassby, Australia's commissioner for community relations, called for the withdrawal of the *Australian Pocket Oxford Dictionary* from circulation because it contained a number of words applied in a derogatory way to ethnic or religious groups: words like *wog, wop,* and *dago.*

Knowing very little, if anything, about lexicographical policy, he   17
thought it deplorable that there was no entry for *Italy* but one for *dago,* none for Brazil as a country but one for *Brazil nut,* and so on. This wholly simplistic notion was rejected with humor and scorn by the Australian press. A cartoon in the *Australian* showed two European migrants looking very unhappy, and the caption read: "Did you hear what those ignorant Aussie dingoes called us?" And a headline in the Melbourne *Sunday Press* makes its point quite simply: "You are on a loser, pal Grassby."

The most recent example of hostility toward dictionary definitions   18
occurred a short time ago. On this occasion, as with *Pakistan,* the criticized definition *was* inadequate, and, curiously, the concession of its inadequacy merely transferred the attack from one quarter to another. In the sixth edition of the *Concise Oxford Dictionary,* published in July 1976, the word *Palestinian* was defined as "(native or inhabitant) of Palestine; (person) seeking to displace Israelis from Palestine." Early in 1977, the definition provoked angry editorial comment in newspapers in the Middle East, and threats were made that if the Oxford University Press did not agree to amend it at once, the matter would be brought to the attention of the Arab League, with a proposal to place the OUP on the Arab boycott list.

Each day's post brought fresh evidence of what appeared to be a   19 severe reaction throughout Arabic-speaking countries, if the newspapers were anything to go by. The sales records for the *Concise Oxford Dictionary* in Egypt showed that all of eleven copies had been sold there in the financial year 1976–1977! But, sales apart, what was clear was that the Arabs considered the definition to be partisan, and that, in my opinion, would have been the attitude of the man on the Clapham omnibus, too.

In two lines of the *COD*—because that was all the space available   20
in such a small dictionary—we concluded that it was not possible to arrive at other than a formulaic definition of *Palestinian.* Any form of words ascribing motives to "Palestinians" simply failed by one test or another when the space available was so limited. We therefore decided to adopt another type of definition, one of the type that is used in every desk dictionary in the world, and the new definition reads as follows: "*n.* Native or inhabitant of Palestine. *a.* Of, pertaining to, or connected with Palestine."

The Arabs were satisfied ("it represents a victory for truth and ob-   21
jectivity," declared the *Egyptian Gazette* of 3 May 1977) and, had the matter rested there, without further publicity, that would probably have been the end of it. Not content with severing the head, however, the Arabs wished to fix it upon the battlements. A press statement was issued to British national newspapers by a London-based Arab organization, and even though this statement was factually and unemotionally expressed, it brought an instant reaction from the other side.

Letters of protest began to arrive from various Jewish organiza-   22
tions, and the scholarly lexicographers of the OUP had to endure the kind of concerted campaign with which politicians have always been familiar. The letters expressed "profound distress" and declared that the lexicographers "had departed from their usual standards of scholarly objectivity in yielding to pro-Arab pressure groups." The "selfsame tune and words" came from several directions. "We consider this an encroachment on traditional British integrity and on British values," "political appeasement for commercial considerations," "I wish to register the strongest protest against such abject and cowardly behaviour on the part of your organization," and so on. It dawned on us, as the letters arrived, that we were dealing with an organized petition. The individuals and groups writing to us had been urged to write to us by some central body. The same phrases occurred in several of the letters; for example: "In describing a Palestinian as a native or inhabitant of Palestine, you impliedly deny the existence of the State of Israel." That "impliedly" rather gave the game away.

This Palestinian affair is for all practical purposes over, though not   23
without bruises on all sides. Dictionary editors are now at last aware

that they must give maximum attention to sensitive words, like *Palestinian, Jap,* and so on. Politically sensitive words like *Palestine* and *Kashmir* can be entered only as geographical, and not as political entities unless there is adequate space to describe the claims and counterclaims and there are facilities for the frequent updating of the entries.

For the most part lexicographers are agreed about the necessity of   24 recording derogatory applications of words even if some sections of the general public are not. Since the 1960s or so most dictionaries (other than the smallest ones and those prepared for the use of children) have also included most of the more commonly heard expressions used in contexts describing sexual or excretory matters. A different practice, which I believe to be mistaken, is defended in classical manner by David B. Guralnik in the foreword to his *Webster's New World Dictionary of the American Language* (Second College Edition, 1972), p. viii:

> *The absence from this dictionary of a handful of old, well-known vulgate terms for sexual and excretory organs and functions is not due to a lack of citations for these words from current literature. On the contrary, the profusion of such citations in recent years would suggest that the terms in question are so well known as to require no explanation. The decision to eliminate them as part of the extensive culling process that is the inevitable task of the lexicographer was made on the practical grounds that there is still objection in many quarters to the appearance of these terms in print and that to risk keeping this dictionary out of the hands of some students by introducing several terms that require little if any elucidation would be unwise. In a similar vein, it was decided in the selection process that this dictionary could easily dispense with those true obscenities, the terms of racial or ethnic opprobrium, that are, in any case, encountered with diminishing frequency these days.*

In respect of such vocabulary, inclusion or exclusion should be   25 governed by the size of the dictionary or by the educational market envisaged for it. In large dictionaries like the *OED,* the *Shorter Oxford English Dictionary* and *Webster's Third New International Dictionary,* such vocabulary should be automatically included, with suitable indications of the status of each item. In desk dictionaries like the *Concise Oxford Dictionary* and *Webster's New Collegiate Dictionary* the editors normally have sufficient space to include such words: a wide range of suitable status labels is available to indicate the degree of vulgarity of words like *crap, cunt, fart, fuck, turd,* and so on; and for terms of racial abuse a special symbol meaning "regarded as offensive in varying degrees by a person to whom the word is applied" is long overdue. Such dictionaries should aim to be regulative or normative in such matters only by the use of cautionary labels and/or symbols and not by censorship. In smaller dictionaries, and in school dictionaries, the absence of such vocabulary needs no defense.

In the end, in their function as "marshallers of words," lexicogra- 26 phers responsible for the compilation of the larger dictionaries must aim to include vocabulary from the disputed areas of vocabulary as well as from safe or uncontroversial subject areas, words that are gracefully formed as well as those that are not, words from sets of religious, political, or social beliefs with which one has no sympathy beside those that one finds acceptable. And to the list of words that must not be excluded I should add those that are explosive and dangerous, like words of ethnic abuse, as well.

QUESTIONS ON CONTENT

1. What for Burchfield is the duty of the lexicographer? How does this position cause a dilemma for the lexicographer when it comes to words with racial or ethnic overtones? How did H. W. Fowler solve the problems surrounding *Jew* in 1924?

2. Explain the problems caused by the entries for *Pakistan* and *Palestinian* in the *Concise Oxford Dictionary*. How was each dispute resolved?

3. Certainly the presence of derogatory definitions in dictionaries does nothing to prevent the persistence of negative stereotypes. But would the elimination of these terms from the dictionary eliminate the negative stereotypes? If not, what else is necessary?

4. If censorship is not the answer, how does Burchfield think terms of racial and ethnic abuse should be handled by lexicographers? Do you agree with his proposal? Explain.

QUESTIONS ON RHETORIC

1. What is Burchfield's purpose in this essay? Does he seem to be more interested in explaining or arguing his position? (Glossary: *Purpose*)

2. How has Burchfield organized his material? Why does this particular pattern seem appropriate? (Glossary: *Organization*)

3. Explain Burchfield's allusion to *Macbeth* in the opening paragraph. How is this paragraph related to the rest of his essay? (Glossary: *Allusion*)

4. In paragraph 24, Burchfield quotes a passage from David B. Guralnik's foreword to *Webster's New World Dictionary of the American Language*. Why do you suppose he uses this quote; doesn't it directly contradict his thesis?

5. Robert Burchfield is English. What is there about his diction that is especially British? (Glossary: *Diction*)

VOCABULARY

ferocity (2)	intractable (4)	colloquial (12)
ideological (2)	antipathy (5)	animus (13)
deference (3)	uncongenial (7)	envisaged (25)
opprobrious (4)	exacerbated (8)	normative (25)

WRITING TOPICS

1. In her essay "Sexism in English: A Feminist View" (pp. 301–308), Alleen Pace Nilsen seeks to show that the English language is inherently sexist. Those in the women's movement are not the only ones to have made this kind of charge; blacks have asserted that English is also inherently racist. For example, they have been concerned about the way desk dictionaries define the words *black* and *white*. Study the complete entries for both of these terms in two or three recently published desk dictionaries. Write an essay in which you discuss any reasons why blacks might find fault with these entries. Be sure to consider what has been omitted as well as what has been included in each of the definitions.

2. Have you ever been victimized by racial or ethnic slurs? Describe your experience and the effect that the slurs had on you.

3. We have all encountered racial and ethnic slurs in the movies, television, and books. In attempting to "depict reality" do the writers involved contribute to the growth of prejudicial language and the continuation of racial and ethnic stereotypes? Is censorship a possible answer? If not, what are the alternatives?

WRITING ASSIGNMENTS FOR "PREJUDICE AND STEREOTYPES"

1. Members of a group often have different perceptions of the characteristics of that group from those held by outsiders. What is your own image of the racial, national, religious, and social groups to which you belong? How do nonmembers view these groups? Write an essay in which you compare the two images and attempt to account for the differences.

2. Write an essay in which you compare and/or contrast the discussions of prejudice and language by Allport and Hayakawa.

3. Since the early 1960s black Americans have sought a self-identifying label for themselves. After suffering for years under the labels *nigger, colored,* and *Negro* imposed by the dominant white society, they have experimented with such labels as *Afro-American* and *black.* Write an essay in which you trace the shifts that have taken place and construct a reasonable linguistic explanation for these shifts.

4. Write an essay in which you discuss what your name means to you. Some questions you might consider include: How did your parents decide on your name? How do you like your name? What does your name mean? How do others respond to your name? Are there any stereotypes associated with your first name? Are there any racial or ethnic stereotypes associated with your last name?

5. Show-business people often change their names. Here are the professional names and the original names of a number of celebrities.

Professional Name	Original Name
Tony Curtis	Bernard Schwartz
Mick Jagger	Michael Philip
Simone Signoret	Simone Kaminker
Roy Rogers	Leonard Slye
Raquel Welch	Raquel Tejada
James Garner	James Bumgarner
Bob Dylan	Robert Zimmerman
Doris Day	Doris von Kappelhoff
Fred Astaire	Frederick Austerlitz
John Wayne	Marion Michael Morrison
Cyd Charisse	Tula Finklea
Anne Bancroft	Annemaria Italiano
Michael Caine	Maurice J. Micklewhite
Jack Benny	Benjamin Kubelsky

Professional Name	Original Name
Connie Francis	Concetta Franconero
Ringo Starr	Richard Starkey
Hugh O'Brian	Hugh J. Krampe

Write an essay in which you speculate about the reasons for these name changes. Why, do you think, such changes are less common among younger performers?

6. CBS news commentator Charles Osgood once wrote, "To hate somebody, to hate them enough to kill them, you must first dehumanize them in your mind. . . . That is why racial and religious epithets are so evil. To call somebody a nigger or a kike or a spic or wop is to rob a human being of his humanity. It is a form of hate, a form of murder." Write an essay in which you discuss the dehumanizing effects of racial, ethnic, and religious labels.

7. The following news item appeared in the Burlington *Free Press* on June 4, 1977:

'NIGGER' CAN BE ERASED IN MAINE

AUGUSTA, Maine (AP)—Names such as Nigger Hill and Nigger Island could be erased from the Maine map under a new law approved Friday by Gov. James B. Longley.

Longley signed a measure into law which allows people to complain to the Maine Human Rights Commission when they feel that the use of the term "nigger" in the name of a geographic site is offensive.

About 10 geographic features in Maine—hills, brooks and islands—include the term.

Rep. Gerald Talbot, D-Portland, the state's only black lawmaker, introduced the bill after he said he tried in vain to have the names changed by other means.

His measure originally called for banning the use of any name which is offensive to a nationality or racial group, but lawmakers amended the bill when they said it was too broad.

They said the original plan could have been extended to include terms such as "squaw."

The law will take effect in the fall.

In an essay discuss whether this is an example of censorship or a sincere attempt to eradicate prejudice. In your opinion, was the law as originally proposed "too broad"? Why, or why not?

NOTE: Suggested topics for research papers appear on p. 446.

NOTABLE QUOTATIONS

The following quotations are drawn from the essays in this section. They are presented as additional topics for classroom discussion or for writing assignments.

"Most people are unaware of this basic law of language—that every label applied to a given person refers properly only to one aspect of his nature." *Allport* (5)

"Especially in a culture where uniformity is prized, the name of *any* deviant carries with it *ipso facto* a negative value-judgment." *Allport* (17)

"Until we label an out-group it does not clearly exist in our minds." *Allport* (19)

"When symbols provoke strong emotions they are sometimes regarded no longer as symbols, but as actual things." *Allport* (34)

"In dealing with subjects about which strong feelings exist, we are compelled to talk in roundabout terms if we wish to avoid traditional prejudices, which hinder clear thinking." *Hayakawa* (3)

"Sometimes it is necessary to violate verbal taboos as an aid to clearer thinking, but more often 'calling a spade a spade' is to provide our minds with a greased runway down which we may slide back into old *and discredited* patterns of evaluation and behavior." *Hayakawa* (11)

"Have you ever noticed how language seems to discriminate against left-handed people?" *English Highlights* (1)

"These aspersions on the one out of twenty—the estimated number of left-handed people in the world—have been cast for too long for there to be much hope of stopping them." *English Highlights* (6)

"As many have learned the hard way, it can be unhealthy using the wrong term. You cannot call a Mexican a Chicano. And although all Chicanos are said to be Mexican-Americans, not all Mexican-Americans are Chicanos." *Guillen* (2)

"Ethnic groups do not often name themselves." *Guillen* (4)

"Of course, many persons feel there would be no need to look for self-identifying expressions if everyone could simply say: 'I'm an American.' " *Guillen* (25)

"It is the duty of lexicographers to record actual usage, as shown by collected examples, not to express moral approval or disapproval of usage; dictionaries cannot be regulative in matters of social, political, and religious attitudes. . . ." *Burchfield* (13)

"To the list of words that must not be excluded [from dictionaries] I should add those that are explosive and dangerous, like words of ethnic abuse, as well." *Burchfield* (26)

VII

Language and Sexism

A conscious effort to diminish the use of the language of sexism may be an important step towards eradicating man's inhumanity to women.

Haig A. Bosmajian

Words, phrases, and sentence patterns are not inherently strong or weak. They acquire these attributes only in a particular cultural context. If our society views female speech as inferior it is because of the subordinate role assigned to women. Our culture is biased to interpret sex differences in favor of men.

Cheris Kramer

When a woman says of her husband, who has drawn up plans for a new bedroom wing and left out closets, "Just like a man," her language is as sexist as the man's who says, after his wife has changed her mind about needing the new wing after all, "Just like a woman."

Casey Miller and Kate Swift

It isn't the language that is sexist; it is society.

Victoria Fromkin and Robert Rodman

1

Sexism in English: A Feminist View

ALLEEN PACE NILSEN

Because culture influences language and language infleunces culture, we cannot reasonably study one subject without also studying the other. In an effort to see what role the dictionary plays in reflecting and influencing attitudes toward women in America, Alleen Pace Nilsen studied all the words relating to males and females in a recently published desk dictionary. Her division and classification of these dictionary entries reveal deep-seated biases against women. Her findings, several of which were totally unexpected, raise important questions about the possibility of establishing equal rights for women in this country.

Does culture shape language? Or does language shape culture? This 1 is as difficult a question as the old puzzler of which came first, the chicken or the egg, because there's no clear separation between language and culture.

A well-accepted linguistic principle is that as culture changes so 2 will the language. The reverse of this—as a language changes so will the culture—is not so readily accepted. This is why some linguists smile (or even scoff) at feminist attempts to replace *Mrs.* and *Miss* with *Ms.* and to find replacements for those all-inclusive words which specify masculinity, e.g., *chairman, mankind, brotherhood, freshman,* etc.

Perhaps they are amused for the same reason that it is the doctor at 3 a cocktail party who laughs the loudest at the joke about the man who couldn't afford an operation so he offered the doctor a little something to touch up the X-ray. A person working constantly with language is likely to be more aware of how really deep-seated sexism is in our communication system.

Last winter I took a standard desk dictionary and gave it a place of 4 honor on my night table. Every night that I didn't have anything more interesting to do, I read myself to sleep making a card for each entry that seemed to tell something about male and female. By spring I had a rather dog-eared dictionary, but I also had a collection of note cards filling two shoe boxes. The cards tell some rather interesting things about American English.

First, in our culture it is a woman's body which is considered important while it is a man's mind or his activities which are valued. A woman is sexy. A man is successful.

I made a card for all the words which came into modern English from somebody's name. I have a two-and-one-half inch stack of cards which are men's names now used as everyday words. The women's stack is less than a half inch high and most of them came from Greek mythology. Words coming from the names of famous American men include *lynch, sousaphone, sideburns, Pullman, rickettsia, Schick test, Winchester rifle, Franklin stove, Bartlett pear, teddy bear,* and *boysenberry.* The only really common words coming from the names of American women are *bloomers* (after Amelia Jenks Bloomer) and *Mae West jacket.* Both of these words are related in some way to a woman's physical anatomy, while the male words (except for *sideburns* after General Burnside) have nothing to do with the namesake's body.

This reminded me of an earlier observation that my husband and I made about geographical names. A few years ago we became interested in what we called "Topless Topography" when we learned that the Grand Tetons used to be simply called *The Tetons* by French explorers and *The Teats* by American frontiersmen. We wrote letters to several map makers and found the following listings: *Nippletop* and *Little Nipple Top* near Mt. Marcy in the Adirondacks, *Nipple Mountain* in Archuleta County, Colorado, *Nipple Peak* in Coke County, Texas, *Nipple Butte* in Pennington, South Dakota, *Squaw Peak* in Placer County, California (and many other places), *Maiden's Peak* and *Squaw Tit* (they're the same mountain) in the Cascade Range in Oregon, *Jane Russell Peaks* near Stark, New Hampshire, and *Mary's Nipple* near Salt Lake City, Utah.

We might compare these names to Jackson Hole, Wyoming, or Pikes Peak, Colorado. I'm sure we would get all kinds of protests from the Jackson and Pike descendants if we tried to say that these topographical features were named because they in some way resembled the bodies of Jackson and Pike, respectively.

This preoccupation with women's breasts is neither new nor strictly American. I was amused to read the derivation of the word *Amazon.* According to Greek folk etymology, the *a* means "without" as in *atypical* or *amoral* while *mazon* comes from *mazōs* meaning "breast." According to the legend, these women cut off one breast so that they could better shoot their bows. Perhaps the feeling was that the women had to trade in part of their femininity in exchange for their active or masculine role.

There are certain pairs of words which illustrate the way in which   10
sexual connotations are given to feminine words while the masculine
words retain a serious, businesslike aura. For example, being a *callboy*
is perfectly respectable. It simply refers to a person who calls actors
when it is time for them to go on stage, but being a *call girl* is being a
prostitute.

Also we might compare *sir* and *madam*. *Sir* is a term of respect   11
while *madam* has acquired the meaning of a brothel manager. The
same thing has happened to the formerly cognate terms, *master* and
mistress. Because of its acquired sexual connotations, *mistress* is now
carefully avoided in certain contexts. For example, the Boy Scouts
have *scoutmasters* but certainly not *scoutmistresses*. And in a dog show
the female owner of a dog is never referred to as the *dog's mistress*, but
rather as the *dog's master*.

Master appears in such terms as *master plan, concert master,*   12
schoolmaster, mixmaster, master charge, master craftsman, etc. But *mis-*
tress appears in very few compounds. This is the way it is with dozens
of words which have male and female counterparts. I found two hundred such terms, e.g., *usher-usherette, heir-heiress, hero-heroine*, etc. In
nearly all cases it is the masculine word which is the base with a feminine suffix being added for the alternate version. The masculine word
also travels into compounds while the feminine word is a dead end;
e.g., from *king-queen* comes *kingdom* but not *queendom*, from *sports-*
man-sportslady comes *sportsmanship* but not *sportsladyship*, etc. There
is one—and only one—semantic area in which the masculine word is
not the base or more powerful word. This is in the area dealing with
sex and marriage. Here it is the feminine word which is dominant.
Prostitute is the base word with *male prostitute* being the derived term.
Bride appears in *bridal shower, bridal gown, bridal attendant, brides-*
maid, and even in *bridegroom,* while *groom* in the sense of *bridegroom*
does not appear in any compounds, not even to name the groom's attendants or his prenuptial party.

At the end of a marriage, this same emphasis is on the female. If it   13
ends in divorce, the woman gets the title of *divorcée* while the man is
usually described with a statement, such as, "He's divorced." When
the marriage ends in death, the woman is a *widow* and the *-er* suffix
which seems to connote masculine (probably because it is an agentive
or actor type suffix) is added to make *widower. Widower* doesn't appear
in any compounds (except for *grass widower,* which is another companion term), but *widow* appears in several compounds and in addition has some acquired meanings, such as the extra hand dealt to the
table in certain card games and an undesirable leftover line of type in
printing.

If I were an anthropological linguist making observations about a   14
strange and primitive tribe, I would duly note on my tape recorder that
I had found linguistic evidence to show that in the area of sex and
marriage the female appears to be more important than the male, but
in all other areas of the culture, it seems that the reverse is true.

But since I am not an anthropological linguist, I will simply go on   15
to my second observation, which is that women are expected to play a
passive role while men play an active one.

One indication of women's passive role is the fact that they are   16
often identified as something to eat. What's more passive than a plate
of food? Last spring I saw an announcement advertising the Indiana
University English Department picnic. It read "Good Food! Delicious
Women!" The publicity committee was probably jumped on by local
feminists, but it's nothing new to look on women as "delectable mor-
sels." Even women compliment each other with "You look good
enough to eat," or "You have a peaches and cream complexion."
Modern slang constantly comes up with new terms, but some of the
old standbys for women are: *cute tomato, dish, peach, sharp cookie,
cheese cake, honey, sugar,* and *sweetie-pie.* A man may occasionally be
addressed as *honey* or described as a *hunk of meat,* but certainly men
are not laid out on a buffet and labeled as women are.

Women's passivity is also shown in the comparisons made to   17
plants. For example, to *deflower* a woman is to take away her virginity.
A girl can be described as a *clinging vine,* a *shrinking violet,* or a *wall-
flower.* On the other hand, men are too active to be thought of as
plants. The only time we make the comparison is when insulting a man
we say he is like a woman by calling him a *pansy.*

We also see the active-passive contrast in the animal terms used   18
with males and females. Men are referred to as *studs, bucks,* and
wolves, and they go *tomcatting around.* These are all aggressive roles,
but women have such pet names as *kitten, bunny, beaver, bird, chick,
lamb,* and *fox.* The idea of being a pet seems much more closely related to females than to males. For instance, little girls grow up wearing *pigtails* and *ponytails* and they dress in *halters* and *dog collars.*

The active-passive contrast is also seen in the proper names given   19
to boy babies and girl babies. Girls are much more likely to be given
names like *Ivy, Rose, Ruby, Jewel, Pearl, Flora, Joy,* etc., while boys
are given names describing active roles such as *Martin* (warlike), *Leo*
(lion), *William* (protector), *Ernest* (resolute fighter), as so on.

Another way that women play a passive role is that they are de-   20
fined in relationship to someone else. This is what feminists are protesting when they ask to be identified as *Ms.* rather than as *Mrs.* or
Miss. It is a constant source of irritation to women's organizations that

when they turn in items to newspapers under their own names, that is, Susan Glascoe, Jeanette Jones, and so forth, the editors consistently rewrite the item so that the names read Mrs. John Glascoe, Mrs. Robert E. Jones.

In the dictionary I found what appears to be an attitude on the part 21 of editors that it is almost indecent to let a respectable woman's name march unaccompanied across the pages of a dictionary. A woman's name must somehow be escorted by a male's name regardless of whether or not the male contributed to the woman's reason for being in the dictionary, or in his own right, was as famous as the woman. For example, Charlotte Brontë is identified as Mrs. Arthur B. Nicholls, Amelia Earhart is identified as Mrs. George Palmer Putnam, Helen Hayes is identified as Mrs. Charles MacArthur, Zona Gale is identified as Mrs. William Llwelyn Breese, and Jenny Lind is identified as Mme. Otto Goldschmidt.

Although most of the women are identified as Mrs. ——— or as the 22 wife of ———, other women are listed with brothers, fathers, or lovers. Cornelia Otis Skinner is identified as the daughter of Otis, Harriet Beecher Stowe is identified as the sister of Henry Ward Beecher, Edith Sitwell is identified as the sister of Osbert and Sacheverell, Nell Gwyn is identified as the mistress of Charles II, and Madame Pompadour is identified as the mistress of Louis XV.

The women who did get into the dictionary without the benefit of a 23 masculine escort are a group sort of on the fringes of respectability. They are the rebels and the crusaders: temperance leaders Frances Elizabeth Caroline Willard and Carry Nation, women's rights leaders Carrie Chapman Catt and Elizabeth Cady Stanton, birth control educator Margaret Sanger, religious leader Mary Baker Eddy, and slaves Harriet Tubman and Phillis Wheatley.

I would estimate that far more than 50 percent of the women listed 24 in the dictionary were identified as someone's wife. But of all the men—and there are probably ten times as many men as women—only one was identified as "the husband of. . . ." This was the unusual case of Frederic Joliot who took the last name of Joliot-Curie and was identified as "husband of Irene." Apparently Irene, the daughter of Pierre and Marie Curie, did not want to give up her maiden name when she married and so the couple took the hyphenated last name.

There are several pairs of words which also illustrate the more 25 powerful role of the male and the relational role of the female. For example a *count* is a high political officer with a *countess* being simply the wife of a count. The same is true for a *duke* and a *duchess* and a *king* and a *queen*. The fact that a king is usually more powerful than a queen might be the reason that Queen Elizabeth's husband is given the title of *prince* rather than *king*. Since *king* is a stronger word than *queen*, it is reserved for a true heir to the throne because if it were given to someone coming into the royal family by marriage, then the subjects might forget where the true power lies. With the weaker word of *queen*, this would not be a problem; so a woman marrying a ruling monarch is given the title without question.

My third observation is that there are many positive connotations   26
connected with the concept of masculine, while there are either trivial or negative connotations connected with the corresponding feminine concept.

Conditioning toward the superiority of the masculine role starts   27
very early in life. Child psychologists point out that the only area in which a girl has more freedom than a boy is in experimenting with an appropriate sex role. She is much freer to be a *tomboy* than is her brother to be a *sissy*. The proper names given to children reflect this same attitude. It's perfectly all right for a girl to have a boy's name, but not the other way around. As girls are given more and more of the boys' names parents shy away from using boy names that might be mistaken for girl names, so the number of available masculine names is constantly shrinking. Fifty years ago *Hazel, Beverly, Marion, Francis,* and *Shirley* were all perfectly acceptable boys' names. Today few parents give these names to baby boys and adult men who are stuck with them self-consciously go by their initial or by abbreviated forms such as *Haze* or *Shirl*. But parents of little girls keep crowding the masculine set and currently popular girls' names include *Jo, Kelly, Teri, Cris, Pat, Shawn, Toni,* and *Sam*.

When the mother of one of these girls tells her to *be a lady,* she   28
means for her to sit with her knees together. But when the father of a little boy tells him to *be a man,* he means for him to be noble, strong, and virtuous. The whole concept of manliness has such positive connotations that it is a compliment to call a male a *he-man,* a *manly man,* or a *virile man* (*virile* comes from the Indo-European *vir,* meaning "man"). In each of these three terms, we are implying that someone is doubly good because he is doubly a man.

Compare *chef* with *cook, tailor* and *seamstress,* and *poet* with *poet-*   29
ess. In each case, the masculine form carries with it an added degree of excellence. In comparing the masculine *governor* with the feminine *governess* and the masculine *major* with the feminine *majorette,* the added feature is power.

The difference between positive male and negative female conno-   30
tations can be seen in several pairs of words which differ denotatively only in the matter of sex. For instance compare *bachelor* with the terms *spinster* and *old maid*. *Bachelor* has such positive connotations

that modern girls have tried to borrow the feeling in the term *bache-lor-girl*. *Bachelor* appears in glamorous terms such as *bachelor pad, bachelor party,* and *bachelor button*. But *old maid* has such strong negative feelings that it has been adopted into other areas, taking with it the feeling of undesirablity. It has the metaphorical meaning of shriveled and unwanted kernels of popcorn, and it's the name of the last unwanted card in a popular game for children.

Patron and *matron* (Middle English for *father* and *mother*) are an-   31
other set where women have tried to borrow the positive masculine connotations, this time through the word *patroness,* which literally means "female father." Such a peculiar term came about because of the high prestige attached to the word *patron* in such phrases as *"a patron of the arts"* or *"a patron saint."* *Matron* is more apt to be used in talking about a woman who is in charge of a jail or a public restroom.

Even *lord* and *lady* have different levels of connotation. *Our Lord* is   32
used as a title for deity, while the corresponding *Our Lady* is a relational title for Mary, the mortal mother of Jesus. *Landlord* has more dignity than *landlady* probably because the landlord is more likely to be thought of as the owner while the landlady is the person who collects the rent and enforces the rules. *Lady* is used in many insignificant places where the corresponding *lord* would never be used, for example, *ladies room, ladies sizes, ladies aid society, ladybug,* etc.

This overuse of *lady* might be compared to the overuse of *queen*   33
which is rapidly losing its prestige as compared to *king*. Hundreds of beauty queens are crowned each year and nearly every community in the United States has its *Dairy Queen* or its *Freezer Queen,* etc. Male homosexuals have adopted the term to identify the "feminine" partner. And advertisers who are constantly on the lookout for euphemisms to make unpleasnt sounding products salable have recently dealt what might be a death blow to the prestige of the word *queen*. They have begun to use it as an indication of size. For example, *queen-size* panty hose are panty hose for fat women. The meaning comes through a comparison with *king-size,* meaning big. However, there's a subtle difference in that our culture considers it desirable for males to be big because size is an indication of power, but we prefer that females be small and petite. So using *king-size* as a term to indicate bigness partially enhances the prestige of *king,* but using *queen-size* to indicate bigness brings unpleasant associations to the word *queen*.

Another set that might be compared are *brave* and *squaw*. The   34
word *brave* carries with it the connotations of youth, vigor, and courage, while *squaw* implies almost opposite characteristics. With the set *wizard* and *witch,* the main difference is that *wizard* implies skill and

wisdom combined with magic, while *witch* implies evil intentions combined with magic. Part of the unattractiveness of both *squaw* and *witch* is that they suggest old age, which in women is particularly undesirable. When I lived in Afghanistan (1967–1969), I was horrified to hear a proverb stating that when you see an old man you should sit down and take a lesson, but when you see an old woman you should throw a stone. I was equally startled when I went to compare the connotations of our two phrases *grandfatherly advice* and *old wives' tales.* Certainly it isn't expressed with the same force as in the Afghan proverb, but the implication is similar.

In some of the animal terms used for women the extreme undesirability of female old age is also seen. For instance consider the unattractiveness of *old nag* as compared to *filly,* of *old crow* or *old bat* as compared to *bird,* and of being *catty* as compared to being *kittenish.* The chicken metaphor tells the whole story of a girl's life. In her youth she is a *chick,* then she marries and begins feeling *cooped up,* so she goes to *hen parties* where she *cackles* with her friends. Then she has her *brood* and begins to *henpeck* her husband. Finally she turns into *an old biddy.*

35

QUESTIONS ON CONTENT

1. What are the three main conclusions about sexism in the English language that Nilsen draws based on her study of the entries in a desk dictionary?
2. What point does Nilsen make about each of the following:
    a. English words derived from the name of a person
    b. geographical names
    c. pairs of words, one masculine and the other feminine
    d. the use of words referring to foods, plants, and animals in connection with women
    e. the first names given to male and female infants
    f. the use of *Ms.*
    g. dictionary entries concerning famous women
    h. positive and negative connotations connected with the concepts "masculine" and "feminine."

3. Most dictionary makers try to describe accurately the ways in which speakers of English use the language. Can we, therefore, reasonably fault them for reflecting cultural attitudes in word definitions?
4. According to Nilsen, in what two areas does the English language reveal the importance of women?
5. In the sentences that follow, each of the italicized words is a generic term—that is, a term that supposedly refers to all people, male and fe-

male, that it designates. Explain why each of the these uses is or is not sexist:

a. My favorite anthropology course is "The Cultures of *Man.*"
b. Over three hundred *bachelor's* degrees were awarded at the last commencement.
c. "Madam *Chairman,*" he said; "I protest the ruling of the chair."
d. All *men* are created equal.
e. Usually women executives are just *yesmen.*
f. "Don't try to make me your *whipping boy,*" Caroline protested.

Rewrite the sentences substituting an unobjectable term for each italicized phrase to eliminate potentially sexist language. Observe the difference between sexist language and sexist sentiment.

QUESTIONS ON RHETORIC

1. What techniques does Nilsen use to support her conclusions? Is her evidence convincing? Why, or why not? (Glossary: *Examples*)

2. How has Nilsen organized her essay? (Glossary: *Organization*) You may find it helpful to make a scratch outline of her main ideas.

3. What is the tone of this essay? How does Nilsen maintain this tone? Is her tone appropriate for her subject and audience? (Glossary: *Tone*)

4. In essays of substantial length such as this one, short transitional paragraphs are often used to link the main sections of the essay. Identify two such paragraphs in Nilsen's article. Are they effective? When would you use a transitional paragraph? When would you avoid doing so? (Glossary: *Transition*)

5. Explain how the chicken metaphor in the last paragraph works. (Glossary: *Figures of Speech*) Is it an effective ending? Why, or why not?

VOCABULARY

scoff (2)	cognate (11)	temperance (23)
atypical (9)	counterparts (12)	shriveled (30)
amoral (9)	delectable (16)	

WRITING TOPICS

1. Nilsen provides us with an extensive catalogue of words that reveal a disparaging attitude toward women. It is not her purpose, however, to offer any solutions to the problem of bias in the language. Write an essay in which you discuss the possible improvements that you as a user of the language, lexicographers as makers of dictionaries, and women and men as leaders of the equal rights movement can bring about.

2. Like any attempt to change the status quo, women's attempts to change language have aroused a great deal of opposition. Who is the opposition? To what do they seem to be reacting? Does the opposition seem justified in any of its objections? What techniques does the opposition employ?

2

You Are What You Say

ROBIN LAKOFF

One early expression of the contemporary feminist movement was the founding in 1972 of Ms *magazine. Its purpose was to raise women's consciousness of their place in society, and the magazine's title symbolized that purpose:* Ms. *represented a new form of address for women, less prejudicial than* Miss *or* Mrs., *which indicate marital status in a way that* Mr. *does not. In the following essay, Robin Lakoff, a professor of linguistics at the University of California at Berkeley and an early contributor to* Ms, *argues that women are socially handicapped by the very language they have been conditioned to speak.*

"Women's language" is that pleasant (dainty?), euphemistic   1
never-aggressive way of talking we learned as little girls. Cultural bias
was built into the language we were allowed to speak, the subjects we
were allowed to speak about, and the ways we were spoken of. Having
learned our linguistic lesson well, we go out in the world, only to discover that we are communicative cripples—damned if we do, and
damned if we don't.

If we refuse to talk "like a lady," we are ridiculed and criticized for   2
being unfeminine. ("She thinks like a man," is, at best, a left-handed
compliment.) If we do learn all the fuzzy-headed, unassertive language
of our sex, we are ridiculed for being unable to think clearly, unable to
take part in a serious discussion, and therefore unfit to hold a position
of power.

It doesn't take much of this for a woman to begin feeling she de-   3
serves such treatment because of inadequacies in her own intelligence
and education.

"Women's language" shows up in all levels of English. For exam-   4
ple, women are encouraged and allowed to make far more precise discriminations in naming colors than men do. Words like *mauve, beige,
ecru, aquamarine, lavender,* and so on, are unremarkable in a woman's
active vocabulary, but largely absent from that of most men. I know of
no evidence suggesting that women actually *see* a wider range of colors
than men do. It is simply that fine discriminations of this sort are

relevant to women's vocabularies, but not to men's; to men, who control most of the interesting affairs of the world, such distinctions are trivial—irrelevant.

In the area of syntax, we find similar gender-related peculiarities of   5
speech. There is one construction, in particular, that women use conversationally far more than men: the tag question. A tag is midway between an outright statement and a yes-no question; it is less assertive than the former, but more confident than the latter.

A *flat statement* indicates confidence in the speaker's knowledge   6
and is fairly certain to be believed; a *question* indicates a lack of knowledge on some point and implies that the gap in the speaker's knowledge can and will be remedied by an answer. For example, if, at a Little League game, I have had my glasses off, I can legitimately ask someone else: "Was the player out at third?" A *tag question,* being intermediate between statement and question, is used when the speaker is stating a claim, but lacks full confidence in the truth of that claim. So if I say, "Is Joan here?" I will probably not be surprised if my respondent answers "no"; but if I say, "Joan is here, isn't she?" instead, chances are I am already biased in favor of a positive answer, wanting only confirmation. I still want a response, but I have enough knowledge (or think I have) to predict that response. A tag question, then, might be thought of as a statement that doesn't demand to be believed by anyone but the speaker, a way of giving leeway, of not forcing the addressee to go along with the views of the speaker.

Another common use of the tag question is in small talk when the   7
speaker is trying to elicit conversation: "Sure is hot here, isn't it?"

But in discussing personal feelings or opinions, only the speaker   8
normally has any way of knowing the correct answer. Sentences such as "I have a headache, don't I?" are clearly ridiculous. But there are other examples where it is the speaker's opinions, rather than perceptions, for which corroboration is sought, as in "The situation in Southeast Asia is terrible, isn't it?"

While there are, of course, other possible interpretations of a sen-   9
tence like this, one possibility is that the speaker has a particular answer in mind—"yes" or "no"—but is reluctant to state it baldly. This sort of tag question is much more apt to be used by women than by men in conversation. Why is this the case?

The tag question allows a speaker to avoid commitment, and   10
thereby avoid conflict with the addressee. The problem is that, by so doing, speakers may also give the impression of not really being sure of themselves, or looking to the addressee for confirmation of their views. This uncertainty is reinforced in more subliminal ways, too. There is a peculiar sentence-intonation pattern, used almost exclu-

sively by women, as far as I know, which changes a declarative answer into a question. The effect of using the rising inflection typical of a yes-no question is to imply that the speaker is seeking confirmation, even though the speaker is clearly the only one who has the requisite information, which is why the question was put to her in the first place:

(Q) When will dinner be ready?
(A) Oh . . . around six o'clock. . . ?

It is as though the second speaker were saying, "Six o'clock—if that's okay with you, if you agree." The person being addressed is put in the position of having to provide confirmation. One likely consequence of this sort of speech pattern in a woman is that, often unbeknownst to herself, the speaker builds a reputation of tentativeness, and others will refrain from taking her seriously or trusting her with any real responsibilities, since she "can't make up her mind," and "isn't sure of herself."

Such idiosyncrasies may explain why women's language sounds much more "polite" than men's. It is polite to leave a decision open, not impose your mind, or views, or claims, on anyone else. So a tag question is a kind of polite statement, in that it does not force agreement or belief on the addressee. In the same way a request is a polite command, in that it does not force obedience on the addressee, but rather suggests something be done as a favor to the speaker. A clearly stated order implies a threat of certain consequences if it is not followed, and—even more impolite—implies that the speaker is in a superior position and able to enforce the order. By couching wishes in the form of a request, on the other hand, a speaker implies that if the request is not carried out, only the speaker will suffer; noncompliance cannot harm the addressee. So the decision is really left up to the addressee. The distinction becomes clear in these examples: 11

Close the door.
Please close the door.
Will you close the door?
Will you please close the door?
Won't you close the door?

In the same ways as words and speech patterns used *by* women undermine her image, those used to *describe* women make matters even worse. Often a word may be used of both men and women (and perhaps of things as well); but when it is applied to women, it assumes a special meaning that, by implication rather than outright assertion, is derogatory to women as a group. 12

The use of euphemisms has this effect. A euphemism is a substitute for a word that has acquired a bad connotation by association with 13

---

something unpleasant or embarrassing. But almost as soon as the new word comes into common usage, it takes on the same old bad connotations, since feelings about the things or people referred to are not altered by a change of name; thus new euphemisms must be constantly found.

There is one euphemism for *woman* still very much alive. The [14] word, of course, is *lady*. *Lady* has a masculine counterpart, namely *gentleman*, occasionally shortened to *gent*. But for some reason *lady* is very much commoner than *gent(leman)*.

The decision to use *lady* rather than *woman*, or vice versa, may [15] considerably alter the sense of a sentence, as the following examples show:

(a) A woman (lady) I know is a dean at Berkeley.
(b) A woman (lady) I know makes amazing things out of shoelaces and old boxes.

The use of *lady* in (a) imparts a frivolous, or nonserious, tone to the [16] sentence: the matter under discussion is not one of great moment. Similarly, in (b), using *lady* here would suggest that the speaker considered the "amazing things" not to be serious art, but merely a hobby or an aberration. If *woman* is used, she might be a serious sculptor. To say *lady doctor* is very condescending, since no one ever says *gentleman doctor* or even *man doctor*. For example, mention in the San Francisco *Chronicle* of January 31, 1972, of Madalyn Murray O'Hair as the *lady atheist* reduces her position to that of scatterbrained eccentric. Even *woman atheist* is scarcely defensible: sex is irrelevant to her philosophical position.

Many women argue that, on the other hand, *lady* carries with it [17] overtones recalling the age of chivalry: conferring exalted stature on the person so referred to. This makes the term seem polite at first, but we must also remember that these implications are perilous: they suggest that a "lady" is helpless, and cannot do things by herself.

Lady can also be used to infer frivolousness, as in titles of organiza- [18] tions. Those that have a serious purpose (not merely that of enabling "the ladies" to spend time with one another) cannot use the word *lady* in their titles, but less serious ones may. Compare the *Ladies' Auxiliary* of a men's group, or the *Thursday Evening Ladies' Browning and Garden Society* with *Ladies' Liberation* or *Ladies' Strike for Peace*.

What is curious about this split is that *lady* is in origin a euphe- [19] mism—a substitute that puts a better face on something people find uncomfortable—for *woman*. What kind of euphemism is it that subtly denigrates the people to whom it refers? Perhaps *lady* functions as a euphemism for *woman* because it does not contain the sexual implications present in *woman:* it is not "embarrassing" in that way. If this is so, we may expect that, in the future, *lady* will replace woman as the primary word for the human female, since *woman* will have become too blatantly sexual. That this distinction is already made in some contexts at least is shown in the following examples, where you can try replacing *woman* with *lady:*

(a) She's only twelve; but she's already a woman.
(b) After ten years in jail, Harry wanted to find a woman.
(c) She's my woman, see, so don't mess around with her.

Another common substitute for *woman* is *girl.* One seldom hears a   20
man past the age of adolescence referred to as a boy, save in expressions like "going out with the boys," which are meant to suggest an air of adolescent frivolity and irresponsibility. But women of all ages are "girls": one can have a man—not a boy—Friday, but only a girl— never a woman or even a lady—Friday; women have girlfriends, but men do not—in a nonsexual sense—have boyfriends. It may be that this use of *girl* is euphemistic in the same way the use of *lady* is: in stressing the idea of immaturity, it removes the sexual connotations lurking in *woman.* *Girl* brings to mind irresponsibility: you don't send a girl to do a woman's errand (or even, for that matter, a boy's errand). She is a person who is both too immature and too far from real life to be entrusted with responsibilities or with decisions of any serious or important nature.

Now let's take a pair of words which, in terms of the possible rela-   21
tionships in an earlier society, were simple male-female equivalents, analogous to *bull:cow.* Suppose we find that, for independent reasons, society has changed in such a way that the original meanings now are irrelevant. Yet the words have not been discarded, but have acquired new meanings, metaphorically related to their original senses. But suppose these new metaphorical uses are no longer parallel to each other. By seeing where the parallelism breaks down, we discover something about the different roles played by men and women in this culture. One good example of such a divergence through time is found in the pair, *master:mistress.* Once used with reference to one's power over servants, these words have become unusable today in their original master-servant sense as the relationship has become less prevalent in our society. But the words are still common.

Unless used with reference to animals, *master* now generally refers   22
to a man who has acquired consummate ability in some field, normally nonsexual. But its feminine counterpart cannot be used this way. It is practically restricted to its sexual sense of "paramour." We start out with two terms, both roughly paraphrasable as "one who has power

over another." But the masculine form, once one person is no longer able to have absolute power over another, becomes usable metaphorically in the sense of "having power over *something.*" *Master* requires as its object only the name of some activity, something inanimate and abstract. But *mistress* requires a masculine noun in the possessive to precede it. One cannot say: "Rhonda is a mistress." One must be *someone's* mistress. A man is defined by what he does, a woman by her sexuality, that is, in terms of one particular aspect of her relationship to men. It is one thing to be an *old master* like Hans Holbein, and another to be an *old mistress.*

The same is true of the words *spinster* and *bachelor*—gender words   23
for "one who is not married." The resemblance ends with the definition. While *bachelor* is a neuter term, often used as a compliment, *spinster* normally is used pejoratively, with connotations of prissiness, fussiness, and so on. To be a bachelor implies that one has the choice of marrying or not, and this is what makes the idea of a bachelor existence attractive, in the popular literature. He has been pursued and has successfully eluded his pursuers. But a spinster is one who has not been pursued, or at least not seriously. She is old, unwanted goods. The metaphorical connotations of *bachelor* generally suggest sexual freedom; of *spinster,* puritanism or celibacy.

These examples could be multiplied. It is generally considered a   24
faux pas, in society, to congratulate a woman on her engagement, while it is correct to congratulate her fiancé. Why is this? The reason seems to be that it is impolite to remind people of things that may be uncomfortable to them. To congratulate a woman on her engagement is really to say, "Thank goodness! You had a close call!" For the man, on the other hand, there was no such danger. His choosing to marry is viewed as a good thing, but not something essential.

The linguistic double standard holds throughout the life of the re-   25
lationship. After marriage, bachelor and spinster become man and wife, not man and woman. The woman whose husband dies remains "John's widow"; John, however, is never "Mary's widower."

Finally, why is it that salesclerks and others are so quick to call   26
women customers "dear," "honey," and other terms of endearment they really have no business using? A male customer would never put up with it. But women, like children, are supposed to enjoy these endearments, rather than being offended by them.

In more ways than one, it's time to speak up.   27

QUESTIONS ON CONTENT

1. In her first paragraph Lakoff says, "Cultural bias was built into the language we were allowed to speak, the subjects we were allowed to speak about, and the ways we were spoken of." Of the three limitations, which one receives the most attention, and which the least?

2. What do you suppose Lakoff intends when she calls women "communicative cripples" (1)? Does she convince you that this is so? If so, how? If not, why not?

3. What, in Lakoff's view, is the effect of referring to a woman as a *lady?* In what circumstances would you use the word *lady?* What makes phrases like "lady lawyer," "lady minister," or "woman professor" condescending?

4. In paragraph 11 Lakoff discusses the differences between requests and commands. Explain the differences among the five examples she gives for getting a door closed.

5. What are "tag questions"? What, according to Lakoff, do they reveal about the speaker?

6. For you, is the word *master* still an exclusively masculine form, or can it now be used with reference to women as in "master teacher" or "master gardener"?

7. In paragraphs 21–25 Lakoff describes what she calls the "linguistic double standard." What does she mean by this phrase? Does this "double standard" still exist? Is it as strong as Lakoff claims it to be? Explain with examples from your own experience.

QUESTIONS ON RHETORIC

1. What is Lakoff's purpose in this essay? (Glossary: *Purpose*) Do you think it was written primarily to inform or to persuade? What leads you to your conclusion?

2. Lakoff uses examples to document each of the points in her presentation. Is she able to convince you on all of her points? If not, which ones lack convincing examples? (Glossary: *Examples*)

3. How would you describe Lakoff's style? (Glossary: *Style*) Does Lakoff herself use "women's language"? If so, give some examples. If not, how would you classify the language she does use?

4. Make a scratch outline of Lakoff's essay. What logical order do you see in her presentation of her main points? (Glossary: *Organization*)

5. In paragraph 13 Lakoff defines the term *euphemism.* Why do you suppose she felt the need to define it? What does this tell you about her intended audience? (Glossary: *Audience*)

6. Lakoff concludes her essay with a one-sentence paragraph. Does it serve to end her essay effectively? (Glossary: *Beginnings/Endings*) Why, or why not?

VOCABULARY

bias (1)
leeway (6)
elicit (7)
corroboration (8)

subliminal (10)
idiosyncrasies (11)
blatantly (19)

frivolity (20)
metaphorical (21)
consummate (22)

WRITING TOPICS

1. Since 1974 when this essay was first published, many would say that women's legal status and attitudes toward themselves have significantly changed. Do you find that women today still use "women's language"? How would you describe women's language today? Are Lakoff's claims of behavioral conditioning still valid? Provide examples from your own experience and observation in your essay.

2. What is "men's language"? Are there any disadvantages in talking "like a man"? In not doing so? Write an essay in which you first describe men's talk and then show how it differs from women's talk.

3. Lakoff says that "women's language" sounds much more polite than men's. Is politeness necessarily a sign of weakness or uncertainty? Explain. What is politeness good for? Is it ever desirable to be impolite? If so, when.

3
Women and Work

CASEY MILLER and KATE SWIFT

Casey Miller and Kate Swift have written many articles on sexism and language for national newspapers and magazines. They are well aware of the power of language to shape our thinking and to discriminate against women. In the following selection from The Handbook of Nonsexist Writing, *Miller and Swift examine the language used to describe women working at home or outside the home and offer many practical suggestions on how to replace exclusive, distorting, ambiguous, and injurious words.*

> "Do you talk to a working woman any differently than a housewife?"
> Advertising executive

What are housewives if not working women? According to a recent 1
study, the average housewife works 99.6 hours a week at a variety of
jobs (purchasing agent, cook, cleaner, economist, chauffeur, etc.) for
which the combined hourly pay scales would have earned her an annual salary of $17,351.88 in the 1978 job market.

Advertisers, along with other speakers and writers, might achieve 2
better communication with women who are full-time homemakers if
they used terms like *salaried women, wage-earning women,* or *women
employed outside the home* when referring to women in the paid work
force. The executive quoted above might have said

> Do you talk to a woman who works outside the home any differently than
> to a housewife?

It is interesting and probably significant that many women do not 3
use the term *work* to describe their housekeeping or homemaking activities. Nor, in general, do members of their families. A woman "stays
home" rather than "works at home." She "fixes dinner" rather than
"works in the kitchen." In contrast, activities men traditionally undertake around the house are usually dignified by the name *work*. A man
"works on the car" or "does his own electrical work." He may have a
"workshop" in the basement.

HOUSEWIFE

While the job a housewife performs is greatly undervalued, the word   4
housewife itself is overworked and often used with disparaging connotations. An insurance agency advertises that its agents take the time to
explain homeowners' insurance

"in terms even a housewife can understand."

The patronizing tone of the ad would be softened if it were revised to
read

in terms the average householder can understand.

A newspaper article on the making of an animated motion picture   5
described the vast amount of work required to produce 250,000 separate images on celluloid transparencies:

"On four floors of a Los Angeles office building, more than 150 artists did
the actual animating. Two hundred housewives with steady hands did the
routine work of painting the images onto cels."

Since steady hands and an aptitude for routine work are less characteristic of housewives as a class than they are of, say, watch repairers, the
use of the term *housewives* here is either irrelevant or insulting: this
chore is so simple even a housewife can do it. Or was the writer trying
to say that after the salaried artists had completed the animation, another 200 people finished the routine painting at home on a piecework
basis? If so, why not say so? If not, a better alternative would have
been

Two hundred assistants selected for their steady hands did the routine
work. . . .

Housewife is also usually out of place as a primary descriptive for a   6
woman who does something newsworthy.

The counterfeit credit cards were traced to a 47-year-old Denver housewife

gives no more pertinent information than would have been conveyed
by "a 47-year-old Denver woman," and it could leave some readers
with the impression that a connection exists between housewifery and
the use of counterfeit credit cards.

The misuse of *housewife* was epitomized a few years ago when   7
Margaret Thatcher, who had just been elected head of the Conservative Party in Great Britain, was regularly identified in the news media
as "a housewife." As it happens Thatcher, a tax lawyer and former
cabinet minister, ran her own household and so was in fact a house-

wife. To single out that term in describing her, however, was to imply that homemaking was her chief or only skill and the primary reason the Conservatives chose her to be their leader. It is hard to imagine any circumstance in which a comparable reference would be made to a man.

Perhaps the Thatcher example should be taken as evidence of the high esteem in which the Western world holds the homemaker's job. On the contrary. About the same time Thatcher was being described as "a housewife" an American newspaper ran an article about the growing number of men who are now full-time homemakers and headed it "The Nonworkers." If in the eyes of society *housework* and *nonwork* are equated, no wonder so many women whose chosen job is to maintain a home feel obliged to describe their occupation as "just housewife." 8

WORKING WIFE, WORKING MOTHER

"What is a working wife? One whose arms and legs move?"

An editor

"Working mothers? Are there any other kind?"

A *Little Leary* cartoon

In a series of articles entitled "Women at Work," a financial newspaper presented much well-researched factual information about women's increased participation in the labor market. But the series also reinforced some common assumptions: first, that it is always preferable in a marriage for the husband to be the breadwinner, the wife to be the homemaker and chief parent; second, that although it is acceptable for a man to hold a paid job even when he has other, adequate sources of income, a married woman who works outside the home for satisfaction rather than necessity contributes both to the unemployment of others and to growing inequities between rich and poor. Yet by omitting any consideration of the monetary value of homemaking—a figure that can be reckoned according to its replacement cost in the gross national product—the articles strengthened the widespread attitude that the unpaid work homemakers do is not an essential factor in the economy. 9

Whatever the merits of these assumptions, the language of the series demonstrated how deeply they have become ingrained in our thinking—and therefore in our patterns of writing and speech. This was particularly apparent in the use throughout the series of the terms *working wives* and *working mothers.* 10

When used to describe someone employed in a paying job, such   11
phrases define a woman primarily in terms of her domestic role; they
imply that her main responsibilities are toward something other than
her employment. Though the implication is often true, it can be
equally true of many men. Yet in the articles men were rarely identified as *working husbands* or *working fathers.*

> "Armed with surveys showing that working wives tend to get more help
> around the house from husbands . . ."

and, quoting a husband,

> "Working wives offer their husbands the flexibility to do what they want
> with their lives."

would have been more accurately phrased

> Armed with surveys showing that wives who work outside the home tend
> to get more help around the house from husbands . . . '

and

> Wives who bring home a paycheck offer their husbands the flexibility to
> do what they want with their lives.

(In the first instance housework is still assumed to be the wife's responsibility, and in the second she is still assigned a secondary, supporting
role; but the language itself is no longer ambiguous.)

An eight-part series on the subject of women in the work force,   12
especially one which drew on many interviews, could probably not be
expected to avoid terms like *working wife* or *women who work* completely, and to their credit the writers of the series used many alternatives such as "women holding jobs," "women who work for pay,"
"job-holding wife," "working parents," and "the husband-wife working family." Phrases like "women who work at home" also indicated
that work done by full-time homemakers was not being ignored. Nevertheless, the underlying assumption that women belong at home was
reinforced both by the language of the writers themselves and of the
people they quoted.

For example, one woman who works for a tree-spraying company   13
was described by the writer as doing

> "a man's job for equal pay,"

implying that when women compete for better-paid jobs they are in-
vading male territory. However, a later reference in the same article
used quotation marks to reflect an awareness—at least on the part of
the writer and the women being interviewed—that men do not have
exclusive rights to certain jobs:

"But many working women say they still have to walk softly on the job, particularly if they're doing 'man's work.' "

Women tended to be seen as wives, whereas men were called 14 "men" more often than "husbands." In each of the following sentences, for example, *husband* (or *husbands*) would have been the appropriate parallel to *wife* (or *wives*).

"It can be an uncomfortable feeling for a man when his wife goes to work."

"There are some less obvious benefits as well that men might gain through their working wives."

"With a working wife, a man can refuse a transfer, quit his job or just tell his boss to go to hell. . . . A wife's job provides a lot of freedom if men are just willing to accept it."

And so ingrained as the image of woman as wife that she continues to be seen as a wife even when she is divorced:

"Mrs. Doe, 53, was divorced three years ago. . . . As head of a household, [she] is a member of the most underprivileged group of working wives."

Married women are seen as blameworthy in a manner not shared 15 by men, whatever their marital, economic, or job status, or by unmarried women:

"Also disturbing are the tensions now arising between wives who work because of strict financial need and those who work because they want the status, satisfaction and adventure of carving a niche in the labor market."

Not surprisingly, wives, even when employed full time, are responsible for the smooth running of the household, as in the example already quoted and in the following:

"Local repairmen . . . get frequent requests nowadays to fix broken appliances after 4 P.M. or on Saturdays, because the customers are working wives."

Actually the reason no one is at home is

. . . because both the husband and wife have jobs,

and

"the day-time absence of employed wives"

is every bit as much

the day-time absence of husband and wife, both of whom are employed.

Even the children tend to be more the mother's children than the 16 father's. Following a description of youngsters waiting outside an elementary school before it opens in the morning, the copy reads

"Occasionally, a teacher or the principal also will come early to mind these offspring of working mothers."

Since the implication was not that these particular children are from single-parent families, but families in which both mother and father are employed, the sentence might have been phrased more equitably:

Occasionally, a teacher or the principal also will come early to mind these children whose parents both have jobs.

When the financial contribution of both spouses is the focus of attention, there is no more reason to single out women as workers (*working mothers, working wives*) than to single out men: 17

Most of the houses in the new development are being built by two-income families.

A two-paycheck family usually has less trouble getting a mortgage.

HOMEMAKING AND PARENTING

In the small percentage of one-parent families where the parent is a man, and in two-parent families where both parents are employed, fathers increasingly perform or share the work traditionally done by mothers. In addition, the Internal Revenue Service lists some 200,000 men in the United States who are full-time homemakers. Thus the disparity in the once commonly understood meanings of the verbs *to mother* (the social act of nurturance) and *to father* (the biological act of insemination) is disappearing. *Fathering,* too, has acquired the meaning "caring for or looking after someone" previously ascribed only to *mothering,* and a new word, *parenting,* is gaining acceptance.   18

New words come into being because enough people feel a need for them. *Parenting* serves two purposes: it describes the role of single parents who have to try to be both mother and father to their children, and it de-emphasizes the stereotype so frequently found in two-parent families that only mothers are responsible for "mothering." Like the familiar word *parenthood, parenting* conveys a sense of mutuality and shared responsibility.   19

Parents can help each other learn the arts of mothering and fathering

makes an arbitrary distinction between two prescribed roles. A father's ability to nurture and a mother's experiences in a world wider than the home are not denied when the sentence is rephrased

Mothers and fathers can help each other learn the art of parenting.

QUESTIONS ON CONTENT

1. What seems to be the problematic confusion between "working woman" and "housewife"? What alternatives do Miller and Swift suggest for "working woman" that are not demeaning to housewives?

2. What for you are the connotations of "housewife"? How do you think the word came to acquire these associations?

3. How, according to Miller and Swift, is the word *housewife* misused?

4. Why are Miller and Swift concerned about the language of the "Women at Work" series, which appeared in the *Wall Street Journal* between August 28 and September 22, 1978? How does the language of the articles reflect the major assumptions behind the series?

5. On what grounds do Miller and Swift object to the terms "working wives" and "working mothers"? What alternatives do the writers of the "Women at Work" series use? Explain why each alternative is preferable.

6. Why is the word *parenting* gaining widespread acceptance? What purposes does this word fulfill?

QUESTIONS ON RHETORIC

1. How are most of Miller and Swift's paragraphs organized? How effective do you find this organizational pattern? (Glossary: *Organization*)

2. What is the function of the Margaret Thatcher example in paragraphs 7 and 8? (Glossary: *Examples*)

3. What is the relationship between paragraphs 12 and 13?

4. What is the tone of this essay? (Glossary: *Tone*) Does the tone influence the way you react to Miller and Swift's suggestions for changing exclusive, distorting, ambiguous, and injurious words? Explain.

VOCABULARY

chauffeur (1)   celluloid (5)   epitomized (7)
connotations (4) pertinent (6)   marital (15)

WRITING TOPICS

1. Carefully read each of the following sentences.

   a. The average person finds it no problem at all to have three head colds, one sunburn, twenty headaches, and two hangovers, and still get in his sixty-one hours of shaving.

   b. Man can do several things which the animal cannot do. . . . His vital interests are not only life, food, access to females, but also. . . .

   c. A three-year-old may be able to feed and dress himself.

    d. The dolphin, a friendly and talkative creature, has a built-in sonar system of his own.

    e. It's the great secret among doctors, known only to their wives, that most things get better by themselves.

    f. ... explained in terms even a housewife can understand.

    g. With a working wife, a man can refuse a transfer, quit his job. ...

    h. The salutation Dear Sir is always permissible when addressing a person not known to the writer.

    i. The author exerts his magnetism on the small boy in all of us.

    j. James Brown will serve as chairman of the Planning Commission and Catherine Roe will serve as chairperson of the Zoning Board.

    k. TV listing: Powerful lady attorney and confident young lawyer team up to defend wealthy contractor.

Did you recognize the sexism in each one? Write an essay in which you describe your own speech and writing. Is it sexist? Can you always recognize the sexism in your own language? How do you feel when you try to avoid or circumvent sexism?

2. Miller and Swift state that "new words come into being because enough people feel a need for them" (19). Using examples from your own experiences or observations, write an essay in which you show the basic truth of this generalization.

4

In Defense of Gender

CYRA McFADDEN

For almost two decades now, feminist linguists have spearheaded the movement against language that discriminates against women. Although their attempts to eradicate sexism have been largely applauded, some people do not like what has happened to English in the process. Such a person is novelist and columnist Cyra McFadden. In the following essay, she argues that the "neutering" of English is both awkward and ludicrous.

So pervasive is the neutering of the English language on the   1
progressive West Coast, we no longer have people here, only persons:
male persons and female persons, chairpersons and doorpersons, wait-
persons, mailpersons—who may be either male or female mailpersons—and refuse-collection persons. In the classified ads, working
mothers seek childcare persons, though one wonders how many men
(archaic for "male person") take care of child persons as a full-time
occupation. One such ad, fusing nonsexist language and the most popular word in the California growth movement, solicits a "nurtureper-
son."

Dear gents and ladies, as I might have addressed you in less trou-   2
bled times, this female person knows firsthand the reasons for scourging sexist bias from the language. God knows what damage was done
me, at fifteen, when I worked in my first job—as what is now known as
a newspaper copyperson—and came running to the voices of men
barking, "Boy!"

No aspirant to the job of refuse-collection person myself, I none-   3
theless take off my hat (a little feathered number, with a veil) to those
of my own sex who may want both the job and a genderless title with
it. I argue only that there must be a better way, and I wish person or
persons unknown would come up with one.

Defend it on any grounds you choose; the neutering of spoken and   4
written English, with its attendant self-consciousness, remains ludicrous. In print, those "person" suffixes and "he/she's" jump out from
the page, as distracting as a cloud of gnats, demanding that the reader

note the writer's virtue. "Look what a nonsexist writer person I am, voiding the use of masculine forms for the generic."

Spoken, they leave conversation fit only for the Coneheads on "Saturday Night Live." "They have a daily special," a woman at the next table told her male companion in Perry's, a San Francisco restaurant. "Ask your waitperson." In a Steig cartoon, the words would have marched from her mouth in the form of a computer printout. 5

In Berkeley, Calif., the church to which a friend belongs is busy stripping its liturgy of sexist references. "They've gone berserk," she writes, citing a reading from the pulpit of a verse from 1 Corinthians. Neutered, the once glorious passage becomes "Though I speak with the tongues of persons and of angels. . . ." So much for sounding brass and tinkling cymbals. 6

The parson person of the same church is now referring to God as "He/She" and changing all references accordingly—no easy undertaking if he intends to be consistent. In the following, the first pronoun would remain because at this primitive stage of human evolution, male persons do not give birth to babies: "And she brought forth her firstborn son/daughter, and wrapped him/her in swaddling clothes, and laid him/her in a manger; because there was no room for them in the inn. . . ." 7

As the after-dinner speaker at a recent professional conference, I heard a text replete with "he/she's" and "his/her's" read aloud for the first time. The hapless program female chairperson stuck with the job chose to render these orally as "he-slash-she" and "his-slash-her," turning the following day's schedule for conference participants into what sounded like a replay of the Manson killings. 8

Redress may be due those of us who, though female, have answered to masculine referents all these years, but slashing is not the answer; violence never is. Perhaps we could right matters by using feminine forms as the generic for a few centuries, or simply agree on a per-woman lump-sum payment. 9

Still, we would be left with the problem of referring, without bias, to transpersons. These are not bus drivers or Amtrak conductors but persons in transit from one gender to the other—or so I interpret a fund-drive appeal asking me to defend their civil rights, along with those of female and male homosexuals. 10

Without wishing to step on anyone's civil rights, I hope transpersons are not the next politically significant pressure group. If they are, count on it, they will soon want their own pronouns. 11

In the tradition of the West, meanwhile, feminists out here wrestle the language to the ground, plant a foot on its neck and remove its masculine appendages. Take the local art critic Beverly Terwoman. 12

She is married to a man surnamed Terman. She writes under 13 "Terwoman," presumably in the spirit of *vive la différence.* As a letter to the editor of the paper for which she writes noted, however, "Terwoman" is not ideologically pure. It still contains "man," a syllable reeking of all that is piggy and hairy-chested.

Why not Beverly Terperson? Or better, since "Terperson" contains 14 "son," Terdaughter"? Or a final refinement, Beverly Ter?

Beverly Terwoman did not dignify this sexist assault with a reply. 15 The writer of the letter was a male person, after all, probably the kind who leaves his smelly sweat socks scattered around the bedroom floor.

No one wins these battles anyway. In another letter to the same 16 local weekly, J. Seibert, female, lets fire at the printing of an interview with Phyllis Schlafly. Not only was the piece "an offense to everything that Marin County stands for," but "it is even more amusing that your interview was conducted by a male.

"This indicates your obvious assumption that men understand 17 women's issues better than women since men are obviously more intelligent (as no doubt Phyllis would agree)."

A sigh suffuses the editor's note that follows: "The author of the 18 article, Sydney Weisman, is a female."

So the war of the pronouns and suffixes rages, taking no prisoners 19 except writers. Neuter your prose with all those clanking "he/she's," and no one will read you except Alan Alda. Use masculine forms as the generic, and you have joined the ranks of the oppressor. None of this does much to encourage friendly relations between persons, transpersons or—if there are any left—people.

I also have little patience with the hyphenated names more and 20 more California female persons adopt when they marry, in the interests of retaining their own personhood. These accomplish their intention of declaring the husband separate but equal. They are hell on those of us who have trouble remembering one name, much less two. They defeat answering machines, which can't handle "Please call Gwendolyn Grunt-Messerschmidt." And in this culture, they retain overtones of false gentility.

Two surnames, to me, still bring to mind the female writers of bad 21 romances and Julia Ward Howe.

It's a mug's game, friends, this neutering of a language already fat, 22 bland and lethargic, and it's time we decide not to play it. This female person is currently writing a book about rodeo. I'll be dragged behind a saddle bronc before I will neuter the text with "cowpersons."

QUESTIONS ON CONTENT

1. Why does McFadden object to the "neutering" of English? Does she think that this neutering process is just another language fad? How do you know?

2. How does McFadden react to "person" suffixes and "he/she's" in print? In speech? Do you have similar reactions?

3. On what grounds does McFadden object to hyphenated names? Do you share her objections? Why, or why not?

4. What does McFadden mean when she says "so the war of the pronouns and suffixes rages, taking no prisoners except writers" (19)?

5. McFadden believes there must be a "better way" to eliminate sexism than to "slash" English to death. Does she offer any solutions? Can you think of any solutions?

QUESTIONS ON RHETORIC

1. What is McFadden's thesis? (Glossary: *Thesis*) Where is it stated? How does she support it?

2. How would you describe McFadden's tone in this essay? (Glossary: *Tone*) Is it appropriate given her subject and purpose?

3. In paragraph 2 McFadden says that "this female person knows firsthand the reasons for scourging sexist bias from the language." How does this claim function in the context of her argument? Did you find it effective? Why, or why not?

4. Identify several metaphors and similes that McFadden uses and explain how each one works. (Glossary: *Figures of Speech*)

5. McFadden claims that "person" suffixes and "he/she's" are both awkward and ridiculous. In what ways does her essay itself illustrate this point?

6. Why do you think McFadden chose to use the word "neuter" to describe the process of eliminating sexism from English? What are the connotations of this word? (Glossary: *Connotation*) Is it an appropriate choice? Explain.

VOCABULARY

fusing (1)	replete (8)	appendages (12)
scourging (2)	render (8)	suffuses (18)
aspirant (3)	generic (9)	lethargic (22)
liturgy (6)		

WRITING TOPICS

1. When McFadden wrote her essay in 1981, she believed that the neutering of English was largely a West Coast phenomenon. How widespread is it today? Do you come into contact with neutered English on a daily basis? Or, has such usage started to die out? Write an essay in which you discuss neutering as a language fad or as a "here-to-stay" change. Feel free to take issue with McFadden and show the serious intent of the changes that have occurred. You might also want to consider other negative reactions to feminist "over-zealousness."

2. Select a passage from the *Bible,* an essay in this book, or a legal document and rewrite it so as to eliminate all sexist language. What do you think of the revised version? What has been lost in the rewriting? Which version do you prefer?

5

Solutions to the Great *He/She* Problem

MARTHA KOLLN

As the controversy about sexism in language swirls around us, it is easy to become extremely self-conscious about the words that we use, self-conscious to the point of sounding either awkward or funny in speech or writing. In the following selection from Understanding English Grammar, *Martha Kolln tells us how to handle situations when making reference to a person of unknown gender. It is reassuring just to know that there are many alternatives to "person" suffixes and "he/she's."*

An invitation to membership recently sent by the Smithsonian Institution included a "registered number" for the addressee only, along with the following statement:

> This registered number is not transferable. If *a friend* wishes to become a member, please ask *them* to write for information.

The gender of *a friend* is unknown, but its referent is clearly singular, so in terms of agreement *them* appears ungrammatical. To avoid *him,* with its masculine designation—and apparently to avoid the awkwardness of *him or her*—the Smithsonian has chosen to use *them* with an indefinite, singular meaning.

A few years ago neither the Smithsonian's writer nor anyone else would have hesitated to use *him:*

> If a friend wishes to become a member, please ask *him* to write for information.

Long-established usage in English calls for the masculine pronoun to refer to either sex in this structure, just as the word *man* has long been used in reference to both sexes in such words as *mankind* and such statements as *"Man* is the thinking animal." This custom was even institutionalized by an Act of Parliament in 1850 with "An Act for shortening the language used in acts of Parliament" which announced that in all acts words importing the masculine gender shall be deemed and taken to include females, and the singular to include the plural, and the plural the singular, unless the contrary as to gender and number is expressly provided.[1]

But times and attitudes change. We have come to recognize the power of language in shaping attitudes. So an important step in reshaping society's view of women is to eliminate the automatic use of *he* and *his* and *him* when the person referred to could just as easily be female:

> *Someone* should lend *his* coat to the accident victim.
> Ask *a friend* to get *his* own number.

This situation comes up time and time again, in writing as well as in conversation. In some cases, the choice of the pronoun is fairly automatic in our society:

> "My son's *kindergarten teacher* just called."
> "What did *she* want?"

> *"My doctor* just called me."
> "What did *he* want?"

> *"The nurse* just called me."
> "What did *she* want?"

The second speaker has no problem in responding, even though the gender of the person referred to is not known. In such conversations, however, if the doctor is a woman or the nurse a man, the first speaker can simply correct the error.

But what should the writer do? The pronoun system simply does not provide a singular version of *they/their/them* in reference to people. For inanimate nouns and for animals we can use *it;* sometimes we even use *it* for very small babies of unknown gender:

> "Isn't *it* cute!"
> "When is *it* due?"

In reference to grownup people we seem to have two choices: Like the Smithsonian, we can become language liberals and use *they* or we can be awkward and use *he or she (his or her)* or, as some writers do, *s/he* (which has no possessive or objective case so far):

> Someone should lend *their* coat to the victim.
> Someone should lend *his or her* coat to the victim.

3

4

5

6

---

[1] Quoted in Robert C. Pooley, *The Teaching of English Usage,* (Urbana, Ill.: The National Council of Teachers of English, 1974), p. 86.

Eventually, perhaps, the plural pronoun will be common for both singular and plural; in the second person (*you/your/you*) we make no distinction between singular plural, so it's not unreasonable to do the same in the third person. But such changes come about very slowly.

Meanwhile, what shall the writer do who wants to be not only logical and conservative but nonsexist as well? A number of current publications have adopted a policy of nonsexism in their pages, and more and more books are doing so as well, so it obviously can be done.

One alternative that often works when referring to students or teachers or people in general is to use the plural. The Smithsonian could easily have avoided the issue;

> If you have *friends* who wish to become members, please ask *them* to write for information.

The plural will not solve the problem in the sentence about the coat: "Someone should lend their coat." But sometimes in such cases another determiner can be substituted for the possessive pronoun:

> Someone should lend *a* coat to the victim.

The authors of the following passages could easily have found ways to avoid the masculine pronoun:

> Of all the developments in the history of m~~an~~ the human race, surely the most remarkable was language, for with it ~~he was~~ Our ancestors were able to pass on ~~his~~ their cultural heritage to succeeding generations who then did not have to rediscover how to make a fire, where to hunt, or how to build another wheel.[2]

> For thousands of years philosophers have been pondering the meaning of "meaning." Yet, everyone who knows a language can understand what is said to ~~him~~ and can produce strings of words which convey meaning.[3]

> It has been said that whenever ~~a person~~ people speak~~s~~, ~~he is~~ they are either mimicking or analogizing.[4]

It is a rare sentence, indeed, that cannot be stated in an alternative way. English is enormously versatile; we almost always have a choice.

---

[2] Charles B. Martin and Curt M. Rulon, *The English Language, Yesterday and Today* (Boston: Allyn and Bacon, Inc., 1973), p. 1.

[3] Victoria Fromkin and Robert Rodman, *An Introduction to Language* (New York: Holt, Rinehart and Winston, Inc., 1974), p. 100.

[4] Charles F. Hockett, "Analogical Creation," in Wallace L. Anderson and Norman C. Stageberg, Eds, *Introductory Readings on Language,* 3rd Edition (New York: Holt, Rinehart and Winston, Inc., 1970), p. 101.

QUESTIONS ON CONTENT

1. Why does Kolln believe that it is important to "eliminate the automatic use of *he* and *his* and *him* when the person referred to could just as easily be female" (3)?

2. How does the sexism problem differ for speakers and writers? How does a faulty pronoun reference get corrected when two people are talking?

3. What, according to Kolln, are the two choices available to the writer who wants to be nonsexist? Which choice does she prefer? Why?

4. Is it reasonable to expect that the third person plural pronoun will in time be common for both singular and plural references? Explain.

5. What logical and conservative suggestions does Kolln provide the writer who wants to be nonsexist?

6. Why, according to Kolln, is it a relatively easy task to avoid sexist usage?

QUESTIONS ON RHETORIC

1. How do the first two paragraphs serve to introduce Kolln's subject? Did you find it an effective introduction? Why, or why not? (Glossary: *Beginnings*)

2. Identify the transitions that Kolln uses to connect her paragraphs. (Glossary: *Transitions*)

3. What would be lost if Kolln had not provided the numerous examples that she does? Why are examples particularly helpful in this essay? (Glossary: *Examples*)

4. Why do you suppose Kolln uses the label "language liberals" in reference to the Smithsonian? How does this label affect you?

5. How would you describe Kolln's tone in this essay? (Glossary: *Tone*) Is her tone appropriate for both her subject and her purpose? Explain.

VOCABULARY

designation (1)   referent (1)   inanimate (5)

WRITING TOPICS

1. Write an essay in which you discuss the power of language to shape society's attitudes toward women.

2. Kolln claims that "English is enormously versatile," yet many native speakers feel restricted or limited by English. They seem to think that there is only one correct way to say or write things. Are you aware of the tremendous flexibility in the English language, or are you one of those who seems to be stuck in a language rut? Write an essay in which you discuss what this flexibility means or could mean for you as a speaker and/or writer.

WRITING ASSIGNMENTS FOR "LANGUAGE AND SEXISM"

1. Consider the following passage from Thomas Szasz's *The Second Sin:*

> The struggle for definition is veritably the struggle for life itself. In the typical Western two men fight desperately for the possession of a gun that has been thrown to the ground: whoever reaches the weapon first, shoots and lives; his adversary is shot and dies. In ordinary life, the struggle is not for guns but for words: whoever first defines the situation is the victor; his adversary, the victim. for example, in the family, husband and wife, mother and child do not get along; who defines whom as troublesome or mentally sick? Or, in the apocryphal story about Emerson visiting Thoreau in jail; Emerson asks: "Henry, what are you doing over there?" Thoreau replies: "Ralph, what are you doing over there?" In short, he who first seizes the word imposes reality on the other: he who defines thus dominates and lives; and he who is defined is subjugated and may be killed.

In what ways does what Szasz is saying apply to women's attempts to eliminate sexism from the English language? Is their struggle a "struggle for definition," a "struggle for life itself"?

2. Find twenty-five words in your desk dictionary that have some relation to males and females, and study the words in the way Nilsen studied her words. (Try to avoid overlapping her examples.) Using Nilsen's article "Sexism in English: A Feminist View" as a model, write a short paper in which you discuss the biases, if any, that you see in the language.

3. Since its beginning, the feminist movement has been surrounded with controversy. One commentator, for example, in a recent essay in *Time,* said, "The feminist attack on social crimes [sexual harassment, sex discrimination, etc.] may be as legitimate as it was inevitable. But the attack on words is only another social crime—one against the means and the hope of communication." Write an essay in which you agree or disagree with this writer's view of women's attempts to change language. Be sure to use examples to support your position.

4. It has been said that the words Americans use to describe old women are more derisive than those for old men because the words for women represent them as thoroughly repugnant and disgusting. Compile a list of words that you use or that you have heard used to refer to old people. Are the words for women more derogatory and demeaning? Write an essay in which you discuss the words on your list.

5. Write an essay in which you analyze Cyra McFadden's arguments in "In Defense of Gender." Does she ever seem to have missed the

point of the language changes? Which of her objections seem to you valid?

6. Write an essay in which you consider one or more of the following potentially sexist words or groups of words in English:

    a. feminine suffixes *-ess* or *-trix*
    b. fellow
    c. old wives' tale
    d. coed
    e. salutations in letters
    f. *Ms, Miss,* and *Mrs.*
    g. *girl* and *gal*

7. Consider the language used to describe the institution of marriage. Write an essay in which you discuss any sexist attitudes that are revealed in the words we use to write and talk about marriage.

NOTE: Suggested topics for research papers appear on p. 446.

NOTABLE QUOTATIONS

The following quotations are drawn from the essays in this section. They are presented as additional topics for classroom discussion or for writing assignments.

"A well-accepted linquistic principle is that as culture changes so will the language." *Nilsen* (2)

"If I were an anthropological linguist making observations about a strange and primitive tribe, I would duly note on my tape recorder that I had found linguistic evidence to show that in the area of sex and marriage the female appears to be more important than the male, but in all other areas of the culture, it seems that the reverse is true." *Nilsen* (14)

" 'Women's language' is that pleasant (dainty?), euphemistic never-aggressive way of talking we learned as little girls." *Lakoff* (1)

"The linguistic double standard holds throughout the life of the relationship. After marriage, a bachelor and spinster become man and wife, not man and woman. The woman whose husband dies remains "John's widow'; John, however, is never 'Mary's widower.' " *Lakoff* (25)

"What are housewives if not working women?" *Miller* and *Swift* (1)

"It is interesting and probably significant that many women do not use the term *work* to describe their housekeeping or homemaking activities." *Miller* and *Swift* (3)

"Defend it on any grounds you choose; the neutering of spoken and written English, with its attendant self-consciousness, remains ludicrous." *McFadden* (4)

"Perhaps we could right matters by using feminine forms as the generic for a few centuries, or simply agree on a per-woman lump-sum payment." *McFadden* (9)

"It is a rare sentence, indeed, that cannot be stated in an alternative way. English is enormously versatile; we almost always have a choice." *Kolln* (10)

VIII

Euphemisms and Professional Jargon

Euphemisms persist because lying is an indispensable part of making life tolerable.

Bergen Evans

The language of bureaucracy is essentially a professional jargon. Like other professional jargons it lends itself to exclusiveness, defensiveness, and laziness.

Henry A. Barnes

Until recent times, doctors talked a magic language, usually Latin, and its mystery was part of your cure. But modern doctors are rather in the situation of modern priests; having lost their magic languages, they run the risk of losing their magic powers too.

Diane Johnson

Most lawyers recognize better than the lay public the problems of impoverished and abused language. We should. We labor through many dozens of pages of it daily.

David S. Levine

Stilted language is as natural and inevitable a hallmark of bureaucracy as garlic is of an Italian restaurant.

Louis B. Lundborg

1
Euphemism

NEIL POSTMAN

In the following essay taken from his book Crazy Talk, Stupid Talk, *Neil Postman, professor of media ecology at New York University, defines euphemism and explains the often disapproved process of euphemizing. He believes that "euphemisms are a means through which a culture may alter its imagery and by so doing subtly change its style, its priorities, and its values." There are those people, however, for whom all euphemisms are bad. Postman argues that many euphemisms serve worthwhile social purposes.*

A euphemism is commonly defined as an auspicious or exalted term (like "sanitation engineer") that is used in place of a more down-to-earth term (like "garbage man"). People who are partial to euphemisms stand accused of being "phony" or of trying to hide what it is they are talking about. And there is no doubt that in some situations the accusation is entirely proper. For example, one of the more detestable euphemisms I have come across in recent years is the term "Operation Sunshine," which is the name the U.S. Government gave to some experiments it conducted with the hydrogen bomb in the South Pacific. It is obvious that the government, in choosing this name, was trying to expunge the hideous imagery that the bomb evokes and in so doing committed, as I see it, an immoral act. This sort of process—giving pretty names to essentially ugly realities—is what has given euphemizing such a bad name. And people like George Orwell have done valuable work for all of us in calling attention to how the process works. But there is another side to euphemizing that is worth mentioning, and a few words here in its defense will not be amiss.

To begin with, we must keep in mind that things do not have "real" names, although many people believe that they do. A garbage man is not "really" a "garbage man," any more than he is really a "sanitation engineer." And a pig is not called a "pig" because it is so dirty, nor a shrimp a "shrimp" because it is so small. There are things, and then there are the names of things, and it is considered a fundamental error in all branches of semantics to assume that a name and a thing are one and the same. It is true, of course, that a name is usually so firmly associated with the thing it denotes that it is extremely difficult to separate one from the other. That is why, for example, advertising is so effective. Perfumes are not given names like "Bronx Odor," and an automobile will never be called "The Lumbering Elephant." Shakespeare was only half right in saying that a rose by any other name would smell as sweet. What we call things affect how we will perceive them. It is not only harder to sell someone a "horse mackerel" sandwich than a "tuna fish" sandwich, but even though they are the "same" thing, we are likely to enjoy the taste of the tuna more than that of the horse mackerel. It would appear that human beings almost naturally come to *identify* names with things, which is one of our more fascinating illusions. But there is some substance to this illusion. For if you change the names of things, you change how people will regard them, and that is as good as changing the nature of the thing itself.

Now, all sorts of scoundrels know this perfectly well and can make   3
us love almost anything by getting us to transfer the charm of a name to whatever worthless thing they are promoting. But at the same time and in the same vein, euphemizing is a perfectly intelligent method of generating new and useful ways of perceiving things. The man who wants us to call him a "sanitation engineer" instead of a "garbage man" is hoping we will treat him with more respect than we presently do. He wants us to see that he is of some importance to our society. His euphemism is laughable only if we think that he is not deserving of such notice or respect. The teacher who prefers us to use the term "culturally different children" instead of "slum children" is euphemizing, all right, but is doing it to encourage us to see aspects of a situation that might otherwise not be attended to.

The point I am making is that there is nothing in the process of eu-   4
phemizing itself that is contemptible. Euphemizing is contemptible when a name makes us see something that is not true or diverts our attention from something that is. The hydrogen bomb kills. There is nothing else that it does. And when you experiment with it, you are trying to find out how widely and well it kills. Therefore, to call such an experiment "Operation Sunshine" is to suggest a purpose for the bomb that simply does not exist. But to call "slum children" "culturally different" is something else. It calls attention, for example, to legitimate reasons why such children might feel alienated from what goes on in school.

I grant that sometimes such euphemizing does not have the in-   5
tended effect. It is possible for a teacher to use the term "culturally different" but still be controlled by the term "slum children" (which the

teacher may believe is their "real" name). "Old people" may be called "senior citizens," and nothing might change. And "lunatic asylums" may still be filthy, primitive prisons though they are called "mental institutions." Nonetheless, euphemizing may be regarded as one of our more important intellectual resources for creating new perspectives on a subject. The *attempt* to rename "old people" "senior citizens" was obviously motivated by a desire to give them a political identity, which they not only warrant but which may yet have important consequences. In fact, the fate of euphemisms is very hard to predict. A new and seemingly silly name may replace an old one (let us say, "chairperson" for "chairman") and for years no one will think or act any differently because of it. And then, gradually, as people begin to assume that "chairperson" is the "real" and proper name (or "senior citizen" or "tuna fish" or "sanitation engineer"), their attitudes begin to shift, and they will approach things in a slightly different frame of mind. There is a danger, of course, in supposing that a new name can change attitudes quickly or always. There must be some authentic tendency or drift in the culture to lend support to the change, or the name will remain incongruous and may even appear ridiculous. To call a teacher a "facilitator" would be such an example. To eliminate the distinction between "boys" and "girls" by calling them "childpersons" would be another.

But to suppose that such changes never "amount to anything" is to 6 underestimate the power of names. I have been astounded not only by how rapidly the name "blacks" has replaced "Negroes" (a kind of euphemizing in reverse) but also by how significantly perceptions and attitudes have shifted as an accompaniment to the change.

The key idea here is that euphemisms are a means through which a 7 culture may alter its imagery and by so doing subtly change its style, its priorities, and its values. I reject categorically the idea that people who use "earthy" language are speaking more directly or with more authenticity than people who employ euphemisms. Saying that someone is "dead" is not to speak more plainly or honestly than saying he has "passed away." It is, rather, to suggest a different conception of what the event means. To ask where the "shithouse" is, is no more to the point than to ask where the "restroom" is. But in the difference between the two words, there is expressed a vast difference in one's attitude toward privacy and propriety. What I am saying is that the process of euphemizing has no moral content. The moral dimensions are supplied by what the words in question express, what they want us to value and see. A nation that calls experiments with bombs "Operation Sunshine" is very frightening. On the other hand, a people who call "garbage men" "sanitation engineers" can't be all bad.

QUESTIONS ON CONTENT

1. If, as Postman says, "there is nothing in the process of euphemizing itself that is contemptible" (4), why do euphemisms have such a bad name?

2. Postman states, "There are things, and then there are the names of things, and it is considered a fundamental error in all branches of semantics to assume that a name and a thing are one and the same" (2). What does he mean? What happens when people think that a name and a thing are the same?

3. Postman believes that "euphemizing may be regarded as one of our more important intellectual resources for creating new perspectives on a subject" (5) How can you change people's perception of something by simply changing its name? Give several examples of your own which substantiate Postman's claim.

4. What does Postman mean when he says that the change from "Negroes" to "blacks" is "a kind of euphemizing in reverse" (6)?

5. Why does Postman "reject categorically the idea that people who use 'earthy' language are speaking more directly or with more authenticity than people who employ euphemisms" (7)? Do you agree with him?

QUESTIONS ON RHETORIC

1. What is Postman arguing for in this essay?

2. Postman presents a dictionary definition of *euphemism* in the first sentence of the essay. Why is it appropriate that he begin with a definition of the term? (Glossary: *Beginnings*)

3. What would be lost if Postman hadn't used all the examples that he includes? (Glossary: *Examples*) Are they all functional and necessary? Explain.

4. In what ways has Postman used transitions to make paragrah 2 coherent? (Glossary: *Transitions*)

5. Why are Postman's last two sentences an appropriate conclusion to his essay? (Glossary: *Beginnings/Endings*)

VOCABULARY

auspicious (1)	evokes (1)	illusions (2)
exalted (1)	amiss (1)	contemptible (4)
expunge (1)	semantics (2)	categorically (7)
hideous (1)		

WRITING TOPICS

1. Postman says, "Euphemizing is contemptible when a name makes us see something that is not true or diverts our attention from something that is" (4). Which of the euphemisms listed below do you find contemptible? Why are they contemptible? Why are the others not contemptible?

pre-owned ("used")
broadcast journalist ("news reporter")
Internal Revenue Service ("tax collector")
nervous wetness ("sweat")
facial blemishes ("pimples")
orderly withdrawal ("retreat")
resources control program ("defoliation")
health alteration committee ("assassination team")
convenient terms ("18 percent annual interest")
queen-size ("large")

Write an essay discussing the uses to which euphemisms can be put. Be sure to include some examples of your own.

2. Several years ago, the editors of *Time* said that "despite its swaggering sexual candor, much contemporary speech still hides behind that traditional enemy of plain talk, the euphemism." Using examples from your own experience or observation, write an essay in which you agree or disagree with the editors of *Time*.

2

Occupational Euphemisms

H. L. MENCKEN

The editors of Time *magazine reported not so long ago on an attempt in Germany to merchandise and make more respectable the "oldest profession in the world." Large, comfortable hotels for prostitution are now called "Eros-centers," and the women who work in them are called "Erostesses." This amusing use of euphemisms is only one more in a long history of attempts by people to elevate themselves by retitling their occupations. In this selection, H. L. Mencken, outspoken journalist, social critic, and commentator on American English during the 1920s and 1930s, has provided us with what has become a classic discussion of this topic.*

The American, probably more than any other man, is prone to be   1
apologetic about the trade he follows. He seldom believes that it is
quite worthy of his virtues and talents; almost always he thinks that he
would have adorned something far gaudier. Unfortunately, it is not always possible for him to escape, or even for him to dream plausibly of
escaping, so he soothes himself by assuring himself that he belongs to a
superior section of his craft, and very often he invents a sonorous name
to set himself off from the herd. Here we glimpse the origin of a multi-
tude of characteristic American euphemisms, e.g., *mortician* for *under-
taker, realtor* for *real-estate agent, electragist* for *electrical contractor,
aisle manager* for *floor-walker, beautician* for *hairdresser, exterminating
engineer* for *rat-catcher,* and so on. *Realtor* was devised by a high-
toned real-estate agent of Minneapolis, Charles N. Chadbourn by
name. He thus describes its genesis:

> It was in November 1915, on my way to a meeting of the Minneapolis
> Real Estate Board that I was annoyed by the strident peddling of a scan-
> dal sheet. "All About the Robbery of a Poor Widow by a Real Estate
> Man." The "real estate man" thus exposed turned out to be an obscure
> hombre with desk-room in a back office in a rookery, but the incident set
> me to thinking. "Every member of our board," I thought, "is besmirched
> by this scandal article. Anyone, however unworthy or disreputable, may
> call himself a real estate man. Why do not the members of our board de-

serve a distinctive title? Each member is vouched for by the board, subscribes to its Code of Ethics, and must behave himself or get out." So the idea incubated for three or four weeks, and was then sprung on the local brethren.

As to the etymology of the term, Mr. Chadbourn says: 2

Real estate originally meant a royal grant. It is so connected with land in the public mind that *realtor* is easily understood, even at a first hearing. The suffix -or means a doer, one who performs an act, as in *grantor, executor, sponsor, administrator.*

The Minneapolis brethren were so pleased with their new name   3
that Mr. Chadbourn was moved to dedicate it to the whole profession. In March 1916, he went to the convention of the National Association of Real Estate Boards at New Orleans, and made a formal offer of it. It was accepted gratefully, and is now defined by the association as follows:

A person engaged in the real estate business who is an active member of a member board of the National Association of Real Estate Boards, and as such, an affiliated member of the National Association, who is subject to its rules and regulations, who observes its standards of conduct, and is entitled to its benefits.

In 1920 the Minneapolis Real Estate Board and the National Asso-   4
ciation of Real Estate Boards applied to Judge Joseph W. Molyneaux of Minneapolis for an injunction restraining the Northwestern Telephone Exchange Company from using *realtor* to designate some of its hirelings, and on September 10 the learned judge duly granted this relief. Since then the National Association has obtained similar injunctions in Virginia, Utah and other States. Its general counsel is heard from every time *realtor* is taken in vain, and when, in 1922, Sinclair Lewis applied it to George F. Babbitt, there was an uproar. But when Mr. Chadbourn was appealed to he decided that Babbitt was "fairly well described," for he was "a prominent member of the local board and of the State association," and one could scarcely look for anything better in a "book written in the ironic vein of the author of 'Main Street.' " Mr. Chadbourn believes that *realtor* should be capitalized, "like *Methodist* or *American*," but so far it has not been generally done. In June, 1925, at a meeting of the National Association of Real Estate Boards in Detroit, the past presidents of the body presented him with a gold watch as a token of their gratitude for his contribution to the uplift of their profession. On May 30, 1934, the following letter from Nathan William MacChesney, general counsel of the National Association, appeared in the *New Republic:*

[*Realtor*] is not a word, but a trade right, coined and protected by law by the National Association of Real Estate Boards, and the term is a part of the trade-mark as registered in some forty-four States and Canada. Something over $200,000 has been spent in its protection by the National Association of Real Estate Boards in attempting to confine its use to those real estate men who are members of the National Association of Real Estate Boards, subject to its code of ethics and to its discipline for violation. It has been a factor in making the standards of the business generally during the past twenty years, and the exclusive right of the National Association of Real Estate Boards has been sustained in a series of court decisions, a large number of injunctions having been issued, restraining its improper use.

In 1924 the *Realtor's Bulletin* of Baltimore reported that certain 5 enemies of realtric science were trying to show that *realtor* was derived from the English word *real* and the Spanish word *toro,* a bull, and to argue that it thus meant *real bull.* But this obscenity apparently did not go far; probably a hint from the alert general counsel was enough to stop it. During the same year I was informed by Herbert U. Nelson, executive secretary of the National Association, that "the real-estate men of London, through the Institute of Estate Agents and Auctioneers, after studying our experience in this respect, are planning to coin the word *estator* and to protect it by legal steps." This plan, I believe, came to fruition, but *estator* never caught on, and I can't find it in the Supplement to the Oxford Dictionary. *Realtor,* however, is there—and the first illustrative quotation is from *Babbitt!* In March, 1927, J. Foster Hagan, of Ballston, Va., reported to *American Speech* that he had encountered *realtress* on the window of a real-estate office there, but this charming derivative seems to have died a-bornin'. In 1925 or thereabout certain ambitious insurance solicitors, inflamed by *realtor,* began to call themselves *insurors,* but it, too, failed to make any progress.

Electragist, like realtor, seems to be the monopoly of the lofty tech- 6 nicians who affect it: "it is copyrighted by the Association of Electragists International, whose members alone may use it." But *mortician* is in the public domain. It was proposed by a writer in the *Embalmers' Monthly* for February, 1895, but the undertakers, who were then *funeral-directors,* did not rise to it until some years later. On September 16, 1916, some of the more eminent of them met at Columbus O., to form a national association, on the lines of the American College of Surgeons, the American Association of University Professors, and the Society of the Cincinnati, and a year later they decided upon National Selected *Morticians* as its designation. To this day the association remains so exclusive that, of the 24,000 undertakers in the United States, only 200 belong to it. But any one of the remaining 23,800 is free to call himself a *mortician,* and to use all the other lovely words that the advance of human taxidermy has brought in. *Mortician,* of course, was suggested by *physician,* for undertakers naturally admire and like to pal with the resurrection men, and there was a time when some of them called themselves *embalming surgeons.* A *mortician* never handles a *corpse;* he *prepares a body* or *patient.* This business is carried on in a *preparation-room* or *operating room,*and when it is achieved the patient is put into a *casket* and stored in the *reposing-room* or *slumber-room* of a *funeral-home.* On the day of the funeral he is moved to the *chapel* therein for the last exorcism, and then hauled to the cemetery in a *funeral-car* or *casket-coach.* The old-time shroud is now a *négligé* or *slumber-shirt* or *slumber-robe,* the mortician's worktruck is an *ambulance,* and the cemetery is fast becoming a *memorial-park.* In the West cemeteries are being supplanted by public mausoleums, which sometimes go under the names of *cloisters, burial-abbeys,* etc. To be laid away in one runs into money. The vehicle that morticians use for their expectant hauling of the ill is no longer an *ambulance,* but an *invalid-coach.* *Mortician* has been a favorite butt of the national wits, but they seem to have made no impression on it. In January, 1932, it was barred from the columns of the Chicago *Tribune.* "This decree goes forth," announced the *Tribune,* "not for lack of sympathy with the ambition of undertakers to be well regarded, but because of it. If they haven't the sense to save themselves from their own lexicographers, we shall not be guilty of abetting them in their folly." But *mortician* not only continues to flourish; it also begets progeny, e.g., *beautician, cosmetician, radiotrician* and *bootician.* The barbers, so far, have not devised a name for themselves in *-ician,* but they may be trusted to do so anon. In my youth they were *tonsorial artists,* but in recent years some of them have been calling themselves *chirotonsors.* Practically all American press-agents are now *public relations counsels, contact-managers* or *publicists,* all tree-trimmers are *tree-surgeons,* all milk-wagon and bakery-wagon drivers have become *salesmen,* nearly all janitors are *superintendents,* many gardeners have become *landscape-architects* (in England even the whales of the profession are simple landscape-gardeners), cobblers are beginning to call themselves *shoe-rebuilders,* and the corn-doctors, after a generation as *chiropodists,* have burst forth as *podiatrists.* The American fondness for such sonorous appellations arrested the interest of W. L. George, the English novelist, when he visited the United States in 1920. He said:

> Business titles are given in America more readily than in England. I know one *president* whose staff consists of two typists. Many firms have four *vice-presidents.* In the magazines you seldom find merely an *editor;* the

others need their share of honor, so they are *associate* (not *assistant*) editors. A dentist is called a *doctor*. I wandered into a university, knowing nobody, and casually asked for the *dean*. I was asked, "Which *dean?*" In that building there were enough deans to stock all the English cathedrals. The master of a secret society is *royal supreme knight commander*. Perhaps I reached the extreme at a theatre in Boston, when I wanted something, I forgot what, and was told that I must apply to the *chief of the ushers*. He was a mild little man, who had something to do with people getting into their seats, rather a comedown from the pomp and circumstance of his title. Growing interested, I examined my programme, with the following result: It is not a large theatre, but it has a *press-representative*, a *treasurer* (box-office clerk), an *assistant treasurer* (box-office junior clerk), an *advertising-agent*, our old friend the *chief of the ushers*, a *stage-manager*, a *head electrician*, a *master of properties* (in England called *props*), a *leader of the orchestra* (pity this—why not *president*) and a *matron* (unknown).

George might have unearthed some even stranger magnificoes in   7
other playhouses. I once knew an ancient bill-sticker, attached to a Baltimore theatre, who boasted the sonorous title of *chief lithographer*. Today, in all probability, he would be called a *lithographic-engineer*. For a number of years the *Engineering News-Record,* the organ of the legitimate engineers, used to devote a column every week to just such uninvited invaders of the craft, and some of the species it unearthed were so fantastic that it was constrained to reproduce their business cards photographically in order to convince its readers that it was not spoofing. One of its favorite exhibits was a bedding manufacturer who first became a *mattress-engineer* and then prompted himself to the lofty dignity of *sleep-engineer*. No doubt he would have called himself a *morphician* if he had thought of it. Another exhilarating specimen was a tractor-driver who advertised for a job as a *caterpillar-engineer*. A third was a beautician who burst out as an *appearance-engineer*. In an Atlanta department-store the *News-Record* found an *engineer of good taste*—a young woman employed to advise newly-married couples patronizing the furniture department, and elsewhere it unearthed *display-engineers* who had been lowly window-dressers until some visionary among them made the great leap, *demolition-engineers* who were once content to be house-wreckers, and *sanitary-engineers* who had an earlier incarnation as garbage-men. The *wedding-engineer* is a technician employed by florists to dress churches for hymeneal orgies. The *commencement-e.* arranges college and high-school commencements; he has lists of clergymen who may be trusted to pray briefly, and some sort of fire-alarm connection, I suppose, with the office of Dr. John H. Finley, the champion commencement orator of this or any other age. The *packing-e.* is a scientist who crates clocks, radios and chinaware for shipment. The *correspondence-e.* writes selling-letters guaranteed

to pull. The *income-e.* is an insurance solicitor in a new falseface. The *dwelling-e.* replaces lost keys, repairs leaky roofs, and plugs up ratholes in the cellar. The *vision-e.* supplies spectacles at cut rates. The *dehorning-e.* attends to bulls who grow too frisky. The *Engineering News-Record* also discovered a *printing-e.*, a *furniture-e.*, a *photographic-e.*, a *financial-e.* (a stock-market tipster), a *paint-e.*, a *clothing-e.*, a *wrapping-e.* (a dealer in wrapping-paper), a *matrimonial-e.* (a psychoanalyst specializing in advice to the lovelorn), a *box-e.* (the *packing-e.* under another name), an *automotive-painting-e.*, a *blasting-e.*, a *dry-cleaning-e.* a *container-e.*, a *furnishing-e.*, a *socioreligious-e.* (an uplifter), a *social-e.* (the same), a *feed-plant-e.*, a *milk-e.*, a *surface-protection-e.*, an *analyzation-e.*, a *fiction-e.*, a *psychological-e.* (another kind of psychoanalyst), a *casement-window-e.* a *shingle-e.*, a *fumigating-e.*, a *laminated-wood-e.*, a *package-e.* (the *packing-e.* again), a *horse-e.*, a *podiatric-e.* (a corn-doctor), an *ice-e.*, a *recreation-e.*, a *tire-e.*, a *paint-maintenance-e.*, a *space-saving-e.*, a *film-e.*, (or *film-gineer*), a *criminal-e.* (a criminologist), a *diet-kitchen-e.*, a *patent-e.*, an *equipment-e.*, a *floor-covering-e.*, a *society-e.*, a *window-cleaning-e.*, a *dust-e.*, a *hospitalization-e.*, a *baking-e.*, a *directory-e.*, an *advertising-e.*, a *golf-e.* (a designer of golf courses), a *humane-e.* (another variety of psychoanalyst), an *amusement-e.*, an *electric-sign-e.*, a *household-e.*, a *pageant-e.*, an *idea-e.*, a *ballistics-e.*, a *lace-e.* and a *sign-e.* Perhaps the prize should go to the *dansant-e.* (an agent supplying dancers and musicians to nightclubs), or to the *hot-dog-e.* The exterminating-engineers have a solemn national association and wear a distinguishing pin; whether or not they have tried to restrain non-member rat-catchers from calling themselves *engineers* I do not know. In 1923 the *Engineering News-Record* printed a final blast against all the pseudo-engineers then extant, and urged its engineer readers to boycott them. But this boycott apparently came to nothing, and soon thereafter it abated its indignation and resorted to laughter. Next to *engineer, expert* seems to be the favorite talisman of Americans eager to augment their estate and dignity in this world. Very often it is hitched to an explanatory prefix, e.g., *housing-, planning-, hog-, erosion-, marketing-, boll-weevil-,* or *sheepdip-,* but sometimes the simple adjective *trained-* suffices. When the Brain Trust came into power in Washington, the town began to swarm with such quacks, most of them recent graduates of the far-flung colleges of the land. One day a humorous member of Congress printed an immense list of them in the *Congressional Record,* with their salaries and academic dignities. He found at least one whose expertness was acquired in a seminary for chiropractors. During the John Purroy Mitchel "reform" administration in New York City (1914–18) so many bogus *experts* were put upon the payroll that special designations for them ran out, and in prodding through the Mitchel records later on

Bird S. Coler discovered that a number had been carried on the books as *general experts.*

QUESTIONS ON CONTENT

1. A euphemism is a supposedly pleasant or higher-status term that is used in place of a blunt or lower-status term. Do you think there is a substantial difference between "real estate man" and "realtor"? Why do you think that Chadbourn was offended by "real estate man"?

2. Why, according to Mencken, do Americans use so many occupational euphemisms?

3. Usually it is those who are in the occupations themselves who call for occupational euphemisms. Do you feel that Mencken or anyone else is justified in criticizing such desires or euphemistic usages? Explain.

4. In paragraph 6 Mencken discusses morticians and the euphemisms associated with their business. What is the total effect of these words?

5. In paragraph 1, Mencken draws attention to a basic contradiction of American life. What is this contradiction? Can it be resolved?

QUESTIONS ON RHETORIC

1. What is the relationship of paragraph 1 to the rest of Mencken's essay? (Glossary: *Beginnings*)

2. How does Mencken introduce his lengthy discussion of the use of the term *engineer?* Do you consider this method effective? What did you think of Mencken's long list of "engineer" examples. Has he given us too much of a good thing? Why, or why not?

3. How does Mencken reveal his attitude toward occupational euphemisms? Consider carefully the language of the essay—for example, "undertakers naturally admire and like to pal with the resurrection men" (6); "in England even the whales of the profession are simple *landscape-gardeners*" (6); "sonorous appellations" (6); "hymeneal orgies" (7). (Glossary: *Diction*)

4. Throughout this essay, Mencken writes of the person involved in an occupation as "he"; the essay begins:

> The American, probably more than any other *man,* is prone to be apologetic about the trade *he* follows. *He* seldom believes that it is quite worthy of *his* virtues and talents; almost always *he* thinks that *he* would have adorned something far gaudier. Unfortunately, it is not always possible for *him* to escape, or even for *him* to dream plausibly of escaping, so *he* soothes *himself* by assuring *himself* that *he* belongs to a superior section of *his* craft . . . [italics added].

Mencken wrote at a time when use of the male pronouns and the generic *man* was not considered sex-biased. Today many people object to the use of exclusively male references. How can the sentences be rewritten to eliminate the italicized references? You may find it helpful to read the short essay by Martha Kolln (p. 332) before rewriting Mencken's paragraph.

5. The paragraphs in Mencken's essay are rather long by contemporary standards. Do you have any suggestions about where he could have divided a long paragraph into two or more shorter ones? Explain.

VOCABULARY

adorned (1)	fruition (5)	progeny (6)
plausibly (1)	derivative (5)	abated (7)
injunction (4)	domain (6)	augment (7)
solicitors (5)		

WRITING TOPICS

1. If you worked as a writer for a newspaper, would you prefer to be called a journalist, reporter, or newspaperman (newspaperwoman)? In a brief essay, explain your preference and your reasons for rejecting the other terms.

2. If euphemisms are a way of covering up something ugly, then occupational euphemisms indicate workers' attitudes toward their jobs. In his best-selling book *Working,* Studs Terkel collects the statements of workers from virtually every job field. What insights does this excerpt from Terkel's introduction offer about why people need occupational euphemisms?

> This book, being about work, is, by its very nature, about violence—to the spirit as well as to the body. It is about ulcers as well as accidents, about shouting matches as well as fistfights, about nervous breakdowns as well as kicking the dog around. It is, above all (or beneath all), about daily humiliations. To survive the day is triumph enough for the walking wounded among the great many of us. . . .
>
> It is about a search, too, for daily meaning as well as daily bread, for recognition as well as cash, for astonishment rather than torpor; in short, for a sort of life rather than a Monday through Friday sort of dying. Perhaps immortality, too, is part of the quest. To be remembered was the wish, spoken and unspoken, of the heroes and heroines of this book.

Now, write an essay in which you discuss the euphemisms associated with your summer job or with your job during the academic year. How do these euphemisms affect your attitude toward your work?

3
Jargon
and the Professions

KENNETH HUDSON

What is jargon, and how is it different from technical language? In the following selection from The Jargon on the Professions, *Kenneth Hudson explains the differences and argues against jargon that is meant only to impress or hide the truth. The best way to keep jargon under control, Hudson believes, is to offer students a broadly-based education that encourages a "pride in handling words really well."*

Technical language is not, in itself, jargon, and it is not a criminal or moral offence to write or speak in a way which is not immediately understood by the man in the street. Every profession necessarily has its own terminology, without which its members cannot think or express themselves. To deprive them of such words would be to condemn them to inactivity. If one wished to kill a profession, to remove its cohesion and its strength, the most effective way would be to forbid the use of its characteristic language. 1

On the other hand, there are people, possibly many people, whose supposedly technical language does not stand up to close examination. It is bogus, existing only to impress the innocent and unwary, and interfering with the process of communication instead of improving it. It may well suggest this profession, rather than that, and it may, in small doses, have a certain exotic charm, provided one is in the mood to accept and enjoy it. But it is not essential, cannot be justified on practical grounds and fulfils no purpose, except possibly to act as a kind of masonic glue between different members of the same profession. The solidarity-value of such nonsense-language certainly should not be underestimated. 2

With these possibilities in mind, one might suggest that jargon, in the last quarter of the twentieth century, contains four essential elements: 3

1. It reflects a particular profession or occupation.
2. It is pretentious, with only a small kernel of meaning underneath it.

356

3. It is used mainly by intellectually inferior people, who feel a need to convince the general public of their importance.
4. It is, deliberately or accidentally, mystifying.

The best minds in any profession are never guilty of jargon, except   4
when they are very tired. Pedestrian minds are drawn towards it automatically and to the most frightening extent. Jargon, one could suggest, is the natural weapon of highly paid people with very little of any value to say. It is a sad and ironical comment on our society that many people feel released from the pressure to use jargon only when they have reached the top of their profession, by which time it may be too late to change one's habits, however much one might wish to. Ambitious people, still busy climbing the ladder, may well consider it professionally dangerous to use straightforward language. One therefore has the paradox that only the person who has finally arrived, with his reputation secure, can afford to be simple and jargon-free. Lesser mortals appear to need their jargon, as a membership-badge of their profession. They do not have the confidence to face the world without it.

There is always the possibility, alas, that people use jargon because   5
they have never learnt or been taught to write properly. At a discussion which took place in Cambridge in 1958, Dr. C. F. A. Pantin spoke with some feeling on the point, as editor of a scientific periodical.

> The most important part of my editorial work [he said] consists of trying to help contributors to say clearly and concisely what they have to say. Many Universities encourage the production of long-winded theses for the degree of Doctor of Philosophy. All too often it is left to the editors to show the contributor how to winnow this stuff and to extract from it the lucid and cogent statement of fact and argument that is worth publication. Nor is this difficulty confined to the young. I have yet to attend an international conference which did not illustrate how firmly men and women believe, perhaps correctly, that professional advancement is closely knit with long-winded and excessive publication, particularly in the highly specialized fields of learning.

Editors, can, however, exercise a pressure different from, and much   6
less beneficial than that suggested by Dr. Pantin, especially nowadays when all forms of publication are expensive. In their anxiety to save space, they may well encourage the German-type double and triple adjectives and the absence of prepositions which produce such overcompressed and disagreeable-sounding prose.

No professional publication contains less jargon, in our sense of the   7
term, than the *British Medical Journal*. What there is is usually very mild, of the "ambulant patient" type. Two generations of editors have conducted a vigorous compaign against it and the results are there to be seen in any issue one cares to select. Some editorial blue-pencilling

is still carried out, but a quarter of a century of campaigning and of rejection of potential contributions has had its effect. Once it becomes generally known that the well-written article is likely to be published and the badly-written one sent back, an improvement in style is almost inevitable.

One cannot say the same about a number of the journals devoted   8 to psychiatry and psychology, especially in the United States. *Archives of General Psychiatry*, Chicago, for instance, is full of dreadful stuff, of which one example will be, for the moment, more than sufficient.

> Other group modalities often used with children are play, behavior modification, and the verbal approach. . . . Play materials are selected to evoke group members' expression and resolution of personal conflicts. Therapeutic ingredients are the therapist-child relationship and therapist clarification—interpretation of feelings expressed through the child's play. Member-to-member interaction is seen as less important in play than in activity-group treatment. In behavior modification groups, the armentarium of behavioral techniques is applied. Treatment goals are limited to the modification of specific behavior patterns. The verbal group therapies include client-centered counseling and insight-oriented psychotherapy. Definitive features of these modalities are discussion of the patients' problems and mobilization of member-to-member and member-to-therapist interaction to improve psychobehavioral functioning.

The key test for jargon is the question: "Could this have been ex-   9 pressed more simply without communication suffering in the process?" If the answer is "Yes," then the probability is that one is faced with a piece of jargon. The passage just quoted from *Archives of General Psychiatry* contains a good deal of jargon, measured by this standard. The following, from the same journal, is not jargon, however.

> If concomitant antiparkinson medication is required, it may have to be continued after HALDOL haloperidol is discontinued, because of the difference in excretion rates. If both are discontinued simultaneously, extrapyramidal symptoms may occur. Intraocular pressure may increase when anticholinergic drugs, including antiparkinson agents, are administered concomitantly with HALDOL haloperidol.

This is technical medical language, a professional code which is   10 perfectly intelligible to anyone who has learnt its elements and who knows how to interpret them. The information cannot be translated into anything simpler.

It is important, however, to distinguish different levels of technical-   11 ity. One can easily illustrate this from the medical field. An example of high-technicality language, which is not jargon, is:

> Normal women had higher mean (this is gamma) γ-globulin levels than males. There was evidence of connective-tissue disease in 10% of female

relatives of patients with systematic lupus erythematosus. A bimodal distribution of serum γ-globulin levels and a raised incidence of antinuclear factor was found in relatives of patients with systematic lupus erythematosus. Rheumatoid factor was slightly more common in female relatives of patients with systemic lupus than would be expected. In addition to familial factors, environmental factors such as hyrallazine therapy might be important in systematic lupus erythematosus.

This is medium-technicality language: 12

Eczema and other common skin conditions, whether wet or dry, usually respond rapidly to treatment with "Hydroderm" ointment. It provides the anti-inflammatory, anti-allergic and antipruritic actions of hydrocortisone; and the anti-bacterial cover of neomycin and bacitiacin, which are effective against most common skin pathogens.

Low-technicality language has a different flavour and texture: 13

Depression becomes more common with advancing age and is all too often overlooked as a diagnosis. This is an important omission, as effective treatment is possible. The diagnosis may be overlooked, because an elderly person, particularly one with physical illness or disability, may be regarded as having sufficient circumstances in his life situation to account for the observed happiness or pessimism. In other patients hypochondriacal symptoms may throw the emphasis on to physical disease, so that the mental diagnosis is missed. Alternatively, very severe depression with withdrawal and apathy may be mistaken for dementia. Many depressed old people may remain unrecognized because they put on a brave front for the doctor and appear cheerful superficially, but specific questioning about mood, appetite and sleep may show the true state of affairs.

One finds three kinds of defence of professional jargon, especially   14
of the jargon and near-jargon employed by doctors, lawyers and economists. Such language is said to be more condensed and therefore time-saving; morale-raising and supportive, in that it allows one professional to recognise another without waste of time; and, often though but rarely expressed, an indispensable means of keeping the public at a respectful distance. The last argument, however, is wearing rather thin, as education spreads. In Western society, the expert no longer has the priestly function he once possessed. He is required to justify his privileged position. The magic of jargon has lost much of its power.

In 1942 the Chief Justice of the United States, Mr. Justice Frank-   15
furter, received a letter from a boy of twelve who announced his ambition to be a lawyer one day and asked for advice on how to proceed in the meantime. The Chief Justice wrote back encouragingly, telling the boy to forget about the law for several years and to concentrate on improving his mind and his appreciation of language by reading good

literature, looking at good pictures and generally learning to be a cultured, civilised person. Only then, he said, would the young man be prepared to begin his legal studies with any prospect of real success. "No one," he wrote, "can be a truly competent lawyer unless he is a cultivated man. The best way to prepare for the law is to come to the study of the law as a well-read person. Thus alone can one acquire the capacity to use the English language on paper and in speech and with the habits of clear thinking which only a truly liberal education can give." The advice is not only applicable to would-be lawyers. Jargon is the product of an insensitive, uneducated mind. A properly educated person cannot bring himself to use it, and the sad truth is that a very large number of the highly educated people who control our lives today and to whom society gives the greatest prestige and reward have received a most inadequate and unbalanced education. Among other failings, they have never acquired a mastery of their mother-tongue.

For both professional and philosophical reasons, scientists and   16
near-scientists have come to believe that the best kind of language is one which betrays no sign of the author's personality or even existence and which is hard, clear and unambiguous, a language which is tidy and exact, with no synonyms and with all possibilities of misunderstanding removed. Confined to the scientific and technical fields, and possibly the legal field, too, such thinking may be entirely reasonable.

There is, however, a danger in the situation. It is that people may   17
come to believe that all human activities can be satisfactorily analysed and described in this same "hard, clear and unambiguous language" and that what cannot be proved by methods of science cannot be true. If routine tests can be devised for chemicals, then one must be found for hunger or the intelligence of children. The untested part is not allowed to be built into the engine and the untested child cannot enter the school. The human personality, according to some modern investigators, can be examined in substantially the same way as the physical structure of a hydrocarbon. "The essence of high F is a placid, unemotional, realistic cheerfulness, with talkativeness, geniality, enthusiasm and a witty originality. All factorizations stress cheerful joyousness, gregariousness, friendly assertiveness and talkativeness, adaptability, quick resourcefulness, humour that tends to wit, and (less definite) sympathy, curiosity and trustfulness."

The nineteenth century was not exposed to this appalling tempta-   18
tion partly because scientists and technicians were relatively few and unimportant and partly for a reason which has been excellently stated by Professor Lionel Trilling: "In the nineteenth century, in this country as in Europe, literature underlay every activity of mind. The scientist, the philosopher, the historian, the theologian, the economist, the

social theorist, and even the politician were required to command literary abilities which would now be thought irrelevant to their respective callings."

Half-way through the twentieth century there can be no doubt at all that literature does not "underlie every activity of mind." The various professions do not move with the same community of culture. There is, broadly speaking, a scientific culture and there is a culture based on letters. The last three-quarters of a century has tried hard, but on the whole without success, to achieve some kind of synthesis between them. Nowadays many observers believe that such a synthesis is impossible, that either science or humanism must conquer the other. And science seems determined to win. The technological revolution of the twentieth century shows signs of handling the humanities much more roughly than the Industrial Revolution of the nineteenth did. It has been stressing the intellect to a degree which is both dangerous and absurd. [19]

In our world of violent emotions and dogmas there is—and it is as well to admit it—something attractive about the kind of language which makes real understanding more likely. There is a genuine feeling of pride in being able to handle a specialised vocabulary properly. We should be careful of attacking any kind of mental discipline. If the generous but correct use of technical terms tones up a man's mind, there is clearly much to be said for it. It is interesting to find technical writing defended in much the same terms that were frequently heard used in praise of a classical education: "For though technical terms form only a small fraction of the words used in any piece of writing, the precision with which they have to be employed has, I think, had a good effect on the thinking and writing of engineers. When he is forced to exercise extreme care with some of his most important words an author will acquire the habit of exercising similar care with others." [20]

This may be so, but it seems equally likely that logic will kill subtlety, that language will lose its overtones and therefore its possibilities. It was George Orwell's nightmare when he envisaged Newspeak, the English in which "every concept that can ever be needed will be expressed by exactly *one* word, with its meaning rigidly defined and all its subsidiary meanings rubbed out and forgotten." [21]

The scientific-technological revolution could quite well lead to this result. It has produced large numbers of people who rate the logical, no-synonym language highly, including many routine research workers who are little more than post-graduate slaves, whether they are employed in University laboratories or by industrial firms. It could develop a mechanised way of spending leisure which would make indi- [22]

vidual effort seem old fashioned. Anyone who, like Orwell, sits down to see how far the process has gone already may come to frightening conclusions.

But it is not inevitable that the logical conclusion will be reached.   23 Since the dropping of the first atomic bomb, scientists have become aware of the dangers of rational, scientific man. They have come to realise that the mind of the complete man needs more than science to feed it. If a person cannot see the virtues of scientific language, he is out of tune with his age. If, on the other hand, he is unable to appreciate the poet's language, he is cut off from much of his national heritage. He must acknowledge that both kinds of language are important to him.

The only way of keeping jargon under control is to make sure that   24 people of the highest intelligence receive a broadly-based education, the most important part of which is the development of a pride in handling words really well. If we could achieve this, we could forget about jargon. It would simply wither away, as the members of our old and new professional groups got the linguistic chip off their shoulders.

QUESTIONS ON CONTENT

1. What, according to Hudson, are the four essential elements of jargon? What question does he think is the key test for jargon?

2. According to Hudson, what kind of people use jargon? Why do you suppose they use it?

3. Hudson states that "only the person who has finally arrived, with his reputation secure, can afford to be simple and jargon-free" (4). Explain the paradox of this situation.

4. What is technical language? When is technical language appropriate?

5. What for Hudson are the dangers of a "logical, no-synonym language"(22)? Why is it important for people not only to see the virtues of scientific language but also to appreciate the beauty of the poet's language?

QUESTIONS ON RHETORIC

1. What is Hudson's thesis in this essay, and where is it stated? (Glossary: *Thesis*)

2. Hudson's essay falls roughly into two parts, one part that is essentially expository and the other that is argumentative. Identify the two parts and explain how they are related (Glossary: *Exposition* and *Argument*)

3. Why do you suppose Hudson chose to present examples of jargon and technical language in paragraphs 8, 9, 11, 12, and 13? (Glossary: *Examples*) What else could he have done? Do you think any of the alternatives would have been more effective? Why, or why not?

4. In paragraph 15 Hudson narrates the story of Chief Justice Frankfurter and the twelve-year-old boy who wanted to become a lawyer. What is the point of the story, and how is it related to his overall argument?

5. What kind of audience do you think Hudson had in mind for his essay? What evidence in the text supports your conclusion? (Glossary: *Audience*)

VOCABULARY

cohesion (1)	paradox (4)	gregariousness (17)
bogus (2)	unambiguous (16)	dogmas (20)
ironical (4)	placid (17)	subsidiary (21)

WRITING TOPICS

1. Select a profession that you are familiar with, and describe the jargon that is used by its members. How much of the jargon is necessary? What seems to be the intent of most of it?

2. Hudson admits that there is "something attractive about the kind of language which makes real understanding more likely" (20). Write an essay in which you support Hudson's claim by using examples from one or more of your academic courses.

3. Hudson is quite outspoken in making the connection between jargon and an improper education. He believes that "Jargon is the product of an insensitive, uneducated mind. A properly educated person cannot bring himself to use it." Write an essay in which you argue for the notion of a liberal education, perhaps one in which "literature underlies every activity of mind."

4
Gobbledygook

STUART CHASE

The late Stuart Chase, well-known commentator on the dynamics of our language and author of The Power of Words *and* The Tyranny of Words, *worked as a consultant for the federal government to help bureaucrats write "plain" English. In this now classic essay, Chase examines the world of obscure language, or gobbledygook, as it has come to be called. Chase believes "Gobbledygook not only flourishes in government bureaus but grows wild and lush in the law, the universities, and sometimes among the literati." He tells us how to recognize "windy and pretentious language," and offers some practical advice about "reducing the gobble."*

Said Franklin Roosevelt, in one of his early presidential speeches: "I   1
see one-third of a nation ill-housed, ill-clad, ill-nourished." Translated
into standard bureaucratic prose his statement would read:

> It is evident that a substantial number of persons within the Continental
> boundaries of the United States have inadequate financial resources with
> which to purchase the products of agricultural communities and industrial
> establishments. It would appear that for a considerable segment of the
> population, possibly as much as 33.3333* of the total, there are inadequate
> housing facilities, and an equally significant proportion is deprived of the
> proper types of clothing and nutriment.

This rousing satire on gobbledygook—or talk among the bureau-   2
crats—is adapted from a report[1] prepared by the Federal Security
Agency is an attempt to break out of the verbal squirrel cage. "Gobbledygook" was coined by an exasperated Congressman, Maury Maverick of Texas, and means using two, or three, or ten words in the place
of one, or using a five-syllable word where a single syllable would suffice. Maverick was censuring the forbidding prose of executive depart-
ments in Washington, but the term has now spread to windy and pretentious language in general.

---

* Not carried beyond four places.
[1] This and succeeding quotations from F.S.A. report by special permission of the
author, Milton Hall.

"Gobbledygook" itself is a good example of the way a language 3
grows. There was no word for the event before Maverick's invention;
one had to say: "You know, that terrible, involved, polysyllabic language those government people use down in Washington." Now one
word takes the place of a dozen.

A British member of Parliament, A. P. Herbert, also exasperated 4
with bureaucratic jargon, translated Nelson's immortal phrase,
"England expects every man to do his duty":

> England anticipates that, as regards the current emergency, personnel will
> face up to the issues, and exercise appropriately the functions allocated to
> their respective occupational groups.

A New Zealand official made the following report after surveying a 5
plot of ground for an athletic field:[2]

> It is obvious from the difference in elevation with relation to the short
> depth of the property that the contour is such as to preclude any reason-
> able development potential for active recreation.

Seems the plot was too steep.

An office manager sent this memo to his chief. 6

> Verbal contact with Mr. Blank regarding the attached notification of pro-
> motion has elicited the attached representation intimating that he prefers
> to decline the assignment.

Seems Mr. Blank didn't want the job.

> A doctor testified at an English trial that one of the parties was suffering
> from "circumorbital haematoma."

Seems the party had a black eye.

> In August 1952 the U.S. Department of Agriculture put out a pamphlet
> entitled: "Cultural and Pathogenic Variability in Single-Condial and Hy-
> phaltip Isolates of Hemlin-Thosporium Turcicum Pass."

Seems it was about corn leaf disease.

On reaching the top of the Finsteraarhorn in 1845, M. Dollfus- 7
Ausset, when he got his breath, exclaimed:

> The soul communes in the infinite with those icy peaks which seem to
> have their roots in the bowels of eternity.

Seems he enjoyed the view.

A governmental department announced: 8

---

[2] This item and the next two are from the piece on gobbledygook by W.E. Farb-
stein, *New York Times*, March 29, 1953.

> Voucherable expenditures necessary to provide adequate dental treatment required as adjunct to medical treatment being rendered a pay patient in in-patient status may be incurred as required at the expense of the Public Health Service.

Seems you can charge your dentist bill to the Public Health Service. Or can you?

LEGAL TALK

Gobbledygook not only flourishes in government bureaus but grows wild and lush in the law, the universities, and sometimes among the literati. Mr. Micawber was a master of gobbledygook, which he hoped would improve his fortunes. It is almost always found in offices too big for face-to-face talk. Gobbledygook can be defined as squandering words, packing a message with excess baggage and so introducing semantic "noise." Or it can be scrambling words in a message so that meaning does not come through. The directions on cans, bottles, and packages for putting the contents to use are often a good illustration. Gobbledygook must not be confused with double talk, however, for the intentions of the sender are usually honest.   9

I offer you a round fruit and say, "Have an orange." Not so an expert in legal phraseology, as parodied by editors of *Labor:*   10

> I hereby give and convey to you, all and singular, my estate and interests, right, title, claim and advantages of and in said orange, together with all rind, juice, pulp, and pits, and all rights and advantages therein ... anything hereinbefore or hereinafter or in any other deed or deeds, instrument or instruments of whatever nature or kind whatsoever, to the contrary, in any wise, notwithstanding.

The state of Ohio, after five years of work, has redrafted its legal code in modern English, eliminating 4,500 sections and doubtless a blizzard of "wherases" and "hereinafters." Legal terms of necessity must be closely tied to their referents, but the early solons tried to do this the hard way, by adding synonyms. They hoped to trap the physical event in a net of words, but instead they created a mumbo-jumbo beyond the power of the layman, and even many a lawyer, to translate. Legal talk is studded with tautologies, such as "cease and desist," "give and convey," "irrelevant, incompetent, and immaterial." Furthermore, legal jargon is a dead language; it is not spoken and it is not growing. An official of one of the big insurance companies calls their branch of it "bafflegab." Here is a sample from his collection.[3]   11

[3] Interview with Clifford B. Reeves by Sylvia F. Porter, New York *Evening Post*, March 14, 1952.

One-half to his mother, if living, if not to his father, and one-half to his mother-in-law, if living, if not to his mother, if living, if not to his father. Thereafter payment is to be made in a single sum to his brothers. On the one-half payable to his mother, if living, if not to his father, he does not bring in his mother-in-law as the next payee to receive, although on the one-half to his mother-in-law, he does bring in the mother or father.

You apply for an insurance policy, pass the tests, and instead of a 12 straightforward "here is your policy," you receive something like this:

This policy is issued in consideration of the application therefor, copy of which application is attached hereto and made part hereof, and of the payment for said insurance on the life of the above-named insured.

ACADEMIC TALK

The pedagogues may be less repetitious than the lawyers, but many 13 use even longer words. It is a symbol of their calling to prefer Greek and Latin derivatives to Anglo-Saxon. Thus instead of saying: "I like short clear words," many a professor would think it more seemly to say: "I prefer an abbreviated phraseology, distinguished for its lucidity." Your professor is sometimes right, the longer word may carry the meaning better—but not because it is long. Allen Upward in his book *The New Word* warmly advocates Anglo-Saxon English as against what he calls "Mediterranean" English, with its polysyllables built up like a skyscraper.

Professional pedagogy, still alternating between the Middle Ages 14 and modern science, can produce what Henshaw Ward once called the most repellent prose known to man. It takes an iron will to read as much as a page of it. Here is a sample of what is known in some quarters as "pedageese":

Realization has grown that the curriculum or the experiences of learners change and improve only as those who are most directly involved examine their goals, improve their understandings and increase their skill in performing the tasks necessary to reach newly defined goals. This places the focus upon teacher, lay citizen and learner as partners in curricular improvement and as the individuals who must change, if there is to be curriculum change.

I think there is an idea concealed here somewhere. I think it means: 15 "If we are going to change the curriculum, teacher, parent, and student must all help." The reader is invited to get out his semantic decoder and check on my translation. Observe there is no technical language in this gem of pedageese, beyond possibly the word "curriculum." It is just a simple idea heavily oververbalized.

In another kind of academic talk the author may display his learn- 16
ing to conceal a lack of ideas. A bright instructor, for instance, in need
of prestige may select a common sense proposition for the subject of a
learned monograph—say, "Modern cities are hard to live in" and
adorn it with imposing polysyllables: "Urban existence in the perpen-
dicular declivities of megalopolis . . ." etc. He coins some new terms to
transfix the reader—"mega-decibel" or "strato-cosmopolis"—and
works them vigorously. He is careful to add a page or two of differen-
tial equations to show the "scatter." And then he publishes, with 147
footnotes and a bibliography to knock your eye out. If the authorities
are dozing, it can be worth an associate professorship.

While we are on the campus, however, we must not forget that the 17
technical language of the natural sciences and some terms in the social
sciences, forbidding as they may sound to the layman, are quite necessary. Without them, specialists could not communicate what they find.
Trouble arises when experts expect the uninitiated to understand the
words; when they tell the jury, for instance, that the defendant is suffering from "circumorbital haematoma."

Here are two authentic quotations. Which was written by a distin- 18
guished modern author, and which by a patient in a mental hospital?
You will find the answer at the end of this essay.

> 1. Have just been to supper. Did not knowing what the woodchuck sent
> me here. How when the blue blue blue on the said anyone can do it that
> tries. Such is the presidential candidate.
> 2. No history of a family to close with those and close. Never shall he be
> alone to be alone to be alone to be alone to be alone to lend a hand and
> leave it left and wasted.

REDUCING THE GOBBLE

As government and business offices grow larger, the need for doing 19
something about gobbledygook increases. Fortunately the biggest office in the world is working hard to reduce it. The Federal Security
Agency in Washington,* with nearly 100 million clients on its books,
began analyzing its communication lines some years ago, with gratifying results. Surveys find trouble in three main areas: correspondence
with clients about their social security problems, office memos, official
reports.

Clarity and brevity, as well as common humanity, are urgently 20
needed in this vast establishment which deals with disability, old age,

* *Ed. note:* Later the Department of Health, Education, and Welfare and subse-
quently the Department of Health and Human Resources.

and unemployment. The surveys found instead many cases of long-windedness, foggy meanings, clichés, and singsong phrases, and gross neglect of the reader's point of view. Rather than talking to a real person, the writer was talking to himself. "We often write like a man walking on stilts."

Here is a typical case of long-windedness: 21

> *Gobbledygook as found:* "We are wondering if sufficient time has passed so that you are in a position to indicate whether favorable action may now be taken on our recommendation for the reclassification of Mrs. Blank, junior clerk-stenographer, CAF 2, to assistant clerk-stenographer, CAF 3?" *Suggested improvement:* "Have you yet been able to act on our recommendation to reclassify Mrs. Blank?"

Another case: 22

> Although the Central Efficiency Rating Committee recognizes that there are many desirable changes that could be made in the present efficiency rating system in order to make it more realistic and more workable than it now is, this committee is of the opinion that no further change should be made in the present system during the current year. Because of conditions prevailing throughout the country and the resultant turnover in personnel, and difficulty in administering the Federal programs, further mechanical improvement in the present rating system would require staff retraining and other administrative expense which would seem best withheld until the official termination of hostilities, and until restoration of regular operation.

The F.S.A. invites us to squeeze the gobbledygook out of this statement. Here is my attempt:

> The Central Efficiency Rating Committee recognizes that desirable changes could be made in the present system. We believe, however, that no change should be attempted until the war is over.

This cuts the statement from 111 to 30 words, about one-quarter of   23
the original, but perhaps the reader can do still better. What of importance have I left out?

Sometimes in a book which I am reading for information—not for   24
literary pleasure—I run a pencil through the surplus words. Often I can cut a section to half its length with an improvement in clarity. Magazines like *The Reader's Digest* have reduced this process to an art. Are long-windedness and obscurity a cultural lag from the days when writing was reserved for priests and cloistered scholars? The more words and the deeper the mystery, the greater their prestige and the firmer the hold on their jobs. And the better the candidate's chance today to have his doctoral thesis accepted.

The F.S.A. surveys found that a great deal of writing was obscure   25 although not necessarily prolix. Here is a letter sent to more than 100,000 inquirers, a classic example of murky prose. To clarify it, one needs to *add* words, not cut them:

> In order to be fully insured, an individual must have earned $50 or more in covered employment for as many quarters of coverage as half the calendar quarters elapsing between 1936 and the quarter in which he reaches age 65 or dies, whichever first occurs.

Probably no one without the technical jargon of the office could translate this: nevertheless, it was sent out to drive clients mad for seven years. One poor fellow wrote back: "I am no longer in covered employment. I have an outside job now."

Many words and phrases in officialese seem to come out automatically, as if from lower centers of the brain. In this standardized prose people never *get jobs,* they "secure employment"; *before* and *after* become "prior to" and "subsequent to"; one does not *do,* one "performs"; nobody *knows* a thing, he is "fully cognizant"; one never *says,* he "indicates." A great favorite at present is "implement."

Some charming boners occur in this talking-in-one's-sleep. For instance:

> The problem of extending coverage to all employees, regardless of size, is not as simple as surface appearances indicate.
> Though the proportions of all males and females in ages 16–45 are essentially the same. . . .
> Dairy cattle, usually and commonly embraced in dairying. . . .

In its manual to employees, the F.S.A. suggests the following:

Instead of	Use
give consideration to	consider
make inquiry regarding	inquire
is of the opinion	believes
comes into conflict with	conflicts
information which is of a confidential nature	confidential information

Professional or office gobbledygook often arises from using the passive rather than the active voice. Instead of looking you in the eye, as it were, and writing "This act requires . . ." the office worker looks out of the window and writes: "It is required by this statute that. . . ." When the bureau chief says, "We expect Congress to cut your budget," the message is only too clear; but usually he says, "It is expected that the departmental budget estimates will be reduced by Congress."

> *Gobbled:* "All letters prepared for the signature of the Administrator will be single spaced."
> *Ungobbled:* "Single space for all letters for the Administrator." (Thus cutting 13 words to 7.)

ONLY PEOPLE CAN READ

The F.S.A. surveys pick up the point that human communication in-   30
volves a listener as well as a speaker. Only people can read, though a
lot of writing seems to be addressed to beings in outer space. To whom
are you talking? The sender of the officialese message often forgets the
chap on the other end of the line.

A woman with two small children wrote the F.S.A. asking what she   31
should do about payments, as her husband had lost his memory. "If he
never gets able to work," she said, "and stays in an institution would I
be able to draw any benefits? . . . I don't know how I am going to live
and raise my children since he is disable to work. Please give me some
information. . . ."

To this human appeal, she received a shattering blast of gobbledy-   32
gook, beginning, "State unemployment compensation laws do no provide any benefits for sick or disabled individuals . . . in order to qualify
an individual must have a certain number of quarters of coverage . . ."
etc., etc. Certainly if the writer had been thinking about the poor
woman he would not have dragged in unessential material about old-
age insurance. If he had pictured a mother without means to care for
her children, he would have told her where she might get help—from
the local office which handles aid to dependent children, for instance.

Gobbledygook of this kind would largely evaporate if we thought   33
of our messages as two way—in the above case, if we pictured ourselves talking on the doorstep of a shabby house to a woman with two
children tugging at her skirts, who in her distress does not know which
way to turn.

RESULTS OF THE SURVEY

The F.S.A. survey showed that office documents could be cut 20 to 50   34
percent, with an improvement in clarity and a great saving to taxpayers in paper and payrolls.

A handbook was prepared and distributed by key officials.[4] They   35
read it, thought about it, and presently began calling section meetings
to discuss gobbledygook. More booklets were ordered, and the local
output of documents began to improve. A Correspondence Review
Section was established as a kind of laboratory to test murky messages.
A supervisor could send up samples for analysis and suggestions. The
handbook is now used for training new members; and many employees keep it on their desks along with the dictionary. . . .

[4] By Milton Hall.

The handbook makes clear the enormous amount of gobbledygook 36
which automatically spreads in any large office, together with ways
and means to keep it under control. I would guess that at least half of
all the words circulating around the bureaus of the world are "irrelevant, incompetent, and immaterial"—to use a favorite legalism; or are
just plain "unnecessary"—to ungobble it.

My favorite story of removing the gobble from gobbledygook con- 37
cerns the Bureau of Standards at Washington. I have told it before but
perhaps the reader will forgive the repetition. A New York plumber
wrote the Bureau that he had found hydrochloric acid fine for cleaning
drains, and was it harmless? Washington replied: "The efficacy of hydrochloric acid is indisputable, but the chlorine residue is incompatible with metallic permanence."

The plumber wrote back that he was mighty glad the Bureau 38
agreed with him. The Bureau replied with a note of alarm: "We cannot
assume responsibility for the production of toxic and noxious residues
with hydrochloric acid, and suggest that you use an alternate proce-
dure." The plumber was happy to learn that the Bureau still agreed
with him.

Whereupon Washington exploded: "Don't use hydrochloric acid; it 39
eats hell out of the pipes!"

NOTE: The second quotation [paragraph 18] comes from Gertrude Stein's *Lucy
Church Amiably*.

QUESTIONS ON CONTENT

1. What is gobbledygook? Give three examples of gobbledygook not
mentioned by Chase. Why does Chase object to gobbledygook? What
does he mean when he says, "Gobbledygook . . . would largely evaporate if we thought of our messages as two way . . ." (33).

2. Why do bureaucrats, lawyers, and professors, among others, use
gobbledygook? Is its use ever justified? Explain.

3. Do you agree with Chase's paraphrases or translations of bureaucratic jargon in paragraphs 4 through 10? Try to rewrite the passages
differently from the way Chase has. How effective are Chase's attempts to "reduce the gobble" in paragraphs 21–22?

4. Chase's statement "It is almost always found in offices too big for
face-to-face talk" (9) emphasizes that gobbledygook goes hand in
hand with the dehumanizing character of most of our institutions.
What is the connection between this statement and George Orwell's

recommendation in "Politics and the English Language" (p. 116) to use concrete terms when writing?

QUESTIONS ON RHETORIC

1. What is Chase's purpose in this essay? (Glossary: *Purpose*)

2. What methods does Chase use to define gobbledygook? Why is it important for him to establish a defintion for the term? What does Chase see as the main distinction between gobbledygook and double-talk (sometimes also referred to as *doublespeak*)? (Glossary: *Definition*)

3. What is the function of the many examples and quotations that Chase uses? Why are they important? (Glossary: *Examples*)

4. Chase concludes his essay with the story of the New York plumber. Is this conclusion effective? Why, or why not? What alternatives did Chase have to end his essay? (Glossary: *Beginnings/Endings*)

VOCABULARY

pretentious (2)	tautologies (11)	murky (25)
immortal (4)	advocates (13)	clients (25)
squandering (9)	proposition (16)	

WRITING TOPICS

1. In his essay "The Marks of an Educated Man" (*Context,* Spring 1961), Alan Simpson presents the following example of inflated prose, or, as he aptly dubs it, "verbal smog."

> It is inherent to motivational phenomena that there is a drive for more gratification than is realistically possible, on any level or in any type of personality organization. Likewise it is inherent to the world of objects that not all potentially desirable opportunities can be realized within a human life span. Therefore, any personality must involve an organization that allocates opportunities for gratifications, that systematizes precedence relative to the limited possibilities. The possibilities of gratification, simultaneously or sequentially, of all need dispositions are severely limited by the structure of the object system and by the intrasystemic incompatibility of the consequences of gratifying them all.

What is the author of this passage trying to say? Rewrite the paragraph eliminating the unnecessary verbiage.

2. The following item appears in the *San Francisco Chronicle.*

STATE MAKES IT PERFECTLY CLEAR

SACRAMENTO For some time the public has wondered what to make of most bureaucratic twaddle—but a new State law has set the record straight at last.

STUART CHASE

From the revised State code of the Division of Consumer Services, Department of Consumer Affairs, Title 4: subsection 2102, comes the official word:

"Tenses, Gender and Number: For the purpose of the rules and regulations contained in this chapter, the present tense includes the past and future tenses, and the future, the present; the masculine gender includes the feminine, and feminine, the masculine; and the singular includes the plural, and the plural the singular."

Our Correspondent

Comment on this example of gobbledygook. Why is bureaucratic and legal writing particularly prone to gobbledygook?

3. Using examples from Chase's essay, Kenneth Hudson's "Jargon and the Professions," and other reading you have done, write an essay in which you discuss the differences between "jargon," "technical language," and "gobbledygook."

5

How to Interpret
an Annual Report

MARY RUTH YOE

*Each year corporations and institutions across the United States publish annual
reports, glossily produced summaries of earnings and expenditures, profits and
losses; and each year thousands of shareholders and prospective investors try to
figure out just how each company actually did. Was it a good year financially, or
was it a bad one? In order to ensure investor confidence, annual reports are generally designed to make every fiscal year sound the same—successful—no matter
what the bottom line indicates. So, "to find out if a company is really in the
black," writes Mary Ruth Yoe, "a reader must tune in to linguistic clues." In the
following essay, Yoe analyzes the euphemisms and jargon American corporations
and educational institutions use to put the best face on each year's fiscal activity.*

" **A**nd they lived happily ever after." You'll never find that sen-   1
tence in an annual report. The institutions and corporations that publish such yearly accountings do believe in fairy-tale endings, but they
strive to achieve the same effect through more subtle methods. That
means you should read an annual report as a piece of literature, carefully, circling the text. Reading between the lines, you may discover
the bottom line. (Sometimes skillfully buried.)

The business of America, said Calvin Coolidge, is business. But the   2
business of American corporations is making money. Even nonprofit
institutions—such as independent colleges and universities—want to
stay solvent. (Rather than sell a product, they make money by building
endowments.) And each year brings a fresh flood of annual reports—
assuring shareholders and other constituencies that everything is basically OK.

Nevertheless, annual reports almost never mention money.   3

You can turn to the back of an annual report and find pages   4
crammed with figures and balance sheets, with notes on nonperform-
ing assets, borrowed funds, long-term debts, dividends, and operating
expenses. But "money"—the word itself—stays firmly out of the lime-

light. Up front, the explanatory text that runs between glossy photographs—smiling employees, freshly polished antique equipment, inspirational nature scenes—is dotted with euphemisms for the company's *raison d'être,* its dirty little secret of success: funds, earnings, revenues, cash flow, returns, profits.

On the other side of the ledger, of course, lurk losses. Rather than 5 mention losses directly, most reports write of events "having a negative impact on earnings." A reader in search of red ink soon picks up on clues, like the adverbs "regrettably" and "disappointingly." Losses— otherwise known as "downturns" or "substantial write-offs"—are sure to follow.

While most euphemisms found in annual reports have to do with 6 money ("a *very* [italics mine] substantial write-off" translates to a $78.5 million loss after tax benefits), felicitous phrasing can smooth over other pimples on the corporate facade. (Someday, corporations may echo gracefully aging beauties and admit that a few flaws add character.) The world presented by the annual report is the best of all possible worlds. There are no "problems," only "challenges" and "opportunities." When the going gets really rough, there are "significant" or "major" opportunities.

So a company admits that it has not been a good year for the entire 7 industry, which "experienced its most difficult year as profitability was reduced by XX percent." A reminder quickly follows that Company A is an industry leader when it comes to adjusting to adversity: "The Company took a number of decisive actions to help weather the economic downturn and prepare for better results in the future."

Bad things do happen to good companies, and sometimes bad 8 things can even be good news. Enter another use for the euphemism, as when a college president explains to alumni and other friends of Alma Mater just how the institution has garnered a record year in gifts and grants: "This outstanding result was substantially aided by the maturation of 23 bequests." For a bequest to mature, somebody—in this case, 23 somebodies—had to die, or otherwise complete a career.

Another species of euphemism: the welded word. In annual report-age, certain words seldom appear without amplifying mates. A corporation never baldly "takes steps." At the very least, a company may admit to taking "further steps." Better still are "prudent steps," "economically sound steps," or—most purposeful of all—"strategically important steps."

In much the same way, the noun "emphasis" seems to lack emphasis. So it is never used alone. Annual reports speak of "increased emphasis" or "continued emphasis." "Commitments" are almost always "continuing," and "analysis" is "in-depth." Even words that can stand alone take on extra meaning when coupled with a few all-purpose adjectives. Current adjectives of choice: "significant," "substantial," and "enhanced."

Overly enthusiastic users of the all-purpose adjective do run the   11
risk of redundancy. One Ivy League university recently boasted of "the positive enhancements" made possible by a corporate benefactor. If the benefactor hadn't come through, one wonders, would that have meant "negative enhancements"?

Annual reports, like other assembly-line products, change models   12
from year to year. In the early 1980s, corporations fought their way out of a recession, and annual reports picked up on the military metaphor. Another plus: military and sexual metaphor overlap, and every company president knows that Sex Sells. So in a competitive marketplace, corporations and universities have abandoned "planning for the future" in favor of "strategic positioning" or, at the very least, "strategic planning." Companies talk of strategies, aggressive tactics, taking action on several fronts. Products are "developed to *penetrate* [italics mine] the evolving corporate market." There are objectives, advances, alliances, new territories. The action verbs are "deploy" and, when things don't go according to strategic planning, "redeploy."

As a subspecies of annual reports, those produced by colleges and   13
universities are generally less glossy than their corporate counterparts. Love of euphemism prevails, but the tone is slightly different. While corporate reports are often written by anonymous pens, at colleges and universities the task falls most often to either the president or to someone connected with the annual giving campaign.

The three little words most likely to appear on the tombstone of an   14
annual giving officer: "Another Record Year." That headline and its variations—"Contributions Break All Records," "Campaign Raises Record Amount"—sound, over and over, like a broken record. Sometimes the writer will dredge up a synonym, like "all-time high" or "new mark." But the device most often used to convert record-breaking ennui into enthusiasm is the exclamation point—frequently preceded by an excited "ever"; "Again, the Highest Ever!" "The most successful fund campaign ever!"

Presidents don't use exclamation points. They emphasize the long   15
view, the fact that education is a *process*. "Discussion of the curriculum is continuing." "Further steps were taken [by whom, the cynic wonders] in the University's program to achieve long-range financial stability." "Dean X and his colleagues are currently engaged in a num-

ber of conversations to this end." And, in summation: "Much, however, remains to be done." Since near-term prospects can't be ignored,
marketing jargon now shows up in presidential prose. "Suddenly the
student is a scarce commodity." Which means that "in an increasingly
competitive college marketplace," a college can't afford to have "an in-
sufficient national presence." Send in the direct-mail experts. . . .

Above all, the president is an institutional Pollyanna. He or she   16
accentuates the positive—a university's "tradition of excellence," a
phrase that encompasses "excellent faculty," "outstanding students,"
"dramatic achievements." But the president must also point to challenges: "maintaining a leadership role," "ensuring the continued excellence of its programs," "enhancing our preeminent position."

Finally, to assure supporters that they have picked a winner, even   17
on a tough track, the president often puts in a leader-in-adversity reminder: "Many other schools face greater perils than we do."

The bottom line: "Much, however, remains to be done."   18

QUESTIONS ON CONTENT

1. Why is it that annual reports almost never make mention of
money? What do they use instead of the word *money?*

2. What does Yoe mean when she says, "the company's *raison d'être,*
its dirty little secret of success"(4)?

3. Illustrate your understanding of what Yoe calls the "welded
word"(9) by giving several examples in addition to the ones she cites.
What is one of the risks faced by users of the "all-purpose adjective"?

4. How, according to Yoe, do corporate annual reports differ from
those produced by colleges and universities? What seems to be the
purpose of annual reports?

5. What, according to Yoe, is the chief advantage of the passive voice
for writers of annual reports?

6. Explain what use annual reports make of military and sexual metaphors.

QUESTIONS ON RHETORIC

1. What is Yoe's thesis, and where is it stated? (Glossary: *Thesis*)

2. Could paragraphs 2 and 3 be combined? What does Yoe gain by
separating them?

3. Cite passages in the essay that show that Yoe's style is informal and
that her tone is conversational. (Glossary: *Style* and *Tone*)

4. In her introductory paragraph Yoe directs the reader to "discover the bottom line." And in her concluding paragraph she returns to "the bottom line." How effectively do these two paragraphs open and close this essay? Explain. (Glossary: *Beginnings/Endings*)

5. Identify several similes that Yoe uses, and explain how each one works. (Glossary: *Figures of Speech*)

VOCABULARY

subtle (1)	garnered (8)	dredge (14)
solvent (2)	amplifying (9)	cynic (15)
endowments (2)	subspecies (13)	preeminent (16)
felicitous (6)		

WRITING TOPICS

1. Carefully read Yoe's satiric "Annual Report Starter Kit." Using the verbs, adverbs, adjectives, and nouns she suggests, write several paragraphs of an annual report for a commercial enterprise you are familiar with. (Your choice may be as sophisticated as IBM or as accessible as a corner lemonade stand.) How do the words Yoe provides get in the way of direct expression?

ANNUAL REPORT STARTER KIT

You, too, can write an annual report. (Though why you'd want to is another subject.) Fourscore verbs, adverbs, adjectives, and nouns, culled from state-of-the-art annual reports, await your ventures.

Simply pretend that you are dining at a Chinese-American restaurant and pick one from Column A, one from Column B, and so on. With experience, you'll be able to string two or more nouns together ("profitability options," "growth postures," "progress enhancement initiatives"). Adjectives also benefit from such coupling ("strategic near-term," "sophisticated evolutionary," "continuing competitive").

A more fundamentally integrated utilization: Shareholders can consult the chart to evaluate the mainstream positioning of their companies' strategic public relations efforts.

Verbs*	Adverbs	Adjectives	Nouns**
Impact	Considerably	Integrated	Action
Enhance	Virtually	Competitive	Change
Restructure	Significantly	Substantial	Progress
Position	Substantially	Strategic	Initiatives
Deploy	Fundamentally	Significant	Options

*The most important verb is, of course, *to be;* and the present perfect, *has been,* is a virtually invaluable form. "The Company has been an actively flexible organization, able to anticipate the challenges of its highly competitive

Verbs*	Adverbs	Adjectives	Nouns**
Redeploy	Aggressively	Flexible	Strategy
Implement	Increasingly	High-growth	Profitability
Complement	Greatly	Long-term	Utilization
Seek	Actively	Evolutionary	Positioning
Finalize	Relatively	Near-term	Expenditures
Outperform	Highly	Sophisticated	Advances
Maintain	Ultimately	Invaluable	Growth
Anticipate	Adversely	Negative	Challenges
Initiate	Creatively	Continuing	Postures
Sustain	Vigorously	Responsive	Enhancement
Explore	Sufficiently	Synergistic	Infrastructures
Reconfigure	Intensively	Extraordinary	Excellence
Expand	Positively	Key	Ventures
Participate	Importantly	Outstanding	Packages
Respond	Imaginatively	Mainstream	Opportunity

environment and thus to position itself creatively for significant long-term high-growth challenges."

The passive voice, in all its variations, is key. While it may not seem to complement the active image sought by the typical corporation or institution, creatively positioned the passive voice has its utilizations. Most importantly, it allows a corporation or its officers to escape out-and-out responsibility: "Disappointingly, profitability has been impacted by the downward pressures of increasingly negative near-term markets."

**In deploying a noun, you should remember that more is more, and try to implement plurals over singulars, thus maintaining a synergistic posture of expanding option packages.

2. Locate a copy of your school's most recent annual report and read it. How closely does it fit Yoe's description of annual reports? In what ways is it significantly different? In an essay analyze the report's use of euphemism and jargon.

3. Write an essay in which you attack or defend the following statement: "Writers of annual reports should not use euphemisms and jargon meant to impress, hide the truth, or cover-up insecurities."

6

The Language of Nuclear War Strategists

STEPHEN HILGARTNER,
RICHARD C. BELL,
and RORY O'CONNOR

What are the ramifications of nuclear capability? How might nuclear warfare be triggered and fought? Who would survive? What are the consequences of "thinking the unthinkable"? Because the threat of full-scale nuclear war is real, our military analysts must deal with that possibility and make predictions accordingly. The following essay offers a view of the "reality" of nuclear warfare suggested by the highly specialized language of nuclear war strategists.

The world of nuclear warfare is a world of doublethink, a hall of mirrors, where *peace* is preserved through the constant threat of war, *security* is obtained through mutual insecurity, and nuclear war planners "think about the *unthinkable*," holding millions of civilians hostage to the most powerful death machines in history.

Nuclear war strategists have developed an esoteric, highly specialized vocabulary. In their ultrarational world, they talk in cool, clinical language about *megatons* and *megadeaths.* Cities are *bargaining chips;* they are not destroyed, they are *taken out* with *clean, surgical strikes*— as if they were tumors.

Since there is no way to defend cities and industry against nuclear attack, *global stability* is now preserved through a system called the *balance of terror.* The balance of terror is based upon the principle of *deterrence.* Nuclear deterrence is, in effect, a mutual suicide pact: if you attack me, it may kill me, but I will kill you before I die. The civilian population of each superpower is held hostage by the opposite power. The same is true of the allies covered by the *nuclear umbrellas* of the superpowers. If either side attacks, all the hostages will be destroyed.

The U.S. Department of *Defense* (known as the War Department   4
until 1948) is incapable of defending the United States against a nuclear attack by the USSR. But it is capable of killing many millions of
Russian citizens at the push of a button, and the Russians are incapable of doing anything to prevent the carnage. If the Russians were to
attack the U.S. or its allies with nuclear weapons, the U.S. would retaliate by attacking the USSR. Since the Russians know this, the reasoning goes, they will be deterred from striking first. A mirror-image argument describes how Russia deters the U.S. from striking its people.

Military analysts classify nuclear attacks as either *counterforce* or   5
countervalue attacks. A counterforce attack is one that is directed primarily against the other side's military forces; countervalue attacks are
directed against cities and industry.

That a counterforce attack is directed primarily against military   6
forces does not mean that there would be few civilian casualties. On
the contrary, counterforce attacks could leave millions of civilians
dead from the fallout produced by attacks on missile silos. A large airport might be construed as a military target because it could serve as a
base for military planes. A naval base situated in a metropolitan area is
another example of a target that could be interpreted as either counterforce or countervalue. The difference between a counterforce and a
countervalue attack is not whether civilians die, but whether this is the
main goal or a side effect. The deaths of civilians and the destruction
of nonmilitary property in a counterforce attack is called *collateral
damage.*

Nuclear war planners have always been afraid that the other side   7
might try to launch a *preemptive first strike* (also known as a *splendid
first strike*), that is, a counterforce attack designed to cripple the
enemy's ability to retaliate. The reasoning behind a preemptive first-
strike strategy goes as follows: If country X can destroy a large enough
number of country Y's missiles in a first-strike attack, then X can also
threaten to destroy Y's remaining cities in a second *nuclear salvo* if Y
retaliates with any remaining missiles. It is assumed that Y will be *rational* and surrender to X rather than ensure its total destruction by
launching an attack for revenge. X can then impose its will on Y, thus
winning the nuclear war.

In its public statements, the USSR has renounced the *first use* of   8
nuclear weapons; the United States has not. Nevertheless, military
planners in both countries prepare for *worst-case* situations and tend
not to believe verbal declarations. In war, the argument goes, *capabili-
ties* count more than *intentions,* since intentions change without warning.

As a result of this perception of the possibility of an enemy at-   9
tempting a splendid first strike, the two superpowers have engaged in a

massive *arms race,* reaching higher and higher levels of destructive power. Some years ago, each superpower attained *overkill,* the ability to kill every citizen on the other side more than once. Nevertheless, the arms race continues, and each side continues to expand and *modernize* its nuclear arsenal.

The driving force behind the arms race is a treacherous double-bind known as the *security dilemma.* Since X is afraid of Y's weapons. X adds to its arsenal. X's arms buildup, which is conceived of as *defensive* by X, is perceived as *offensive* by Y, prompting Y to build more weapons to deter an attack by X. X looks at this and concludes that Y must be planning to attack; otherwise Y would not have expanded its arsenal. X therefore decides to build still more weapons, and the cycle continues.   10

The security dilemma has led to the creation of huge military establishments in both the U.S. and the USSR. The superpowers' *hawks* watch each other closely, passing what they see through the gloomy filter of worst-case *scenarios.* The hawks of one nation contribute to the prestige and power of the hawks of the other, and arms budgets climb.   11

The arms race has produced a wide array of nuclear weapons and delivery systems for getting them to their targets. The weapons are designed for use in different situations and vary considerably in explosive power. Nuclear warriors generally divide these weapons into three categories: strategic, tactical, and theater.   12

Strategic nuclear weapons have high-yield warheads; each warhead may be hundreds of times as powerful as the bomb that destroyed Hiroshima. The Hiroshima bomb had a *yield* of 13,000 tons of TNT, or 13 *kilotons;* strategic weapons often have a yield measured in *megatons*—millions of tons of TNT. Strategic weapons are capable of striking targets many thousands of miles away. Both superpowers have deployed their strategic weapons in bombers, in land-based missiles, and in submarines. In the U.S., this three-legged war machine is called the *strategic TRIAD.* Bombers armed with nuclear weapons wait for the *go code.* Land-based *Intercontinental Ballistic Missiles* (*ICBMs*) are ready to strike at the push of a button. Submarines bearing nuclear-armed missiles are *on-station,* waiting for a transmission that would order them to launch their cargo. Radar systems scan the sky for incoming missiles or bombers. At least one of the *Strategic Air Command's* flying command posts, officially called the *Looking Glass Planes* and unofficially known as the *Doomsday Planes,* is in the air at all times. And overhead, a network of satellites circles the earth, watching Soviet ICBM fields and maintaining *command, control and communications,* or C^3 (*C cubed*)—the capability to transmit and receive information and orders.   13

Tactical nuclear weapons are designed for use on the *nuclear battle-* 14 *field.* They have much smaller yields than strategic weapons; their yields usually range from as low as one kiloton to several times the yield of the Hiroshima bomb. Tactical nuclear weapons are designed for use in conjunction with *conventional military forces.* In a land war, tactical nuclear weapons might be used to *take out* enemy tank columns. On the sea, they could be used to sink enemy warships. They can be shot from artillery, dropped from planes, shot in short-range missiles, used in depth charges or torpedoes, or placed in land mines.

Theater nuclear weapons have powerful warheads like those of 15 strategic weapons. They do not have intercontinental range, however, and are designed for use in a *limited theater of operations*—like Europe, for example. These weapons include bombers and missiles with medium to long ranges. They are *deployed* on land and on aircraft carriers.

The U.S. government has also developed a new kind of nuclear 16 weapon called the *neutron bomb* or *enhanced radiation warhead.* Neutron bombs produce less explosive blast than other nuclear weapons, releasing a greater fraction of their energy in a deadly burst of neutron radiation. Neutron bombs purportedly make it possible to kill enemy troops while reducing blast damage to the surrounding countryside. In its war games, the Defense Department envisions using neutron bombs to stop Soviet tank attacks in western Europe.

Equipped with this array of armaments, nuclear warriors are ready 17 to play the game of *escalation,* using threats and counterthreats to deter, influence, coerce, and block their opponents.

The theory of *limited war*—war which the combatant nations limit 18 in scope or intensity by tacit or explicit agreement—is important to escalation strategy. This theory holds that war can be limited by restricting the geographic region in which it is conducted, by limiting the kinds of weapons used, or by limiting the kinds of targets attacked.

Nuclear war strategist Herman Kahn outlined a theory of escala- 19 tion and limited war in a 1965 book called *On Escalation: Metaphors and Scenarios.* Kahn developed an *escalation ladder* with forty-four rungs, or levels of conflict. The rungs Kahn described range from "Political, Economic and Diplomatic *Gestures*" through "*Nuclear 'Ultimatums'* " and limited evacuation of cities, before crossing the *"No Nuclear Use Threshold."* From *"Local Nuclear War,"* the ladder rises to *"Exemplary Attacks"* on property and population, before reaching *"Slow-Motion Countercity War."* As the intensity of the conflict climbs, the level of *"Countervalue Salvo"* is reached, and finally, the orgasmic release of *"Spasm or Insensate War,"* as everyone lets loose with everything they have got.

Escalation strategy is a complex game of *nuclear chicken.* Opposing   20
strategists, like two drivers headed on a collision course, try to force
each other to back down by threatening terrible consequences for both
unless somebody backs down. A disagreement might escalate into a
crisis, a crisis into a conventional war. The use of tactical nuclear
weapons would escalate conventional war into *limited nuclear war.* If
this happens, no one knows whether the use of nuclear force could be
neatly contained. Some analysts fear that crossing the *no-nuclear-use
threshold* would ultimately lead to a *spasm war.*

Escalation strategy, also known as *brinksmanship,* is ripe with   21
paradox. Survival depends on everyone being *rational,* yet it is hard to
tell what the word rational means. Sometimes it seems rational to pretend to be irrational, even to act irrationally, making the illusion more
credible by making it more real. In a game of chicken, the driver who
throws his steering wheel out the window has won control of the road.
Similarly, the nuclear warrior can seize the advantage by throwing
away options, or by convincing the opponent he is willing to plunge
over the brink. President Nixon, for example, developed a strategy he
called the *"Madman Theory"* to try to force the North Vietnamese to
negotiate. According to Nixon operative H. R. Haldeman, convicted in
the Watergate coverup, Nixon said:

> I want the North Vietnamese to believe I've reached the point where I
> might do *anything* [original emphasis] to stop the war. We'll just slip the
> word to them that "for God's sake, you know Nixon is obsessed about
> Communism. We can't restrain him when he's angry—and he has his
> hand on the *nuclear button"*—and Ho Chi Minh himself will be in Paris in
> two days begging for peace.

Over the years, the U.S. government has developed a number of   22
theories about how to maintain deterrence; these are known as *strategic doctrines.* The best known is the strategy of *mutually assured destruction (MAD),* developed by Robert McNamara, Secretary of Defense during the Kennedy and Johnson administrations. Under this
strategy, nuclear war is deterred by the threat that any attack would
promptly lead to a *nuclear exchange* that would destroy both superpowers.

For the balance of terror to remain *stable,* nuclear war strategists   23
must keep escalation under control. Each side must believe that everyone's nuclear forces have *survivability,* the ability to survive a counterforce attack and still deliver a crippling retaliatory blow. Both sides
must believe that the *costs of striking* would be greater than the *costs of
not striking.*

If the survivability of either side's forces is in question, the whole   24
situation becomes a hall of mirrors. What if X thinks Y thinks X could

take out Y's weapons in a preemptive first strike? Should X strike? If X doesn't, Y might strike first, because X thinks Y might think it has nothing to lose. And what might Y think about all this? A terrifying web of perceptions and misperceptions is possible. *Spiraling tensions* could start a thermonuclear war even if no one wanted it.

During the late 1960s and the early 1970s, the survivability of each 25 superpower's nuclear forces was not in question. In the past decade, however, improvements in weapons technology have made the survivability of land-based missiles less certain. This erosion of survivability is the result of what is known as *technological creep,* improvements in weapons technology that seem to have a momentum of their own.

One of the most *destabilizing* technological developments of the 26 1970s was the deployment of *MIRVs, multiple independently targetable reentry vehicles.* MIRVs make it possible for a single missile to carry a number of nuclear warheads, each of which can be aimed at a separate target. The U.S. began deploying MIRVs in 1970, and the Soviet Union began in 1975.

MIRVs tend to give the advantage to the side which strikes first in 27 a nuclear exchange. A quick look at the following example will illustrate why this is so. Imagine a situation in which each side has 1,000 missiles with 10 MIRVed warheads on each missile. By striking first with 100 missiles—MIRVed with 1,000 warheads—the attacker could eliminate all of the other side's missiles. This would leave the attacker 900 missiles to use as a deterrent against retaliation. While this example is hypothetical, the message is clear; MIRVs are destablizing.

A second case of technological creep has occurred in the area of 28 missile accuracy. Extreme accuracy is not important for *city-busting,* since the target is large and *soft*—unprotected and easily destroyed. Accuracy is important for counterforce attacks, however. Underground missile silos, with their heavy shieldings, and very *hard* targets, and to destroy them, it is necessary to make a *direct hit.* Over the past decade, each superpower has greatly improved the accuracy of its missiles, so much so that they can now land within a few hundred feet of their targets. Weapons specialists refer to this increase in accuracy as a decrease in the *CEP,* or the *circular error probable,* which is the radius of the circle in which a missile has a 50 percent chance of landing if aimed at its center. As a result of the increase in accuracy, land-based missiles in both the U.S. and the USSR are vulnerable to counterforce attack.

No one has developed *antisubmarine warfare (ASW)* technology 29 capable of threatening the survivability of either U.S. or USSR submarines, and the subs remain a *credible* deterrent. Work to *improve* antisubmarine warfare is under way in both countries, however.

The C^3 systems both superpowers depend on to coordinate their   30
nuclear forces might be vulnerable to nuclear attack. This could provide a *strong incentive* to strike first. As the newsletter of the Federation of American Scientists (FAS) noted in October 1980,

> A nation that strikes first with strategic forces does so with its command
> structure, control mechanisms, and communications devices wholly intact,
> alerted, and ready. Each and every telephone line, satellite, and antenna is
> functioning and every relevant person is alive and well. By contrast, the
> nation which seeks to launch a retaliatory attack may find its chain of
> command highly disrupted, its telephone lines dead, its satellites inopera-
> tive, its radio signals interfered with, and its communications officers out
> of action.

The FAS called attacks on C^3 "a kind of supercounterforce and   31
correspondingly destabilizing." The Federation predicted: "Should
either side carry out deliberate efforts to attack the C^3 of the other, it
appears almost certain that a spasm war would result in which the attacked nation gave its military commanders either by prior agreement
or by last desperate message, the authority to *fire at will.* As its ability
to communicate gave out, it could and would do no less than use its
last communications channel for *the final order.*

Another threat to the stability of deterrence is the possibility that a   32
system failure in either superpower's nuclear-war-fighting computers
could trigger an accidental nuclear war. Three recent *alerts* caused by
computer errors show that this threat may not be as insignificant as the
Department of Defense claims:

> In November of 1979, data from a computer *war game* accidentally flowed
> into a live warning and command network, triggering a low-level alert.
> The computer's mistake was not detected for six minutes. In the mean-
> time, B-52 pilots were told to man their planes, and the launch officers in
> ICBM silos unlocked a special strong box, removed the *attack verification
> codes,* and inserted the *keys* into their slots. When two keys ten feet apart
> are turned within two seconds of each other, the missiles blast off.
>
> In June, 1980, on two separate occasions, a computer error caused by a
> faulty circuit chip worth 46¢ sent out false signals that the USSR had
> launched missiles headed for the U.S. In both cases, some of the B-52 fleet
> started its engines before the error was detected.

The Pentagon maintains that there is *"no chance* that any *irretriev-*   33
able actions would be taken on the basis of *ambiguous computer infor-*
mation," noting that the computers do not make decisions alone and
that *human intervention* has always detected the errors.

Nevertheless, there is little time for the people involved to read the   34
signals properly and make decisions. Land-based missiles can reach

the U.S. in about thirty minutes, while submarine-launched missiles might take only half that time. Moreover, the threat exists that an erroneous alert could generate a nuclear attack as if by a trick of mirrors. If in response to a computer error the B-52s were suddenly to take off from their air bases, the Russians would immediately detect the maneuver. Soviet officers would have even less time to reach a judgment about how to respond, since their *early warning systems* are not as sophisticated as those of the U.S. If the Soviets dispatched their bombers, the U.S. warning system would in turn detect the planes, and the computer's message, though originally erroneous, would be *confirmed*.

The Pentagon claims that such a *chain reaction is a "highly unlikely* ₃₅ *scenario."* A full public discussion of the issues involved is impossible because most of the relevant information is classified.

QUESTIONS ON CONTENT

1. What do the authors mean when they state that "the world of nuclear warfare is a world of doublethink"(1)? Explain how the image of a "hall of mirrors" works in this essay?

2. The authors describe the language of nuclear war strategist as "cool" and "clinical." Do you agree with their assessment? Why do you suppose war strategists choose to use such language? How is their language related to the War Department's name change in 1948?

3. Explain the principle of "deterrence." Why are nuclear war planners afraid of a "preemptive first strike"? And how is the threat of a preemptive first strike related to what we know as the "arms race"?

4. What is the difference between a neutron bomb and a conventional nuclear bomb?

5. What developments in the 1970s destabilized the situation between the United States and the USSR? What other threats to deterrence exist?

6. Choose a paragraph or two from the essay and try to substitute words for those italicized. What is the effect?

QUESTIONS ON RHETORIC

1. What seems to be the authors' purpose in this essay—to explain the highly specialized vocabulary of the nuclear strategies or to argue against the use of such language? Explain your answer with examples from the essay. (Glossary: *Purpose*)

2. Identify passages in which the authors make use of the strategies of classification and analyzing cause and effect. (Glossary: *Division and Classification* and *Cause and Effect*)

3. In paragraphs 20 and 21 the authors use the analogy of two drivers competing in a game of chicken to explain "escalation strategy." Explain how the analogy works. How helpful did you find it in understanding the complexities of escalation strategy? (Glossary: *Analogy*)

4. In paragraphs 21, 30, and 32, the authors use examples. Explain the function of each example within the context of its paragraph. (Glossary: *Examples*)

VOCABULARY

esoteric (2)	conjunction (14)	orgasmic (19)
carnage (4)	purportedly (16)	insensate (19)
retaliate (4)	arrray (17)	hypothetical (27)
construed (6)	tacit (18)	vulnerable (28)
arsenal (9)		

WRITING TOPICS

1. Using examples from the essay you've just read and examples of your own if you have them, write an essay in which you argue that the language of the nuclear war strategists gives us an inaccurate picture of the realities of nuclear warfare.

2. Using the definitions of technical language and jargon given by Kenneth Hudson (pp. 356–362), how would you describe the language of nuclear war strategists, particularly the words italicized by Hilgartner and his coauthors? How much of this language meets Hudson's criteria for jargon, and how much is legitimate technical vocabulary? How much would you call euphemism?

3. Is it acceptable to use euphemisms to deal with matters, such as nuclear warfare, that pose psychological difficulties? Or is such action simply immoral? How do you think Neil Postman (pp. 343–345) would react to the language of the nuclear war strategists?

WRITING ASSIGNMENTS FOR "EUPHEMISMS AND PROFESSIONAL JARGON"

1. Select one of the following situations, and write a dialogue that accurately uses the language of the people involved:

   a. a conference between a student and a teacher about the first paper of the semester
   b. a discussion between an executive and an auto mechanic about repairs to the former's Cadillac
   c. a conversation between a ten-year-old child and his or her parent about the condition of the child's room
   d. an interview by a newspaper reporter with the chief of police of a small town concerning a recent crime

2. Watch episodes from three different television shows featuring detectives, doctors, lawyers, or persons in some other occupation. Write an essay in which you analyze the professional language used in these shows, commenting on the general accuracy of the language and the similarities among the shows.

3. Interview an athlete or a coach about the prospects for the season, a recent game, an upcoming opponent, or any other aspect of the sport. Write an essay based on this interview, making sure that you accurately capture the sports jargon used by the athlete or coach.

4. Linguist Benjamin Lee Whorf has pointed out that "the structure of a given language determines, in part, how the society that speaks it views reality." Explain how our use of euphemisms affects both our behavior and our opinion of our behavior. Consider, for example, the following expressions and the euphemisms for them:

   false teeth ("dental appliance")
   typist ("information processor")
   bombing raid ("limited duration protective reaction strike")
   lie ("inoperative statement")
   rerun ("encore telecast")
   fire ("terminate")
   constipation ("occasional irregularity")

List other euphemisms used by government, big business, and professions. How may the use of such euphemisms influence behavior?

5. Study a copy of the *New York Times* or another major newspaper for its use of euphemisms in editorials, news articles, commercial ads, classified ads, etc. Write an essay based on what you find in the newspaper, and then draw some conclusions regarding the frequency and

types of euphemisms you have found. For what purposes are the euphemisms used in the different parts of the newspaper?

6. Write an essay in which you use the following quote from *Time* magazine as your thesis: "Like stammers or tears, euphemisms will be created whenever men doubt, or fear, or do not know."

7. In an article called "Public Doublespeak," Terence Moran presented the following list of recommendations given to the faculty of an elementary school in Brooklyn:

FOR PARENT INTERVIEWS AND REPORT CARDS

Harsh Expression (Avoid)	Acceptable Expression (Use)
Does all right if pushed	Accomplishes tasks when interest is stimulated.
Too free with fists	Resorts to physical means of winning his point or attracting attention.
Lies (Dishonest)	Shows difficulty in distinguishing between imaginary and factual material.
Cheats	Needs help in learning to adhere to rules and standards of fair play.
Steals	Needs help in learning to respect the property rights of others.
Noisy	Needs to develop quieter habits of communication.
Lazy	Needs ample supervision in order to work well.
Is a bully	Has qualities of leadership but needs help in learning to use them democratically.
Associates with "Gangs"	Seems to feel secure only in group situations; needs to develop sense of independence.
Disliked by other children	Needs help in learning to form lasting friendships.

After reading Neil Postman's essay on euphemisms and Stuart Chase's on bureaucratic language, write an essay in which you discuss what this list recommends and the possible effects of its use on teachers, students, and parents.

8. One of the fascinating aspects of American English is its diversity, and one of the causes of this diversity is the specialized vocabularies of different occupations in America. Russell Baker's report of a fictitious symposium dealing with Little Miss Muffet, taken from *Poor Russell's Almanac,* illustrates several varieties of occupational Americanese:

Little Miss Muffet, as everyone knows, sat on a tuffet eating her curds and whey when along came a spider who sat down beside her and frightened Miss Muffet away. While everyone knows this, the significance of the event had never been analyzed until a conference of thinkers recently brought their special insights to bear upon it. Following are excerpts from the transcript of their discussion:

Sociologist: We are clearly dealing here with a prototypical illustration of a highly tensile social structure's tendency to dis- or perhaps even de-structure itself under the pressures created when optimum minimums do not obtain among the disadvantaged. Miss Muffet is nutritionally under-privileged, as evidenced by the subliminal diet of curds and whey upon which she is forced to subsist, while the spider's cultural disadvantage is evidenced by such phenomena as legs exceeding standard norms, odd mating habits, and so forth.

In this instance, spider expectations lead the culturally disadvantaged to assert demands to share the tuffet with the nutritionally underprivi-leged. Due to a communications failure, Miss Muffet assumes without evidence that the spider will not be satisfied to share her tuffet, but will also insist on eating her curds and perhaps even her whey. Thus, the fail-ure to preestablish selectively optimum norm structures diverts potentially optimal minimums from the expectation levels assumed to. . . .

Militarist: Second-strike capability, sir! That's what was lacking. If Miss Muffet had developed a second-strike capability instead of squan-dering her resources on curds and whey, no spider on earth would have dared launch a first strike capable of carrying him right to the heart of her tuffet. I am confident that Miss Muffet had adequate notice from experts that she could not afford both curds and whey and, at the same time, sup-port an early-spider-warning system. Yet curds alone were not good enough for Miss Muffet. She had to have whey, too. Tuffet security must be the first responsibility of every diner. . . .

Book Reviewer: Written on several levels, this searing and sensitive ex-ploration of the arachnid heart illuminates the agony and splendor of Jew-ish family life with a candor that is at once breathtaking in its simplicity and soul-shattering in its implied ambiguity. Some will doubtless be shocked to see such subjects as tuffets and whey discussed without flinch-ing, but hereafter writers too timid to call a curd a curd will no longer. . . .

Editorial Writer: Why has the Government not seen fit to tell the public all it knows about the so-called curds-and-whey affair? It is not enough to suggest that this was merely a random incident involving a lonely spider and a young diner. In today's world, poised as it is on the knife edge of. . . .

Psychiatrist: Little Miss Muffet is, of course, neither little nor a miss. These are obviously the self she has created in her own fantasies to escape the reality that she is a gross divorcee whose superego makes it impossible for her to sustain a normal relationship with any man, symbolized by the spider, who, of course, has no existence outside her fantasies. Little Miss Muffet may, in fact, be a man with deeply repressed Oedipal impulses, who sees in the spider the father he would like to kill, and very well may some day unless he admits that what he believes to be a tuffet is, in fact, probably the dining room chandelier, and that the whey he thinks he is eating is, in fact, probably. . . .

Flower Child: Like this beautiful kid is on a bad trip, dig? Like. . . .

Student Demonstrator: Little Miss Muffet, tuffets, curds, whey and spi-ders are what's wrong with education today. They're all irrelevant. Tuffets are irrelevant. Curds are irrelevant. Whey is irrelevant. Meaningful experience! How can you have relevance without meaningful experience? And how can there ever be meaningful experience without understanding? With understanding and meaningfulness and relevance, there can be love and good and deep seriousness and education today will be freed of slavery and Little Miss Muffet, and life will become meaningful and. . . .

Child: This is about a little girl who gets scared by a spider.

(The child was sent home when the conference broke for lunch. It was agreed that he was too immature to subtract anything from the sum of human understanding.)

Note: Suggested topics for research papers appear on p. 446.

Try your hand at retelling the story of George Washington and the cherry tree from the standpoint of several of the following: police officer, social worker, clergyman, psychiatrist, George's teenage friend, forester, or some other person who uses a distinctive jargon. Share your versions of the story with other members of the class.

NOTABLE QUOTATIONS

The following quotations are drawn from the essays in this section. They are presented as additional topics for classroom discussion or for writing assignments.

"What we call things affects how we will perceive them." *Postman* (2)

"The process of euphemizing has no moral content. The moral dimensions are supplied by what the words in question express, what they want us to value and to see." *Postman* (7)

"The American, probably more than any other man, is prone to be apologetic about the trade he follows." *Mencken* (1)

"Next to *engineer, expert* seems to be the favorite talisman of Americans eager to augment their estate and dignity in this world." *Mencken* (7)

"The best minds in any profession are never guilty of jargon, except when they are very tired. Pedestrian minds are drawn towards it automatically and to the most frightening extent." *Hudson* (4)

"The only way of keeping jargon under control is to make sure that people of the highest intelligence receive a broadly-based education, the most important part of which is the development of a pride in handling words really well." *Hudson* (24)

"Many words and phrases in officialese seem to come out automatically, as if from lower centers of the brain." *Chase* (26)

"Professional or office gobbledygook often arises from using the passive rather than the active voice." *Chase* (29)

"You should read an annual report as a piece of literature, carefully, circling the text." *Yoe* (1)

"While most euphemisms found in annual reports have to do with money . . ., felicitous phrasing can smooth over other pimples on the corporate facade." *Yoe* (6)

"Nuclear war strategists have developed an esoteric, highly specialized vocabulary." *Hilgartner, Bell, and O'Connor* (2)

"If the survivability of either side's forces is in question, the whole situation becomes a hall of mirrors." *Hilgartner, Bell, and O'Connor* (24)

IX
Taboos

There can't be anything about a particular string of sounds which makes it intrinsically clean or dirty, ugly or beautiful. The filth or beauty of language must be in the ear of the listener, or in the collective ear of society.

Victoria Fromkin and Robert Rodman

The infamous *four-letter words* . . . form part of the vocabulary of practically everyone above the age of six or seven. They are not slang terms, but legitimate Standard English of the oldest stock, and they are euphemized in many ways, typically by conversion into pseudo-Latin (e.g., *copulation, defecation, urination*), into slang (*make love, number two, pee*), or into socially acceptable dashes (*f----, s----, p----*, etc.).

Hugh Rawson

The real argument against the use of dirty words . . . is not that they shock or disturb the listener but that they are a limiting, self-deceiving form of expression that reveals insecurity rather than unconventionality. There is nothing *more* conventional than dirty words.

Dr. Joyce Brothers

When you're lying awake with a dismal
    headache, and repose is tabooed by anxiety,
I conceive you may use any language
    you choose to indulge in, without impropriety.

William Schwenck Gilbert

1
Verbal Taboo

S. I. HAYAKAWA

S. I. Hayakawa, formerly president of San Francisco State University and United States Senator from California, is one of the leading semanticists in this country. In this excerpt from Language in Thought and Action, *Hayakawa examines the verbal taboo, the phenomenon that occurs in almost all languages when the distinction between languages and reality becomes confused.*

In every language there seem to be certain "unmentionables"—words of such strong affective connotations that they cannot be used in polite discourse. In English, the first of these to come to mind are, of course, words dealing with excretion and sex. We ask movie ushers and filling-station attendants where the "lounge" or "rest room" is, although we usually have no intention of lounging or resting. "Powder room" is another euphemism for the same facility, also known as "toilet," which itself is an earlier euphemism. Indeed, it is impossible in polite society to state, without having to resort to baby talk or medical vocabulary, what a "rest room" is for. (It is "where you wash your hands.") Another term is "John." There is now a book on the best "Johns" in New York.

Money is another subject about which communication is in some ways inhibited. It is all right to mention *sums* of money, such as $10,000 or $2.50. But it is considered in bad taste to inquire directly into other people's financial affairs, unless such an inquiry is really necessary in the course of business. When creditors send bills, they almost never mention money, although that is what they are writing about. There are many circumlocutions: "We beg to call your attention to what might be an oversight on your part." "We would appreciate your early attention to this matter." "May we look forward to an early remittance?"

The fear of death carries over, quite understandably in view of the widespread confusion of symbols with things symbolized, into fear of the *words* having to do with death. Many people, therefore, instead of saying "died," substitute such expressions as "passed away," "went to his reward," "departed," and "went west." In Japanese, the word for death, *shi,* happens to have the same pronunciation as the word for the number four. This coincidence results in many linguistically awkward situations, since people avoid *"shi"* in the discussion of numbers and prices, and use *"yon,"* a word of different origin, instead.

Words having to do with anatomy and sex—and words even   4
vaguely suggesting anatomical or sexual matters—have, especially in American culture, remarkable affective connotations. Ladies of the nineteenth century could not bring themselves to say "breast" or "leg"—not even of chicken—so that the terms "white meat" and "dark meat" were substituted. It was thought inelegant to speak of "going to bed," and "to retire" was used instead. In rural America there are many euphemisms for the word "bull"; among them are "he-cow," "cow-critter," "male cow," "gentleman cow." But Americans are not alone in their delicacy about such matters. When D. H. Lawrence's first novel, *The White Peacock* (1911), was published, the author was widely and vigorously criticized for having used (in innocuous context) the word "stallion." "Our hearts are warm, our bellies are full" was changed to "Our hearts are warm, and we are full" in a 1962 presentation of the Rodgers and Hammerstein musical *Carousel* before the British Royal Family.

These verbal taboos, although sometimes amusing, also produce   5
serious problems, since they prevent frank discussion of sexual matters. Social workers, with whom I have discussed this question, report that young people of junior high school and high school age who contact venereal disease, become pregnant out of wedlock, and get into other serious trouble of this kind are almost always profoundly ignorant of the most elementary facts about sex and procreation. Their ignorance is apparently due to the fact that neither they nor their parents have a vocabulary with which to discuss such matters: the nontechnical vocabulary of sex is to them too coarse and shocking to be used, while the technical, medical vocabulary is unknown to them. The social workers find, therefore, that the first step in helping these young people is usually a linguistic one: the students have to be taught a vocabulary in which they can talk about their problems before they can be helped further.

The stronger verbal taboos have, however, a genuine social value.   6
When we are extremely angry and we feel the need of expressing our anger in violence, uttering these forbidden words provides us with a relatively harmless verbal substitute for going beserk and smashing furniture; that is, the words act as a kind of safety valve in our moments of crisis.

It is difficult to explain why some words should have such powerful   7
affective connotations while others with the same informative conno-

tations do not. Some of our verbal reticences, especially the religious ones, have the authority of the Bible: "Thou shalt not take the name of the Lord thy God in vain; for the Lord will not hold him guiltless that taketh his name in vain" (Exodus 21:7). "Gee," "gosh almighty," and "gosh darn" are ways to avoid saying, "Jesus," "God Almighty," and "God damn"; and carrying the biblical injunction one step further, we also avoid taking the name of the Devil in vain by means of such expressions as "the deuce," "the dickens," and "Old Nick." It appears that among all the people of the world, among the civilized as well as the primitive, there is a feeling that the names of the gods are too holy, and the names of evil spirits too terrifying, to be spoken lightly.

The primitive confusion of word with thing, of symbol with thing   8
symbolized, manifests itself in some parts of the world in a belief that the name of a person is *part of* that person. To know someone's name, therefore, is to have power over him. Because of this belief, it is customary among some peoples for children to be given at birth a "real name" known only to the parents and never used, as well as a nickname or public name to be called by in society. In this way the child is protected from being put in anyone's power. The story of Rumpelstiltskin is a European illustration of this belief in the power of names. . . .

QUESTIONS ON CONTENT

1. Into what categories does Hayakawa classify taboo words? Give an example of each subject area.

2. What does Hayakawa mean when he says that taboo words have "strong affective connotations"(1)? How do affective connotations differ from informative connotations?

3. According to Hayakawa, what problems result from the existence of verbal taboos?

4. Hayakawa says that the "stronger verbal taboos have . . . a genuine social value" (6). What is it?

5. What does Hayakawa mean when he says there is "widespread confusion of symbols with things symbolized" (3)?

6. What is the relationship between taboo words and euphemisms? Provide several examples to illustrate your answer.

QUESTIONS ON RHETORIC

1. Which sentence in paragraph 4 is the topic sentence? How does Hayakawa support this idea? (Glossary: *Topic Sentence*)

2. How does Hayakawa make the transition between paragraphs 5 and 6? What other transitional devices does he use in this essay? (Glossary: *Transitions*)

3. Hayakawa assumes that his readers are familiar with the story of Rumpelstiltskin, a children's classic, and therefore does not retell the story to make his point. Is Hayakawa's assumption correct? Do you know the story?

4. In what ways do Hayakawa's numerous examples function in this essay? (Glossary: *Examples*) Which ones are most effective for you? Why?

VOCABULARY

inhibited (2)   coincidence (3)   ignorant (5)
symbols (3)   anatomical (4)

WRITING TOPICS

1. There is an important distinction between symbols and the things they stand for, that is, their referents. For example, a person should not confuse an actual chair (physical object) with the word *chair* (symbol). Nevertheless, as Hayakawa observes, there is "widespread confusion of symbols with things symbolized" (3). In this connection, discuss the following episode in which a small child is talking to her mother: "Mommy! I'm scared of *death*. I don't like to hear that word. It frightens me! If only it were called something else, like *looma*." What in your opinion would happen if the word were changed? Can you suggest other examples to support your view?

2. In recent years "concerned citizens" across the country have attempted to remove the *Dictionary of American Slang* as well as certain desk dictionaries from schools and libraries. They have done so to keep their children from being exposed to taboo language. What underlying assumption about the relationship between words and things do such efforts reflect? If these citizens were successful in removing these books, would their children be protected? Why, or why not?

2
Four-Letter Words Can Hurt You

BARBARA LAWRENCE

Barbara Lawrence was born in Hanover, New Hampshire, and graduated from Connecticut College. Before becoming a professor of humanities at the State University of New York at Old Westbury, she worked as an editor at McCall's, Redbook, *and the* New Yorker. *In the following essay, published in the* New York Times *in 1973, she defines "obscenity" and explains why she finds the obscene language some people use to be "implicitly sadistic or denigrating to women."*

Why should any words be called obscene? Don't they all describe natural human functions? Am I trying to tell them, my students demand, that the "strong, earthy, gut-honest"—or, if they are fans of Norman Mailer, the "rich, liberating, existential"—language they use to describe sexual activity isn't preferable to "phony-sounding, middle-class words like 'intercourse' and 'copulate'?" "Cop You Late!" they say with fancy inflections and gagging grimaces. "Now, what is *that* supposed to mean?"

Well, what is it supposed to mean? And why indeed should one group of words describing human functions and human organs be acceptable in ordinary conversations and another, describing presumably the same organs and functions, be tabooed—so much so, in fact, that some of these words still cannot appear in print in many parts of the English-speaking world?

The argument that these taboos exist only because of "sexual hang-ups" (middle-class, middle-age, feminist), or even that they are a result of class oppression (the contempt of the Norman conquerors for the language of their Anglo-Saxon serfs), ignores a much more likely explanation, it seems to me, and that is the sources and functions of the words themselves.

The best known of the tabooed sexual verbs, for example, comes from the German *ficken,* meaning "to strike"; combined, according to

Partridge's etymological dictionary *Origins,* with the Latin sexual verb *futuere;* associated in turn with the Latin *fustis,* "a staff or cudgel"; the Celtic *buc,* "a point, hence to pierce"; the Irish *bot,* "the male member"; the Latin *battuere,* "to beat"; the Gaelic *batair,* "a cudgeller"; the Early Irish *bualaim,* "I strike"; and so forth. It is one of what etymologists sometimes call "the sadistic group of words for the man's part in copulation."

The brutality of this word, then, and its equivalents ("screw," "bang," etc.), is not an illusion of the middle class or a crotchet of Women's Liberation. In their origins and imagery these words carry undeniably painful, if not sadistic, implications, the object of which is almost always female. Consider, for example, what a "screw" actually does to the wood it penetrates; what a painful, even mutilating, activity this kind of analogy suggests. "Screw" is particularly interesting in this context, since the noun, according to Partridge, comes from words meaning "groove," "nut," "ditch," "breeding sow," "scrofula" and "swelling," while the verb, besides its explicit imagery, has antecedent associations to "write on," "scratch," "scarify," and so forth—a revealing fusion of a mechanical or painful action with an obviously denigrated object.   5

Not all obscene words, of course, are as implicitly sadistic or denigrating to women as these, but all that I know seem to serve a similar purpose: to reduce the human organism (especially the female organism) and human functions (especially sexual and procreative) to their least organic, most mechanical dimension; to substitute a trivializing or deforming resemblance for the complex human reality of what is being described.   6

Tabooed male descriptives, when they are not openly denigrating to women, often serve to divorce a male organ or function from any significant interaction with the female. Take the word "testes," for example, suggesting "witnesses" (from the Latin *testis*) to the sexual and procreative strengths of the male organ; and the obscene counterpart of this word, which suggests little more than a mechanical shape. Or compare almost any of the "rich," "liberating" sexual verbs, so fashionable today among male writers, with that much-derided Latin word "copulate" ("to bind or join together") or even that Anglo-Saxon phrase (which seems to have had no trouble surviving the Norman Conquest) "make love."   7

How arrogantly self-involved the tabooed words seem in comparison to either of the other terms, and how contemptuous of the female partner. Understandably so, of course, if she is only a "skirt," a "broad," a "chick," a "pussycat" or a "piece." If she is, in other words, no more than her skirt, or what her skirt conceals; no more than a   8 breeder, or the broadest part of her; no more than a piece of a human being or a "piece of tail."

The most severely tabooed of all the female descriptives, inciden- 9 tally, are those like a "piece of tail," which suggest (either explicitly or through antecedents) that there is no significant difference between the female channel through which we are all conceived and born and the anal outlet common to both sexes—a distinction that pornographers have always enjoyed obscuring.

This effort to deny women their biological identity, their individu- 10 ality, their humanness, is such an important aspect of obscene language that one can only marvel at how seldom, in an era preoccupied with definitions of obscenity, this fact is brought to our attention. One problem, of course, is that many of the people in the best position to do this (critics, teachers, writers) are so reluctant today to admit that they are angered or shocked by obscenity. Bored, maybe, unimpressed, aesthetically displeased, but—no matter how brutal or denigrating the material—never angered, never shocked.

And yet how eloquently angered, how piously shocked many of 11 these same people become if denigrating language is used about any minority group other than women; if the obscenities are racial or ethnic, that is, rather than sexual. Words like "coon," "kike," "spic," "wop," after all, deform identity, deny individuality and humanness in almost exactly the same way that sexual vulgarisms and obscenities do.

No one that I know, least of all my students, would fail to question 12 the values of a society whose literature and entertainment rested heavily on racial or ethnic pejoratives. Are the values of a society whose literature and entertainment rest as heavily as ours on sexual pejoratives any less questionable?

QUESTIONS ON CONTENT

1. How does Lawrence explain the existence of taboos? What other explanations does she mention and then dismiss?

2. Why does Lawrence, as a woman, object to obscene language? Could men object to obscene language on the same grounds?

3. Do you agree with Lawrence's argument? Why, or why not? Would it be fair to consider Lawrence's view of obscenity as strictly feminist?

4. In paragraph 4 Lawrence details the origin of "the best known of the tabooed sexual verbs." In what way is this presentation of the word's etymology related to her central argument? How did you respond to this paragraph? Why?

QUESTIONS ON RHETORIC

1. Lawrence begins her essay with a series of questions. What functions do these questions serve? (Glossary: *Beginnings* and *Rhetorical Questions*)

2. Lawrence consciously avoids using "obscene" words. What, in your opinion, is gained or lost as a result of this strategy? Explain.

3. Comment on the connotations of the words which have been italicized in the following sentence: (Glossary: *Connotation*)

> And yet how *eloquently* angered, how *piously* shocked many of these same people become if denigrating language is used about any minority group other than women. . . .(11)

4. Should paragraphs 11 and 12 have been combined? Why do you feel Lawrence has made separate paragraphs?

5. What is the effect of Lawrence's final question? How would you answer it?

VOCABULARY

preferable (1)	analogy (5)	contemptuous (8)
grimaces (1)	antecedent (5)	pejoratives (12)
oppression (3)	implicitly (6)	

WRITING TOPICS

1. Discuss the pros and cons of the proposition that women's use of "liberated" language is self-defeating. Why, in your opinion, do some women make a point of using such language?

2. Do you commonly use sexual obscenities and feel justified in doing so? Or do such words offend you? How would you describe your feelings about obscenities? Defend your feelings to someone who does not share them.

3. Lawrence observes that "some of these words still cannot appear in print in many parts of the English-speaking world" (2)—and books that contain these words, including some dictionaries, are banned from

many school libraries and bookstores. What reasons can be given for and against censoring obscene words, or banning publications in which they appear? Does such action really eradicate the problem, or merely force it underground? What is your position? How would you support it?

3

On the Use of "Dirty" Words

WILLIAM F. BUCKLEY, JR.

William F. Buckley, Jr., is best known as an articulate spokesman for the political right. For thirty years he has edited the National Review, *America's leading conservative magazine, and he is published three times weekly in a widely syndicated newspaper column. In the following essay from the* National Review, *Buckley takes issue with the maxim we've all heard at one time or another: "Only people with a small vocabulary use 'dirty' words." He comes to the defense of "dirty" words on the grounds that they let us all express certain kinds of emotion that are not otherwise readily communicable.*

I guess I was seven when I first heard the maxim that only people 1
with a small vocabulary use "dirty" words. I am forty-seven and have just received a communication from a reader delivering that maxim as though he had invented it. The trouble with the cliché is (a) it isn't true; (b) it doesn't take into account the need to use the resources of language; and (c) the kind of people who use it are almost always engaged in irredentist ventures calculated to make "dirty," words and expressions that no longer are, and even some that never were.

The first point is easily disposed of by asking ourselves the ques- 2
tion, Did Shakespeare have a good vocabulary? Yes; and he also used, however sparingly, profane and obscene words.

The second point raises the question of whether a certain kind of 3
emotion is readily communicable with the use of other than certain kinds of words. Let us assume the only thing it is safe to assume about the matter, namely that every emotion is experienced by everyone, from the darkest sinner to the most uplifted saint. The sinner, having no care at all for people's feelings, let alone for propriety abstractly considered, lets loose a profanity not only on occasions when his emotions are acutely taxed, but even when they are mildly stirred. The saint—or so I take it from their published writings—manages to exclude the profane word from his vocabulary, and does not resort to it under any circumstances. It was for the saint that the tushery was invented. "Tush! tush!" the saint will say to his tormentors, as he is eased into the cauldron of boiling oil.

Non-saints, it is my thesis, have a difficult time adopting the man-   4
ners of saints; and even if they succeed most of the time in suppressing
obnoxious words, they will probably not succeed all of the time. Moreover, as suggested above, they are up against a community some of
whose members are always seeking to repristinate the world of language back to the point where you could not even say, "Gosh, Babe
Ruth was a good baseball player," because Gosh is quite clearly a
sneaky way of saying God, the use of which the purists would hold to
be impermissible under any circumstances—indeed they, plus the Supreme Court, reduce the permissible use of the word to the innermost
tabernacles.

The context in which a bad word is used does much to deter-   5
mine the quality of its offensiveness, and the usefulness of the word.
Reviewing Norman Mailer's first novel many years ago, Professor
John Roche objected that the recurring use of barracks language,
while it reproduced faithfully the language of the barracks, in fact dis-
torts the prose for readers outside the barracks set who are emotionally or psychologically interrupted every time they run into a word
they are not used to seeing on the printed page. It is as if a poet were
handicapped by the miscadencing of his verse by a reader who suddenly paused at unexpected places, as if to walk around a puddle
of water.

I had reason to reach, a while back, for a word to comment upon a   6
line of argument I considered insufferably sanctimonious. "Crap," I
wrote: And the irredentist hordes descended upon me all in their fury.
I have replied to them that the word in question is defined in a current
dictionary in several ways. That among these are meaning 2: "nonsense; drivel: *Man, don't hand me that crap.* 3. a lie; an exaggeration:
Bah, you don't believe that crap, do you?" Notwithstanding that the
word has these clearly non-scatalogical uses, there is an Anglo-Saxon
earthiness to it which performs for the writer a function altogether different from such a retort as, say, "Flapdoodle."

There are those of us who feel very strongly that the cheapest and   7
most indefensible way to give offense is to direct obscenities wantonly,
and within the earshot of those who seek protection from that kind of
thing. There will always be a certain healthy tension between Billingsgate and the convent, but in the interest of the language, neither side
should win the war completely. Better a stalemate, with a DMZ that
changes its bed meanderingly, like the Mississippi River.

QUESTIONS ON CONTENT

1. What problems does Buckley have with the maxim that "only people with a small vocabulary use 'dirty' words" (1)?

2. What, according to Buckley, determines both the offensiveness and the usefulness of "dirty" words?

3. What contrast does Buckley draw between saints and sinners? Where do non-saints fit in to the scheme of things? Which do you think Buckley considers himself to be?

4. In the preceding essay, Barbara Lawrence claims that "four-letter words can hurt you." How do you think Buckley would respond to Lawrence's position?

QUESTIONS ON RHETORIC

1. What is Buckley's thesis, and where is it stated? (Glossary: *Thesis*)

2. How has Buckley organized his essay? (Glossary: *Organization*) Which sentence in the opening paragraph serves to set up the organization?

3. In paragraph 6 Buckley recalls an occasion when he used a "dirty" word to comment on a line of argument. How well does he defend his use of "crap"? Why is "crap" a more effective word than "flapdoodle" in this case?

4. Did you find Buckley's defense of dirty words persuasive? Why, or why not?

5. How would you describe Buckley's own vocabulary? Is he a person with a small vocabulary? Would you expect him to rely heavily on "dirty" words in conversation and writing?

6. Identify several metaphors and similes that Buckley uses, and explain how each works. (Glossary: *Figures of Speech*)

VOCABULARY

maxim (1)   cauldron (3)   sanctimonious (6)
irredentist (1)   repristinate (4)   wantonly (7)
tushery (3)

WRITING TOPICS

1. Write an essay in which you discuss the use of dirty words. In what kinds of situations are they permissible? When are they impermissible? Be sure to support your reasons with examples from your own experience or observation.

2. Why do you think dirty words have come to be considered so? Do some ever become generally acceptable? In other words, are there some words that your parents and grandparents consider "dirty" that are not considered such by your generation? Write an essay in which you discuss such words and speculate about why your generation no longer considers them offensive.

3. What does Buckley mean when he states "There will always be a certain healthy tension between Billingsgate and the convent" (7)? Write an essay in which you explain what the tension is and why it may be considered healthy.

4

Institution Is Not a Dirty Word

FERN KUPFER

Fern Kupfer is the mother of Zachariah, a child severely brain-damaged from birth. She and her husband, knowing that his care precluded any semblance of normal family life, decided to institutionalize their son. Their position is not a very popular one currently. In the following essay, Kupfer takes an open and honest look at a subject that is generally considered taboo and dealt with euphemistically if at all.

I watched Phil Donahue recently. He had on mothers of handicapped children who talked about the pain and blessing of having a "special" child. As the mother of a severely handicapped six-year-old boy who cannot sit, who cannot walk, who will be in diapers all of his days, I understand the pain. The blessing part continues to elude me—notwithstanding the kind and caring people we've met through this tragedy.

What really makes my jaws clench, though, is the use of the word "special." The idea that our damaged children are "special," and that we as parents were somehow picked for the role, is one of the myths that come with the territory. It's reinforced by the popular media, which present us with heartwarming images of retarded people who marry, of quadriplegics who fly airplanes, of those fortunate few who struggle out of comas to teach us about the meaning of courage and love. I like these stories myself. But, of course, inspirational tales are only one side of the story. The other side deals with the daily care of a family member who might need more than many normal families can give. Parents who endure with silent stoicism or chin-up good humor are greeted with kudos and applause. "I don't know how you do it," the well-wishers say, not realizing, of course, that no one has a choice in this matter. No one would consciously choose to have a child anything less than healthy and normal. The other truth is not spoken aloud: "Thank God, it's not me."

410

One mother on the Donahue show talked about how difficult it was 3 to care for her severely brain-damaged daughter, but in the end, she said serenely, "She gives much more than she takes from our family." And no, she would never institutionalize her child. She would never "put her away." For "she is my child," the woman firmly concluded as the audience clapped in approval. "I would never give her up."

Everyone always says how awful the institutions are. Don't they 4 have bars on the windows and children lying neglected in crowded wards? Aren't all the workers sadists, taking direction from the legendary Big Nurse? Indeed, isn't institutionalizing a child tantamount to locking him away? Signing him out of your life forever? Isn't it proof of your failure as a parent—one who couldn't quite measure up and love your child, no matter what?

No, to all of the above. And love is beside the point. 5

Our child Zachariah has not lived at home for almost four years. I 6 knew when we placed him, sorry as I was, that this was the right decision, for his care precluded any semblance of normal family life for the rest of us. I do not think that we "gave him up," although he is cared for daily by nurses, caseworkers, teachers and therapists, rather than by his mother and father. When we come to visit him at his "residential facility," a place housing fifty severely physically and mentally handicapped youngsters, we usually see him being held and rocked by a foster grandma who has spent the better part of the afternoon singing him nursery rhymes. I do not feel that we have "put him away." Perhaps it is just a question of language. I told another mother who was going through the difficult decision regarding placement for her retarded child, "Think of it as going to boarding school rather than institutionalization." Maybe euphemisms help ease the pain a little bit. But I've also seen enough to know that institution need not be a dirty word.

The media still relish those institution horror stories: a page-one 7 photo of a retarded girl who was repeatedly molested by the janitor on night duty. Oh, the newspapers have a field day with something like that. And that is how it should be, I suppose. To protect against institutional abuse we need critical reporters with sharpened pencils and a keen investigative eye. But there are other scenes from the institution as well. I've seen a young caseworker talk lovingly as she changed the diapers of a teen-age boy. I've watched as an aide put red ribbons into the ponytail of a cerebral-palsied woman, wipe away the drool and kiss her on the cheek. When we bring Zach back to his facility after a visit home, the workers welcome him with hugs and notice if we gave him a haircut or a new shirt.

The reporters don't make news out of that simple stuff. It doesn't 8 mesh with the anti-institutional bias prevalent in the last few years, or the tendency to canonize the handicapped and their accomplishments. This anti-institutional trend has some very frightening ramifications. We force mental patients out into the real world of cheap welfare hotels and call it "community placement." We parole youthful offenders because "jails are such dangerous places to be," making our city streets dangerous places for the law-abiding. We heap enormous guilt on the families that need, for their own survival, to put their no-longer-competent elderly in that dreaded last stop: the nursing home.

Another danger is that in a time of economic distress for all of us, funds could be cut for human-service programs under the guise of anti-institutionalization. We must make sure, before we close the doors of those "awful" institutions, that we have alternative facilities to care for the clientele. The humanitarians who tell us how terrible institutions are should be wary lest they become unwilling bedfellows to conservative politicians who want to walk a tight fiscal line. It takes a lot of money to run institutions. No politician is going to say he's against the handicapped, but he can talk in sanctimonious terms about efforts to preserve the family unit, about families remaining independent and self-sufficient. Translated, this means, "You got your troubles, I got mine."

Most retarded people do not belong in institutions any more than most people over sixty-five belong in nursing homes. What we need are options and alternatives for a heterogeneous population. We need group homes and halfway houses and government subsidies to families who choose to care for dependent members at home. We need accessible housing for independent handicapped people; we need to pay enough to foster-care families to show that a good home is worth paying for. We need institutions. And it shouldn't have to be a dirty word.

QUESTIONS ON CONTENT

1. Why do Americans use the word "special" to refer to handicapped children? Why does the use of this word bother Kupfer?

2. In paragraph 5, what does Kupfer mean when she states: "And love is beside the point?"

3. In what ways do "euphemisms help ease the pain" of placing a child in an institution? Explain the euphemisms "put her away" and "boarding school." Will we always need euphemisms if we can come to accept institutions as a real option or alternative for the care of the handicapped?

4. What arguments does Kupfer have with the media? How, according to Kupfer, have the media helped to make "institution" a dirty word?

5. Why is Kupfer frightened by the current anti-institutional trend in the United States? What solutions does she offer?

QUESTIONS ON RHETORIC

1. Where does Kupfer first introduce the issue of institutionalizing the handicapped? Why do you suppose she did not introduce it earlier in the essay? How does she lead up to the statement of her position?

2. What exactly is Kupfer arguing for? Has she managed to change your thinking? What aspects of her argument do you find most persuasive? Least persuasive? (Glossary: *Argument*)

3. What is Kupfer's tone in this essay? (Glossary: *Tone*) Is it appropriate given her subject and purpose? Why, or why not?

4. Kupfer's fifth paragrah consists of two short sentences. How does this paragraph function in the context of the essay?

VOCABULARY

quadriplegics (2)	tantamount (4)	clientele (9)
stoicism (2)	semblance (6)	sanctimonious (9)
kudos (2)	canonize (8)	heterogeneous (10)
sadists (4)		

WRITING TOPICS

1. Write an essay in which you discuss to what extent our reactions to and treatment of the handicapped are "just a question of language" (6). Is the public becoming more understanding of the situation, or do we still need to shroud the subject in euphemisms and taboos?

2. Handicapped children are not the only social issue talked about in euphemism or not talked about at all. Certainly drugs, venereal disease, divorce, homosexuality, pornography, sexual abuse, rape, and incest have been treated as taboo. Using Kupfer's essay as a model, write an essay in which you advocate a strong position about one of the above topics, a position that cuts through the euphemisms and taboos that surround the subject.

WRITING ASSIGNMENTS FOR "TABOOS"

1. Write an essay in which you compare and contrast the analyses of taboo words by Hayakawa and Lawrence.

2. Write an essay in which you argue that the euphemism, when used honestly, is "a handy verbal tool to avoid making enemies needlessly or shocking friends."

3. People use euphemisms when they want to avoid talking directly about subjects that make them uncomfortable, although what makes people uncomfortable changes. For example, we have been able to mention the words *legs* and *breasts* for quite a while and *venereal disease* for a shorter time, but many people still avoid the words *die* and *death*. Identify some other subjects for which euphemisms are still prevalent, and list several euphemisms for each. Do you use the same euphemisms as your parents? As your grandparents?

4. Write an essay in which you attempt to persuade your readers either that censorship is never justifiable or that it is sometimes justifiable. Be sure to provide sound reasons rather than emotional responses.

5. Many people complain about books, movies, rock songs, and television shows on the ground that they are "obscene" and/or "pornographic." But, too often, people can't seem to agree what they mean by these two terms—what's obscene for one person is not for another. Write an essay in which you define your perspective of these two terms in a detailed, convincing way.

6. Areas of American life that are taboo—and regarding which a great number of euphemistic terms are used—include death, money, sex, and disease (anything from acne to cancer). Choose one of these taboo subjects, or one of your own, and write an essay in which you discuss the euphemisms that are frequently used in writing or talking about the subject. Why are such euphemisms necessary?

7. Eugene Goodheart has said that "language unwittingly reflects on the man who uses it rather than on the object of its use" (*The Nation*, April 6, 1970). Write an essay in which you comment on a person who uses four-letter words when others might be seen as more "appropriate."

8. Consider the following list of euphemisms for *toilet:*

    rest room
    john
    lavatory
    wash room

little boy's (or girl's) room
men's (or women's) room
powder room
bathroom

Write an essay in which you discuss what the widespread use of these euphemisms and others suggests about us and our culture.

9. The following news item, first published in *Time* (December 11, 1972), is another example of efforts to "clean-up" our language:

BOWDLER IN OREGON

Some American place names have a unique resonance about them—places like Maggie's Nipples, Wyo., or Greasy Creek, Ark., Lickskillet, Ky., or Scroungeout, Ala. Collectors of Americana also savor Braggadocio, Mo., the Humptulips River in Washington, Hen Scratch, Fla., Dead Irishman Gulch, S. Dak., Cut 'N Shoot, Texas, Helpmejack Creek, Ark., Bastard Peak, Wyo., Goon Dip Mountain, Ark., Tenstrike, Minn., Laughing Pig, Wyo., Two Teats, Calif., or Aswaguscawadic, Me.

Not the least flavorsome was a sylvan place called Whorehouse Meadows, outside of Ontario, Ore. The meadow was named, with admirable directness, for some local women who once profitably entertained sheepherders there. But last week, the Oregon Geographic Names Board filed an official objection to a bit of bowdlerization by the Federal Bureau of Land Management. It discovered that the bureau, in drawing up a map of the area, had changed the name from Whorehouse Meadows to Naughty Girl Meadows. The bureau also cleaned up a nearby spot, deftly retitling it Bullshirt Springs, a change so small that the natives see no reason to contest it.

Write an essay in which you discuss the way name changes reflect Americans' perceptions of themselves and their culture. You may use examples from "Bowdler in Oregon" as well as other name changes that you know about in writing your essay.

Note: Suggested topics for research papers appear on p. 446.

NOTABLE QUOTATIONS

The following quotations are drawn from the essays in this section. They are presented as additional topics for classroom discussion or for writing assignments.

"Money is another subject about which communication is in some ways inhibited." *Hayakawa* (2)

"The stronger verbal taboos have . . . a genuine social value." *Hayakawa* (6)

"Why should any words be called obscene? Don't they all describe natural human functions?" *Lawrence* (1)

"Non-saints, it is my thesis, have a difficult time adopting the manners of saints; and even if they succeed most of the time in suppressing obnoxious words, they will probably not succeed all of the time." *Buckley* (4)

"There will always be a certain healthy tension between Billingsgate and the convent, but in the interest of the language, neither side should win the war completely." *Buckley* (7)

"What really makes my jaws clench, though, is the use of the word 'special.' The idea that our damaged children are 'special,' and that we as parents were somehow picked for the role, is one of the myths that come with the territory." *Kupfer* (2)

"We need institutions. And it shouldn't have to be a dirty word." *Kupfer* (10)

X
Writing Well: Using Language Responsibly

In order to be a great writer a person must have a built-in, shock-proof crap detector.

Ernest Hemingway

Originality does not consist in saying what no one has ever said before, but in saying exactly what you think yourself.

James Stephens

In many ways writing is the act of saying *I,* of imposing oneself upon other people, of saying *listen to me, see it my way, change your mind.* It's an aggressive, even a hostile act.

Joan Didion

A writer is not so much someone who has something to say as he is someone who has found a process that will bring about new things he would not have thought of it he had not started to say them.

William Stafford

I am never as clear about any matter as when I have just finished writing about it.

James Van Allen

1
Writing Honestly

DONALD HALL

Donald Hall is a poet, essayist, and teacher of writing. After graduating from Harvard and Oxford Universities, he taught at the University of Michigan until 1976, when he moved to his farm in New Hampshire to devote all his time to his writing. In the following essay, taken from his college textbook Writing Well, *Hall discusses the importance of the interrelationship of sincerity, inspiration, and discipline for the writer.*

W riting well is the art of clear thinking and honest feeling. The phrase *honest feeling* implies an opposite, dishonest feeling, which no one admits to but which we sometimes see clearly in others. We are all aware of honest and dishonest expression. We have grown up on the false laughter of television, the fake enthusiasm of advertising, the commercial jollity and condolences of greeting cards, and the lying assertions of politicians. If some falsity has not entered our prose, we are made of aluminum.

We can be false in a thousand ways. We do it with handshakes and we do it with grunts. We do it by saying outright lies and we do it by keeping silent. But in these examples we understand our own falsity. When we fool *ourselves* we are in more trouble. We fool ourselves with words that can mean almost anything. How much have we said when we call someone *liberal?* We fool ourselves when we avoid blame by leaving *I* out of the sentence, as when we knock over a lamp and claim that "The lamp was knocked over" or that "The lamp fell," as if it acted by itself. We also fool ourselves by using clichés, trite expressions that have become meaningless substitutes for feeling and thought.

impressionable age	bottom line
startling conclusion	name of the game
a vital part of our future	get a point across
made it what it is today	a changing society

Clichés are little cinder blocks of crushed and reprocessed experience. When we use them in writing, we violate our agreement to construct sentences in order to reach someone else. We appear to make contact, but the appearance is not a reality. Clichés are familiar and comfortable; they *seem* to mean something, but when I reach the *startling conclusion* that the *bottom line* is the *name of the game* in a *changing society,* I say nothing to anyone. Clichés prevent true contact by making false contact in its place.

Every profession—medicine, law, theater, business—has its own   3
clichés. We call the clichés that belong to a profession its *jargon.* One set of clichés appears especially at graduations, from primary school through graduate school.

> The future belongs to you.
> The challenge of new . . .
> In today's world . . .
> Responsibility, good citizenship, service to the community . . .

The university, in fact, is one of the great sources of jargon. Here are two paragraphs from a letter addressed by a newly elected college president to his faculty.

> Dear Members of the State College Community:
>   I am deeply honored and challenged by the opportunity to join State College as its seventh president. The hospitality and spontaneous warmth of everyone we have met has made both Barbara and me feel very welcome. We look forward to making State our home as quickly as we can arrange an orderly transition from our current responsibilities.
>   State College is rich in tradition: it is an institution with a past, and, more importantly, it is a College with a future. Building on its heritage, and maximizing its resources, State College can continue to achieve distinction by providing educational opportunities for young men and women.

Not all college presidents write this sort of thing, but many do. It is the language we expect from officials—from politicians and bureaucrats, from the presidents of colleges and the presidents of corporations. It says nothing, and it says it with maximum pomposity. It took this man years to learn the trick of empty jargon, the style of interlocking cliché. Every phase is trite, and the phrases are stuck together with mortar like *is* and *and* and *with.* The edifice is reprocessed garbage.

> deeply honored
> challenged by the opportunity
> spontaneous warmth
> making . . . our home
> orderly transition
> current responsibilities

rich in tradition
Building on its heritage
maximizing its resources
achieve distinction
providing educational opportunities

One should mention as well the trite and meaningless contrast between the past, as in *heritage*—a word as hokey as *home*—and *a college with a future*. The contrast says nothing. Unless the collegiate doors are closing tomorrow, of course it has *a future*. The word *future*—like *heritage* and *home*—carries vaguely positive connotations. A candidate for president of the United States used as a slogan, *The future lies before us,* trying to associate himself with this positive connotation; no one found the slogan offensive, but he lost.

In the college president's letter, the smoothness of the masonry is   4
exceptional, but the passage is without content and without feeling. The paragraphs are insincere because they do not represent a person's feelings. Of course the author did not *intend* insincerity, nor did he feel that he was lying.

We must look closely at the notion of sincerity; otherwise, we   5
might use it to justify its opposite. The worst liars sincerely say, to themselves and to the world, that they are the most honest. Yet sincerity can be a valuable idea if we think clearly about it, and sincerity has everything to do with the reasons for writing well. Peter Elbow, quoted in Ken Macrorie's book *Uptaught,* says:

> I warm against defining sincerity, as telling true things about oneself. It is more accurate to define it functionally as the sound of a writer's voice or self on paper—a general sound of authenticity in words. The point is that self-revelation . . . is an easy route in our culture and therefore can be used as an evasion: it can be functionally insincere even if substantially true and intimate. To be precise, *sincerity is the absence of "noise" or static—the ability or courage not to hide the real message.*

The static is the distance between what the words say and what we   6
sense lies behind them. The person with a pose of sincerity fixes us with his eyes, saying, "I am going to be wholly honest with you. I am a bastard. I cheat on my girlfriend and I steal my roommate's toothpaste." The real message: "Love me, I'm so *honest.*"

The distance between the meaning (the apparently stated) and the   7
expression (the really implied) ruins the statement and prevents real communication between people. In the college president's letter, the meaning has something to do with expressing pleasure in a new task; the expression is an exhibition of academic smoothness; it is a little

dance performed by a well-trained educationist seal. It says, "Look at me. Admit me to your ranks. I am one of you."

We cannot accept sincerity as a standard if we are going to take the writer's word for it. We can take it seriously if we listen to his *words* for it. Sincerity is *functional* (Elbow's word) if we believe it, if we hear the voice of a real person speaking forth in the prose—whether of speech or of the written word. The reader must feel that the prose is sincere. And sincerity comes from the self-knowledge we earn by self-exploration. When we express self-knowledge in our writing, we speak in a voice which sounds natural and which reaches the ears of other people. Finding this voice is not easy. It requires self-examination and hard thinking or analysis. It is worth it. Socrates made the commitment: the life which is unexamined is not worth living. 8

EXAMINING THE WORDS

By learning to write well, we learn methods of self-discovery and techniques for self-examination. Understanding the self allows us to move outside the self, to read, to analyze, to define, and thus to make contact outside the self, with others. Writing well can be a starting point for all thinking. Self-examination finds what we have inside us that is our own. Of course we are stuffed with clichés—we have been exposed to them all our lives—but clichés are not "our own." We have swallowed everything that has ever happened to us: we dropped the bottle to the floor at the age of eight weeks and cried for the lack of it; the telephone did not ring last week, and we cried for the lack of it; the toy shines under the tree, the toy rusts behind the garage; the smell of bacon, the smell of roses, the smell of kittens that have been careless, the flowers and the beer cans emerging from the snow. Everything that ever happened to us remains on file in our heads. As a professor at MIT put it: the human brain is a big computer made of meat. 9

If the brain is a computer, we are all engaged in learning how to operate it. For the college president quoted above, the task of writing was simple; he was programmed to write that kind of prose; he pushed the right keys and his brain computer turned out preassembled units of academic jargon. The commencement speaker, or the student writing home for money, presses other keys for printouts of ready-made pseudothoughts and pseudofeelings. But let us suppose that we are interested in something genuine, the voice without static, the utterance in which expression and meaning are the same. We must learn new ways to use the accumulation of words, sense impressions, and ideas 10 that we keep in the floppy discs of the brain. Our words must not make rows of identical houses like the subdivision prose of cliché. "New" is fresh, genuine, ourselves, our own experience. Making it new, we make contact with the reader.

Freshness is not, however, the inevitable result of spontaneity. Writing freely, without pausing for correction, is a good way to practice writing, to learn to flow, and to uncover material you didn't know was in you. It can be important to develop a sense of freedom in writing. But then there is the second half of genuine expression, the half that applies the map maker's self-examination to the new country of self-exploration. This self-examination, leading to revision, allows the writer to communicate with other human beings. Revising the map, we think of the reader; we revise to make contact with the reader. 11

REVISING THE MAP

Almost all writers, almost all the time, need to revise. We need to revise because spontaneity is never adequate. Writing that is merely emotional release for the writer becomes emotional chaos for the reader. Even when we write as quickly as our hand can move, we slide into emotional falsity, into cliché or other static. And we make leaps by private association that leave our prose unclear. And we often omit steps in thinking or use a step that we later recognize as bad logic. Sometimes we overexplain the obvious. Or we include irrelevant detail. First drafts remain first drafts. They are the material that we must shape, a marble block that the critical brain chisels into form. We must shape this material in order to pass it from mind to mind; we shape our material into a form that allows other people to receive it. This shaping often requires us, in revising, to reorganize whole paragraphs, both the order of sentences and the sentences themselves. We must drop sentences and clauses that do not belong; we must expand or supply others necessary to a paragraph's development. Often we must revise the order of paragraphs; often we must write new paragraphs to provide coherent and orderly progress. 12

Good writing is an intricate interweaving of inspiration and discipline. A student may need one strand more than the other. Most of us continually need to remember both sides of writing: *we must invent, and we must revise.* In these double acts, invention and revision, we are inventing and revising not just our prose style but our knowledge of ourselves and of the people around us. When Confucius recommended "Make it new," he told us to live what Socrates called "the examined life." It was a moral position. By our language, we shall know our- 13 selves—not once and for all, by a breakthrough, but continually, all our lives. Therefore, the necessity to write well arises from the need to understand and to discriminate, to be genuine and to avoid what is not genuine, in ourselves and in others. By understanding what our words reveal, we can understand ourselves; by changing these words until we arrive at our own voices, we change ourselves; by arriving at our own voices, we are able to speak to others and be heard.

QUESTIONS FOR STUDY AND DISCUSSION

1. What is Hall's thesis in this essay, and where is it stated? (Glossary: *Thesis*)

2. How, according to Hall, do people fool themselves by using the passive voice, personification, clichés, and jargon?

3. What does Hall mean when he says, "We must look closely at the notion of sincerity; otherwise, we might use it to justify its opposite"(5)? Explain Peter Elbow's definition of sincerity, which Hall quotes in paragraph 5.

4. Explain Hall's use of the computer analogy in paragraph 10. Is the analogy effective? Why, or why not? (Glossary: *Analogy*)

5. What role does Hall believe spontaneity plays in writing? What does he believe are its benefits? Its limitations?

6. In what ways is Hall's final paragraph an appropriate conclusion for his essay? (Glossary: *Endings*)

7. To what extent would you say that Hall practices what he preaches? Explain.

2
Writing for an Audience

LINDA FLOWER

Linda Flower is an Associate Professor of English at Carnegie-Mellon University, where she directed the Business Communication program for a number of years. Her widely recognized research on the composing process resulted in the textbook Problem-Solving Strategies for Writing *(2nd edition, 1985). In the following selection taken from that text, Flower discusses the importance of defining your audience of readers before you start writing.*

The goal of the writer is to create a momentary common ground between the reader and the writer. You want the reader to share your knowledge and your attitude toward that knowledge. Even if the reader eventually disagrees, you want him or her to be able for the moment to *see things as you see them*. A good piece of writing closes the gap between you and the reader.

ANALYZE YOUR AUDIENCE

The first step in closing that gap is to gauge the distance between the two of you. Imagine, for example, that you are a student writing your parents, who have always lived in New York City, about a wilderness survival expedition you want to go on over spring break. Sometimes obvious differences such as age or background will be important, but the critical differences for writers usually fall into three areas: the reader's *knowledge* about the topic; his or her *attitude* toward it, and his or her personal or professional *needs*. Because these differences often exist, good writers do more than simply express their meaning; they pinpoint the critical differences between themselves and their reader and design their writing to reduce those differences. Let us look at these three areas in more detail.

KNOWLEDGE This is usually the easiest difference to handle. What does your reader need to know? What are the main ideas you hope to teach? Does your reader have enough background knowledge to really understand you? If not, what would he or she have to learn?

425

ATTITUDES When we say a person has knowledge, we usually refer   4
to his conscious awareness of explicit facts and clearly defined concepts. This kind of knowledge can be easily written down or told to
someone else. However, much of what we "know" is not held in this
formal, explicit way. Instead it is held as an attitude or image—as a
loose cluster of associations. For instance, my image of lakes includes
associations many people would have, including fishing, water skiing,
stalled outboards, and lots of kids catching night crawlers with flash-
lights. However, the most salient or powerful parts of my image, which
strongly color my whole attitude toward lakes, are thoughts of cloudy
skies, long rainy days, and feeling generally cold and damp. By contrast, one of my best friends has a very different cluster of associations:
to him a lake means sun, swimming, sailing, and happily sitting on the
end of a dock. Needless to say, our differing images cause us to react
quite differently to a proposal that we visit a lake. Likewise, one reason
people often find it difficult to discuss religion and politics is that terms
such as "capitalism" conjure up radically different images.

As you can see, a reader's image of a subject is often the source of   5
attitudes and feelings that are unexpected and, at times, impervious to
mere facts. A simple statement that seems quite persuasive to you,
such as "Lake Wampago would be a great place to locate the new
music camp," could have little impact on your reader if he or she simply doesn't visualize a lake as a "great place." In fact, many people
accept uncritically any statement that fits in with their own attitudes—
and reject, just as uncritically, anything that does not.

Whether your purpose is to persuade or simply to present your   6
perspective, it helps to know the image and attitudes that your reader
already holds. The more these differ from your own, the more you will
have to do to make him or her *see* what you mean.

NEEDS When writers discover a large gap between their own   7
knowledge and attitudes and those of the reader, they usually try to
change the reader in some way. Needs, however, are different. When
you analyze a reader's needs, it is so that you, the writer, can adapt to
him. If you ask a friend majoring in biology how to keep your fish tank
from clouding, you don't want to hear a textbook recitation on the life
processes of algae. You expect the friend to adapt his or her knowledge
and tell you exactly how to solve your problem.

The ability to adapt your knowledge to the needs of the reader is   8
often crucial to your success as a writer. This is especially true in writing done on a job. For example, as producer of a public affairs program for a television station, 80 percent of your time may be taken up
planning the details of new shows, contacting guests, and scheduling
the taping sessions. But when you write a program proposal to the station director, your job is to show how the program will fit into the cost

guidelines, the FCC requirements for relevance, and the overall pro-gramming plan for the station. When you write that report your role in the organization changes from producer to proposal writer. Why? Be-cause your reader needs that information in order to make a decision. He may be *interested* in your scheduling problems and the specific content of the shows, but he *reads* your report because of his own needs as station director of that organization. He has to act.

In college, where the reader is also a teacher, the reader's needs are   9 a little less concrete but just as important. Most papers are assigned as a way to teach something. So the real purpose of a paper may be for you to make connections between two historical periods, to discover for yourself the principle behind a laboratory experiment, or to de-velop and support your own interpretation of a novel. A good college paper doesn't just rehash the facts; it demonstrates what your reader, as a teacher, needs to know—that you are learning the thinking skills his or her course is trying to teach.

Effective writers are not simply expressing what they know, like a   10 student madly filling up an examination bluebook. Instead they are *using* their knowledge: reorganizing, maybe even rethinking their ideas to meet the demands of an assignment or the needs of their reader.

QUESTIONS FOR STUDY AND DISCUSSION

1. What for Flower should be the goal of the writer?

2. What does Flower mean by the "distance" between the writer and the reader? How, according to Flower, do writers close the gap be-tween themselves and their readers?

3. What does Flower see as the three critical differences between writ-ers and readers? Why do you suppose she devotes so little attention to "knowledge" and so much more to both "attitude" and "needs"?

4. What is the difference between "knowledge" and "attitude"? Why is it important to know the difference?

5. Why is it so important for writers to adapt their knowledge to their readers' needs? How do you determine what your reader's needs are? Explain.

6. What, according to Flower, does a good college paper do? What does she mean when she says that effective writers do not simply express what they know, they *use* their knowledge?

7. Flower wrote this selection for college students. How well did she assess your knowledge, attitude, and needs about the subject of a writer's audience?

3
Simplicity

WILLIAM ZINSSER

The following essay is taken from William Zinsser's On Writing Well: An Informal Guide to Writing Nonfiction. *In it Zinsser, a longtime writer, editor, critic, and teacher of writing, advises and demonstrates that self-discipline and hard work are necessary to achieve clear, simple prose. No matter what your experience as a writer has been, you will find Zinsser's observations sound and his advice practical.*

Clutter is the disease of American writing. We are a society strangling in unnecessary words, circular constructions, pompous frills and meaningless jargon. 1

Who can understand the viscous language of everyday American commerce and enterprise: the business letter, the interoffice memo, the corporation report, the notice from the bank explaining its latest "simplified" statement? What member of an insurance or medical plan can decipher the brochure that tells him what his costs and benefits are? What father or mother can put together a child's toy—on Christmas Eve or any other eve—from the instructions on the box? Our national tendency is to inflate and thereby sound important. The airline pilot who announces that he is presently anticipating experiencing considerable precipitation wouldn't dream of saying that it may rain. The sentence is too simple—there must be something wrong with it. 2

But the secret of good writing is to strip every sentence to its cleanest components. Every word that serves no function, every long word that could be a short word, every adverb that carries the same meaning that's already in the verb, every passive construction that leaves the reader unsure of who is doing what—these are the thousand and one adulterants that weaken the strength of a sentence. And they usually occur, ironically, in proportion to education and rank. 3

During the late 1960s the president of a major university wrote a letter to mollify the alumni after a spell of campus unrest. "You are probably aware," he began, "that we have been experiencing very considerable potentially explosive expressions of dissatisfaction on issues 4 only partially related." He meant that the students had been hassling them about different things. I was far more upset by the president's English than by the students' potentially explosive expressions of dissatisfaction. I would have preferred the presidential approach taken by Franklin D. Roosevelt when he tried to convert into English his own government's memos, such as this blackout order of 1942:

> Such preparations shall be made as will completely obscure all Federal buildings and non-Federal buildings occupied by the Federal government during an air raid for any period of time from visibility by reason of internal or external illumination.

"Tell them," Roosevelt said, "that in buildings where they have to   5
keep the work going to put something across the windows."

Simplify, simplify. Thoreau said it, as we are so often reminded,   6
and no American writer more consistently practiced what he preached. Open *Walden* to any page and you will find a man saying in a plain and orderly way what is on his mind:

> I love to be alone. I never found the companion that was so companionable as solitude. We are for the most part more lonely when we go abroad among men than when we stay in our chambers. A man thinking or working is always alone, let him be where he will. Solitude is not measured by the miles of space that intervene between a man and his fellows. The really diligent student in one of the crowded hives of Cambridge College is as solitary as a dervish in the desert.

How can the rest of us achieve such enviable freedom from clutter?   7
The answer is to clear our heads of clutter. Clear thinking becomes clear writing: one can't exist without the other. It is impossible for a muddy thinker to write good English. He may get away with it for a paragraph or two, but soon the reader will be lost, and there is no sin so grave, for he will not easily be lured back.

Who is this elusive creature the reader? He is a person with an at-   8
tention span of about twenty seconds. He is assailed on every side by forces competing for his time: by newspapers and magazines, by television and radio, by his stereo and videocassettes, by his wife and children and pets, by his house and his yard and all the gadgets that he has bought to keep them spruce, and by that most potent of competitors, sleep. The man snoozing in his chair with an unfinished magazine open on his lap is a man who was being given too much unnecessary trouble by the writer.

It won't do to say that the snoozing reader is too dumb or too lazy   9
to keep pace with the train of thought. My sympathies are with him. If the reader is lost, it is generally because the writer has not been careful enough to keep him on the path.

This carelessness can take any number of forms. Perhaps a sentence is so excessively cluttered that the reader, hacking his way through the verbiage, simply doesn't know what it means. Perhaps a sentence has been so shoddily constructed that the reader could read it in any of several ways. Perhaps the writer has switched pronouns in mid-sentence, or has switched tenses, so the reader loses track of who is talking or when the action took place. Perhaps Sentence B is not a logical sequel to Sentence A—the writer, in whose head the connection is clear, has not bothered to provide the missing link. Perhaps the writer has used an important word incorrectly by not taking the trouble to look it up. He may think that "sanguine" and "sanguinary" mean the same thing, but the difference is a bloody big one. The reader can only infer (speaking of big differences) what the writer is trying to imply. 10

Faced with these obstacles, the reader is at first a remarkably tenacious bird. He blames himself—he obviously missed something, and he goes back over the mystifying sentence, or over the whole paragraph, piecing it out like an ancient rune, making guesses and moving on. But he won't do this for long. The writer is making him work too hard, and the reader will look for one who is better at his craft. 11

The writer must therefore constantly ask himself: What am I trying to say? Surprisingly often, he doesn't know. Then he must look at what he has written and ask: Have I said it? Is it clear to someone encountering the subject for the first time? If it's not, it is because some fuzz has worked its way into the machinery. The clear writer is a person clear-headed enough to see this stuff for what it is: fuzz. 12

I don't mean that some people are born clear-headed and are therefore natural writers, whereas others are naturally fuzzy and will never write well. Thinking clearly is a conscious act that the writer must force upon himself, just as if he were embarking on any other project that requires logic: adding up a laundry list or doing an algebra problem. Good writing doesn't come naturally, though most people obviously think it does. The professional writer is forever being bearded by strangers who say that they'd like to "try a little writing sometime" when they retire from their real profession. Or they say, "I could write a book about that." I doubt it. 13

Writing is hard work. A clear sentence is no accident. Very few sentences come out right the first time, or even the third time. Remember this as a consolation in moments of despair. If you find that writing is hard, it's because it *is* hard. It's one of the hardest things that people do. 14

QUESTIONS FOR STUDY AND DISCUSSION

1. What is the relationship that Zinsser sees between thinking and writing?

2. What is clutter? How does Zinsser think that we can free ourselves of clutter?

3. What assumptions does Zinsser make about readers? According to Zinsser, what responsibilities do writers have to readers?

4. What questions should the writer constantly ask? Why are these questions so important?

5. What does Zinsser mean by "simplicity"? Would you agree with him that "our national tendency is to inflate and thereby sound important"(2)? Why, or why not?

6. Zinsser uses short sentences (seven or fewer words) effectively in his essay. Locate several examples of short sentences, and explain the function of each within its paragraph.

7. The following two pages show a passage from the final manuscript for this essay. Carefully study the manuscript, and then discuss the ways in which Zinsser has been able to eliminate clutter.

5 --

is too dumb or too lazy to keep pace with the ~~writer's~~ train of thought. My sympathies are ~~entirely~~ with him.) ~~He's not so dumb.~~ (If the reader is lost, it is generally because the writer ~~of the article~~ has not been careful enough to keep him on the ~~proper~~ path.

This carelessness can take any number of ~~different~~ forms. Perhaps a sentence is so excessively ~~long and~~ cluttered that the reader, hacking his way through ~~all~~ the verbiage, simply doesn't know what *it* ~~the writer~~ means. Perhaps a sentence has been so shoddily constructed that the reader could read it in any of *several* ~~two or three different~~ ways. ~~He thinks he knows what the writer is trying to say, but he's not sure.~~ Perhaps the writer has switched pronouns in mid-sentence, or ~~perhaps he~~ has switched tenses, so the reader loses track of who is talking ~~to whom~~ or ~~exactly~~ when the action took place. Perhaps Sentence B is not a logical sequel to Sentence A -- the writer, in whose head the connection is ~~perfectly~~ clear, has not *bothered to provide* ~~given enough thought to providing~~ the missing link. Perhaps the writer has used an important word incorrectly by not taking the trouble to look it up ~~and make sure.~~ He may think that "sanguine" and "sanguinary" mean the same thing, but) ~~I can assure you that~~ (the difference is a bloody big one ~~to the reader.~~ *The reader* ~~He~~ can only ~~try to~~ infer ~~what~~ (speaking of big differences) what the writer is trying to imply.

Faced with *these* ~~such a variety of~~ obstacles, the reader is at first a remarkably tenacious bird. He ~~tends to~~ blame*s* himself. ~~He~~ obviously missed something, ~~he thinks,~~ and he goes back over the mystifying sentence, or over the whole paragraph,

6 --

piecing it out like an ancient rune, making guesses and moving on. But he won't do this for long. ~~He will soon run out of patience.~~ (The writer is making him work too hard ~~--~~ →harder ~~than he should have to work --~~ (and the reader will look for ~~a writer~~ one who is better at his craft.

The writer must therefore constantly ask himself: What am I trying to say ~~in this sentence?~~ (Surprisingly often, he doesn't know.) ~~And~~ Then he must look at what he has ~~just~~ written and ask: Have I said it? Is it clear to someone ~~who is coming upon~~ encountering the subject for the first time? If it's not ~~clear,~~ it is because some fuzz has worked its way into the machinery. The clear writer is a person ~~who is~~ clear-headed enough to see this stuff for what it is: fuzz.

I don't mean ~~to suggest~~ that some people are born clear-headed and are therefore natural writers, whereas ~~other people~~ others are naturally fuzzy and will ~~therefore~~ never write well. Thinking clearly is ~~an entirely~~ conscious act that the writer must ~~keep forcing~~ force upon himself, just as if he were ~~starting out~~ embarking on any other ~~kind of~~ project that ~~calls for~~ requires logic: adding up a laundry list or doing an algebra problem ~~or playing chess.~~ Good writing doesn't ~~just~~ come naturally, though most people obviously think ~~it's as easy as walking.~~ it does. The professional

4

The Maker's Eye: Revising Your Own Manuscripts

DONALD M. MURRAY

Donald M. Murray is a writer who currently teaches writing at the University of New Hampshire. He served as an editor at Time *magazine and won the Pulitzer Prize in 1954 for editorials that appeared in the Boston* Globe. *His works include poetry, novels, short stories, and sourcebooks for teachers of writing, like* A Writer Teaches Writing *and* Learning by Teaching, *where he explores aspects of the writing process. In the following essay first published in* The Writer, *Murray discusses the importance of revision to the work of a writer.*

When students complete a first draft, they consider the job of writing done—and their teachers too often agree. When professional writers complete a first draft, they usually feel that they are at the start of the writing process. When a draft is completed, the job of writing can begin. 1

That difference in attitude is the difference between amateur and professional, inexperience and experience, journeyman and craftsman. Peter F. Drucker, the prolific business writer, calls his first draft "the zero draft"—after that he can start counting. Most writers share the feeling that the first draft, and all of those which follow, are opportunities to discover what they have to say and how best they can say it. 2

To produce a progression of drafts, each of which says more and says it more clearly, the writer has to develop a special kind of reading skill. In school we are taught to decode what appears on the page as finished writing. Writers, however, face a different category of possibility and responsibility when they read their own drafts. To them the words on the page are never finished. Each can be changed and rearranged, can set off a chain reaction of confusion or clarified meaning. This is a different kind of reading which is possibly more difficult and certainly more exciting. 3

Writers must learn to be their own best enemy. They must accept   4
the criticism of others and be suspicious of it; they must accept the
praise of others and be even more suspicious of it. Writers cannot depend on others. They must detach themselves from their own pages so
that they can apply both their caring and their craft to their own work.

Such detachment is not easy. Science-fiction writer Ray Bradbury   5
supposedly puts each manuscript away for a year to the day and then
rereads it as a stranger. Not many writers have the discipline or the
time to do this. We must read when our judgment may be at its worst,
when we are close to the euphoric moment of creation.

Then the writer, counsels novelist Nancy Hale, "should be critical   6
of everything that seems to him most delightful in his style. He should
excise what he most admires, because he wouldn't thus admire it if he
weren't . . . in a sense protecting it from criticism." John Ciardi, the
poet, adds, "The last act of the writing must be to become one's own
reader. It is, I suppose, a schizophrenic process, to being passionately
and to end critically, to begin hot and to end cold; and, more important, to be passion-hot and critic-cold at the same time."

Most people think that the principal problem is that writers are too   7
proud of what they have written. Actually, a greater problem for most
professional writers is one shared by the majority of students. They are
overly critical, think everything is dreadful, tear up page after page,
never complete a draft, see the task as hopeless.

The writer must learn to read critically but constructively, to cut   8
what is bad, to reveal what is good. Eleanor Estes, the children's book
author, explains: "The writer must survey his work critically, coolly, as
though he were a stranger to it. He must be willing to prune, expertly
and hard-heartedly. At the end of each revision, a manuscript may
look . . . worked over, torn apart, pinned together, added to, deleted
from, words changed and words changed back. Yet the book must
maintain its original freshness and spontaneity."

Most readers underestimate the amount of rewriting it usually   9
takes to produce spontaneous reading. This is a great disadvantage to
the student writer, who sees only a finished product and never watches
the craftsman who takes the necessary step back, studies the work
carefully, returns to the task, steps back, returns, steps back, again and
again. Anthony Burgess, one of the most prolific writers in the
English-speaking world, admits, "I might revise a page twenty times."
Roald Dahl, the popular children's writer, states, "By the time I'm
nearing the end of a story, the first part will have been reread and altered and corrected at least 150 times. . . . Good writing is essentially
rewriting. I am positive of this."

Rewriting isn't virtuous. It isn't something that ought to be done. It   10 is simply something that most writers find they have to do to discover what they have to say and how to say it. It is a condition of the writer's life.

There are, however, a few writers who do little formal rewriting, 11 primarily because they have the capacity and experience to create and review a large number of invisible drafts in their minds before they approach the page. And some writers slowly produce finished pages, performing all the tasks of revision simultaneously, page by page, rather than draft by draft. But it is still possible to see the sequence followed by most writers most of the time in rereading their own work.

Most writers scan their drafts first, reading as quickly as possible to 12 catch the larger problems of subject and form, then move in closer and closer as they read and write, reread and rewrite.

The first thing writers look for in their drafts is *information*. They 13 know that a good piece of writing is built from specific, accurate, and interesting information. The writer must have an abundance of information from which to construct a readable piece of writing.

Next writers look for *meaning* in the information. The specifics 14 must build to a pattern of significance. Each piece of specific information must carry the reader toward meaning.

Writers reading their own drafts are aware of *audience*. They put 15 themselves in the reader's situation and make sure that they deliver information which a reader wants to know or needs to know in a manner which is easily digested. Writers try to be sure that they anticipate and answer the questions a critical reader will ask when reading the piece of writing.

Writers make sure that the *form* is appropriate to the subject and 16 the audience. Form, or genre, is the vehicle which carries meaning to the reader, but form cannot be selected until the writer has adequate information to discover its significance and an audience which needs or wants that meaning.

Once writers are sure the form is appropriate, they must then look 17 at the *structure,* the order of what they have written. Good writing is built on a solid framework of logic, argument, narrative, or motivation which runs through the entire piece of writing and holds it together. This is the time when many writers find it most effective to outline as a way of visualizing the hidden spine by which the piece of writing is supported.

The element on which writers may spend a majority of their time is 18 *development*. Each section of a piece of writing must be adequately developed. It must give readers enough information so that they are satisfied. How much information is enough? That's as difficult as asking how much garlic belongs in a salad. It must be done to taste, but most beginning writers underdevelop, underestimating the reader's hunger for information.

As writers solve development problems, they often have to con- 19
sider questions of *dimension*. There must be a pleasing and effective proportion among all the parts of the piece of writing. There is a continual process of subtracting and adding to keep the piece of writing in balance.

Finally, writers have to listen to their own voices. *Voice* is the force 20
which drives a piece of writing forward. It is an expression of the writer's authority and concern. It is what is between the words on the page, what glues the piece of writing together. A good piece of writing is always marked by a consistent, individual voice.

As writers read and reread, write and rewrite, they move closer and 21
closer to the page until they are doing line-by-line editing. Writers read their own pages with infinite care. Each sentence, each line, each clause, each phrase, each word, each mark of punctuation, each section of white space between the type has to contribute to the clarification of meaning.

Slowly the writer moves from word to word, looking through lan- 22
guage to see the subject. As a word is changed, cut, or added, as a construction is rearranged, all the words used before that moment and all those that follow that moment must be considered and reconsidered.

Writers often read aloud at this stage of the editing process, mut- 23
tering or whispering to themselves, calling on the ear's experience with language. Does this sound right—or that? Writers edit, shifting back and forth from eye to page to ear to page. I find I must do this careful editing in short runs, no more than fifteen or twenty minutes at a stretch, or I become too kind with myself. I begin to see what I hope is on the page, not what actually is on the page.

This sounds tedious if you haven't done it, but actually it is fun. 24
Making something right is immensely satisfying, for writers begin to learn what they are writing about by writing. Language leads them to meaning, and there is the joy of discovery, of understanding, of making meaning clear as the writer employs the technical skills of language.

Words have double meanings, even triple and quadruple mean- 25
ings. Each word has its own potential for connotation and denotation. And when writers rub one word against the other, they are often rewarded with a sudden insight, an unexpected clarification.

The maker's eye moves back and forth from word to phrase to 26
sentence to paragraph to sentence to phrase to word. The maker's eye sees the need for variety and balance, for a firmer structure, for a more

appropriate form. It peers into the interior of the paragraph, looking for coherence, unity, and emphasis, which make meaning clear.

I learned something about this process when my first bifocals were 27 prescribed. I had ordered a larger section of the reading portion of the glass because of my work, but even so, I could not contain my eyes within this new limit of vision. And I still find myself taking off my glasses and bending my nose toward the page, for my eyes unconsciously flick back and forth across the page, back to another page, forward to still another, as I try to see each evolving line in relation to every other line.

When does this process end? Most writers agree with the great 28 Russian writer Tolstoy, who said, "I scarcely ever reread my published writings, if by chance I come across a page, it always strikes me: all this must be rewritten; this is how I should have written it."

The maker's eye is never satisfied, for each word has the potential 29 to ignite new meaning. This article has been twice written all the way through the writing process, and it was published four years ago. Now it is to be republished in a book. The editors made a few small suggestions, and then I read it with my maker's eye. Now it has been re-edited, re-revised, re-read, re-re-edited, for each piece of writing to the writer is full of potential and alternatives.

A piece of writing is never finished. It is delivered to a deadline, 30 torn out of the typewriter on demand, sent off with a sense of accomplishment and shame and pride and frustration. If only there were a couple more days, time for just another run at it, perhaps then. . . .

QUESTIONS FOR STUDY AND DISCUSSION

1. Why does Murray see revision as such an important element in the process of writing?

2. What is Murray's purpose in writing this essay? (Glossary: *Purpose*)

3. What, according to Murray, are the eight things a writer must be conscious of in the process of revision? Describe the process you generally go through when you revise your writing. How does your process compare with Murray's?

4. What does Murray mean when he says, "Writers must learn to be their own best enemy"(4)?

5. What does Murray gain from frequently quoting professional writers? What seems to be the common message from the professionals?

6. How do professionals view first drafts? Why is it important for you to adopt a similar attitude?

7. What does Murray see as the connection between reading and writing? How does reading help the writer?

8. When, according to Murray, does revision end? Why do you suppose he concludes his essay in mid-sentence?

5

Notes on Punctuation

LEWIS THOMAS

Lewis Thomas has had a distinguished career as a physician, administrator, researcher, teacher, and writer. He is currently president of the Memorial Sloan-Kettering Cancer Center in New York City. Thomas began his writing career in 1971 with a series of essays for the New England Journal of Medicine; *many of these have been collected in* The Lives of a Cell: Notes of a Biology Watcher *and* The Medusa and the Snail: More Notes of a Biology Watcher. *"Notes on Punctuation" is taken from* The Medusa and the Snail. *In this selection Thomas demonstrates the value, meaning, and practical usefulness of various punctuation marks.*

There are no precise rules about punctuation (Fowler lays out some   1
general advice (as best he can under the complex circumstances of
English prose (he points out, for example, that we possess only four
stops (the comma, the semicolon, the colon and the period (the question mark and exclamation point are not, strictly speaking, stops; they
are indicators of tone (oddly enough, the Greeks employed the semicolon for their question mark (it produces a strange sensation to read a
Greek sentence which is a straightforward question: Why weepest
thou; (instead of Why weepest thou? (and, of course, there are parentheses (which are surely a kind of punctuation making this whole matter much more complicated by having to count up the left-handed parentheses in order to be sure of closing with the right number (but if
the parentheses were left out, with nothing to work with but the stops,
we would have considerably more flexibility in the deploying of layers
of meaning than if we tried to separate all the clauses by physical bar-
riers (and in the latter case, while we might have more precision and
exactitude for our meaning, we would lose the essential flavor of language, which is its wonderful ambiguity)))))))))))).

The commas are the most useful and usable of all the stops. It is   2
highly important to put them in place as you go along. If you try to
come back after doing a paragraph and stick them in the various spots
that tempt you you will discover that they tend to swarm like minnows

into all sorts of crevices whose existence you hadn't realized and before you know it the whole long sentence becomes immobilized and lashed up squirming in commas. Better to use them sparingly, and with affection, precisely when the need for each one arises, nicely, by itself.

I have grown fond of semicolons in recent years. The semicolon   3
tells you that there is still some question about the preceding full sentence; something needs to be added; it reminds you sometimes of the Greek usage. It is almost always a greater pleasure to come across a semicolon than a period. The period tells you that that is that; if you didn't get all the meaning you wanted or expected, anyway you got all the writer intended to parcel out and now you have to move along. But with a semicolon there you get a pleasant little feeling of expectancy; there is more to come; read on; it will get clearer.

Colons are a lot less attractive, for several reasons: firstly, they give   4
you the feeling of being rather ordered around, or at least having your nose pointed in a direction you might not be inclined to take if left to yourself, and, secondly, you suspect you're in for one of those sentences that will be labeling the points to be made: firstly, secondly and so forth, with the implication that you haven't sense enough to keep track of a sequence of notions without having them numbered. Also, many writers use this system loosely and incompletely, starting out with number one and number two as though counting off on their fingers but then going on and on without the succession of labels you've been led to expect, leaving you floundering about searching for the ninethly or seventeenthly that ought to be there but isn't.

Exclamation points are the most irritating of all. Look! they say,   5
look at what I just said! How amazing is my thought! It is like being forced to watch someone else's small child jumping up and down crazily in the center of the living room shouting to attract attention. If a sentence really has something of importance to say, something quite remarkable, it doesn't need a mark to point it out. And if it is really, after all, a banal sentence needing more zing, the exclamation point simply emphasizes its banality!

Quotation marks should be used honestly and sparingly, when   6
there is a genuine quotation at hand, and it is necessary to be very rigorous about the words enclosed by the marks. If something is to be quoted, the *exact* words must be used. If part of it must be left out because of space limitations, it is good manners to insert three dots to indicate the omission, but it is unethical to do this if it means connecting two thoughts which the original author did not intend to have tied together. Above all, quotation marks should not be used for ideas that you'd like to disown, things in the air so to speak. Nor should they be

put in place around clichés; if you want to use a cliché you must take full responsibility for it yourself and not try to fob it off on anon., or on society. The most objectionable misuse of quotation marks, but one which illustrates the dangers of misuse in ordinary prose, is seen in advertising, especially in advertisements for small restaurants, for example "just around the corner," or "a good place to eat." No single, identifiable, citable person ever really said, for the record, "just around the corner," much less "a good place to eat," least likely of all for restaurants of the type that use this type of prose.

The dash is a handy device, informal and essentially playful, telling you that you're about to take off on a different tack but still in some way connected with the present course—only you have to remember that the dash is there, and either put a second dash at the end of the notion to let the reader know that he's back on course, or else and the sentence, as here, with a period.   7

The greatest danger in punctuation is for poetry. Here it is necessary to be as economical and parsimonious with commas and periods as with the words themselves, and any marks that seem to carry their own subtle meanings, like dashes and little rows of periods, even semicolons and question marks, should be left out altogether rather than inserted to clog up the thing with ambiguity. A single exclamation point in a poem, no matter what else the poem has to say, is enough to destroy the whole work.   8

The things I like best in T. S. Eliot's poetry, especially in the *Four Quartets,* are the semicolons. You cannot hear them, but they are there, laying out the connections between the images and the ideas. Sometimes you get a glimpse of a semicolon coming, a few lines farther on, and it is like climbing a steep path through woods and seeing a wooden bench just at a bend in the road ahead, a place where you can expect to sit for a moment, catching your breath.   9

Commas can't do this sort of thing; they can only tell you how the different parts of a complicated thought are to be fitted together, but you can't sit, not even take a breath, just because of a comma.   10

QUESTIONS FOR STUDY AND DISCUSSION

1. What point does Thomas make about punctuation in his opening paragraph? How does he continue to develop this point throughout his essay?

2. Point out the four similes that Thomas uses in this essay. What is being compared in each? Why is each comparison appropriate? Why do you suppose Thomas chose to use figurative language in an essay on punctuation? (Glossary: *Figures of Speech*)

NOTES ON PUNCTUATION   **443**

3. In paragraph 5, Thomas personifies exclamation points. What other examples of personification can you find in the essay? Why is this figure of speech particularly useful for Thomas's purposes? (Glossary: *Figures of Speech*)

4. In the course of explaining its function, Thomas actually uses each mark of punctuation. This is an interesting example of illustration, of "showing" while explaining. When did you become aware of what he was doing? Did this strategy help you to understand and appreciate the uses of punctuation?

5. What is Thomas's attitude toward writing? Toward punctuation? What in his diction reveals his attitude? (Glossary: *Diction*)

WRITING ASSIGNMENTS FOR "WRITING WELL: USING LANGUAGE RESPONSIBLY"

1. Each of the essays in this section is concerned with the importance of writing well, of using language responsibly. Write an essay in which you discuss the common themes which are emphasized in two or more of the essays.

2. Write an essay in which you discuss the proposition that honesty, while it does not guarantee good writing, is a prerequisite of good writing.

3. Philosopher Ludwig Wittgenstein once said, "The limits of my language are the limits of my world." What do you think he meant? Write an essay in which you support Wittgenstein's generalization with carefully selected examples from your own experience.

4. Write an essay in which you describe the characteristics of good writing. You may use the articles in this section for reference.

5. We are often told that writing is an important means of communication. But the more writing we do, the more we realize that writing is important in other ways as well. Write an essay in which you discuss the particular reasons why you value writing.

6. Some of our most pressing social issues depend for their solutions upon a clear statement of the problem and the precise definition of critical terms. For example, the increasing number of people kept alive by machines has brought worldwide attention to the legal and medical definitions of the word *death*. Debates continue about the meanings of other controversial words, such as *morality, minority* (ethnic), *alcoholism, life* (as in the abortion issue), *pornography, kidnapping, drug, censorship, remedial, insanity, monopoly* (business), and *literacy.* Select one of these words, and write an essay in which you discuss the problems associated with the term and its definition.

NOTABLE QUOTATIONS

The following quotations are drawn from the essays in this section. They are presented as additional topics for classroom discussion or for writing assignments.

"Writing well is the art of clear thinking and honest feeling." *Hall* (1)

"Good writing is an intricate interweaving of inspiration and discipline." *Hall* (13)

"A good piece of writing closes the gap between you and the reader." *Flower* (1)

"The ability to adapt your knowledge to the needs of the reader is often crucial to your success as a writer." *Flower* (8)

"A good college paper doesn't just rehash the facts; it demonstrates what your reader, as a teacher, needs to know—that you are learning the thinking skills his or her course is trying to teach." *Flower* (9)

"But the secret of good writing is to strip every sentence to its cleanest components." *Zinsser* (3)

"A clear sentence is no accident." *Zinsser* (14)

"If you find that writing is hard, it's because it *is* hard. It's one of the hardest things that people do." *Zinsser* (14)

"When a draft is completed, the job of writing can begin." *Murray* (1)

"Writers must learn to be their own best enemy. They must accept the criticism of others and be suspicious of it; they must accept the praise of others and be even more suspicious of it. Writers cannot depend on others." *Murray* (4)

"A good piece of writing is always marked by a consistent, individual voice." *Murray* (20)

"A piece of writing is never finished." *Murray* (30)

"There are no precise rules about punctuation. . . ." *Thomas* (1)

". . . The essential flavor of language . . . is its wonderful ambiguity. . . ." *Thomas* (1)

TOPICS FOR RESEARCH PAPERS

The following is a list of suggested research-paper topics. Because each topic is broad, you will need to limit and focus the subject you choose for your paper.

1. the language of college catalogues
2. how children learn language
3. the difference between the language of males and the language of females
4. the history of English
5. stereotyping in the language of cartoons
6. the values conveyed by song lyrics
7. the language of political propaganda
8. names and naming: people, places, or things
9. advertising and children
10. the language of the funeral industry: death, dying, or burial
11. insults, taunts, and jeers
12. greeting-card verse
13. advertising jingles
14. obscenities
15. censorship
16. Bowdler and bowdlerization
17. the Sapir-Whorf hypothesis
18. college slang on your campus
19. sports jargon
20. language games (such as pig Latin, rhyming slang, and "op" languages)
21. the language of menus
22. language pollution
23. public doublespeak
24. nonverbal communications
25. medical jargon: the language of doctors, dentists, and nurses
26. the language of science fiction
27. the language of disc jockeys
28. the language of soap operas
29. black English
30. words in English borrowed from other languages
31. social or regional dialect variations
32. the language of legal documents (such as insurance policies, sales agreements, and leases)
33. language in women's magazines and in men's magazines
34. body language and advertising
35. the jargon of a subculture
36. how a dictionary is made
37. advertising techniques today and fifty years ago
38. English as a world language
39. contemporary propaganda
40. the power of words

41. Intensify/Downplay in advertisements
42. the slanting of the news
43. sexist language
44. nicknames
45. etymologies
46. slips of the tongue and other bloopers
47. contemporary euphemisms
48. prejudice and language
49. parody
50. verbal taboos in America

Glossary of Rhetorical Terms

Abstract   See *Concrete/Abstract.*

Allusion   An allusion is a passing reference to a familiar person, place, or thing drawn from history, the Bible, mythology, or literature. An allusion is an economical way for a writer to capture the essence of an idea, atmosphere, emotion, or historical era, as in "The scandal was his Watergate," or "He saw himself as a modern Job," or "Everyone there held those truths to be self-evident." An allusion should be familiar to the reader, for if it is not, it will add nothing to the meaning.

Analogy   Analogy is a special form of comparison in which the writer explains something complex or unfamiliar by comparing it to something familiar: "A transmission line is simply a pipeline for electricity. In the case of a water pipeline, more water will flow through the pipe as water pressure increases. The same is true of a transmission line for electricity." When a subject is unobservable, complex, or abstract—when it is so generally unfamiliar that readers may have trouble understanding it—analogy is particularly useful.

Argument   Argument is one of the four basic types of prose. (Narration, description, and exposition are the other three.) To argue is to attempt to convince a reader to agree with a point of view, to make a given decision, or to pursue a particular course of action. Logical argument is based upon reasonable explanations and appeals to the reader's intelligence. See also *Persuasion, Logical Fallacies, Deduction,* and *Induction.*

Attitude   A writer's attitude reflects his or her opinion of a subject. For example, a writer can think very positively or very negatively about a subject. In most cases the writer's attitude falls somewhere between these two extremes. See also *Tone.*

Audience   An audience is the intended readership for a piece of writing. For example, the readers of a national weekly news magazine come from all walks of life and have diverse opinions, attitudes, and

448

educational experiences. In contrast, the readership for an organic chemistry journal is made up of people whose interests and educations are quite similar. The essays in this book are intended for general readers, intelligent people who may lack specific information about the subjects being discussed.

Beginnings/Endings   A *beginning* is that sentence, group of sentences, or section that introduces the essay. Good beginnings usually identify the thesis or controlling idea, attempt to interest the reader, and establish a tone. Some effective ways in which writers begin essays include (1) telling an anecdote that illustrates the thesis, (2) providing a controversial statement or opinion which engages the reader's interest, (3) presenting startling statistics or facts, (4) defining a term that is central to the discussion that follows, (5) asking thought-provoking questions, (6) providing a quotation that illustrates the thesis, (7) referring to a current event that helps to establish the thesis, or (8) showing the significance of the subject or stressing its importance to the reader.

An *ending* is that sentence or group of sentences which brings an essay to closure. Good endings are purposeful and well planned. Endings satisfy readers when they are the natural outgrowths of the essays themselves and give the readers a sense of finality or completion. Good essays do not simply stop; they conclude.

Cause and Effect Analysis   Cause and effect analysis is one of the types of exposition. (Process analysis, definition, division and classification, and comparison and contrast are the others.) Cause and effect analysis answers the question *why*. It explains the reasons for an occurrence or the consequences of an action. Whenever a question asks *why*, answering it will require discovering a *cause* or series of causes for a particular *effect;* whenever a question asks *what if,* its answer will point out the effect or effects that can result from a particular cause.

Classification   See *Division and Classification.*

Cliché   A cliché is an expression that has become ineffective through overuse. Expressions such as *quick as a flash, dry as dust, jump for joy,* and *slow as molasses* are all clichés. Writers normally avoid such trite expressions and seek instead to express themselves in fresh and forceful language. See also *Figures of Speech.*

Coherence   Coherence is a quality of good writing that results when all sentences, paragraphs, and longer divisions of an essay are naturally connected. Coherent writing is achieved through (1) a logical sequence of ideas (arranged in chronological order, spatial order, order of importance, or some other appropriate order), (2) the thoughtful repetition of key words and ideas, (3) a pace suitable for your topic and your reader, and (4) the use of transitional words and expressions. Coherence should not be confused with unity. See also *Unity* and *Transitions.*

Colloquial Expressions A colloquial expression is characteristic of or appropriate to spoken language or to writing that seeks its effect. Colloquial expressions are informal, as *chem, gym, come up with, be at loose ends, won't,* and *photo* illustrate. Thus, colloquial expressions are acceptable in formal writing only if they are used purposefully.

Comparison and Contrast Comparison and contrast make up one of the types of exposition. (Process analysis, definition, division and classification, and cause and effect analysis are the others.) In comparison and contrast, the writer points out the similarities and differences between two or more subjects in the same class or category. The function of any comparison and contrast is to clarify—to reach some conclusion about the items being compared and contrasted. An effective comparison and contrast will not dwell on obvious similarities or differences; it will tell readers something significant that they may not already know.

Conclusions See *Beginnings/Endings*

Concrete/Abstract A concrete word names a specific object, person, place, or action that can be directly perceived by the senses: *car, bread, building, book, John F. Kennedy, Chicago,* or *hiking.* An abstract word, in contrast, refers to general qualities, conditions, ideas, actions, or relationships which cannot be directly perceived by the senses: *bravery, dedication, excellence, anxiety, stress, thinking,* or *hatred.*

Although writers must use both concrete and abstract language, good writers avoid too many abstract words. Instead, they rely on concrete words to define and illustrate abstractions. Because concrete words affect the senses, they are easily comprehended by a reader.

Connotation/Denotation Both connotation and denotation refer to the meanings of words. Denotation is the dictionary meaning of a word, the literal meaning. Connotation, on the other hand, is the implied or suggested meaning of a word. For example, the denotation of *lamb* is "a young sheep." The connotations of lamb are numerous: *gentle, docile, weak, peaceful, blessed, sacrificial, blood, spring, frisky, pure, innocent,* and so on. Good writers are sensitive to both the denotations and the connotations of words and use these meanings to advantage in their writing.

Deduction Deduction is the process of reasoning from stated premises to a conclusion which follows necessarily. This form of reasoning moves from the general to the specific. See also *Syllogism.*

Definition   Definition is one of the types of exposition. (Process analysis, division and classification, comparison and contrast, and cause and effect analysis are the others.) Definition is a statement of the meaning of a word. A definition may be either brief or extended, part of an essay or an entire essay itself.

Denotation   See *Connotation/Denotation.*

Description   Description is one of the four basic types of prose. (Narration, exposition, and argument are the other three.) Description tells how a person, place, or thing is perceived by the five senses. Objective description reports these sensory qualities factually, whereas subjective description gives the writer's interpretation of them.

Diction   Diction refers to a writer's choice and use of words. Good diction is precise and appropriate—the words mean exactly what the writer intends, and the words are well suited to the writer's subject, intended audience, and purpose in writing. The word-conscious writer knows that there are differences among *aged, old,* and *elderly; blue, navy,* and *azure;* and *disturbed, angry,* and *irritated.* Furthermore, this writer knows in which situation to use each word. See also *Connotation/Denotation.*

Division and Classification   Division and classification make up one of the types of exposition. (Process analysis, definition, comparison and contrast, and cause and effect analysis are the others.) Division involves breaking down a single large unit into smaller subunits, or separating a group of items into discrete categories. Classification, on the other hand, involves arranging or sorting people, places, or things into categories according to their differing characteristics, thus making them more manageable for the writer and more understandable for the reader. Division, then, takes apart, while classification groups together. Although the two processes can operate separately, most often they work hand in hand.

Endings   See *Beginnings/Endings.*

Essay   An essay is a relatively short piece of nonfiction in which the writer attempts to make one or more closely related points. A good essay is purposeful, informative, and well organized.

Evidence   Evidence is the data on which a judgment or argument is based or by which proof or probability is established. Evidence usually takes the form of statistics, facts, names, examples or illustrations, and opinions of authorities.

Examples   Examples illustrate a larger idea or represent something of which they are a part. An example is a basic means of developing or clarifying an idea. Furthermore, examples enable writers to show and not simply to tell readers what they mean. The terms *example* and *illustration* are sometimes used interchangeably. An example may be anything from a statistic to a story; it may be stated in a few words or go on for several pages. What is required of an example is that it be closely *relevant* to the idea or generalization it is meant to illustrate. To be most effective, an example should be *representative*. The story it tells or the fact it presents should be typical of many others that readers are sure to think of.

Exposition Exposition is one of the four basic types of prose. (Narration, description, and argument are the other three.) The purpose of exposition is to clarify, explain, and inform. The methods of exposition are process analysis, definition, division and classification, comparison and contrast, and cause and effect analysis. For a detailed discussion of each of these methods of exposition, see the appropriate entries in this glossary.

Fallacy See *Logical Fallacies.*

Figures of Speech Figures of speech are brief, imaginative comparisons which highlight the similarities between things that are basically dissimilar. They make writing vivid and interesting and therefore more memorable. The most common figures of speech are:

> *Simile:* An implicit comparison introduced by *like* or *as.* "The fighter's hands were like stone."
>
> *Metaphor:* An implied comparison which uses one thing as the equivalent of another. "All the world's a stage."
>
> *Personification:* A special kind of simile or metaphor in which human traits are assigned to an inanimate object. "The engine coughed and then stopped."

Idiom An idiom is a word or phrase that is used habitually with a particular meaning in a language. The meaning of an idiom is not always readily apparent to nonnative speakers of that language. For example, *catch cold, hold a job, make up your mind,* and *give them a hand* are all idioms in English.

Illustration See *Examples.*

Induction Induction is the process of reasoning to a conclusion about all members of a class through an examination of only a few members of the class. This form of reasoning moves from a set of specific examples to a general statement or principle. As long as the evidence is accurate, pertinent, complete, and sufficient to represent the assertion, the conclusion of the inductive argument can be regarded as valid; if, however, you can spot inaccuracies in the evidence or point to contrary evidence, you have good reason to doubt the assertion as it stands. Inductive reasoning is the most common of argumentative structures. See also *Deduction.*

Introductions See *Beginnings/Endings.*

Irony The use of words to suggest something different from their literal meaning. A writer can use irony to establish a special relationship with the reader and to add an extra dimension or twist to the meaning.

Jargon See *Technical Language.*

Logical Fallacies A logical fallacy is an error in reasoning that renders an argument invalid. Some of the more common logical fallacies are:

Oversimplification: The tendency to provide simple solutions to complex problems. "The reason we have inflation today is that OPEC has unreasonably raised the price of oil."

Non sequitur ("It does not follow"): An inference or conclusion that does not follow from established premises or evidence. "It was the best movie I saw this year, and it should get an Academy Award."

Post hoc, ergo propter hoc ("After this, therefore because of this"): Confusing chance or coincidence with causation. Because one event comes after another one, it does not necessarily mean that the first event caused the second. "I won't say I caught cold at the hockey game, but I certainly didn't have it before I went there."

Begging the question: Assuming in a premise that which needs to be proven. "If American autoworkers built a better product, foreign auto sales would not be so high."

False analogy: Making a misleading analogy between logically unconnected ideas. "He was a brilliant basketball player; therefore, there's no question in my mind that he will be a fine coach."

Either/or thinking: The tendency to see an issue as having only two sides. "Used car salesmen are either honest or crooked."

Logical Reasoning See *Deduction* and *Induction.*

Metaphor See *Figures of Speech.*

Narration One of the four basic types of prose. (Description, exposition, and argument are the other three.) To narrate is to tell a story, to tell what happened. While narration is most often used in fiction, it is also important in nonfiction, either by itself or in conjunction with other types of prose. A good narrative essay has four essential features. The first is *context:* the writer makes clear when the action happened, where it happened, and to whom. The second is *point of view:* the writer establishes and maintains a consistent relationship to the action, either as a participant or as a reporter simply looking on. The third is *selection of detail:* the writer carefully chooses what to include, focusing on those actions and details that are most important to the story while merely mentioning or actually eliminating others. The fourth is *organization:* the writer organizes the events of the narrative into an appropriate sequence, often a strict chronology with a clear beginning, middle, and end.

Objective/Subjective Objective writing is factual and impersonal, whereas subjective writing, sometimes called impressionistic, relies heavily on personal interpretation.

Organization In writing, organization is the thoughtful arrangement and presentation of one's points or ideas. Narration is often organized chronologically. Exposition may be organized from simplest to most complex or from most familiar to least familiar. Argument may be organized from least important to most important. There is no single correct pattern of organization for a given piece of writing, but good writers are careful to discover an order of presentation suitable for their subject, their audience, and their purpose.

Paradox A paradox is a seemingly contradictory statement that may nonetheless be true. For example, *we little know what we have until we lose it* is a paradoxical statement.

Paragraph The paragraph, the single most important unit of thought in an essay, is a series of closely related sentences. These sentences adequately develop the central or controlling idea of the paragraph. This central or controlling idea, usually stated in a topic sentence, is necessarily related to the purpose of the whole composition. A well-written paragraph has several distinguishing characteristics: a clearly stated or implied topic sentence, adequate development, unity, coherence, and an appropriate organizational strategy.

Personification See *Figures of Speech.*

Persuasion Persuasion, or persuasive argument, is an attempt to convince readers to agree with a point of view, to make a given decision, or to pursue a particular course of action. Persuasion heavily appeals to the emotions whereas logical argument does not. See *Argument, Induction,* and *Deduction.*

Point of View Point of view refers to the grammatical person of the speaker in an essay. For example, a first-person point of view uses the pronoun *I* and is commonly found in autobiography and the personal essay; a third-person point of view uses the pronouns *he, she,* or *it* and is commonly found in objective writing.

Process Analysis Process analysis is a type of exposition. (Definition, division and classification, comparison and contrast, and cause and effect analysis are others.) Process analysis answers the question *how* and explains how something works or gives step-by-step directions for doing something.

Purpose Purpose is what the writer wants to accomplish in a particular piece of writing. Purposeful writing seeks to *relate* or *tell* (narration), to *describe* (description), to *explain* (process analysis, definition, division and classification, comparison and contrast, and cause and effect analysis), or to *convince* (argument).

Rhetorical Questions   A rhetorical question is asked but requires no answer from the reader. "When will nuclear proliferation end?" is such a question. Writers use rhetorical questions to introduce topics they plan to discuss or to emphasize important points.

Simile   See *Figures of Speech.*

Slang   Slang is the unconventional, very informal language of particular subgroups in our culture. Slang, such as *zonk, coke, split, rap, cop,* and *stoned,* is acceptable in formal writing only if it is used purposefully. See Stuart Berg Flexner, "Preface to the *Dictionary of American Slang"* (pp. 180–190).

Specific/General   General words name groups or classes of objects, qualities, or actions. Specific words, on the other hand, name individual objects, qualities, or actions within a class or group. To some extent the terms *general* and *specific* are relative. For example, *dessert* is a class of things. *Pie,* however, is more specific than *dessert* but more general than *pecan pie* or *chocolate cream pie.*

Good writing judiciously balances the general with the specific. Writing with too many general words is likely to be dull and lifeless. General words do not create vivid responses in the reader's mind as concrete specific words can. On the other hand, writing that relies exclusively on specific words may lack focus and direction, the control that more general statements provide.

Style   Style is the individual manner in which a writer expresses his or her ideas. Style is created by the author's particular selection of words, construction of sentences, and arrangement of ideas.

Subjective   See *Objective/Subjective.*

Syllogism   A syllogism is an argument that utilizes deductive reasoning and consists of a major premise, a minor premise, and a conclusion. For example,
All trees that lose leaves are deciduous. (major premise)
Maple trees lose their leaves. (minor premise)
Therefore, maple trees are deciduous. (conclusion)
See also *Deduction.*

Symbol   A symbol is a person, place, or thing that represents something beyond itself. For example, the eagle is a symbol of America, and the bear, a symbol of Russia.

Syntax   Syntax refers to the way in which words are arranged to form phrases, clauses, and sentences as well as to the grammatical relationship among the words themselves.

Technical Language   Technical language is the special vocabulary of a trade or profession. Writers who use technical language do so with an awareness of their audiences. If the audience is a group of peers, technical language may be used freely. If the audience is a more general one, technical language should be used sparingly and carefully so as not to sacrifice clarity. Technical language that is used only to impress, hide the truth, or cover insecurities is termed *jargon* and is not condoned. See *Diction*. For a complete discussion of technical language and jargon, see Kenneth Hudson, "Jargon and the Professions" (pp. 356–362).

Thesis   A thesis is a statement of the main idea of an essay. Also known as the controlling idea, a thesis may sometimes be implied rather than stated directly.

Tone   Tone is the manner in which a writer relates to an audience, the "tone of voice" used to address readers. Tone may be described as friendly, serious, distant, angry, cheerful, bitter, cynical, enthusiastic, morbid, resentful, warm, playful, and so forth. A particular tone results from a writer's diction, sentence structure, purpose, and attitude toward the subject. See also *Attitude*.

Topic Sentence   The topic sentence states the central idea of a paragraph and thus limits and controls the subject of the paragraph. Although the topic sentence normally appears at the beginning of the paragraph, it may appear at any other point, particularly if the writer is trying to create a special effect. Also see *Paragraph*.

Transitions   Transitions are words or phrases that link sentences, paragraphs, and larger units of a composition in order to achieve coherence. These devices include parallelism, pronoun references, conjunctions, and the repetition of key ideas, as well as the many conventional transitional expressions such as *moreover, on the other hand, in addition, in contrast,* and *therefore*. Also see *Coherence*.

Unity   Unity is achieved in an essay when all the words, sentences, and paragraphs contribute to its thesis. The elements of a unified essay do not distract the reader. Instead, they all harmoniously support a single idea or purpose.

"Black Children, Black Speech" by Dorothy Z. Seymour. Reprinted by permission of Commonweal Foundation.

"The Country's Going Through a Rough Spell" from *American Beat,* by Bob Greene. Copyright © 1984 John Deadline Enterprises. Reprinted with the permission of Atheneum Publishers, Inc.

"Caught Between Two Languages" from *Hunger of Memory* by Richard Rodriguez. Copyright © 1981 by Richard Rodriguez. Reprinted by permission of David R. Godine, Publisher, Boston.

III LANGUAGE, POLITICS, AND PROPAGANDA

"Selection, Slanting, and Charged Language" from *Understanding and Using English* by Newman P. Birk and Genevieve B. Birk. Reprinted by permission of the publisher, Bobbs-Merrill Educational Publishing, Birk and Birk, *Understanding and Using English,* 5th Edition, © 1972 Bobbs-Merrill.

"Politics and the English Language" by George Orwell. Copyright 1946 by Sonia Brownell Orwell; renewed 1974 by Sonia Orwell. Reprinted from *Shooting an Elephant and Other Essays* by George Orwell by permission of Harcourt Brace Jovanovich Inc., the estate of the late Sonia Brownell Orwell, and Martin Secker and Warburg, Ltd.

"The Joys of Watergate" by Jim Quinn. From *American Tongue and Cheek,* by Jim Quinn. Copyright © 1981 by Jim Quinn. Reprinted by permission of Pantheon Books, a division of Random House, Inc.

"Propaganda: How Not to Be Bamboozled" by Donna Woolfolk Cross. From *Speaking of Words: A Language Reader.* Reprinted by permission of Donna Woolfolk Cross.

IV WORDS, MEANINGS, AND DICTIONARIES

"The Power of Words" from *The Word-A-Day Vocabulary Builder* by Bergen Evans. Copyright © 1963 by Bergen Evans. Reprinted by permission of Random House, Inc.

"Vogue Words Are Trific, Right?" by William Safire. Copyright © 1976 by The New York Times Company. Reprinted by permission.

"Differences in Vocabulary" from *Discovering American Dialects* by Roger W. Shuy. Copyright © 1967 by the National Council of Teachers of English. Reprinted by permission of the publisher.

"Preface to the *Dictionary of American Slang*" by Stuart Berg Flexner from *Dictionary of American Slang* by Harold Wentworth and Stuart Berg Flexner (Thomas Y. Crowell). Copyright © 1960, 1967, 1975 by Harper & Row, Publishers, Inc. Reprinted by permission of Harper & Row, Publishers, Inc.

"How Dictionaries Are Made" from *Language in Thought and Action,* Fourth Edition by S. I. Hayakawa, copyright © 1978 by Harcourt Brace Jovanovich, Inc. Reprinted by permission of the publisher.

V   ADVERTISING AND LANGUAGE

"Bugs Bunny Says They're Yummy" by Dawn Ann Kurth. Copyright © 1972 by The New York Times Company. Reprinted by permission.

"Weasel Words: God's Little Helpers" by Paul Stevens. From *I Can Sell You Anything* by Carl P. Wrighter. Copyright © 1972 by Ballantine Books, Inc. Reprinted by permission of Ballantine Books, a division of Random House, Inc.

"How to Write Potent Copy" from *Confessions of an Advertising Man* by David Ogilvy. Copyright © 1963 David Ogilvy Trustee. Reprinted with the permission of Atheneum Publishers, Inc.

"It's Natural! It's Organic! Or Is It?" from Consumers Union. Copyright 1980 by Consumers Union of United States, Inc., Mount Vernon, N.Y. 10553. Introduction and Part 1 reprinted by permission from *Consumer Reports,* July 1980.

"Tell Me, Pretty Billboard" from *First Person Rural* by Noel Perrin. Copyright © 1978 by Noel Perrin. Reprinted by permission of David R. Godine, Publisher, Boston.

"Intensify/Downplay" by Hugh Rank, from *Teaching about Doublespeak*, edited by Daniel Dieterich (NCTE, 1976). Copyright © 1976 by the National Council of Teachers of English. Reprinted by permission of the publisher and the author. "Intensify/Downplay" schema, copyright © 1976, by Hugh Rank. Reprinted by permission of the author.

VI   PREJUDICE AND STEREOTYPES

"The Language of Prejudice" by Gordon Allport, © 1954, Addison-Wesley, Reading, Massachusetts. Reprinted with permission.

"Words with Built-in Judgments" from *Language in Thought and Action*, Fourth Edition, by S. I. Hayakawa, copyright © 1978 by Harcourt Brace Jovanovich, Inc. Reprinted by permission of the publisher.

"Does Language Libel the Left-Handed?" from *English Highlights: Words at Work* (March–April 1968).

"What to Call an American of Hispanic Descent" May 4, 1980, by Tomas Guillen, printed with permission of Seattle Times Co., copyright 1980.

"Dictionaries and Ethnic Sensibilities" by Robert Burchfield, from *The State of the Language* (ed. Leonard Michaels and Christopher Ricks), 1980; reprinted by permission of the University of California press.

VII   LANGUAGE AND SEXISM

"Sexism in English: A Feminist View" by Alleen Pace Nilsen from the book *Female Studies VI: Closer to the Ground Women's Classes, Criticism, Programs—1972,* ed.s, Nancy Hoffman, Cynthia Secor, Adrian Tinsley. Copyright © 1972 by Nancy Hoffman, Cynthia Secor, Adrian Tinsley. Reprinted with permission of The Femi-

VIII   EUPHEMISMS AND PROFESSIONAL JARGON

IX   TABOOS

X   WRITING WELL: USING LANGUAGE RESPONSIBLY

ADDITIONAL CREDITS